Media Politics in China

M000200831

Maria Repnikova introduces the webs of Chinese media politics that are hidden beneath the imagery of overarching contention between the omnipowerful state and suppressed dissidents. Drawing on rich empirical data, this novel analysis demonstrates that the relationship between China's critical journalists and the state is that of a fluid collaboration, whereby an ambiguous partnership is sustained through continuous acts of guarded improvisation. Journalists and the state actively reinvent the rules of their engagement, but the latter holds the upper hand in controlling the space and scope of this creative manoeuvring. This improvised cooperative mode of state-society relations differs from other authoritarian contexts, pointing to China's uniqueness when it comes to managing critical voices in the long-term. This book provides fresh empirical and theoretical insights into Chinese politics, comparative authoritarianism and global communication.

Maria Repnikova is a scholar of comparative authoritarianism and political communication in illiberal contexts, with a focus on China and Russia. She holds a Doctorate in Politics from Oxford University where she was a Rhodes Scholar. In the past, Maria has researched Chinese migration to Russia as a Fulbright Fellow, has held the Overseas Press Club fellowship in Beijing and was a post-doctoral fellow at the Annenberg School for Communication. Maria speaks fluent Mandarin and Russian. She teaches international communication, Chinese media politics and society, and information politics in non-democratic regimes.

Media Politics in China

Improvising Power under Authoritarianism

Maria Repnikova

Georgia State University

CAMBRIDGE UNIVERSITY PRESS

CAMBRIDGE
UNIVERSITY PRESS

University Printing House, Cambridge CB2 8BS, United Kingdom

One Liberty Plaza, 20th Floor, New York, NY 10006, USA

477 Williamstown Road, Port Melbourne, VIC 3207, Australia

314-321, 3rd Floor, Plot 3, Splendor Forum, Jasola District Centre, New Delhi - 110025, India

79 Anson Road, #06-04/06, Singapore 079906

Cambridge University Press is part of the University of Cambridge.

It furthers the University's mission by disseminating knowledge in the pursuit of education, learning and research at the highest international levels of excellence.

www.cambridge.org
Information on this title: www.cambridge.org/9781316647158
DOI: 10.1017/9781108164474

First published 2017
First paperback edition 2018

A catalogue record for this publication is available from the British Library

ISBN 978-1-107-19598-1 Hardback
ISBN 978-1-316-64715-8 Paperback

To Change-Makers Within the System

Contents

Preface

This book examines the relationship between China's critical journalists and the party-state in the past decade, under the Hu-Wen leadership. In contrast to existing scholarship on comparative authoritarianism and Chinese politics and society, which tends to analyse the perspectives of societal actors and the state separately from one another, this study brings the two together, unveiling the intricacies of their interactions. It portrays the engagement between critical journalists and central officials as a fluid, state-dominated partnership characterised by continuous improvisation. Party officials grant journalists an ambiguous consultative role, while journalists align their political and professional agenda to the central state. Their collaboration is maintained in large part due to the flexible nature of this arrangement, referred to as 'guarded improvisation'. The two actors make ad hoc adjustments in response to one another, but the party-state consistently directs the process and the scope of this creative manoeuvring.

The analysis draws on unique access to politically sensitive material, including 120 in-depth interviews with critical journalists, media and crisis management experts, and government officials. It also includes multilayered textual analysis of the Chinese Communist Party journal, *Qiushi*, and selected articles in two outspoken media outlets, *Caijing* and *Nanfang Zhoumo*. The data is employed to analyse the routine interactions between critical journalists and the party-state, as well as their dynamics during major crisis events, specifically the Wenchuan earthquake and coal-mining disasters. This study further includes a comparative dimension by drawing contrasts between the case of China and the Soviet Union, as well as between China and Russia, and between the Hu-Wen period and the Xi era.

Through the lens of journalist-state relations, this book theorises the workings of limited openings for political public participation in China and under authoritarianism more broadly. In China, it captures the bottom-up and top-down dimensions of these openings by underscoring the within-the-system nature of China's societal activism, as well as its unequal positioning vis-à-vis the state, and the importance of mutually embraced ambiguity for sustaining the engagement between critical voices and central officials. The book further demonstrates how the top-down management of political openings in China carries both consultative and fluid dimensions as the state opens up some input channels in policy-making while keeping the rules of the game intentionally ambiguous. Finally, the book questions the dichotomy of resilience versus democratisation underlying the study of comparative authoritarianism by highlighting the potential for societal actors to shape authoritarian governance in a constructive manner, even if not managing or intending to pave the way for a democratic transition.

Acknowledgements

This book is a product of intellectual and emotional synergy from many individuals across three continents. The groundwork for the study was laid during my time as a doctoral student at the University of Oxford, under thoughtful supervision of Professors Vivienne Shue and Stephen Whitefield. Professor Shue was the first to spark and sustain my interest in Chinese politics, media and society, and her inspiring intellectual guidance and logistical support over the past eight years made for the nucleus of this project. She has always pushed me to delve deeper into pursuit of puzzles that intrigue me the most in the field this book represents one of these puzzles. Professor Whitefield added a comparative and theoretical lens to the study of China and helped position my ideas in the context of varieties of authoritarianism and political participation in illiberal systems. His perspective transformed the project, and I am very grateful for his supervision.

Encouragement and support from mentors and colleagues, including Andrew Mertha, Guobin Yang, Marwan Kraidy, Harley Balzer, Rana Mitter, Jonathan Sullivan, Jeffrey Wasserstrom, Anne-Marie Brady, Daniel Lynch, Patricia Thornton, Kristen Looney, Christian Sorace, Rachel Murphy, Kevin O'Brien, Rachel Stern, Ashley Esarey, Peter Lorentzen, Daniela Stockmann, Jonathan Hassid, Marina Svensson, Timothy Colton, James Phillips, Floriana Fossato, Karrie Koesel, Rongbin Han, Maria Lipman, Bingchun Meng, Ola Onuch, Victor Pickard, Tania Saeed, Martin Dimitrov, Wang Haiyan, Nancy Bermeo, Monroe Price, Michael D. Carpini, Kecheng Fang, Mohamed Zayani, Omar Al-Ghazzi, Anne Kaun, Yue Hou, Min Jiang, amongst others, have greatly enriched the writing and the analysis. All the mistakes in this book, of course, are solely my own.

Financial support from the Rhodes Trust, the Wai Seng Scholarship Fund, the Contemporary China Studies Programme at Oxford, the Leverhulme Trust Grant, St. Antony's College, Oxford University Department of Politics and International Relations, and most recently the Project for Advanced Research in Global Communication (PARGC) at the Annenberg School for Communication, University of Pennsylvania, has enabled me to carry out the research and writing.

Between 2014 and 2016, as a postdoctoral fellow at the Annenberg School, I received enormous support in the process of completing the manuscript revisions. I am especially grateful to Marina Krikorian who has offered daily doses of encouragement and intellectual exchange, and made me feel welcome, as well as to all the wonderful staff at Annenberg, and of course, to Marwan Kraidy who tirelessly reminded me that the book project is the key objective of my fellowship and has graciously given me enough time to complete it. I would have never come to PARGC were it not for the introduction and support from Guobin Yang. His friendship, mentorship and nuanced approach to scholarship on Chinese media and society have been truly inspiring. Special thank you goes to Michael D. Carpini, the Dean of Annenberg School, who has welcomed and integrated me into the community of communication scholars and encouraged me to pursue the path of global communication.

During the process of manuscript revisions, a number of invited talks have brought new questions and insights into the analysis. A visit to Cornell University in October 2015 is especially memorable, thanks to the invitation of Andrew Mertha, who has become a very supportive mentor and a friend in the past several years. His work on fragmented authoritarianism and policy entrepreneurship has been a rich influence in this book.

From idea development to production stages of the book, Lucy Rhymer at Cambridge University Press has offered timely and consistent support. As a first-time author, it has been a tremendous pleasure to work with her and all the staff at Cambridge University Press in making this book come to fruition. I would also like to thank my current employer, Georgia State University, Department of Communication, for allocating time and resources in these last steps on the book's journey to publication.

Media Politics in China would not have been possible without the help of colleagues and interviewees in China and in Russia. I am forever indebted to the individuals who have selflessly helped me carry out the research on a subject that is sensitive and challenging to investigate for insiders and outsiders alike. A special thank you is due to Professor Zhan Jiang, who has taught me the most I know about China's media politics, and generously shared his contacts and advice throughout my research. Professor Xiao Dongfa at Beijing University has helped with contacts and research support from the very beginning and made Beijing a home each time I visited. He sadly passed away in April 2016, and this book is in part a tribute to his friendship and wisdom. Liu Cong, Anna and Cissy have provided invaluable research assistance and support. Filip Noubel, a close friend and a beautiful writer and translator, as well as a long-time resident and an unbeatable media and society expert in Beijing, has shared rare practitioner insights on the subject, as well as his intricate knowledge of Chinese tea, literature and culture. Wu Wei (Vivian Wu), a relentless media practitioner and intellectual, and has been a part of this project and my China journey throughout, from the first media training she was leading to her days at the New School in New York. Max Duncan hosted me in Beijing and has offered friendship, humour and exposure into the intricacies of Western media reporting in China. Maria Lipman hosted me at the Moscow Carnegie Centre and gracefully facilitated introductions with Russian experts and media professionals. I am also deeply grateful to all the editors, journalists, scholars and officials who agreed to speak to me extensively and openly. I could not imagine such openness was possible when I started this research, and I greatly value their patience with me, as well as their trust and enthusiasm for my project. Out of concern for anonymity, I cannot thank individual journalists, editors and officials who have partaken in this project. I hope I have managed to do them justice by attempting to explain the complicated and often contradictory realities they inhabit.

Finally, this study stands firmly on the foundation of my friends and family. Elena Minina, one of my closest friends and sharpest critics, never failed to highlight potential improvements both in terms of language and content. Elena's enduring friendship, wit, and unwavering sarcastic enthusiasm has been my true rock, as the book went through its metamorphosis from dissertation to published manuscript. My soul-sister and a remarkable thinker and friend, Nadiya Figueroa, has taught me to always seek the higher meaning from the work, to value the human facets of research and writing and to patiently build global and local linkages, while being tightly held on distance with ample doses of love and visionary advice. Nadiya Kravets, another life-long friend and supporter of this idea from the early days of the MPhil, has mulled through my writings and spiritual journeys over coffee pots and unforgettable butter sandwiches at St Antony's college, in Boston and Atlanta. My tiny, resilient, beautiful family Tatiana Repnikova, Galina Alpatova and Dmitri Repnikov, have provided a soft cushion of emotional support and love throughout this endeavour, even if it translated into less time together in the past years. They have patiently lived through the endless phases of this book, as it became a part of them. Arthur Vissing and his parents, Lise and Lars Vissing, have made this journey especially colourful and soulful. From endless conversations about Chinese media over home-cooked meals in Oxford, Rabat, Copenhagen, Lisbon and Bonne, to streams of encouragement and Charlie Chaplin films, this book is fused with beautiful memories.

Part I

Conceptual & Theoretical Frameworks

1 Introduction

Hegemony is 'a relation, not of domination by means of force, but of consent by means of political and ideological leadership. It is the organization of consent'.[1]

A popular depiction of Chinese media in the past decade has been that of a fearful, loyal agent of the ruthless party-state, which exudes no tolerance towards its critics. Indoctrinated to channel official propaganda to the public, silenced by censorship and threatened by coercion, Chinese journalists function in one of the world's toughest places when it comes to media freedom. The few dissidents who are brave enough to challenge China's omnipowerful party apparatus are quickly crushed by it, as manifested by harassment and arrests of activists, widely documented in the Western press.[2] The latest global press freedom assessments rank China at the bottom of their lists, alongside Somalia, Iran and Vietnam.[3]

What goes unnoticed beneath the stark imagery of collision between the mighty state and the fearless, isolated critics, however, is the web of complex negotiations taking place between some Chinese journalists and party officials. Specifically, whereas the majority of Chinese reporting still adheres to the propaganda model, in the past three decades, an exceptional practice of what I term 'critical journalism',[4] including investigative, in-depth, editorial and human-interest coverage of contentious

---

[1] Roger Simon, *Gramsci's Political Thought: An Introduction* (London: ElecBook, 2001): 2.
[2] Most stories in Western media concerning Chinese activists highlight state coercion against them. See, for instance, Scott Neuman, 'Chinese Activist Tells of "Crazy Retaliation" Against His Family', *NPR.org*, 4 July 2014, available at: www.npr.org/blog s/thetwo-way/2012/05/10/152412388/chinese-activist-tells-of-crazy-retailiation-against-his-family; Sandra Schulz, 'The Courage of the Few: Dozens Targeted in Chinese Crackdown on Critical Voices', *Spiegel Online*, 20 April 2011, available at: www.spiegel .de/international/world/the-courage-of-the-few-dozens-targeted-in-chinese-crackdown-o n-critical-voices-a-758152.html.
[3] Reporters without Borders ranked China 176th out of 180 countries in the 2017 press freedom rankings. https://rsf.org/en/ranking.
[4] While 'investigative journalism' is the most commonly used term for reporting that pushes the boundaries, followed by the concept of 'liberal journalism', which is very loosely defined, the term 'critical journalism' also echoes in other writings on journalism in

societal issues, has emerged in China amid the restrictive environment. Critical journalists comprise a diverse group, with the majority of them based at successful commercial news outlets,[5] but some also working for investigative units of official party outlets, and others contributing individual reports as freelancers and social media commentators. The group includes such different individuals as Miss Xi, a twenty four-year-old Beijinger and recent journalism graduate who has dug into high-level official corruption cases at *Nanfang Dushibao* and *Caixin*, and Mr He, a fifty-year-old Gansu native who never studied journalism but has headed investigative bureaus at the *China Economic Times* and *The Economic Observer*, where he exposed issues ranging from coal mine disasters to improper vaccinations in Shanxi. While their professional pressures, regional bases and personal struggles may differ, what unites these journalists is their pursuit of social justice and their quest to push the envelope of permissible reporting.

Their photographs rarely appear in Western newspapers, as they tend to avoid exposure while carrying out enduring battles within the system. Instead of protesting on the streets, they often gather and share their experiences on university campuses or in the Western-style coffee houses that are mushrooming all over Beijing. You are more likely to find them in

democratic and authoritarian societies. As for democracies, critical journalism parallels scholarly conceptions of journalism 'as an act of critique', as opposed solely to that of communication and culture. See Barbie Zelizer, 'How Communication, Culture, and Critique Intersect in the Study of Journalism', *Communication, Culture & Critique* 1(1) (2008): 86–91. In authoritarian and especially in a Chinese context, the term critical journalism has also been frequently used by scholars analysing media practices that push the boundaries of the permissible. Truex, for instance, in his analysis of Chinese media talks about 'critical media' versus 'official' media. See Rory Truex, 'Who Believes the *People's Daily*? Bias and Trust in Authoritarian Media', paper presented at the Comparative Politics Seminar, University of Pennsylvania, 10 April 2015. Hem refers to the practice of challenging censorship in non-democratic regimes as that of 'critical journalism'. See Mikal Hem, 'Evading the Censors: Critical Journalism in Authoritarian States', Reuters Institute Fellowship Paper, University of Oxford, Trinity Term 2014. Liebman, in his analysis of Chinese media, specifically refers to critical reporting as a new genre that is synonymous with the media's oversight role. See Benjamin L. Liebman, 'Changing Media, Changing Courts', in Susan L. Shirk (ed.), *Changing Media, Changing China* (New York: Oxford University Press, 2011): 150–175. Critical journalism is a more inclusive concept than either investigative or liberal-oriented reporting, as it refers to journalists critically engaging with contentious governance issues in a variety of ways, including, but not limited to, the investigative genre. In this book critical journalism is understood to channel an oversight over political governance.

[5] While all Chinese media is still owned by the party-state, many news outlets are partially commercialised, with up to 49 per cent of private ownership in the media being legally allowed by the state. Some scholars categorise Chinese media into 'commercialized', 'semi-commercialized' and 'official' outlets. See Daniela Stockmann, *Media Commercialization and Authoritarian Rule in China* (Cambridge, New York: Cambridge University Press, 2012). Media commercialisation is discussed in Chapter 3.

dimly lit Soviet-style lecture halls that resemble meeting rooms of propaganda officials, or in corners of a local Starbucks, than in openly subversive spaces for political critique. While not publicly fighting the regime, these journalists delve into sensitive areas, such as corruption and societal inequality, and provide an alternative framing to that deployed by propaganda journalists on issues of high importance to Chinese citizens. In the past decade alone, they exposed stories such as the 2002 AIDS epidemic in Henan province, the 2003 Sun Zhigang case of a migrant worker illegally detained and beaten to death in Guangzhou,[6] the scandalous school demolitions in the 2008 Sichuan earthquake, the 2008 milk-poisoning scandal, widespread environmental protests, and food safety crises, among other contentious issues.[7] In most cases, their stories raised a wide public outcry, as manifested in active discussions online, and in some cases they also produced a moderate policy shift.

Given the obsession of the Chinese party-state with maintaining political stability and its deeply entrenched suspicion of liberal media, what motivates it to tolerate critical voices? And considering the high risks associated with probing the system and the meagre chances of changing the political status quo, what drives some journalists to undertake personal and professional risks and engage in critical journalism? Most importantly, how do the key actors – journalists and central officials – manage their delicate relationship and what explains its continuing perseverance? This book is the first sustained attempt at examining the relations between China's critical journalists and the party-state in the past decade (2002–2012) – a period associated with official effort in building a 'harmonious society' amid rising levels of public discontent.[8] Whereas the 1990s are known as the golden age of watchdog journalism in China,[9] the period since 2000 has been more tumultuous for journalist-state relations. As the costs of the fast economic growth of the past two decades began to sink in and give rise to social mobilisation, critical journalism has carried higher risks and opportunities for both the state and media professionals. The tensions, which are already escalating as China continues to strive for a balance between sustained economic growth and political

---

[6] Sun Zhigang, a young graphic designer from Hubei, was detained and beaten to death by Guangzhou police for not carrying his registration permit. The report by Nanfang Dushibao has sparked widespread public uproar and a legal change whereby all 'custody and repatriation centers' were to be abolished. See 'The Rise of Rights?' *China Digital Times*, May 27, 2005, available at: http://chinadigitaltimes.net/2005/05/rise-of-rights/.

[7] Jingrong Tong, *Investigative Journalism in China: Journalism, Power, and Society* (London: Continuum, 2011).

[8] Mathieu Duchâtel and François Godement, 'China's Politics under Hu Jintao', *Journal of Current Chinese Affairs* 38(3) (2009): 3–11.

[9] Tong, *Investigative Journalism in China*.

stability, make the puzzle of journalist-state relations ever more interesting and timely to examine. In the past three years, under Xi Jinping's leadership, for instance, the coexistence of critical voices and the state is facing new challenges, as manifested in Xi's renewed emphasis on upholding stability and in journalists' persisting push for official accountability, recently demonstrated in courageous investigative reporting of the major chemical explosion in Tianjin.[10]

Beyond correcting popular misconceptions about Chinese media, the pursuit of this book is driven by three overarching intellectual objectives. First, the relationship between critical journalists and the state is an important dimension of Chinese politics on the boundary of the permissible, and thereby can inform us as much about the evolving bottom-up activism as about the modes of adaptation of the Chinese party-state when faced with impending pressures from below. While China's critical journalists constitute a fraction of Chinese media professionals, they are deeply entrenched in the wider network of China's activists, which includes the more contentious non-governmental organisation (NGO) leaders[11] and lawyers,[12] among others who have consistently probed the limits of the regime's tolerance through questioning, criticising and transforming some aspects of governance. At the same time, critical journalists are distinct from other activists or critical actors in a way that makes them theoretically important for analysing the Chinese political system. They carry a heightened political sensitivity for the regime, as they are capable of not only exposing public grievances and governance failures but also of galvanising certain causes and social movements. They can not only provide communication linkages across different activist groups but can also connect these groups with the larger public and empower social movements, especially in the fast-speed age of social media. In the past ten years, the internet has further facilitated the journalists' mediator role, which in turn has arguably spearheaded more contention amongst the Chinese public.[13] Grasping how critical journalists engage with the regime and how the party-state interacts and

---

[10] For more details on the Tianjin explosion, see 'The Tianjin Explosion', A China File Conversation, 18 August 2015, available at: www.chinafile.com/conversation/tianjin-explosion.

[11] For more details on NGOs, see, for instance, Tony Saich, 'Negotiating the State: The Development of Social Organizations in China', *The China Quarterly* 161 (2000): 124–141; Rachel E. Stern and Kevin O'Brien, 'Politics at the Boundary: Mixed Signals and the Chinese State', *Modern China* 38(2) (2011): 174–198.

[12] For more details on law, see Randall Peerenboom, *China's Long March Toward Rule of Law* (Cambridge University Press, 2002); Neil Jeffrey Diamant, Stanley B. Lubman, and Kevin J. O'Brien, *Engaging the Law in China: State, Society, and Possibilities for Justice* (Stanford: Stanford University Press, 2005).

[13] Steinhardt in his analysis of media coverage of protest events argues how protests have been increasingly covered in a sympathetic way by major Chinese news media over the

responds to these critics, therefore, allows us to map out a more comprehensive picture of 'boundary spanning'[14] activity and the mechanisms behind the regime's persisting adaptability and resilience.

More broadly, the study of critical journalists and the state in China is an account of limited political openings for public participation under authoritarianism – a phenomenon widely examined in comparative authoritarianism literature in the context of elections,[15] but much less so with regard to other channels, such as the media. The media is often treated as one of the variables influencing electoral outcomes,[16] or, when analysed in more detail, it is either portrayed as a democratising force,[17] or, on the opposite, as a tool of public opinion manipulation.[18] What is evident is that media openings are always highly contested spaces under authoritarianism, as regimes regard them with schizophrenic vision, both as potential threats to and as necessary tools for their continuing survival in the interconnected world. The aspiration of this book is to examine these tensions in more depth by stepping beyond the analytical focus on the outcomes of liberalisation versus resilience and illuminating the processes of negotiation and mutual adaptation of different actors involved in contesting these openings. A better grasp of these processes in turn facilitates a deeper understanding of potential risks and opportunities that the presence of some critical journalism, and bounded political openings for participation more broadly, entail for authoritarian regimes.

past decade. He attributes this in part to the internet's reshaping of the Chinese public sphere, but also in part to the deliberate policy on behalf of the Chinese state in allowing for more positive protest coverage. See H. Christoph Steinhardt, 'From Blind Spot to Media Spotlight: Propaganda Policy, Media Activism and the Emergence of Protest Events in the Chinese Public Sphere', *Asian Studies Review* 39(1) (2015): 119–137.

[14] 'Boundary-spanning contention' in China was first defined and introduced by O'Brien. See: Kevin J. O'Brien, 'Neither Transgressive Nor Contained: Boundary-Spanning Contention in China', *Mobilization* 8(1) (2002): 51–64.

[15] For more details on 'electoral authoritarianism', see Yonatan L. Morse, 'The Era of Electoral Authoritarianism', *World Politics* 64(1) (2012): 161–198; Andreas Paul Schedler, *Electoral Authoritarianism* (Boulder, Colo: Lynne Rienner Publishers, 2006); Steven Levitsky and Lucan Way, 'The Rise of Competitive Authoritarianism', *Journal of Democracy* 13(2) (2002): 51–65.

[16] Valerie J. Bunce and Sharon L. Wolchik, *Defeating Authoritarian Leaders in Postcommunist Countries* (Cambridge: Cambridge University Press, 2011).

[17] For more details on the importance of media in regime change, see, for instance, Minxin Pei, *From Reform to Revolution: The Demise of Communism in China and the Soviet Union* (Cambridge, MA: Harvard University Press, 1994); Natana J. DeLong-Bas, 'The New Social Media and the Arab Spring', *Oxford Islamic Studies Online*, available at: www.oxfordislamicstudies.com/Public/focus/essay0611_social_media.html; Sahar Khamis and Katherine Vaughn, 'Cyberactivism in the Egyptian Revolution: How Civic Engagement and Citizen Journalism Tilted the Balance', *Arab Media & Society* 14 (2011), available at: www.arabmediasociety.com/?article=769.

[18] For more details on media as a tool of authoritarians, see, for instance, Stockmann, *Media Commercialization and Authoritarian Rule in China*; Evgeny Morozov, *The Net Delusion: The Dark Side of Internet Freedom (Reprint edition)* (New York: Public Affairs, 2012).

By focusing on the case study of media politics in China, moreover, the ulterior objective is to question the conceptual categories of 'hybrid' versus 'full authoritarian' regimes dominating the existing comparative analysis,[19] as will be explained in detail in the following chapter. The China case demonstrates that even those regimes that lack national elections can still combine state control with moderate tolerance of political participation – aspects of which, like the media, can be compared across cases, as demonstrated in the comparison with Russia and the Soviet Union in Chapter 7.

Finally, this book's undertaking is rooted in a motivation to take another step in the direction of de-Westernising media studies[20] by examining the role of media oversight, which is most closely associated with Western liberal democracies, in the radically different and improbable context of China's one-party state. Investigative journalism and critical reporting are largely linked to the notion of the fourth estate and the conception of accountability in democratic systems.[21] The majority of the existing studies on this subject, not surprisingly, are situated in Western contexts.[22] When strides towards non-Western comparisons are made, they tend to be focused on conceptualising and categorising media systems rather than media practices and production processes.[23] Marginalised journalism practices, like critical reporting, often get absorbed into meta-level systemic comparisons. By documenting the micro- and macro-characteristics of critical journalism in China, the analysis presented here not only complements system-level comparisons but also invites more comparative work between Western and non-Western contexts, as well as across non-Western contexts on the

---

[19] Latest scholarship on authoritarian regimes divides them into those that have elections (termed as 'hybrid' or 'competitive' and 'electoral' authoritarian regimes) and those that don't (termed as 'full' or 'closed' authoritarian regimes). This split and the logic driving it are problematised in the following chapter.

[20] James Curran and Myung-Jin Park, *De-Westernizing Media Studies* (London: Routledge, 2000).

[21] Larry Jay Diamond and Leonardo Morlino, *Assessing the Quality of Democracy* (Baltimore: Johns Hopkins University Press, 2005); Doris Appel Graber, *Mass Media and American Politics* (Washington, DC: Cq Press, 2009).

[22] See, for instance, David L. Protess and Fay Lomax Cook, *The Journalism of Outrage: Investigative Reporting and Agenda Building in America* (New York: Guilford Press, 1992); Silvio Ricardo Waisbord, *Watchdog Journalism in South America: News, Accountability, and Democracy* (New York: Columbia University Press, 2000).

[23] Daniel C. Hallin, *Comparing Media Systems: Three Models of Media and Politics* (Cambridge: Cambridge University Press, 2004); Fred S. Siebert, Theodore Peterson, and Wilbur Schramm, *Four Theories of the Press: The Authoritarian, Libertarian, Social Responsibility and Soviet Communist Concepts of What the Press Should Be and Do* (Urbana: University of Illinois Press, 1963).

dimension of journalistic practices and actors engaged in them, which reside beneath the large and often opaque umbrellas of media systems.

A Fluid Collaboration and Guarded Improvisation

In the past decade, the field of Chinese media studies has undergone a revival, with scholars moving beyond the examination of party institutions responsible for media control towards analysing commercial aspects of media practices,[24] and most recently engaging with multifaceted dynamics of the internet, including online activism,[25] modes of internet management by the regime,[26] and the implications of advances in social media for state-society relations.[27] Although the focus of enquiry has expanded and diversified, the dominant frameworks for engaging with Chinese media have not significantly changed over time. They continue to feature an emphasis either on the party-state tactics or on bottom-up practices, resulting in an analytical dichotomy of control versus resistance.[28] Specifically, whereas one set of scholarly works interrogates censorship, ranging from the study of official directives to experiments with keyword filtering, the other illuminates journalists and netizens' contestation of control via a myriad of creative practices.[29] This two-sided analysis of Chinese media, which tends to portray the relationship between the state and liberal-minded journalists and netizens as one of perpetual struggle, reflects the dominant approach in the field of Chinese politics more broadly, whereby either a top-down or a bottom-up lens is

[24] Stockmann, *Media Commercialization and Authoritarian Rule in China* (Cambridge, New York: Cambridge University Press); Ying Zhu, *Two Billion Eyes: The Story of China Central Television* (New York: The New Press, 2014); Daniel C. Lynch, *After the Propaganda State: Media, Politics and 'Thought Work' in Reformed China* (Stanford: Stanford University Press, 1999).

[25] Guobin Yang, *The Power of the Internet in China: Citizen Activism Online* (New York: Columbia University Press, 2011).

[26] Gary King, Jennifer Pan, and Margaret Roberts, 'How Censorship in China Allows Government Criticism but Silences Collective Expression', *American Political Science Review* 107(2) (May 2013): 1–18.

[27] Rebecca MacKinnon, 'China's "Networked Authoritarianism"', *Journal of Democracy* 22 (2) (2011): 32–46; King, Pan, and Roberts, 'How Censorship in China Allows Government Criticism but Silences Collective Expression'; Min Jiang, 'Authoritarian Deliberation on Chinese Internet', *Electronic Journal of Communication* 20(3 &4) (2010), available at: www.cios.org/EJCPUBLIC/020/2/020344.html.

[28] An important exception to that is the work by Han on patriotic commentators online that bridges the gap between the contention and control. See Rongbin Han, 'Manufacturing Consent in Cyberspace: China's Fifty-cent Army', *Journal of Current Chinese Affairs* 44(2) (2015): 105–134.

[29] Yang, *The Power of the Internet in China*; Ashley Esarey and Xiao Qiang, 'Political Expression in the Chinese Blogosphere: Below the Radar', *Asian Survey* 48(5) (2005): 752–772. On journalists creative practices, see Jonathan Hassid, *China's Unruly Journalists: How Committed Professionals are Changing the People's Republic*, London and New York: Routledge, 2015. Specifically on investigative journalists, see: Tong, Investigative Journalism in China.

employed in delineating the modes of control and resistance, as will be explained in detail in Chapter 2.

This study examines the relationship between critical journalists and the state at both the top-down and the bottom-up levels of analysis, and thereby theorises about the key features of their engagement. In fusing the two perspectives together, this book portrays the relationship between critical journalists and central authorities as a fluid, state-dominated partnership characterised by continuous improvisation. The two actors are analysed as operating within a common political framework and aspiring towards a shared goal – the goal of improving governance. Party officials grant journalists an ambiguous consultative role in the system, and journalists align their own agenda to that of the central state. These actors are capable of maintaining collaborative ties in large part due to the flexible nature of this arrangement, which is defined here as 'guarded improvisation'. Journalists and officials make ad hoc creative adjustments in response to one another, with the state maintaining ample room for modification in endorsing, constraining and responding to watchdog reporting, and with journalists improvising by reinterpreting official policies and working to bypass political restrictions in the haze of dynamic ambiguity. The party-state, however, consistently and carefully guards or leads the direction and the scope of this creative manoeuvring,[30] whereas journalists limit their improvised resistance to 'tactical' strategies undertaken within the structures imposed by the state.[31]

In putting forward this new framework for characterising the relations between critical journalists and the party-state, this study doesn't aim to dismiss the importance of contention, but rather to propose that the overriding tensions should be examined in the larger context of a cooperative umbrella fusing the interests of central and occasionally also local officials with those of critical journalists. The cat and mouse game is vivid, but it is only one facet of their relationship. This book invites scholars of Chinese media to question and unpack the dichotomous categories (i.e. contestation versus control) and to deconstruct the

---

[30] The notion of the state guarding the direction of state-media relations echoes Cheek's concept of 'directed public sphere' used in conceptualising the relations between Chinese intellectuals and the party. See Timothy Cheek, 'Introductions: The Making and Breaking of the Party-State in China', in Timothy Cheek and Tony Saich (eds.), *New Perspectives on State Socialism in China* (Armonk, NY: M.E. Sharpe, 1997): 7.

[31] The idea of 'tactics' here is borrowed from Certeau's writing, *The Practice of Everyday Life*, where he asserts that in our daily routines, such as walking in a city, we can only embark on tactical moves whereas the 'strategies' determining the framework of the city are carried out by structures of power, including institutions and corporations.

fluid partnership between the seemingly adversarial forces as an important step in grasping the nuances of the Chinese media system.

This collaborative dimension is not unique to journalists, and feeds into the scholarly analysis of Chinese intellectuals and other activists as being embedded into the political system.[32] While on the surface having more temptations to embark on open subversion, as they are more readily exposed to global influences in contrast to other Chinese activists, journalists are still deeply entrenched in the system, exhibiting a mix of pragmatism and idealism akin to other contemporary change-makers in China who operate on the fringes of the permissible. Specifically, they acknowledge their role as agents of the central state, take advantage of the loopholes in the political system and avoid issues that immediately challenge or question the party's legitimacy. This notion of symbiotic relations between journalists and officials echoes studies of artists under censorship in socialist contexts that argue that in contrast to the widely perceived antagonism, the censors and their subjects are fused together in an intricate dance of acquiescence.[33]

At the same time, the analysis in this book shows that the persisting embedding of societal actors into the political system and their collaboration with the regime are contingent on unequal power dynamics in favour of the state, and the presence of mutually embraced ambiguity that allows for the relationship to be continuously adjusted and reinvented. As for unequal dynamics, the study of journalists suggests that activists and critical voices continue to occupy the weaker advisory role and remain vulnerable to the shifting political objectives and sensitivities. Though journalists can be the ones sparking the improvised engagement with authorities by outrunning censorship and re-navigating the grey zone, the party-state intensely and meticulously guides their relationship. Throughout, the book illuminates how the party crafts the space for media supervision by framing it as a party-led mechanism in the official discourse and by carefully pre-empting and reacting to journalists' improvised acts both on a routine basis and especially in times of major crisis events.

---

[32] For more details on intellectuals, see Timothy Cheek, *The Intellectual in Modern Chinese History* (Cambridge University Press: 2015); for more details on activism, see Peter Ho and Richard Louis Edmonds, *China's Embedded Activism: Opportunities and Constraints of a Social Movement* (Abingdon, NY: Routledge Chapman & Hall, 2008). This dynamic is also not unique to Chinese activists and intellectuals. It echoes writings on relations between artists and intellectuals and the socialist state. In examining Hungarian artists under socialism, for instance, Haraszti writes that 'a new aesthetic culture has emerged in which censors and artists are entangled in a mutual embrace'. See Miklos Haraszti, *The Velvet Prison: Artists Under State Socialism* (New York: Basic Books, 1987): 5.

[33] Haraszti, *The Velvet Prison*.

As for the importance of ambiguity, the arguments put forward here echo and build on other recent works on 'political ambivalence',[34] 'mixed signals'[35] and 'uncertainty'[36] as characterising China's 'politics at the boundary'.[37] As explained in detail in the following chapter, the framework of 'guarded improvisation' is an attempt at further crystallising the process of this fluid engagement between the state and societal actors. While ambiguity undoubtedly limits activism and especially critical journalism to the narrow grey zones demarcated by the party, it also facilitates its continued existence in a system that prioritises political stability above all. Uncertainty, therefore, should not only be understood as a mechanism of control via self-censorship, as already widely documented in other works, but also as an enabling condition for limited forms of activism to coexist with an authoritarian system.

The book further demonstrates that the fluid partnership between journalists and officials appears to be rooted in 'fragmented',[38] 'consultative'[39] and 'adaptive'[40] features of China's political system. As for the fragmented feature, fluid collaboration is in part a product of the decentralised nature of China's political system, which has long been conceptualised as that of 'fragmented authoritarianism',[41] displaying significant gaps between central-level initiatives and their local-level implementation. These gaps create opportunities for alliances to form between central authorities and societal actors, including critical journalists, that target policy gridlocks and governance failures at the local level. Local officials, as demonstrated in the following chapters, often serve as the common target of journalists and central authorities. At the same time, decentralised policy-making inspires opportunistic behaviour on

---

[34] Rachel Stern, *Environmental Litigation in China: A Study in Political Ambivalence* (Cambridge; New York: Cambridge University Press, 2013).

[35] Rachel E. Stern and Kevin J. O'Brien, 'Politics at the Boundary: Mixed Signals and the Chinese State', *Modern China* 38(2) (1 March 2012): 174–198.

[36] Jonathan Hassid, 'Controlling the Chinese Media: An Uncertain Business', *Asian Survey* 48(3) (2008): 414–430.

[37] Stern and O'Brien, 'Politics at the Boundary Mixed Signals and the Chinese State'.

[38] Kenneth Lieberthal and Michel Oksenberg, *Policy Making in China* (Princeton, NJ: Princeton University Press, 1988); Andrew Mertha, ' "Fragmented Authoritarianism" 2.0: Political Pluralization in the Chinese Policy Process', *The China Quarterly* 200 (2009): 995–1012.

[39] Jessica C. Teets, 'Let Many Civil Societies Bloom: The Rise of Consultative Authoritarianism in China', *The China Quarterly* 213 (2013): 19–38.

[40] Sebastian Heilmann and Elizabeth J. Perry, *Mao's Invisible Hand: The Political Foundations of Adaptive Governance in China* (Cambridge, MA; London: Harvard University Press, 2011).

[41] Lieberthal and Oksenberg, *Policy Making in China*; Mertha, '"Fragmented Authoritarianism" 2.0'.

behalf of local officials, who attempt to safeguard their interests by applying pressures on the centre and on individual reporters to halt and mitigate negative coverage. Whereas in the realm of economic policy-making, experimentation has been noted as an important by-product of fragmented governance,[42] when it comes to media and social activism, this book suggests that improvisation is a more fitting term, as it captures the less structured and the more dynamic modes of negotiating political boundaries.

Journalist-state relations are also a manifestation of a fusion of China's consultative and adaptive features, whereby limited public feedback is incorporated into policy-making, while flexibility is prioritised in most dimensions of decision-making and policy implementation. In fact, the analysis of journalists demonstrates how these two parallel but seemingly disparate modes of governance work to reinforce each other in the Chinese context. As the next chapter theorises in more detail, bounded consultations can facilitate the adaptability of the party-state, as they invite prompt adjustments of state policies in accordance with public preferences and help enforce top-down accountability, while a flexible mode of carrying out these consultations is what makes them tolerable to the regime in the first place, as authorities can bend their responses while maintaining a grip on political stability.

Beyond highlighting the persisting characteristics of China's activism and political governance, the analysis of China's critical journalists further links the China case to comparative studies on participatory channels under authoritarianism, offering new ways of understanding this phenomenon. By highlighting the potential for societal actors to shape authoritarian governance in a constructive manner, even if not managing nor intending to pave the way for a democratic transition, this book shows that state-sanctioned openings for political participation can serve different governance purposes, such as those of feedback and accountability channels, beyond destabilising or superficially enhancing a ruling regime. As this account of China's critical journalists demonstrates, the relationship between critical actors and the state under authoritarian rule can embody flexible collaboration, not only the state domination or high contention portrayed in the existing literature.[43]

---

[42] Sebastian Heilmann, 'Policy Experimentation in China's Economic Rise', *Studies in Comparative International Development* 43(1) (2008): 1–26.

[43] Comparative authoritarianism scholarship examines this issue from the top-down perspective focusing either on the incentives and tactics of the regime in containing any dissent or on the most contentious segments of society aiming for breaking the system. The subtler within-the-system activism has been given little attention in the literature. This is explained in more detail in the next chapter.

The Approach and Sources

The book approaches the dynamic puzzle of critical journalism in four parts: conceptual and theoretical frameworks, the key parameters of journalist-state relations in China, case studies of crisis events, and comparative dimensions of state-media relations in Russia and the Soviet Union and of media politics in the Xi Jinping era. The first part of the book which encompasses this introductory chapter and the following theoretical discussion, unpacks the conceptual framework of a fluid partnership and guarded improvisation and explains the theoretical pay-offs of this study for the scholarship on Chinese society, political governance and comparative authoritarianism.

The second part introduces the overarching objectives for media oversight held by central party officials and critical journalists (Chapter 3), followed by the analysis of routine constraints on their relationship, as experienced by practising journalists and editors (Chapter 4). Chapter 3 discusses the notion of a fluid collaboration between critical journalists and the party-state as being rooted in their shared vision of media oversight – a vision that is overshadowed by ambiguity but nonetheless frames critical journalism as a channel for improving the party's governance, mainly at the local level. Chapter 4, illuminates day-to-day improvised interactions between journalists and media-regulating officials through journalists' accounts of political pressures, ranging from pre-publication censorship and withholding of information by authorities to post-publication censorship and coercive punishments.

The third part of the book investigates how the terrain that binds these actors shifts during national-level crisis events.[44] Chapters 5 and 6, expose the reader to the evolving relationship between journalists and officials as it comes under significant pressure. In times of crisis, the party-state is torn between using the media for two somewhat contradictory purposes: propaganda and public feedback. On the one hand, the authorities are driven to shape public opinion through the media, while, on the other, they rely on the media for accurate and objective reporting in order to effectively manage a crisis and pre-empt public discontent. Chinese journalists, in turn, find themselves in an equally precarious position during crisis events, as they come under severe guidance from the state while striving to deliver timely and objective coverage of complex and emotionally-charged events. These mutual challenges experienced by journalists and officials are not unique to China or to authoritarian

---

[44] Crisis events encompass three predominant features: threat, uncertainty and urgency. See Arjen Boin, Eric Stern and Bengt Sundelius, *The Politics of Crisis Management: Public Leadership Under Pressure* (Cambridge, UK: Cambridge University Press, 2005).

contexts. Even in democracies, media plays diverse roles in times of emergency, including that of information provision and investigation, and governments often attempt to set media agenda. In China, these dynamics are amplified. Up until the early 2000s, no major reporting on disasters was tolerated as it was deemed to be potentially destabilising. Historically, major disasters in China were regarded as premonitions of the weakening power of the state or as signs of forthcoming political transformations.[45] To this day, the regime regards them with acute sensitivity, yet it now realises that in the age of social media and globalisation, a complete cover-up is impossible and unfavourable, and a more nuanced treatment of disaster coverage is in order.

The two crises examined here are the Sichuan earthquake (Chapter 5) and repetitive major coal-mining accidents (Chapter 6).[46] The Sichuan earthquake (also named the Wenchuan earthquake after its epicentre) was the deadliest natural catastrophe to affect China in the past decade,[47] with the death of over 5,000 children in poorly constructed schools eliciting wide public scrutiny. Coal-mining safety has been a continuous challenge for the Chinese state throughout the reform era,[48] turning into a national scandal and getting at the forefront of high-level policy discussions by the mid-2000s.[49] By intentionally selecting two different types of disasters, with the earthquake inciting an unexpected, immediate and large-scale exogenous shock to the system, and the coal-mining accidents presenting the cumulative effect of continuous governance failures, this book traces some variation in potentially destabilising political effects and the subsequent interactions between journalists and the state during and in the aftermath of major crises.

The concluding part of this book takes a step in a comparative direction by drawing contrasts across authoritarian cases (Chapter 7) as well as between Hu and Xi periods (Chapter 8). Chapter 7 compares the China case to two contrasting cases of journalist-state relations in the late Soviet Union under Gorbachev and in the Russian Federation under Putin.

---

[45] Gerard Lemos, *The End of the Chinese Dream: Why Chinese People Fear the Future* (New Haven: Yale University Press, 2012).

[46] The analysis includes all major accidents that occurred under the Hu-Wen leadership with fatalities of thirty and higher. For more details, see Table 6.2.

[47] According to the Centre for Research on the Epidemiology of Disasters, the Sichuan earthquake led to 68,858 deaths (and 18,618 people missing) and economic losses of 85 billion dollars (Femke Vos et al., 'Annual Disaster Statistical Review 2008: The Numbers and Trends', Belgium Centre for Research on the Epidemiology of Disasters, 2009).

[48] Olivia Lang, 'The Dangers of Mining around the World', *BBC News*, 14 October 2010, available at: www.bbc.co.uk/news/world-latin-america-11533349.

[49] Wang Shaoguang, 'Regulating Deaths at Coalmines: Changing Mode of Governance', *Journal of Contemporary China* 15(46) (2006): 1–30.

The former is the case of critical journalists playing a democratising role, contributing to the eventual collapse of the Soviet Union, and the latter is the case of them coexisting with the regime but having a highly subdued and marginalised position in the political system. These comparative contexts reflect the two common ways of analysing limited political openings under authoritarianism, introduced earlier, with critical actors either being involved in a contentious battle with the state or being manipulated by the regime into serving an image-boosting function. This chapter demonstrates how the fluid collaboration framework and the variables of shared objectives and guarded improvisation help explain the divergent relations between critical journalists and the state in other authoritarian contexts. Beyond its theoretical significance in linking the analysis of China to the wider comparative universe of non-democracies, this chapter illuminates both an anti-model of China's approach to managing the media – that of the Gorbachev leadership—as well as the new potential model for managing critical voices under authoritarianism—in the form of Putin's leadership. In the past several years, under Xi's rule, the Chinese party-state has revived the study of the Gorbachev example to avoid similar mistakes and disastrous consequences,[50] while closely observing Putin's mode of governing, and in some ways adapting his personalistic features. Chapter 8 concludes the book by revisiting the key arguments and reassessing them in the context of recent changes in media and state-society relations under President Xi. It introduces the latest shifts, and further explains the continuities in journalist-state relations, the flaring of recent tensions, and what the evolving practice of media oversight tells us about China's consultative governance, varieties of authoritarianism and comparability of media oversight role across political spectrums.

The sensitivity of the subject of this book made for a challenging process of data gathering, involving twelve months of fieldwork with multiple trips to Beijing from 2008 to 2016, as well as a research trip to Moscow in April 2010. A total of 120 semi-structured interviews were carried out with media practitioners, media and crisis management experts, and party and state officials, lasting from one hour to an entire day. Interviews were secured through a web of introductions, otherwise known as the snowball technique, with initial interviewees helping arrange additional meetings with their colleagues. All interviews

---

[50] For more details on the Chinese party-state learning from Gorbachev's 'failures', see Anne-Marie Brady, *Marketing Dictatorship: Propaganda and Thought Work in Contemporary China* (Lanham, MD; Plymouth: Rowman & Littlefield, 2008).

were conducted by the author in Chinese and Russian. The anonymity of respondents was ensured by carefully concealing their names throughout the research and the writing process. Some follow-up interviews and informal conversations that inform the concluding part of the book were also conducted via Skype and e-mail correspondence in 2014 and 2015, as well as in person, in the summer of 2016. For the list of guiding interview questions and interviewees, please refer to Appendix B.

Media practitioners, including reporters and editors, who make up the majority of the interviewees, were selected primarily from the outlets nationally renowned for investigative and in-depth reporting on contentious societal issues,[51] ranging from the more commercial outlets like *Nanfang Zhoumo, Nanfang Renwu Zhoukan, Nanfang Dushibao, Caijing* and *Caixin,* to investigative units of official outlets such as that of *Jingji Guanchabao, Bingdian* of *Zhongguo Qingnian Bao* and the *Xinwen Diaocha* programme of China Central Television (CCTV). The analysis also draws on interviews with investigative journalists and op-ed editors at popular mainstream outlets, such as *Xinjing Bao,* freelance journalists who write for established outlets and online platforms, such as *Bolian* and most recently, Sohu and Tencent; as well as retired investigative journalists. In addition, interviews with editors at some official outlets, such as *Huanqiu Shibao* and Xinhua News Agency, were conducted for a contrasting perspective. In Moscow, interviewees included editors and journalists at nationally reputable investigative outlets, including *Novaya Gazeta, The New Times, Agentura.ru, Vlast'* magazine and the editorial section of *Vedomosti* business newspaper. The author has also interacted with retired journalists who were active in the *glasnost* era. In selecting interviewees, the author has largely opted for journalists from established news outlets as opposed to citizen journalists because in-depth reporting in China is still carried out primarily by news outlets, with social media being largely forbidden from embarking on independent investigations.[52] Moreover, focusing on established news outlets has helped to illuminate the evolution of the interaction of critical voices and the party-state over a longer time frame, and to contrast journalists' perceptions with their published writings, which enriches the data and the analysis. At the same time, this study is by no means a synthesis of the workings of the press, but

---

[51] In categorising the outlets, the author relied on secondary literature on Chinese journalism, as well as on preliminary fieldwork carried out in China as part of my master's thesis in 2007–2008, which involved interviews with Chinese media experts and educators closely watching the developments of Chinese media, including critical reporting.

[52] Interviews MNG02; COF01; CSE02. These trends are shifting somewhat under Xi, with some platforms like Tencent publishing and carrying out independent investigative reporting. This is explained in more detail in the Conclusion of this book.

rather it sits at the crossroads of new and traditional media, as the boundaries between the two are increasingly evaporating, with print media actively transitioning to online platforms and well-known newspaper journalists turning into popular online public opinion makers with the help of social media platforms like Weibo and Weixin. It is apparent in this research that the majority of critical reports are read in an online edition, rather than in print, and commercial and official news outlets alike are aggressively adapting to digital audiences. A number of media professionals analysed in this study also have a large individual online following. Hu Shuli, the current editor of *Caixin* magazine, previously at *Caijing*, for instance,[53] has two million followers on Weibo, and Luo Changpin, the former editor of *Caijing* has 680,000 followers.[54] Not all media personalities are this popular amongst the general public, but the gatekeepers of critical publications tend to exert significant influence on online public opinion in sharing their reports, as well as their opinions on current events. The personalised sharing, however, tends to be limited, as explained further in Chapter 4. Throughout this book, the analysis of critical journalists is fused with the discussion of social media, and its interactive effects on the evolution of investigative reporting are explained in detail.

The book further draws on rare encounters with Chinese officials in charge of media regulation at the central level, including high-ranking employees at China's General Administration of Press and Publication (GAPP, *Zhonghua Renmin Gongheguo Xinwen Chuban Zongshu,* 中华人民共和国新闻出版总署) and the Central Propaganda Department (CPD, *zhongyang xuanchuan bu,* 中央宣传部),[55] as well as officials in charge of overseeing mining safety at the State Council. Some interviews were followed up with e-mail correspondence, and a number of conversations were carried out with the same officials over an extensive period (four years). Since the motivation of this book was to sketch a framework of journalist-state relations at the national level, interviews with officials are biased in favour of the centre. The objectives of local officials, however, are richly documented in the study, as they are weaved into the interviews with journalists and central officials, and present an important part of the story.[56]

[53] Hu Shuli left *Caijing* in 2009 and took her top editorial team with her to start another magazine, *Caixin.* Ian Johnson and Sky Canaves, 'Leading Editor Quits China's Top Magazine', *The Wall Street Journal,* 10 November, 2009, available at: www.wsj.com/articles/SB125775561968037983.

[54] These numbers are based on the latest search on Weibo.

[55] It was officially renamed in English as the Publicity Department.

[56] For an in-depth analysis of journalist-state dynamics at the local level, see Wanning Sun and Jenny Chio (eds.), *Mapping China: Region, Province, Locality* (London: Routledge, 2012).

Finally, the perspectives of well-known media and crisis management experts, as well as representatives of media development NGOs, greatly enrich the analysis and complement the discussions with journalists and officials. The scholars and experts interviewed are based at Beijing Foreign Studies University, Beijing University, Renmin University, China Communications University, Tsinghua University, Fudan University, the Chinese Academy of Social Sciences and the School of Government at Nankai University, as well as at commercial firms involved in training officials in communication techniques. Many of these experts provide media training to officials at the central and local levels, and carry out research directly linked to the questions at the heart of this study, including the opportunities and limitations for media oversight in China and the state's evolving approaches to crisis management. A global practitioner perspective is also fused into the analysis through conversations with the director and other employees of the International Centre for Communication Development (ICCD), a Beijing-based international organisation that has led extensive journalism training workshops in China on issues ranging from media ethics to environmental journalism,[57] and through attendance of a number of events and conferences co-sponsored by foreign embassies and Chinese universities on the topic of journalism and media governance. In Moscow, expert interviewees include those based at the Moscow Carnegie Center, Moscow State University and the Glasnost Foundation, as well as independent commentators and activists involved in advancing critical media agenda.

In-depth interviews are complemented by a close textual analysis of the official discourse on the media (Chapter 3), as well as of investigative and in-depth coverage of selected crisis events (Chapters 5 and 6). The former involves a careful study of selected articles in *Qiushi*, a fortnightly magazine managed by the Central Committee of the Chinese Communist Party (CCP) and renowned for representing policy statements and carrying official discourse. The latter includes the examination of crisis coverage by two different nationally reputable investigative outlets: *Nanfang Zhoumo* and *Caijing*.[58] The analysis of writings of officials and journalists distills different discourse strategies employed by the two actors, as well as the key frames used in discussing media oversight (in the case of officials) and in formulating critical comments (in the case of journalists).

---

[57] For more details, see www.iccd.biz/temp/about.html. It is the same organisation that represents the Internews branch in China.

[58] A wider analysis of media reports by a range of critical outlets discussed in the previous section is performed beforehand to determine the scope of investigative coverage. The author then proceeds with a detailed textual analysis of the coverage in the two outlets.

This linguistic component presents a rare attempt at in-depth qualitative study of discourse concerning sensitive issues and subtle contested meanings in the Chinese context.[59] It enriches and diversifies interview analysis, as it further interrogates the concepts and ideas discussed by the interviewees, and demonstrates some of their practical manifestations, especially in the case of journalists' reporting on sensitive issues.

In the past six years of carrying out the research for this book, the author has benefitted tremendously from long-standing relationships with generous Chinese and Russian colleagues, who have not only accepted interview requests, highlighted the appropriate media sources and shared their contacts but also have allowed for observing journalism classes, media training workshops, public lectures, as well as participating in private gatherings at their homes and in public spaces. When not referring to a specific interview or media analysis, this book draws on many observations collected over the course of these interactions. The attendance of several annual investigative journalism conferences (*yulun jiandu huiyi*) was particularly meaningful for this research, as the conference gathered critical journalists and editors from across the country and engaged with different facets of journalists' work on the boundaries of the permissible, including their perceptions of restrictions, negotiation tactics and general understanding of the nature of media oversight in China. Informal meetings and presentations at the Moscow Carnegie Center have also facilitated unique exposure to different voices in the Russian media community. This book attempts to fuse this multifaceted exposure on the ground with critical analysis of primary sources and theoretical and comparative thinking on Chinese governance and authoritarian regimes.

---

[59] Content analysis has been a more popular technique for analysing discourse, especially when it comes to media reports in China. While undoubtedly useful for gauging the larger trends and processing big data, overreliance on content analysis risks missing or confusing the more subtle meanings. When it comes to expressing criticism in an authoritarian system or to advocating for a contentious policy of media oversight, the discourse is ridden with ambiguity that requires more in-depth, qualitative study.

2 Theoretical Pay-offs

This chapter builds on the Introduction and demonstrates how the framework of a fluid collaboration between critical journalists and the party-state can be read at different theoretical levels. Specifically, the analysis that follows shows how the study of China's critical journalists advances our understanding of China's bottom-up activism and political governance, as well as that of the varieties of authoritarianism. This chapter underscores key features of China's bottom-up activism, including its embedded, unequal and ambiguous positioning vis-à-vis the state; theorises about China's political system as at once fragmented, consultative and highly fluid; and introduces the notion of constructive collaboration as an alternative framework for engagement between critical actors and the state in authoritarian regimes. The chapter thereby bridges the top-down and bottom-up approaches to studying bounded political openings for political participation in the Chinese context, as well as the scholarship on Chinese studies and comparative authoritarianism.

China's Societal Activism: The Mode of Creative Collaboration with the State

The analysis of perspectives and practices of China's critical journalists is a window into the wider milieu of China's social activism, as critical journalists are both mediators between the state and society, as well as direct participants in activist movements. Journalists analysed in this book channel societal grievances to authorities and inform the public of official response, but also directly advocate for certain causes, alongside other activists or 'critical actors', including lawyers, non-governmental organisation (NGO) leaders and intellectuals. While they are a minority within the larger group of China's media professionals, critical journalists constitute an integral part of the web of activism and are critical to the workings of politics on the boundary of permissible or 'boundary-spanning contention'[1] in China. The conceptual framework introduced in this book to characterise journalists' relations with the state, therefore, speaks to the larger scholarship on bottom-up activism and state-society relations in China. The notion of a fluid collaboration underscores the within-the-system characteristic of activist movements, and specifies the state-dominated and ambiguous relationship of critical actors with the party-state. While both journalists and central party officials gain from their collaboration, it remains heavily crafted by the latter. The high degree of improvisation permeating their interactions appears to enable some resistance practices by critical journalists, whilst also facilitating their general compliance with political status quo.

The analysis in this book reinforces scholarly arguments about the collaborative stance of China's critical actors and bottom-up activism more broadly by showcasing that even critical journalists, many of whom reside in urban areas and have access to global information flows, position themselves as change-makers *within* the system. While Western media and analysis often emphasise the work of dissidents and lay hope on social activism in overturning China's authoritarian political trajectory, the majority of China's activism, including that in the media sphere, continues to exist alongside, rather than in opposition to the regime. The examination of the political objectives and operational tactics of media practitioners reinforces the notions of 'rightful resistance'[2] and 'embeddedness'[3] attributed to the activities of rural protesters, NGO leaders, lawyers and intellectuals, among other actors. Similarly to the dynamics observed in rural protests, China's critical journalism 'operates near the boundary of authorised channels, employs the rhetoric and commitments of the powerful to curb the exercise of power, hinges on locating and exploiting divisions within the state, and relies on mobilising support from the wider public'.[4] Like other strategic actors walking the labyrinths of China's fragmented political system, Chinese journalists are 'policy entrepreneurs',[5] taking advantage of political loopholes and skilfully aligning themselves with central initiatives to discipline local

---

[1] The phrase 'boundary-spanning contention' in relation to China was coined by Kevin J. O'Brien. See Kevin J. O'Brien, 'Neither Transgressive nor Contained: Boundary-Spanning Contention in China', *Mobilization* 8(1) (2003): 51–64.

[2] Kevin J. O'Brien and Lianjiang Li, *Rightful Resistance in Rural China* (New York: Cambridge University Press, 2006).

[3] Peter Ho and Richard Edmonds, *China's Embedded Activism* (Abingdon; New York: Routledge, 2008).

[4] O'Brien and Li, *Rightful Resistance in Rural China*: 2.

[5] Andrew Mertha, 'Society in the State: China's Nondemocratic Political Pluralization', in Peter Gries and Stanley Rosen (eds.), *Chinese Politics: State, Society and the Market* (London: Routledge, 2010), 69–84.

officials. Like cause lawyers, Chinese journalists seek political connections at both local and central levels to secure protection in pursuing sensitive cases.[6] Like grassroots NGO leaders, journalists attempt to build trust with officials through personal engagement.[7] Like liberally minded intellectuals within the establishment, critical journalists are state employees and are thereby implicitly integrated into the party-system.[8]

In unveiling collaborative attitudes and practices of critical journalists vis-à-vis the party-state, this book further highlights the intermingling of pragmatic reasoning with activists' genuine support for political status quo. On the one hand, the choice to collaborate appears to be a strategic decision to survive within the system. Borrowing on De Certeau's distinction between 'strategies' devised by powerholders and 'tactics' deployed from below, Chinese journalists are 'poaching' but not transforming the rules of the game.[9] This 'tactical' resistance is likely to be in part a product of journalists' failures at 'strategies' or direct confrontation and systemic reform, as experienced in the 1989 Tiananmen movement and in the events leading up to that. For a brief period in May 1989, Chinese journalists across the official and commercial spectrum openly reported on the escalating clash between the student protesters demanding more democratic reforms and the unyielding official reaction and participated in and galvanised protests alongside student activists.[10] In that period, therefore, journalists embodied the dual role of information transmitters and advocates, as described earlier, but aimed at transformation of the system rather than at solely exposing its flaws. The regime's violent crackdown on

---

[6] John W. Givens and Maria Repnikova, 'Advocates of Change in Authoritarian Regimes: How Chinese Lawyers and Chinese and Russian Journalists Stay out of Trouble', http://papers.ssrn.com/sol3/papers.cfm?abstract_id=1911590. For an in-depth study of Chinese lawyers and their embeddedness in the system, see Ethan Michelson, 'Lawyers, Political Embeddedness, and Institutional Continuity in China's Transition from Socialism', *American Journal of Sociology* 113 (2007): 352–414; and Sida Liu and Terence C. Halliday, 'Political Liberalism and Political Embeddedness: Understanding Politics in the Work of Chinese Criminal Defense Lawyers,' *Law & Society Review* 45(4) (2011): 831–866.

[7] Alex Jingwei He and Genghua Huang, 'Fighting for Migrant Labor Rights in the World's Factory: Legitimacy, Resource Constraints and Strategies of Grassroots Migrant Labor NGOs in South China', *Journal of Contemporary China* 24 (2015): 471–492.

[8] Suzanne Ogden, 'From Patronage to Profits: The Changing Relationship of Chinese Intellectuals with the Party-state', in Edward Gu and Merle Goldman (eds.), *Chinese Intellectuals Between State and Market* (London: Routledge, 2004): 111–138.

[9] Michel De Certeau, *The Practice of Everyday Life* (Berkeley: University of California Press, 1984).

[10] For a detailed and personal account of journalists' participation in the Tiananmen movement, see Liu Binyan, 'After Tiananmen Square, a "Dark Age" for Press Freedom in China', *Nieman Reports*, 28 August 2014.

student protesters and its subsequent targeting of journalists has likely served as a warning sign for media practitioners to collaborate or else to risk losing capacity for any political leverage. As Chapter 3 explains in more detail, the Tiananmen incident demonstrated to China's critical journalists across generations that pragmatism and compromise with authorities is the only feasible way of transforming the system.

At the same time, beyond pragmatism, the tactical behaviour of critical journalists towards the party-state appears to have been reinforced by their idealistic vision of contributing to progressive, gradual change. This facet of journalists' collaboration echoes in the attitudes of other societal actors. O'Brien and Li, for instance, argue that rural residents sincerely believe in the benevolent nature of the central state, which represents their interests.[11] Spires characterises many NGO workers as 'patriotic progressives', who consider improving the existing system as the best way forward,[12] and Davies describes China's intellectual thought as 'patriotic worrying',[13] centred on solving China's problems. The analysis of critical journalists, as explained in Chapter 3, similarly uncovers a degree of patriotism, fused with a belief in stability and societal order as integral ingredients for the successful evolution of China in the long term. However, this patriotic allegiance and confidence in the central state amongst critical actors, including journalists, may be waning in the Xi period, as the new leadership has swayed towards centralising power and has displayed less tolerance for bottom-up critique. Some of the interviewees, as discussed in the concluding chapter, privately express disillusion with Xi's leadership, especially his tightening grip on the media and public discourse. At the same time, while the attitudes may be shifting, this has thus far not translated into overt resistance of the party's hegemony, as contention persists largely within the orbit of the party-state. Overall, this book showcases that while in the wide spectrum of activism journalists might be considered as among the most contentious, their behaviour and political objectives are akin to those of other actors furthering their interests and pushing the boundaries locally and nationally.

By describing the relationship between critical journalists and the party-state as that of 'guarded improvisation', this study further underscores the inherently unequal or state-dominated nature of collaborative ties between

---

[11] O'Brien and Li, *Rightful Resistance in Rural China*: 44.

[12] Anthony J. Spires, 'Contingent Symbiosis and Civil Society in an Authoritarian State: Understanding the Survival of China's Grassroots NGOs', *American Journal of Sociology* 117(1) (July 2011): 1–45.

[13] Gloria Davies, *Worrying about China: The Language of Chinese Critical Inquiry* (Cambridge, MA: Harvard University Press, 2007).

critical actors and the ruling regime. The terms 'symbiosis'[14] and 'co-dependence',[15] often applied to conceptualise this relationship, are misleading, as they allude to the presence of a balanced mutual need that unifies the two actors. Though there are gains to collaboration on both sides, the analysis of journalists demonstrates that the power alignments are deeply uneven. This asymmetry is evident in how the party-state takes the upper hand in defining the scope for media oversight, the patterns of interactions between journalists and the state and the limited influence that media investigations exert on short-term and long-term policy change. The concept of 'contingent symbiosis'[16] put forward by Spires in his analysis of the relations between local NGOs and officials comes closest to capturing the dynamics of critical journalists. Spires argues that there is not only a mutual need fuelling the relationship but also a mutual suspicion that makes it contingent and inherently skewed in favour of officials. While the notion of 'contingent symbiosis' signals wider uncertainty underlying cooperative ties, the term 'guarded' stresses the state-crafted nature of this relationship. Echoing the notion of 'directed public sphere' introduced by Cheek in his study of Chinese intellectuals,[17] the analysis in this book demonstrates that the party's capacity to consistently guard its relationship with journalists has allowed for the delicate coexistence. The comparative analysis of media liberalisation under Gorbachev introduced earlier, and developed in Chapter 7, demonstrates further how more equal ties between journalists and high-level officials can endanger the intricate balance sustaining this relationship in an authoritarian context. In contrast to the Chinese party-state engaging critical journalists and other actors in an advisory role on specific, mostly local-level issues, Gorbachev invited liberal journalists to partake in and mobilise large-scale political and economic reforms. His strong dependency on journalists as advocates for his policies placed him in a compromised position, with journalists subsequently taking advantage of their status to overpower the ruling elites and contribute to systemic change. In the case of China, the regime has been obsessively learning from Gorbachev's mistakes[18] by ensuring that in every facet of its relationship with critical actors, it remains at the driving wheel.

---

[14] Tony Saich, 'Negotiating the State: The Development of Social Organizations in China', *The China Quarterly* 161 (2000): 124–141.

[15] Timothy Hildebrandt, *Social Organizations and the Authoritarian State in China* (Cambridge; New York: Cambridge University Press, 2013).

[16] Spires, 'Contingent Symbiosis and Civil Society in an Authoritarian State'.

[17] Timothy Cheek, 'Introductions: The Making and Breaking of the Party-State in China', in Timothy Cheek and Tony Saich (eds.), *New Perspectives on State Socialism in China* (Armonk, NY: M.E. Sharpe, 1997): 7.

[18] Using Gorbachev as an anti-model has been stressed in a number of interviews with Chinese party officials, scholars and journalists. Similar conclusions were drawn by other

Other than the state-dominated nature of this collaboration, the concept of 'guarded improvisation' highlights the importance of ambiguity for critical actors in sustaining and reshaping their relations with the state. The following chapters demonstrate that uncertainty often presents a creative challenge or an opportunity for critical journalists to push the boundaries, while limiting them to resistance within the system. The notion of productive ambiguity complements the arguments made by other scholars on bottom-up activism that underscore how lawlessness as opposed to rule of law can empower grassroots activism in creating room for experimental initiatives,[19] or how murky boundaries can allow activists to reinterpret their responsibilities and take advantage of the loopholes in the system.[20] In analysing journalists' relationship with ambiguity, this book not only highlights their opportunistic treatment of the fragmented political system but also introduces other creative practises they resort to in navigating the fluid political landscape. As for the former, like other critical actors, journalists consistently partner with the centre in exposing local governance failures and tend to play out local interests against those of the centre in advocating for certain political outcomes. As a result of journalists' embeddedness in the system, focusing on local-level failures is a creative strategy to win over the centre's trust and support for their cause. Occasionally, journalists also align with local officials to channel their interests to the centre in exchange for information access and other assistance in their investigations, as demonstrated in Chapter 6. Beyond taking advantage of central-local discrepancies, however, critical journalists play in the shadows of uncertainty by embarking in language politics, practicing strategic timing and taking advantage of technology, namely social media. Like netizens, who frequently resort to satire and ambiguous language in expressing criticism,[21] critical journalists tend to channel sensitive content indirectly through inventive linguistic devices, introduced in Chapters 5 and 6. Unlike citizen journalists who might be alienated from official structures, however, critical journalists work closely with officials on a routine basis and are thereby more prone to strategically timing their reporting in conjuncture with shifting political trends. The chapters that follow show that

scholars. See Anne-Marie Brady, *Marketing Dictatorship: Propaganda and Thought Work in Contemporary China* (Lanham, MD; Plymouth: Rowman & Littlefield, 2008).

[19] Spires, 'Contingent Symbiosis and Civil Society in an Authoritarian State'; Rachel E. Stern, *Environmental Litigation in China: A Study in Political Ambivalence* (Cambridge: Cambridge University Press, 2013).

[20] Ho and Edmonds, *China's Embedded Activism*.

[21] Guobin Yang and Min Jiang, 'The Networked Practice of Online Political Satire in China: Between Ritual and Resistance', *International Communication Gazette*, February 2015.

journalists are highly capable of discerning patterns in the state's fluid management of the media. Finally, journalists' savvy use of social media, as discussed in Chapter 4, can help them outrun the censors, build alliances and networks, instigate public support and occasionally implement alternative activism initiatives to complement their investigative reporting. In short, 'tactics' deployed by critical journalists in a fluid environment feature 'a mobility that must accept the chance offerings of the moment, and seize on the wing of possibilities that offer themselves at any given moment ... it must make use of the cracks that particular conjunctions open in the surveillance of the proprietary powers ...'[22]

While creating space for negotiating the rules of the game, ambiguity also undoubtedly provokes self-censorship amongst media professionals. Aligned with Stern and Hassid's depiction of the state's arbitrary management of society as facilitating a high degree of compliance,[23] the analysis of journalists illuminates the cautious nature of political activism stemming largely out of fear of incorrect assessment of the boundaries or the understanding that improvisation is only feasible within the state-endorsed grey zone. Like artists in socialist Hungary, Chinese journalists reside in a 'velvet prison'[24] that binds them to the political status quo. 'The state is able to domesticate the artist because the artist has already made the state his home', writes Haraszti in his explanation of the mutual embrace between artists and censors in socialist Hungary.[25] A similar dynamic applies to critical journalists and the state in contemporary China. A number of creative tactics deployed by journalists, moreover, such as building personal relationships with local officials or advocating for causes supported from above, end up implicitly translating into self-censorship, as journalists often exchange official collaboration for milder coverage of contentious issues. As argued by De Certeau, 'a tactic is an art of the weak',[26] and journalists' resorting to creativity is a result of their weaker positioning vis-à-vis the powerholders. At the same time, the analysis of journalists' behaviour demonstrates their acceptance of improvised interaction as the underlying reality (or feature) of their relationship with the state – something that has thus far fared them better than transparent rules, which would likely only serve to further constrain them in an authoritarian context. While transparency tends to be

---

[22] De Certeau, *The Practice of Everyday Life*: 37.

[23] Rachel E. Stern and Jonathan Hassid, 'Amplifying Silence: Uncertainty and Control Parables in Contemporary China', *Comparative Political Studies* 45(10) (2012): 1230–1254.

[24] Miklos Haraszti, *The Velvet Prison: Artists Under State Socialism* (New York: Basic Books, 1987).

[25] Ibid: 5.   [26] De Certeau, *The Practice of Everyday Life*: 37.

associated with more room for political activism, therefore, this book makes a somewhat counterintuitive claim that less transparency can make limited activism more sustainable, while also preventing it from evolving into large-scale anti-regime movements, which the Chinese state is clearly intent on avoiding at all costs.

The Chinese Political System: The Intermingling of Consultative and Fluid Governance

Other than theorising about the nature of bottom-up activism in China, the analysis of the state's relationship with critical journalists captures important dimensions of China's top-down management of society. The analytical framework of a fluid collaboration sustained through guarded improvisation depicts the party's approach to critical voices as at once consultative and ambivalent. On the one hand, the regime promotes some deliberative channels, including those in the media, in order to gauge bottom-up feedback and enforce vertical accountability. On the other hand, these consultations are fluid and contradictory, with feedback being incorporated selectively in an ad hoc manner. The analysis of critical journalists suggests that endorsing consultative governance contributes to the adaptability of the regime, while the flexible and state-led nature of these consultations is what makes them tolerable to authorities in the first place. A more institutionalised form of societal feedback is perceived as potentially undermining of political stability.

As for the consultative dimension, like other recent works that argue that participatory channels and bounded civil society activism can coexist with the party-state, the analysis of journalists shows that a limited media oversight role is incorporated into China's model of political governance. Echoing the conceptualisations of the Chinese political system as 'consultative Leninism'[27] and 'consultative authoritarianism',[28] the party's endorsement of the supervision role for the media points to its sanctioning of consultations with society through the media channel. As explained in detail in Chapter 3, the party-state has promoted the policy of media supervision or *yulun jiandu* in the past three decades, alongside the

---

[27] Steve Tsang, 'Consultative Leninism: China's New Political Framework?' *Journal of Contemporary China* 18(62) (2009): 865–880.

[28] Jessica C. Tweets, 'Let Many Civil Societies Bloom: The Rise of Consultative Authoritarianism in China', *The China Quarterly* 213 (2013): 19–38. For more on consultative authoritarianism, see Baogang He and Stig Thøgersen, 'Giving the People a Voice? Experiments with Consultative Authoritarian Institutions in China', *Journal of Contemporary China* 19(66) (2010): 675–692; Rory Truex, 'Consultative Authoritarianism and Its Limits', *Comparative Political Studies* 50 (3) (2014): 329–361.

dominant media role of guiding public opinion. In line with other works highlighting the 'deliberative' nature of China's policy-making,[29] the analysis that follows demonstrates that the party-state encourages public deliberation on some issues through the media in order to align public preferences with those of the state. Beyond invoking some bottom-up feedback through the media, the analysis in Chapters 5 and 6 further points to the selectively 'responsive'[30] nature of China's governance, as manifested in the official partial addressing of problems exposed by journalists. The regime, therefore, both encourages and reacts to media investigations, implicitly assigning journalists an ambiguous advisory role within the system.

In endorsing consultative or deliberative governance when it comes to media oversight, the overarching objective to grasp and accommodate public preferences is combined with or reinforced by the central state's motivation to mitigate accountability failures that are rooted in China's fragmented political system.[31] Congruent with Mertha's astute conclusions about China's policy-making process being 'captured by the fragmented authoritarianism framework',[32] the analysis that follows demonstrates that much of the regime's incentive to allow for some critical voices stems from its challenge to enforce local-level accountability. As with endorsing village-level elections,[33] implementing an

---

[29] Beibei Tang, 'The Discursive Turn: Deliberative Governance in China's Urbanized Villages', *Journal of Contemporary China* 24 (2015): 137–157; Baogang He and Mark E. Warren, 'Authoritarian Deliberation: The Deliberative Turn in Chinese Political Development', *Perspectives on Politics* 9(2) (2011): 269–289; Min Jiang, 'Authoritarian Deliberation on Chinese Internet', *Electronic Journal of Communication* 20(3 and 4) (2010).

[30] A number of recent works on Chinese politics refer to the Chinese regime as 'responsive authoritarianism'. See Robert P. Weller, 'Responsive Authoritarianism', in Bruce Gilley and Larry Diamond (eds.), *Political Change in China: Comparisons with Taiwan* (Boulder and London: Lynne Rienner Publishers, 2008): 117–135; James Reilly, *Strong Society, Smart State: The Rise of Public Opinion in China's Japan Policy* (New York: Columbia University Press, 2011). Daniela Stockmann, *Media Commercialization and Authoritarian Rule in China* (Cambridge: Cambridge University Press, 2012). Responsive authoritarianism comes close to the notion of 'public-pressure model' of policy-making attributed to China, which refers to the state's inclusive approach to wider public opinion preferences (not just elites) in formulating and implementing new policies. See Shaoguang Wang, 'Changing Models of China's Policy Agenda Setting', *Modern China* 34(1) (2008): 56–87.

[31] The concept 'fragmented authoritarianism', coined by Lieberthal and Oksenberg, remains integral to analysing contemporary Chinese politics. See Kenneth Lieberthal and Michel Oksenberg, *Policy Making in China* (Princeton, NJ: Princeton University Press, 1988).

[32] Andrew Mertha, ' "Fragmented Authoritarianism" 2.0: Political Pluralization in the Chinese Policy Process', *The China Quarterly* 200 (2009): 995–1012.

[33] Pierre F. Landry, Deborah Davis and Shiru Wang, 'Elections in Rural China: Competition without Parties', *Comparative Political Studies* 43(6) (2010): 763–790;

administrative litigation act,[34] or tolerating some localised protests,[35] NGO activism[36] and online criticism,[37] the regime's sanctioning of the media oversight role appeals to the objective of disciplining unruly local officials. The media is especially useful in ameliorating the distortions in vertical information filtering, as local officials tend to inflate their reported performance targets to the centre.[38] As the following chapter demonstrates, the party's discourse on investigative journalism either directly or indirectly assigns local officials as targets of media supervision. And as unravelled throughout this book, the higher critical journalists climb up the tower of the party's bureaucracy, the more the sensitivity of their reports escalates in the eyes of the party, and the more likely journalists are to incur a negative reaction from authorities, undermining their space within the system. Echoing recent scholarly arguments about the selective nature of censorship in Chinese media, especially in the online sphere,[39] the analysis that follows in Chapter 4 and in the case study chapters points to the differentiation between central-level and local-level issues when it comes to the tolerance of political critique.

By examining the process of interaction between critical journalists and the party-state, this book further gets at the key feature of consultative governance – its ambivalent or improvised nature. Just as ambiguity creates space for bottom-up creative resistance amongst journalists, it is also at the core of sustaining consultative processes for the state. In maintaining a fluid space to manoeuvre vis-à-vis the journalists, the

Bruce Gilley, 'Democratic Enclaves in Authoritarian Regimes', *Democratization* 17(3) (2010): 389–415.

[34] Tom Ginsburg, 'Administrative Law and the Judicial Control of Agents in Authoritarian Regimes', in Tom Ginsburg and Tamir Moustafa (eds.), *Rule by Law: The Politics of Courts in Authoritarian Regimes* (New York, NY: Cambridge University Press, 2008): 58–73.

[35] O'Brien and Li, *Rightful Resistance in Rural China*.

[36] Weller, 'Responsive Authoritarianism'.

[37] Online exposures of local officials has been termed as the human flesh search engine (HFSE), whereby netizens hunt down and expose individual officials for their corrupt behaviour through photographs of expensive items, fake promises, etc. See Li Gao and James Stanyer, 'Hunting Corrupt Officials Online: The Human Flesh Search Engine and the Search for Justice in China', *Information, Communication and Society* 17 (2014): 814–829. Since most online investigations target local officials, central authorities exude some tolerance and often use them as an opportunity to demonstrate responsiveness to public opinion by punishing corrupt officials.

[38] On distortions in China's internal information system, see Kezhou Xiao and Brantly Womack, 'Distortion and Credibility within China's Internal Information System', *Journal of Contemporary China* 23(88) (2014): 680–697.

[39] See Peter Lorentzen, 'China's Strategic Censorship', *American Journal of Political Science* 58(2) (2014): 402–414; Gary King, Jennifer Pan and Margaret E. Roberts, 'How Censorship in China Allows Government Criticism but Silences Collective Expression', *American Political Science Review* 107(2) (2013): 1–18.

authorities create a buffer for initiating and tolerating some critical reporting. In managing critical journalists, the officials (both local and central,
but especially central) opt for significant flexibility and resist explicit
endorsements, let alone institutionalisation, of media freedoms in the
form of a press law or other legal protections for journalists. Similarly to
its attitude towards commercial media and the internet, the regime exhibits 'deep ambivalence'[40] when it comes to critical journalism, striving to
garner the pay-offs without undermining stability. As shown throughout
the book, the party-state upholds ambiguity in endorsing, restricting and
responding to media investigations and critiques. It keeps the discourse
on media oversight consistently vague, uses an ad hoc management style
in patrolling critical journalists and reacts to media revelations with a mix
of censorship and tacit acknowledgement.

The party's improvised consultations with journalists speak to other
studies that underscore the regime's ambivalence in managing public
participation in politics and in its fluid approach to governance reform
more broadly. As for the former, improvisation echoes in what some
scholars refer to as the state's 'episodic' and experimental guidance of
civic organisations,[41] and what others term as 'political ambivalence'[42]
and 'mixed signals',[43] signifying the presence of conflicting preferences in
the regime's treatment of societal activism. More broadly, some scholars
have characterised the first decade of reform in the post-Mao era in terms
of cycles of *'fang/shou'* (letting go and tightening up),[44] which have
produced a fluid, 'discontinuous' and 'cyclical' reform process. Some
go further and argue that China's flexible approach extends to many
spheres and represents a continuation of Mao's 'guerrilla policy style',
which consistently prioritised 'elasticity' over procedural stability.[45]

---

[40] Qian Gang and David Bandurski, 'China's Emerging Public Sphere: The Impact of
Media Commercialization, Professionalism, and the Internet in an Era of Transition',
in Susan Shirk (ed.), *Changing Media, Changing China* (Oxford; New York: Oxford
University Press, 2011): 38–77.

[41] Nara Dillon, 'Governing Civil Society: Adapting Revolutionary Methods to Serve Post-
Communist Goals', in Sebastian Heilmann and Elizabeth J. Perry (eds.), *Mao's Invisible
Hand: The Political Foundations of Adaptive Governance in China* (Cambridge, MA;
London: Harvard University Asia Center, 2011): 138–165.

[42] Stern, *Environmental Litigation in China.*

[43] Rachel E. Stern and Kevin J. O'Brien, 'Politics at the Boundary: Mixed Signals and the
Chinese State', *Modern China* 38(2) (2012): 174–198.

[44] Richard Baum, *Burying Mao: Chinese Politics in the Age of Deng Xiaoping* (Princeton, NJ:
Princeton University Press, 1994).

[45] Sebastian Heilmann and Elizabeth J. Perry, 'Embracing Uncertainty: Guerrilla Policy
Style and Adaptive Governance in China', in Sebastian Heilmann and Elizabeth J. Perry
(eds.), *Mao's Invisible Hand: The Political Foundations of Adaptive Governance in China*
(Cambridge, MA; London: Published by the Harvard University Asia Center; distributed by Harvard University Press, 2011): 1–30.

China's economic reform, for instance, has been termed the 'point-to-surface' approach or 'experimentation under hierarchy', which means that targeted experiments are conducted and evaluated at the local level before wider economic reforms are initiated, with the central state ordering the experiments.[46] Experimentation was also found to be at the heart of China's rural development policy.[47]

The existing works on China's ambivalent governance, however, whether they concern the political system at large or bottom-up activism in particular, tend to associate ambivalence primarily with domination and control rather than with consultation and deliberation. Perry, for instance, connotes fluidity with an almost Machiavellian discourse of Realpolitik, with decision-makers being driven by power and little regard for accountability. 'Unchecked by institutions of accountability, guerrilla leaders pursue their objectives with little concern for the interests of those who stand in their way', she writes.[48] From this depiction of the roots of experimental governance, one may infer that, if anything, ambiguity is another form of domination over society, as it empowers the party-state to act deliberately and arbitrarily, and fosters self-censorship and general public reluctance to embark on risky political initiatives. Other scholars explicitly link uncertainty to control by arguing that a 'regime of uncertainty' is at the heart of the party's continuing hold on the media,[49] and that arbitrary crackdowns on political activism produce 'control parables' or speculative discussions among activists, which tend to spread fear and compliance.[50] Whilst acknowledging that ambivalence constitutes one of the regime's control tactics in containing critical discourse, the analysis of top-down management of critical journalists also demonstrates that ambiguity is fused with China's consultative governance, as consultations are only initiated in so far as they can be continuously reinvented by the state.

In introducing the concept of 'guarded improvisation', which speaks to the existing terms of 'experimentation under hierarchy',

---

[46] Sebastian Heilmann, 'Policy-Making through Experimentation: The Formation of a Distinctive Policy Process', in Heilmann and Perry, *Mao's Invisible Hand: The Political Foundations of Adaptive Governance in China*: 62–102.

[47] Elizabeth J. Perry, 'From Mass Campaigns to Managed Campaigns: "Constructing a New Socialist Countryside"', in Heilmann and Perry, *Mao's Invisible Hand: The Political Foundations of Adaptive Governance in China*: 30–62.

[48] Heilmann and Perry, *Mao's Invisible Hand: The Political Foundations of Adaptive Governance in China*: 13.

[49] Jonathan Hassid, 'Controlling the Chinese Media: An Uncertain Business', *Asian Survey* 48(3) (2008): 414–430.

[50] Stern and Hassid, 'Amplifying Silence': 1230–1254.

'political ambivalence' and 'mixed signals', this book further specifies the nature of the party's fluid performance in managing critical actors. In contrast to the 'point to surface' approach of economic experiments,[51] when it comes to testing out limited participatory channels in the political domain, such as that of the media oversight, the process features less hierarchy and coordination. Improvisation is not clearly delineated between the centre 'ordering the experiments' and local authorities implementing them, but is undertaken by all actors involved, including journalists and officials (both central and local). Moreover, whereas experiments tend to be planned and organised in advance, improvisation happens on a more spontaneous basis, with participants acting in response to one another. Journalists, for instance, can be the ones initiating improvisation by probing a sensitive issue not previously known to authorities, as well as reacting to ad hoc directives from above by creatively outrunning censorship and other political pressures. These distinctions in fluid governance in economic versus political spheres showcase that when it comes to the latter, the party is less guided by specific long-term agenda in maintaining bounded political openings, but rather tends to adjust its preferences in real time depending on the evolution of other policies and its fluctuating strategic objectives. As demonstrated in the following chapters, while the overarching framework for media supervision is vaguely articulated by the state, the specific functions the media is expected to fulfil shift in accordance with public sentiments and perceived risks of political instability. Building on the notions of 'political ambivalence' and 'mixed signals' that capture the state's preference for fluid treatment of the boundaries of permissible, 'guarded improvisation' further underscores the presence of strategic reasoning on behalf of the party-state in embarking on flexible governance and the fusion of creative ad hoc practices by authorities and critical actors. While illuminating competing voices in the official apparatus, this book approaches ambiguity as less of a contradiction, and more of a strategic conduct on behalf of the state, and an integral feature facilitating the coexistence of otherwise conflicting forces. The concept of guarded improvisation captures the combined efforts by the state and societal actors at sustaining and taking advantage of ambiguity.

The characterisation of China's societal governance as guarded improvisation underscores both the potential resilience and vulnerability of

---

[51] Sebastian Heilmann, 'Policy Experimentation in China's Economic Rise', *Studies in Comparative International Development* 43(1) (2008): 1–26.

China's political system when it comes to managing critical voices. On the one hand, the analysis of critical journalists suggests that this mode of top-down governance empowers the regime to better grasp and respond to societal feedback, as well as to swiftly reinvent the space for political participation when needed. The analysis of media oversight shows that a combination of consultations and flexible response has enabled the party-state to secure certain gains from critical journalism, while thus far bypassing the potential damages to its legitimacy. Both on a routine basis and in times of major disasters, the regime's proactive engagement with journalists has fostered collaborative ties to the advantage of the former.

At the same time, fluid consultative governance carries significant risks for the long-term evolution and survival of the party-state. First, the ad hoc style of consulting with society, including critical actors, undermines the effectiveness of these input channels. While the regime is reactive to public opinion, the actual policy implementation appears to be more questionable, especially when it comes to systemic issues. As Chapters 5 and 6 demonstrate, the authorities are skilful at showcasing acknowledgement of media investigations, but deep-seated governance failures underlined in media reports, such as corruption, are often ignored or buried in projections of official responsiveness. Moreover, fluid consultations give rise to significant improvisation by local officials, whose interests often conflict with those of the centre and who tend to be resistant to media oversight. As shown throughout the book, local officials deploy their own creative acts in negotiating media supervision, which can undermine journalists' capacity to contribute to governance improvements. The analysis in this book, therefore, exposes some of the weaknesses of consultative governance processes in light of the fragmented political system and cautions against closely associating them with the regime's resilience. More attention needs to be paid to investigating the outcomes of these consultations to determine their effects on long-term governance. Finally, the analysis points to the vulnerability of the party-state in setting out a highly interactive framework for engaging with society and critical voices. By opting for constant adaptation, the regime puts itself in a vicious cycle of grasping and responding to societal shifts, which are further amplified by new media. The fluid governance, given its interactive nature, is dependent on the state's capacity to keep up with and manoeuvre these dynamic changes and challenges, which include managing citizens' expectations of official response. By settling for a state of flux, the regime, on the one hand, is securing space for inventive response, but on the other, might be undermining its flexibility in the long term.

China's Critical Journalists and Comparative Authoritarianism

Other than engaging with the scholarship on China's bottom-up activism and top-down political governance, this book also situates the China case in the wider literature on comparative authoritarianism. The analysis of the relationship between China's critical journalists and the party-state expands the conception of participatory channels under authoritarianism, the roles they are assigned by ruling regimes and the types of relationships that can form between critical actors and authorities. Namely, the China case demonstrates that state-sanctioned political participation is present beyond the widely studied electoral domain, challenging the current delineation of authoritarian regimes based on the elections variable. It further shows that these political openings or channels can serve different roles under authoritarianism, including that of an oversight or a feedback mechanism. Finally, the framework of state-dominated fluid partnership between critical journalists and the party-state highlights a possibility for a constructive albeit ambiguous relationship unifying critical actors and the state in non-democratic systems.

As for challenging the narrow scholarly conception of participatory channels or bounded political openings, the China case points to the importance of further shedding the shadow of democratisation in our analysis of authoritarian regimes by shifting the empirical focus beyond the study of elections onto the wider spectrum of spaces for bottom-up participation, including those in the media. While in the past decade, comparative authoritarianism scholarship has evolved from treating limited political liberalisation[52] as a natural pathway to democratic transition,[53] to acknowledging that non-democratic regimes can

---

[52] Limited political liberalisation is understood here as the presence of circumscribed or bounded political openings or channels, which allow for societal actors to participate in and attempt to influence governance processes. It signifies a relaxation of restrictions in a certain sphere that projects a more inclusive approach to policy-making under authoritarian rule.

[53] For other studies linking liberalisation directly to democratic transition, see, for instance, Russell Bova, 'Political Dynamics of the Post-Communist Transition: A Comparative Perspective', in Nancy Bermeo (ed.), *Liberalization & Democratization: Change in the Soviet Union and Eastern Europe* (Baltimore: John Hopkins University Press, 1991); Rex Brynen, Bahgat Korany, and Paul Noble, *Political Liberalization and Democratization in the Arab World* (Boulder; London: Lynne Rienner, 1995); Mehran Kamrava and Frank O. Mora, 'Civil Society and Democratisation in Comparative Perspective: Latin America and the Middle East', *Third World Quarterly* 19(5) (1998): 893–915; Ghassan Salame (ed.), *Democracy Without Democrats? The Renewal of Politics in the Muslim World* (London: I.B. Tauris, 2001).

indefinitely sustain some bounded political openings,[54] the focus of the literature still primarily remains on 'the consequences of regime survival, transformation, or democratization'.[55] Not surprisingly, this focus has translated into the empirical study of elections – the democratic feature conceived of as most critical to transition outcomes – as evident in the burgeoning field of 'electoral authoritarianism' studies.[56] While civil society and critical media are treated as potentially significant accountability mechanisms in the process of consolidating democracies,[57] their capacity to shape authoritarian governance is largely dismissed in the existing studies of mixed or semi-authoritarian regimes. At most, they tend to be regarded as variables indirectly influencing electoral outcomes.[58]

Echoing the arguments of Smulovitz and Peruzzotti about the need to incorporate 'societal accountability' into our comparative assessments of political accountability and governance in democratic systems,[59] this book underscores the importance of non-electoral forms of political liberalisation in constructing a comprehensive evaluation of contemporary authoritarian systems. As Diamond argues, specifically referring to China and its alternative forms of political liberalisation, 'Every step toward political liberalisation matters, both for prospect of a transition to democracy and for quality of political life as it is daily experienced by

---

[54] In his influential article on hybrid regimes, Carothers declared the 'end of the transition paradigm', urging scholars and practitioners to abandon assumptions about democratisation being the obvious outcomes of mixed regimes; see Thomas Carothers, 'The End of the Transition Paradigm', *Journal of Democracy* 13(1) (2003): 5–21. His article gave rise to new scholarship categorising and conceptualising these mixed regimes.

[55] Gilley, 'Democratic Enclaves in Authoritarian Regimes': 389–415.

[56] This is evident by the prominence of an 'electoral authoritarianism' category in recent works on mixed regimes. See, for instance, Yonatan L. Morse, 'The Era of Electoral Authoritarianism', *World Politics* 64(1) (2012): 161–198; Adam Macdonald, 'From Military Rule to Electoral Authoritarianism: The Reconfiguration of Power in Myanmar and its Future', *Asian Affairs: An American Review* 40(1) (2013): 20–36; Cameron Ross, 'Regional Elections and Electoral Authoritarianism in Russia', *Europe-Asia Studies* 63(4) (2011): 641–661; Asli U. Bâli, 'From Subjects to Citizens? The Shifting Paradigm of Electoral Authoritarianism in Egypt', *Middle East Law and Governance* 1(1) (2009): 38–89.

[57] See, for instance, Rafael Lopez-Pintor and Leonardo Morlino, 'Italy and Spain', in Larry J. Diamond and Leonardo Morlino (ed.), *Assessing the Quality of Democracy* (Baltimore: The Johns Hopkins University Press, 2005); Sumit Ganguly, 'Bangladesh and India', in Larry J. Diamond and Leonardo Morlino (ed.), *Assessing the Quality of Democracy* (Baltimore: The Johns Hopkins University Press, 2005).

[58] Steven Levitsky and Lucan A. Way, *Competitive Authoritarianism: Hybrid Regimes After the Cold War*. 1st edn. (Cambridge: Cambridge University Press, 2010); Valerie J. Wolchik and Sharon L. Bunce, *Defeating Authoritarian Leaders in Postcommunist Countries* (Cambridge: Cambridge University Press, 2011).

[59] Enrique Peruzzotti and Catalina Smulovitz, 'Societal Accountability in Latin America', *Journal of Democracy* 11(4) (2000): 147–158.

abused and aggrieved citizens'.[60] Like works on judicial politics under authoritarianism, which show that courts can constitute spaces for political contestation,[61] the analysis of critical journalism in China suggests that media can present a meaningful channel for societal engagement with authorities even in systems lacking national elections. This book, thereby, reinforces the notion of a 'democratic enclave' as a flexible category, varying in the types of spaces (i.e., institutions and actors) and their influence on empowering political participation.[62]

In arguing for a broader conception of participatory channels under authoritarianism, the China case further questions the existing categorisation of authoritarian systems based on the electoral variable, echoing Diamond's critique that such categories 'impose an uneasy order on an untidy empirical world'.[63] Whereas in the current literature China is lumped with North Korea and other non-electoral autocracies in a category of 'closed' political systems,[64] in reality, as demonstrated in Chapter 7, in some ways China appears as more democratic than hybrid authoritarian systems, like Russia, despite the presence of regular elections in the latter. The Chinese regime grants journalists a governance role within the system, unlike the Russian state that isolates them to the margins. The China case suggests that in thinking about and comparing authoritarian regimes it is useful to revert back to Linz's classic distinction of authoritarianism from totalitarianism based on the presence of limited political pluralism in the former,[65] rather than to continue to create new subcategories of mixed regimes based solely on the electoral dimension. While the combination of elections and non-democratic rule is a relatively recent, post-Cold War phenomenon, the presence of some channels for bottom-up input under non-democratic rule is a persistent trend and should be examined comparatively and comprehensively.

Other than calling for a more inclusive conceptualisation and examination of participatory channels, the study of the media oversight role in China presents a distinct analytical framework for grasping the workings of these channels, and the relations between critical voices and the state

[60] Larry Diamond, 'Thinking about Hybrid Regimes', *Journal of Democracy* 13(2) (2002): 33.
[61] Tom Ginsburg and Tamir Moustafa (eds.), *Rule by Law: The Politics of Courts in Authoritarian Regimes* (New York, NY: Cambridge University Press, 2008).
[62] Gilley, 'Democratic Enclaves in Authoritarian Regimes'.
[63] Diamond, 'Thinking About Hybrid Regimes': 33.
[64] Andreas Schedler, *Electoral Authoritarianism: The Dynamics of Unfree Competition* (Boulder, CO: Lynne Rienner Publishers, 2006); Levitsky and Way, *Competitive Authoritarianism*.
[65] Juan J. Linz, *Totalitarian and Authoritarian Regimes* (Boulder, CO; London: Lynne Rienner Publishers, 2000).

under authoritarian rule. By demonstrating that a constructive governance dimension and intensive creative improvisation underpins the
engagement between journalists and the party-state in China, this study
challenges the existing scholarly depictions of political openings as either
merely artificial or destructive, and the subsequent relations between the
state and society as being either entirely state-dominated or highly contentious. As for the artificial versus destructive dichotomy, studies of
participatory channels under authoritarianism largely embrace the top-
down approach and argue that these channels primarily serve a superficial
function of liberal image boosting for autocratic states. The scholarly
consensus is that authoritarian states tolerate these spaces not to eventually undertake a democratic transition but to stave it off and remain
in power by granting democratic institutions and critical actors solely
a nominal or a symbolic role in the system.[66] As Schedler writes in his
analysis of electoral authoritarianism, 'Political institutions that are created by and embedded in an authoritarian regime are never, except by
a slip of language, "democratic institutions"'.[67] In his study of Russia's
hybrid regime, Balzer similarly argues that the goal of Putin's regime in
tolerating some political and societal diversity, including elections
and some independent media, is to avoid, rather than enhance,
accountability.[68] Other works point to the 'co-optation'[69] and
'transparency-boosting'[70] function of pseudo-democratic institutions.

---

[66] A recent possible exception to this consensus is the work by Slater and Wong, who argue
that authoritarian regimes can choose a democratisation path if the ruling party enjoys
substantial incumbent capacity, and thereby a high chance of remaining in power in
a democratic system. Instead of treating democratisation as a desperate choice, therefore,
the two authors argue that it could be a choice of the 'strong', those confident of their
success in a democracy. Their argument, however, primarily focuses on democratisation,
not limited to political liberalisation. Moreover, it does not necessarily contradict the
other works as it still maintains that authoritarian rulers would primarily embark on
liberalisation for the sake of remaining in power. See Dan Slater and Joseph Wong,
'The Strength to Concede: Ruling Parties and Democratization in Developmental
Asia', *Perspectives on Politics* 11(3) (2013): 717–733.

[67] Andreas Schedler, 'The New Institutionalism in the Study of Authoritarian Regimes',
paper presented at the American Political Science Association annual meeting, Toronto,
2009.

[68] Harley Balzer, 'Managed Pluralism: Vladimir Putin's Emerging Regime', *Post-Soviet
Affairs* 19(3) (2003): 189–227.

[69] Jennifer Gandhi and Ellen Lust-Okar, 'Elections under Authoritarianism', *The Annual
Review of Political Studies* 12 (2009): 403–422.

[70] See, for instance, Lilia Shevtsova, 'Ten Years After the Soviet Breakup: Russia's Hybrid
Regime', *Journal of Democracy* 12(1) (2001): 65–70; Andreas Schedler, 'The Menu of
Manipulation', *Journal of Democracy* 13(2) (2002): 36–50; Crawford Young, 'The Third
Wave of Democratization in Africa: Ambiguities and Contradictions', in Richard Joseph
(ed.), *State, Conflict, and Democracy in Africa* (Boulder, CO: Lynne Rienner Publishers,
1999).

As will be explained in more detail in Chapter 7, for instance, some scholars argue that critical press and civil society in Russia produce a more liberal domestic and international image and grant some policy-making flexibility to the regime without posing a challenge to the political system.[71] The scholarship further illuminates a multitude of tactics that regimes use to contain these self-orchestrated openings, emphasising the importance of a strong coercive apparatus.[72] Limited political liberal-isation, therefore, is treated as a strategic but artificial measure that authorities use to create a fake image of transparency in order to enhance domestic and international support for their rule.

When a bottom-up lens is employed in examining the bounded open-ings, the studies look not only at potential subversion of the regime through democratic channels, like elections and protests, but also through activities of NGOs and liberal media.[73] Wolchik and Bunce, for instance, in their rich study of diverse electoral outcomes in post-Soviet states, argue that a strong civil society is an important factor in empowering opposition and facilitating electoral defeat of incumbent non-democratic rulers.[74] Gandhi also examines the potential for opposi-tion to use democratic institutions to challenge the status quo, finding that constitutional rules play an important role in influencing coordina-tion efforts among opposition candidates.[75] Unlike the top-down lens, the bottom-up lens of analysis points to a democratising potential of these channels and actors, as a result of movements not envisioned nor con-tained by the state.

The current scholarship, therefore, positions channels or spaces for political participation in two analytical extremes: either they are comple-tely undemocratic or they indirectly serve to facilitate democratic move-ments. The relationship between critical voices and ruling authorities that ensues from this analysis is either that of an orchestra, with a conductor in the form of the state effectively and comprehensively managing musicians or critical voices and society at large, or that of a clashing performance, with different actors (i.e., authorities and societal forces) aggressively

[71] Balzer, 'Managed Pluralism: Vladimir Putin's Emerging Regime'.

[72] For more details on the variety of tactics used to manipulate elections in mixed regimes, see Schedler, 'The Menu of Manipulation': 36–50.

[73] See, for instance, Nicolas van de Walle, 'Tipping Games: When Do Opposition Parties Coalesce?' in Andreas Schedler (ed.), *Electoral Authoritarianism*; Jennifer Gandhi, 'Coordination Among Opposition Parties in Authoritarian Elections', paper presented at the conference titled 'Dictatorships: Their Governance and Social Consequences', Princeton University, 25–26 April 2008, available at: www.princeton.edu/~piirs/Dictat orships042508/Gandhi.pdf; Wolchik and Bunce, *Defeating Authoritarian Leaders in Postcommunist Countries*.

[74] Wolchik and Bunce, *Defeating Authoritarian Leaders in Postcommunist Countries*.

[75] Gandhi, 'Coordination among Opposition Parties in Authoritarian Elections'.

competing for audience or public support. This study of China's critical journalists presents an alternative way for both analysing and characterising the relations between critical voices and ruling elites. By combining the top-down perspective of Chinese authorities with the bottom-up perspective of critical journalists, it illuminates the process of their engagement, uncovering a dynamic improvisational interaction fusing the two actors in a collaborative framework. The Chinese regime appears to incorporate limited critical voices not solely as a façade of transparency but as a feedback mechanism and a tool for improving local governance and for guiding public opinion, whereas journalists do not directly resist the state but collaborate on governance agenda with the centre, while still challenging selective aspects of official misconduct. The management of journalists, moreover, is not dominated by overt coercion, but more by subtle creative measures that evolve depending on political circumstances and journalists' enterprising behaviour. The framework of a fluid collaboration echoes Migdal's 'state in society' approach to analysing political change, which suggests that the state and society are continuously interacting with each other, and as a result, reshaping one another.[76] Thus, a deeper understanding of different forms of societal interactions with the state informs us of the processes underpinning political change. The comparative chapter (Chapter 7) indicates how divergent engagements between critical journalists and the state in Russia and the Soviet Union can help explain the different forms of authoritarian rule in those two regimes from those present in China, as well as the different outcomes of incorporating bounded political openings (i.e., democratisation in the Soviet Union and increasing confrontation between state and society in Putin's Russia). It is not merely the presence of semi-democratic institutions or spaces for political participation that potentially destabilise an authoritarian regime but the patterns of engagement between the state and society. Specifically, the study of China's critical journalists suggests that how a state and critical actors handle and manoeuvre high levels of uncertainty, inherent to all authoritarian regimes, is critical to understanding their evolution.

Conclusion: Forming the Bridges

By introducing new questions and conceptual frameworks into theoretical debates on China's bottom-up activism, top-down governance and political liberalisation under authoritarian rule, this book also attempts to

---

[76] Joel S. Migdal, *State in Society: Studying How States and Societies Transform and Constitute One Another* (Cambridge: Cambridge University Press, 2001).

create linkages across these otherwise often disparate fields of inquiry. First, it connects the China case to the scholarship on contemporary authoritarianism. It argues for the importance of closely investigating non-electoral political openings and documenting the processes of regime evolution in response to critical voices, as much as explaining its resilience or collapse. Rather than classifying authoritarian regimes on the basis of their apparent progress towards democracy, the China case calls for contrasting the modes of consultation and responsiveness of authoritarian regimes to public preferences, and legitimation mechanisms these regimes incorporate in order to stay in power. As this book uncovers through the prism of journalist-state relations, China's form of authoritarianism appears to differ from that observed in large-N comparative studies, with the Chinese regime adopting a more multifaceted approach in using bounded political openings to bolster its durability. There is an underlying consultative governance dimension attached to these openings that is thus far not apparent in larger comparative studies.[77] At the same time, by placing China in the wider spectrum of authoritarian regimes, this book shows that coexistence of political openings and even pervasive bottom-up activism alongside an authoritarian regime is not unique to China, but is rather a notable feature of many non-democratic regimes. It is not their persisting cohabitation, but the nature of the engagement between critical actors and officials that may distinguish China from other cases.

By capturing the perspectives of both the party-state and critical journalists in the framework of guarded improvisation, this study also bridges the scholarship on China's top-down and bottom-up governance. The interactive and improvised nature of journalists' relations with the party-state highlights not only the dynamism of China's adaptive political system but also the inherent systemic vulnerability resulting from its fluid management of critical actors and society at large, which binds the party-state in an indefinite cycle of rapid adjustments and pre-emptive initiatives. This vulnerability is ever more evident in the Xi era, as explained in detail in the concluding chapter. By identifying the regime's consultative and highly engaged approach towards critical journalists, this study further shows that the emergence of bottom-up activism in China in the reform era partially stems from the specific features of its political system. In other words, while creative attempts by societal actors to stretch the

---

[77] Reilly argues that responsive authoritarianism is a phenomenon that is present beyond China, giving Middle East, particularly Iran as some of the examples. In discussing these cases, however, he mainly refers to the coexistence of vibrant civil society with an authoritarian state as opposed to the state's interest in engaging and responding to bottom-up feedback. See Reilly, *Strong Society, Smart State*.

boundaries of the permissible undoubtedly help expand and sustain political activism, they are also a by-product of the presence of state-initiated, yet highly ambiguous spaces for political participation. Moreover, while critical actors strategically manoeuvre political ambiguity, their activities remain heavily guided by the party, which actively micro-manages the patterns of their engagement. The framework of collaboration and guarded improvisation, therefore, captures the consultative approach of the party-state and the embedded attitudes of critical actors as well as the fluid, state-dominated arrangement that binds the two forces together in an uncertain, tense and dynamic cohabitation.

Part II

Mutual Objectives and Routine Dynamics

3   Unified Objectives
The Official Discourse and Journalistic Interpretation of Media Supervision

Introduction

This chapter examines the driving forces behind the collaborative ties between China's critical journalists and the party-state. It investigates the official thinking on media oversight through the analysis of the party-state's discourse on the policy of 'media supervision' or *yulun jiandu*. The chapter further presents the perspectives of media practitioners, highlighting the societal and political aspirations driving their work. The analysis that follows shows that central authorities and critical journalists hold shared objectives when it comes to the practice of media oversight. The party-state encourages the media supervision role as one of its governance mechanisms aimed at helping expose and solve bureaucratic gridlocks and to guide public opinion, and journalists accept their responsibility of enhancing the party's performance. The congruence in motivations of higher authorities and critical journalists with regard to media oversight is amplified by their mutual improvisation on this concept. The authorities allow for significant ambiguity in their endorsements of media supervision, leaving space for backtracking when needed, and the journalists engage in limited reinterpretation of the official policy to their advantage. The party-state, however, contains the scope of conceptual improvisation by strictly framing media supervision as a mechanism subordinate to the party, while journalists accept their role as agents, rather than as independent watchdogs, of the party.

Background: Transformative Forces behind the Emergence of Critical Journalism

Prior to engaging with the official discourse on media oversight, it is important to introduce the evolution of the Chinese media landscape during the reform period: the economic transformation of print media; the technological shifts and the Westernisation trends in journalism

45

education, all sanctioned by the regime. These changes contributed to the emergence and the evolution of critical journalism.

As for economic transformations, starting in the late 1970s with deregulation and partial privatisation of the media industry, the state-initiated economic reform of the media sector produced a diverse, competitive and decentralised media landscape, conducive to investigative and in-depth reporting. Striving to promote more competition and economic dynamism, the state cut subsidies to the media sector, changed ownership regulations, allowing for up to a 49 per cent stake of private ownership of the media, and issued more media licences, encouraging entrepreneurship.[1] Though some changes took place at the outset of the reform period, more serious transformations were introduced in the 1990s, following the wider economic reforms promoted during Deng Xiaoping's Southern Tour.[2] As a result of these far-reaching reforms, the media sector – particularly print media – has exploded, with the number of newspapers expanding from 69 in 1979 to 1,937 in 1997,[3] and the market share of official papers declining in favour of the newly emerged commercialised and partially commercialised newspapers.[4]

The sharp competition for advertising revenue and readership accompanying the expansion and diversification of the media sector has inspired some media outlets to feature investigative and critical coverage to differentiate themselves and to attract new readership. In fact, in today's China, the publications most reputable for professional in-depth and investigative reporting are either semi-commercialised or fully commercialised,[5] enjoying high circulation and advertising revenues. *Nanfang Zhoumo*, for instance, known from the mid-1980s to the late 2000s as one of China's feistiest newspapers, has a circulation of over

---

[1] Daniela Stockmann and Mary E. Gallagher, 'Remote Control: How the Media Sustain Authoritarian Rule in China', *Comparative Political Studies* 44(4) (2011): 436–467.

[2] Deng Xiaoping's 1992 Southern Tour is considered a turning point in China's economic development. Deng advocated sweeping economic development, particularly of the coastal areas, but also throughout China's major industries.

[3] Guoguang Wu, 'One Head, Many Mouths: Diversifying Press Structures in Reform China', in Chin-Chuan Lee (ed.), *Power, Money, and Media: Communication Patterns and Bureaucratic Control in Cultural China* (Evanston: Northwestern University Press, 2000): 47.

[4] Daniela Stockmann, *Media Commercialization and Authoritarian Rule in China* (Cambridge University Press, 2012); Minxin Pei, *From Reform to Revolution: The Demise of Communism in China and the Soviet Union* (Cambridge: Harvard University Press, 1994).

[5] Even the most commercialised outlets, however, are still technically owned by the Chinese Communist Party (CCP), since the highest private ownership allowed is 49 per cent.

one million and advertising revenue exceeding one billion yuan,[6] while *Caijing*, a famous Beijing-based investigative outlet, made it into the top ten magazines with the highest advertising revenue in 2006.[7] The financial success of investigative publications further helped attract more media professionals to this genre, as they began to perceive it as a career, not only as an advocacy initiative.[8] Intellectuals and liberal-minded journalists, who in the past could only express their opinions in underground publications, now had some public outlets to channel their ideas and they exploited them skilfully.[9]

Decentralisation of the media, which paralleled its expansion, has also enabled more investigative journalism. In the reform era, the media shifted from being mainly concentrated in the capital to spreading across the country, with the majority of newspapers now being published at the provincial and municipal levels. Specifically, whereas in 1979, 24.6 per cent out of a total of 69 newspapers were published in Beijing, by 1997 only 9.6 per cent of 2,149 newspapers were published in the capital.[10] This shift meant that the central press was no longer the sole authority on many subject areas, and new opportunities emerged for provincial media to examine governance issues at a distance from higher officials. Some of the media outlets most renowned for critical coverage in the past decade, including *Nanfang Zhoumo* and *Nanfang Dushibao*, for instance, are based in the southern Guangzhou province, over a thousand miles away from Beijing. Decentralisation also incited journalistic investigations of governance failures outside one's home province – a practice known as extraterritorial supervision, or *yidi jiandu*, which is discussed in detail in the next chapter. On the whole, China's media scholars tend to associate the 1990s with the 'golden period' for watchdog journalism,[11] which parallels state-supported commercialisation of the media sector, and the subsequent emergence of competitive critical outlets. Thus, the party-state has implicitly incentivised watchdog reporting by granting media a limited economic autonomy from the state.[12]

---

[6] Qian Gang, 'Why Southern Weekly?' *China Media Project*, 18 February 2013, available at: http://cmp.hku.hk/2013/02/18/31257/.

[7] James F. Scotton and William A. Hachten, *New Media for a New China* (Oxford: Wiley-Blackwell, 2010).

[8] Jingrong Tong and Colin Sparks, 'Investigative Journalism in China Today', *Journalism Studies* 10 (2009): 337–352.

[9] Pei, *From Reform to Revolution*.

[10] Wu, 'One Head, Many Mouths', in Lee (ed.), *Power, Money, and Media*: 47.

[11] Jingrong Tong, *Investigative Journalism in China: Journalism, Power, and Society* (London: Continuum, 2011).

[12] For more scholarship on media commercialization, see Yuezhi Zhao, 'From Commercialization to Conglomeration: The Transformation of the Chinese Press Within the Orbit of the Party State', *Journal of Communication* 50(2) (2000): 3–26;

Other than the economic reform of the media sector, the state's endorsement of the internet, starting in the mid-1990s, has also indirectly empowered the expansion of critical journalism. The internet, while posing its own competitive challenges for established media publications, has also simultaneously facilitated the production and dissemination of critical discourses. As for the production of investigative reporting, as shown throughout the book, social media has generated unprecedented connectivity across journalist communities as well as between journalists and activists in working on shared agenda and in putting pressure on the state.[13] Starting with BBS forums[14] and blogs in the 1990s and early 2000s, and shifting into microblogging or Weibo in the mid- to late 2000s, and most recently moving into the use of WeChat platforms or Weixin, Chinese media practitioners have consistently employed internet tools to connect, collaborate and spread media reports that in the past had only been available for sale in print editions. Beyond the accessibility of new technological tools, the internet has in part created more active media audiences and co-producers of media content. Internet expansion in the past two decades has facilitated an emergence of what some scholars refer to as 'media citizenship', or a transformation of previously passive media consumers into proactive ones, involved in producing, sharing and analysing information online.[15] This shift has further revitalised and diversified Chinese media industry, as journalists now face more demanding readers and commentators online, as well as competing information sources from netizens and citizen journalists. As a result of social media expansion, journalists' task of informed, balanced and timely

Hu Shuli, 'The Rise of the Business Media in China', in Susan L. Shirk (ed.), *Changing Media, Changing China* (Oxford; New York: Oxford University Press, 2011): 77–91; Qian Gang and David Bandurski, 'China's Emerging Public Sphere: The Impact of Media Commercialization, Professionalism, and the Internet in an Era of Transition', in Shirk (ed.), *Changing Media, Changing China* (Oxford, New York: Oxford University Press): 38–77. China's annual Blue Books provide detailed information on the economic developments in the media industry. See, for example, Cui Baoguo, '2010 nian: zhongguo chuanmei chanye fazhan baogao' ('2010: Report on the Development of China's Media Industry') (Beijing: Social Sciences Academic Press, 2010).

[13] For more details about the positive linkages between the internet and established critical journalism, see Jonathan Hassid and Maria Repnikova, 'Why Chinese Print Journalists Embrace the Internet', *Journalism* 17(7) (2016): 882–898.

[14] BBS or bulletin-board sites are online communities or forums set up by different organisations, including universities and work units to facilitate discussions on topics ranging from sports to politics. For more details on the evolution of BBS, see: Hu Yong, 'BBS sites on China's Changing Web', *China Media Project*, 1 June 2010; available at: http://cmp.hku.hk/2010/06/01/6158/.

[15] Christoph H. Steinhardt 'From Blind Spot to Media Spotlight: Propaganda Policy, Media Activism and the Emergence of Protest Events in the Chinese Public Sphere', *Asian Studies Review* 39(1) (2015): 123.

reporting and interpretation of conflicting information has become ever more critical in recent years. The tensions and the opportunities emerging from the internet expansion are illustrated in the following chapters.

Finally, the state's tolerance for some Western ideas in journalist training spaces and practices has also indirectly empowered the development of media oversight practice in China. In the past two decades, the curricula and training materials used in journalism classes have significantly evolved to include Western materials and teaching approaches, especially in the realm of practical journalism training, such as interviewing, editing and new media usage.[16] The teaching curricula have further shifted from a sole focus on the party's ideology to addressing commercial and global facets of journalism. In some cases, the umbrella of Western and commercial teachings has also created new spaces for discussion of media ethics, professionalism and strategies for investigative journalism.[17] Outside the classrooms, as highlighted in parts of the book, China's opening up to the world has allowed for a number of practicing journalists to partake in exchanges in Western media and journalism programmes and to build new information and professional networks that spread beyond China's borders.

The economic, technological and pro-Western transformations that have taken place in China in the past three decades, therefore, had a significant impact on the development of the media industry and the subsequent appearance, expansion and reinvention of critical journalism. Beyond providing the commercial impetus, and indirectly facilitating the emergence of digital platforms and new audiences and co-producers of media content, as well as sanctioning an infusion of Western ideas in journalism training, the party-state has also directly endorsed limited media oversight in the past three decades. The following section engages with the explicit endorsement in detail by examining the official discourse on watchdog journalism or media supervision.

Part I: The Media Supervision Role in the Official Discourse

The Emergence of the Official Concept

While the predominant role of the media advocated under Mao was that of the party mouthpiece (*houshe* 喉舌) and a tool for public

---

[16] Maria Repnikova, 'Thought Work Contested: Ideology and Journalism Education in China', *China Quarterly* 230 (2017).
[17] Ibid.

mobilisation,[18] a trace of media's oversight role was present in the official discourse during that period, as manifested by some official encouragement of newspapers to engage in limited criticism of the party. Studies tracing the history of investigative journalism in China point to the party's urging of the press to channel public criticisms of official wrongdoings in the early 1950s in order to discipline cadres and elites and to facilitate 'self-improvement'.[19] This state-sanctioned media critique was explicitly termed 'newspaper criticism' or *baozhi piping* (报纸批评), and often resembled an orchestrated attempt by higher officials to weed out certain individuals or factions.[20] The highest point of critical reporting under Mao's rule was during the Hundred Flowers Campaign,[21] which was subsequently suppressed as part of the Anti-Rightist Campaign,[22] and cracked down on still harder during the Cultural Revolution.[23] Liu Binyan, a leading Chinese intellectual who had continuously exposed governance failures in China from the Mao era to the present, described the Hundred Flowers Campaign as a brief opening for unmasking the lived experiences hidden under the propaganda shadow: 'Instead of writing that everyone lived well, they now sought to depict life realistically, with all the contradictions and conflicts of socialist society that "realism" had attempted to suppress'.[24] In addition to these politicised and controversial openings for media critique, the party has long maintained a practice of soliciting internal feedback from the media known as *neican* (内参) or 'internal references'. These internally produced investigative reports would only be accessible to selected party officials, who used them to address specific governance failures, such as

[18] Yuezhi Zhao, *Communication in China: Political Economy, Power, and Conflict* (Lanham, MD; Plymouth: Rowman & Littlefield, 2008).

[19] Tong, *Investigative Journalism in China*: 25.

[20] Li-fung Cho, 'The Emergence, Influence and Limitations of Watchdog Journalism in Post-1992 China: A Case Study of *Southern Weekend*', PhD dissertation (The University of Hong Kong, 2007).

[21] In the Spring of 1957, Mao encouraged more public expression of political criticism. Intellectuals in particular were invited to express their opinions, which led to the outpouring of criticisms towards the party-state, particularly the local authorities. See Kenneth Lieberthal, *Governing China: From Revolution Through Reform* (New York; London: W.W. Norton & Company, Inc., 1995).

[22] This campaign centred on labelling intellectuals as 'rightists', as a result of their actions during the Hundred Flowers Campaign, and purging them to penal camps or to the countryside for forced labour.

[23] A movement launched by Chairman Mao, with the aim to purge the bourgeoisie elements by mobilising young people across the country. The movement took place between 1966 and 1976 and had grave effects on journalism practice and education, with most intellectuals purged to the countryside or banned from expressing their opinions.

[24] Nathan Gardels, 'The Price China Has Paid: The Interview with Liu Binyan', *The New York Review of Books* 35 (21/22), 19 January 1989, available at: www.nybooks.com/articles/4178.

local corruption.[25] The internal reference system is still in place to this day in official news outlets like *Xinhua* and *Renmin Ribao*.[26] The Mao period, therefore, featured some official endorsement of critical reporting, though for the most part it was highly managed by the party-state and missing the important element of public supervision over party officials, which was introduced much later, in the 1980s.

During the reform era, an official yet elusive concept emerged to capture the media's oversight role: *yulun jiandu* (舆论监督). The meaning of this concept is not immediately obvious. The direct translation is public opinion supervision, but Western scholars have also deciphered it as 'supervision by public opinion'[27] and 'public supervision'.[28] Although *yulun jiandu* appears to invoke the relationship between the public and the state, this concept has been used mainly in discussions of the media by Chinese authorities, media scholars and journalists, and is understood to signify a distinct media role, synonymous with media supervision or *meiti jiandu* (媒体监督). As Zhao and Wusan argue, while noting the vagueness of the term: '[A] prevailing definition connotes the use of critical media reports to supervise government officials'.[29] The association of *yulun jiandu* with the media is further reinforced by the existence of other official concepts to describe public supervision more broadly, such as *qunzhong jiandu* (群众监督), directly translated as supervision by the masses, and *shehui jiandu* (社会监督), translated as supervision by society, or societal supervision.

To capture the full meaning of this term, *yulun jiandu* is defined here as media oversight and supervision of authorities through conveying public opinion, whereby media is meant to channel public concerns to the party-state. The shorter versions, 'the media supervision through public opinion' and 'the media supervision role', are used interchangeably in this

---

[25] For more detail on *neican*, see Jennifer Grant, 'Internal Reporting by Investigative Journalists in China and its Influence on Government Policy', *International Communication Gazette* 41 (1988).

[26] During field research, the author has encountered several journalists who were engaged in internal reporting for Xinhua News Agency. For more on the 'neican' system, see Wen-Hsuan Tsai, 'A Unique Pattern of Policymaking in China's Authoritarian Regime: The CCP's Neican/Pishi Model', *Asian Survey* 55(6) (2015): 1093–1115.

[27] Martin Brenderbach, 'Public Opinion: A New Factor Influencing the PRC Press', *Asien* 96 (July 2005): 29–45.

[28] Stevenson Yang, 'The Absent-Minded Reform of China's Media', in David M. Filkenstein and Maryanne Kivlehan (eds.), *China's Leadership in the 21st Century: The Rise of the Fourth Generation* (Armonk, NY: M.E. Sharpe, 2002): 223–249.

[29] Yuezhi Zhao and Sun Wusan, 'Public Opinion Supervision: Possibilities and Limits of the Media in Constraining Local Officials', in Elizabeth J. Perry and Merle Goldman (eds.), *Grassroots Reform in Contemporary China* (Cambridge: Harvard University Press, 2007).

chapter. The official emphasis on public opinion in this concept is important, as it implies that journalists' agenda should be fused with that of the public.[30] As elaborated further in the chapter, however, the party-state does not encourage media to represent all of public opinion, and serving the state's interests is advocated as the core facet of journalists' supervision work.

The concept of *yulun jiandu* emerged in the late 1980s, receded following the 1989 Tiananmen Square incident and reappeared again in the 1990s. The first high-level reference to *yulun jiandu* featured in a speech delivered by China's Premier Zhao Ziyang[31] at the Thirteenth Party Congress[32] in 1987, in which he explicitly called for media supervision of public opinion:

> It is important to enhance reports on government and party activities through a variety of modern propaganda tools to make the media play the role of *yulun jiandu,* to support the mass criticisms of the Party and the government's shortcomings and mistakes, to create opposition to the bureaucracy and to fight against all kinds of unhealthy practices.[33]

Zhao's statement shows that the official endorsement of media oversight as a feedback and a self-correcting mechanism was notable from the start. Specifically, Zhao's remark suggests that by carrying out *yulun jiandu* reporting, the media should channel public concerns to the party-state, which could in turn facilitate the party's self-improvement, including its overcoming of policy gridlocks. Zhao's brief endorsement further alludes to the elusive and contradictory nature of the media supervision role through public opinion. On the one hand, the boundaries for critical reporting are left undefined, suggesting that the media could potentially report on any public grievance. On the other hand, it is apparent that *yulun jiandu* is a party-led mechanism, initiated within the confines of the

---

[30] This assumption resonates with that held by democracy scholars who merge the media's watchdog or accountability role with that of civil society, and conceptualise it as one of the vertical (bottom-up) accountability channels. See Larry Diamond and Leonard Morlino, *Assessing the Quality of Democracy* (Baltimore: The John Hopkins University Press, 2005); Andreas Schedler, 'Conceptualizing Accountability', in Andreas Schedler, Larry Diamond and Marc F. Plattner (eds.), *The Self-Restraining State: Power and Accountability in New Democracies* (Boulder, CO: Lynne Rienner Publishers, 1999): 13–29.

[31] Zhao Ziyang served as premier of the People's Republic of China (PRC) from 1980 to 1987 and the general secretary of the Chinese Communist Party (CCP) from 1987 to 1989.

[32] The party congress takes place only once every five years and is one of the most important policy-making forums, carefully monitored and foreshadowing the direction of the party.

[33] Chen Lidan, 'Wo guo yulun jiandu de lilun yu jiangou' ('Yulun Jiandu's Theoretical Construction in China'), *Xinwen Jie* (April 2004): 24.

party-state. Even though this specific statement was made in the context of freedom of the press and democracy debates taking place in Beijing at that time,[34] Zhao did not link *yulun jiandu* to the wider political liberalisation and democratisation processes.[35] From the outset of the party-state's promotion of the media's supervision role in the reform era, it was characterised by guarded improvisation, with authorities loosely outlining the scope for critical journalism, while still framing it as a governance mechanism of the party.

Not long after the initial official encouragement of media supervision, it suffered a setback following the 1989 Tiananmen incident, with officials, including Jiang Zemin, returning to the 'mouthpiece' conceptualisation of the media role.[36] Although *yulun jiandu* was mentioned in a 1989 speech delivered by Jiang, it was done so strictly in the context of promoting the media's guidance of public opinion or its dominant role of *yulun daoxiang* (輿論导向).[37] That same year, Zhao Ziyang was placed under house arrest under the pretext of his opposition to the Tiananmen military crackdown.[38] Zhao's explicit support for students' demands to enact the law of the press – among other institutional mechanisms facilitating accountability – was not welcomed by the hardliners in the party.[39] His death under house arrest symbolised the limits of the party's tolerance for public opinion input and criticism of its policies. The media crackdown was also in part a reaction to the collapse of the Soviet Union, according to media scholars interviewed at Beijing and Tsinghua universities.[40] As already mentioned in the Introduction and discussed in detail in Chapter 7, a freer Soviet media was seen as instrumental in the breakdown of the Soviet Union.[41] To this day, the debate on the subject remains highly sensitive in China's academic and journalistic circles.[42]

---

[34] The Chinese student pro-democracy movement started in 1987 and culminated in the Tiananmen protests of 1989.

[35] His memoir, however, suggests that he held more radical thoughts about freedom of the press in private. He did express stronger opinions in support of freedom of expression advocated by students in 1989. For more details on Zhao's impressions and documentation of party debates at the time, see Zhao Ziyang, *Prisoner of the State: The Secret Journal of Premier Zhao Ziyang* (London: Simon & Schuster, 2009).

[36] Zhao and Wusan, 'Public Opinion Supervision': 45.

[37] Cho, 'The Emergence, Influence and Limitations of Watchdog Journalism in Post-1992 China'.

[38] Lindsay Beck, 'Zhao's Death Shows Limits of China's Media Freedom', *Reuters*, 27 January 2005, available at: http://chinadigitaltimes.net/2005/01/lindsay-beck-zhao-death-shows-limits-of-chinas-media-freedom/.

[39] Ziyang, *Prisoner of the State*.   [40] Interviews CSE04; CSE01.

[41] Anne-Marie Brady, *Marketing Dictatorship: Propaganda and Thought Work in Contemporary China* (Lanham, MD; Plymouth: Rowman & Littlefield, 2008).

[42] The author has personally witnessed the secret discussion of the media's role in Russia's democratisation. This discussion is explained further in the chapter.

The crackdown, however, was gradually reversed in the 1990s, with *yulun jiandu* re-emerging as one of the party-state's policies to battle corruption within the party and to address social problems associated with rapid economic growth.[43] Enhancing media supervision through public opinion was integrated into the official agenda, along with strengthening the rule of law and top-down oversight over local officials. This was manifested in the inclusion of *yulun jiandu* in party congress reports in 1992 and 1997,[44] as well as in the explicit statements made about media supervision by top officials. In 1997, Premier Li Peng praised *Jiaodian Fangtan* (Focus, 焦点访谈), a popular investigative programme on China Central Television (CCTV),[45] as an 'excellent innovation'.[46] In 1998, the president of China's Supreme Court, Xiao Yang, encouraged media supervision of the courts,[47] which has continued to intensify in the past decade, with media coverage of legal battles often affecting court decisions in favour of public opinion.[48] In the same year, following the Fifteenth National Congress, Premier Zhu Rongji showed support for *yulun jiandu* with an official visit to *Jiaodian Fangtan*. During the visit, he announced that this programme represented the ideal of media supervision through public opinion, as it aggressively battled corruption without endangering the legitimacy of the party.[49] 'I am also one of the officials who should be monitored by Focus', he proclaimed.[50] Other than the support for media supervision by central authorities, some scholars also note the official endorsement of *yulun jiandu* at the provincial level in the 1990s.[51] Specifically, Guangdong and Henan emerged as

---

[43] Zhao Yuezhi, 'Watchdogs on Party Leashes? Contexts and Implications of Investigative Journalism in post-Deng China', *Journalism Studies* 1 (2000): 577–597.

[44] Cho, 'The Emergence, Influence and Limitations of Watchdog Journalism in Post-1992 China'.

[45] *Jiaodian Fangtan*, translated as 'Focus', was launched in 1994, and became a pioneering programme for exposing corruption. This programme, attracting over 300 million viewers every night, had set an example for other TV stations, especially at the local level, to create similar programmes and also inspired more journalists to practise investigative reporting. See Li Xiaoping, ' "Focus" (*Jiaodian Fangtan*) and the Changes in the Chinese Television Industry', *Journal of Contemporary China* 11 (2002): 17–34. For more details on a journalistic account of the programme, see also Elisabeth Rosenthal, 'A Muckraking Program Draws 300 Million Daily', *The New York Times*, 2 July 1998, available at: www.nytimes.com/1998/07/02/world/clinton-in-china-airwaves-a-muckraking-program-draws-300-million-daily.html.

[46] Xiaoping, ' "Focus" and the Changes in the Chinese Television Industry': 22.

[47] Ibid.

[48] This phenomenon is known as 'media judgement' or 'trial by the media'. See Benjamin L. Liebman, 'The Media and the Courts: Towards Competitive Supervision?' *The China Quarterly* 208 (2011): 833–850.

[49] Brenderbach, 'Public Opinion'.

[50] Xiaoping, '"Focus" and the Changes in the Chinese Television Industry': 23.

[51] Tong, *Investigative Journalism in China*.

two provinces with more liberal political attitudes towards investigative reporting. At the same time, it is important to note that while high-level and regional authorities promoted media supervision in the 1990s, they did not advocate it as the media's dominant role, with the guidance of public opinion always taking precedence in the official discourse. The media's watchdog function, therefore, while encouraged, has been framed as secondary to its role of spreading official messages to the public and helping maintain political stability.[52]

The Hu-Wen era has been characterised by some scholars and journalists as marking a relative decline of official support for *yulun jiandu*.[53] Specifically, they argue that the combination of the official promotion of 'harmonious society' (*hexie shehui*, 和谐社会) and growing public discontent, as manifested by the increasing frequency of protests,[54] has made media supervision a more risky endeavour in the eyes of the party. The following analysis, however, demonstrates that despite the seemingly unfavourable environment for media supervision, this policy still featured in the official discourse in the Hu-Wen era, but it has been marked by more ambiguity in contrast to the past.

Yulun Jiandu *in the Hu-Wen Period*

Although unlike the late 1990s, there were no high-level visits to investigative programmes or extensive political statements devoted to *yulun jiandu* in the Hu-Wen period, the concept still featured in key political speeches in the past decade, as manifested by its brief mention at the Sixteenth, Seventeenth and Eighteenth Party Congresses.[55] In all three

---

[52] Cho, 'The Emergence, Influence and Limitations of Watchdog Journalism in Post-1992 China'.

[53] Tong, *Investigative Journalism in China*. The author's interviews with Chinese journalists and media scholars similarly reveal their shared understanding of *yulun jiandu*'s having less scope during the Hu-Wen period than under previous administrations in the reform era, with the exception of the post-Tiananmen crackdown. Some interviewees presented me with a graph of *yulun jiandu* prevalence during the reform period, with the early 2000s being the peak for investigative reporting and the Hu-Wen period presenting a gradual decline. Some specified the reporting on severe acute respiratory syndrome (Sars) cases in 2003 as the peak of the media's supervision through public opinion. Nonetheless, even during the Hu-Wen period, interviewees noted the presence of the so-called openings for and crackdowns on investigative reporting, depending on the sensitivity of the domestic and international political climate.

[54] Alan Taylor, 'Rising Protests in China', *The Atlantic*, 17 February 2012; for more recent scholarly works on protests, see Ching Kwan Lee, *Against the Law: Labor Protests in China's Rustbelt and Sunbelt* (London: University of California Press, 2007).

[55] Full texts of the speeches are available at: www.china.org.cn/english/features/49007.htm; http://news.xinhuanet.com/english/2007-10/24/content_6938749.htm; www.china.org.cn/china/18th_cpc_congress/node_7167318.htm.

speeches delivered by the party secretary (Jiang Zenmin in 2002 and Hu Jintao in 2007 and 2012), *yulun jiandu* appeared in almost identical sentences concerning the need for restraining and supervising the use of power. As these speeches reveal little insight into the official thinking about the workings of *yulun jiandu*, a further analysis was carried out to reconstruct the meaning of this concept, namely the examination of the discussion of the policy in the Chinese Communist Party's (CCP) top journal, *Qiushi*, from the twenty-first issue in 2002 to the fourth issue in 2012,[56] in addition to the analysis of interviews with propaganda officials and media scholars. A close thematic and framing analysis of 306 articles containing the term *yulun jiandu* in *Qiushi* and an examination of the interview data found that the discussion of media supervision is encompassed into a broader theme of either official oversight or media policy. Specifically, *yulun jiandu* was framed as one of the party-state's accountability mechanisms, as well as a media role facilitating effective guidance of public opinion (*yulun yindao*, 舆论引导). The analysis further shows that the official discourse on *yulun jiandu* featured conceptual ambiguity, enabling fluid policy-making when it comes to media oversight.

Yulun Jiandu *and Party Oversight*

Under the theme of official supervision, often incorporated into the anti-corruption rhetoric, *yulun jiandu* is framed as one of the multiple oversight mechanisms endorsed by the party-state, and aimed at improving the party's performance. The following excerpts illustrate how it is positioned within the discussion on supervision:

Carefully put in practice the following supervision mechanisms: sharing information and making reports about important events and one's own work, convening small-scale meetings within your unit, appropriately handling complaint letters and visits . . . seriously researching and establishing a *yulun jiandu* system,[57] as well as a system for requesting information and dismissing incompetent officials . . . [Written by the deputy secretary of the Beijing Municipal Party Committee and the secretary for the Beijing Committee for Inspecting Discipline, 2005.][58]

---

[56] First, the 'full-text researching' function was used to identify the articles in this time period that contained the keyword *yulun jiandu*, which produced a total of 308 articles. This was followed by a close reading of the articles to identify the broader themes and frames associated with the discussion of *yulun jiandu*. The *Qiushi* articles reflect and incorporate the analysis of top leadership speeches, especially those from the three party congresses in 2002, 2007 and 2012.

[57] The original texts did not highlight these phrases. This was done by the author to draw the reader to the mentions of *yulun jiandu*.

[58] Yang Anjiang, 'Qianghua jiandu, tuijin chengfan tixi jianshi' ('Strengthen Supervision, Move Forward the Implementation of the Self-restraint System'), *Qiushi* 5 (2005): 36–37.

Take a step further in moving forward the transparency of the Party's operations, make government affairs open to the public, broaden supervision channels, combine the inner-Party supervision and public supervision, government's specialised supervision organs, Chinese People's Consultative Conference, supervision by law, mass supervision, *yulun jiandu*, and other mechanisms. [Written by the editor-in-chief as part of the analysis of Hu Jintao's speech at the Seventh Plenary Conference of the Central Commission for Inspecting Discipline, 2007.][59]

Continuously perfect various inner-Party supervision institutions, reinforce the supervision of the leading cadres at different levels ... Integrate supervision resources, broaden supervision channels, persist in inner-Party supervision and external (outer Party) supervision, integrate supervision by specialised organs with mass supervision, bring into play the function of *yulun jiandu*, join forces in strengthening the entire supervision system. [Written by the deputy secretary of the Special Commission for Inspecting Discipline, 2010.][60]

These three statements taken from different periods of the Hu-Wen administration indicate the embeddedness of media supervision through public opinion in the larger system of the party's supervision. In each statement, it is mentioned alongside other mechanisms aimed at fostering accountability of party units, especially at the local level. This discourse reflects the emphasis of the leadership on strengthening official discipline by revamping supervision systems and combining the internal mechanisms, such as intra-party democracy, with external channels, like the media, in order to achieve 'scientific' or 'comprehensive, coordinated, and sustainable' development.[61]

The appearance of *yulun jiandu* in conjunction with the Chinese People's Political Consultative Conference (CPPCC), the system for public complaints letters and visits, and the rule of law, seems to position media oversight on an equal footing with these societal mechanisms, echoing the works of Nathan and Lorentzen, which treat media's critical and investigative reporting as part of the wider feedback and bottom-up accountability network created by the state.[62] This discourse also

---

[59] Yang Shaohua, 'Anzhao kexue fazhan guan de yaoqiu qieshi zhuanbian zuofeng: xuexi Hu Jintao tongzhi zai zhongyang ji-wei di-qi ci quanti huiyi shang de zhongyao jianghua' ('Study Comrade Hu Jintao's Speech at the Seventh Plenary Conference of the Central Commission for Inspecting Discipline'), *Qiushi* 5 (2007): 16–19.

[60] Zhang Huixin, 'Jinyibu tigao fanfuchanglian jianshe kexuehua shuiping' ('Go a Step Further in Improving the Scientific Standards of Opposing Corruption and Advocating Honesty'), *Qiushi* 23 (2010): 15–17.

[61] 'Scientific development' was the key development approach in the Hu-Wen era. See Joseph Fewsmith, 'Promoting the Scientific Development Concept', *China Leadership Monitor* 11 (13 July 2004), available at: www.hoover.org/sites/default/files/uploads/documents/clm11_jf.pdf.

[62] Andrew Nathan, 'Authoritarian Resilience', *Journal of Democracy* 14 (2003): 6–17; Peter L. Lorentzen, Pierre F. Landry, and John K. Yasuda, 'Transparent Authoritarianism? An Analysis of Political and Economic Barriers to Greater Government Transparency in

confirms the feedback role played by commercial media, as analysed in Stockmann's groundbreaking work on Chinese media commercialisation.[63] At the same time, the loose mention of *yulun jiandu* signals its uncertain standing in the state's supervision agenda. The mention of the media's supervision through public opinion at the end of long sentences, and more broadly in the middle or in the concluding paragraphs of articles, indicates the 'backgrounding' or de-emphasising of this concept by the authors.[64] The use of phrases like 'bring into play' or 'research' in relation to *yulun jiandu* further suggests that the institutionalisation of this mechanism is still in its early stages. The nature of the workings of *yulun jiandu* with other accountability mechanisms is also left unspecified. While some recent scholarly works point to the emergence of competitive supervision between the courts and the media,[65] for instance, the above official statements do not mention the party's endorsement of this practice or of any other cross-supervision processes. The discussion of public oversight in general, however, is not distinguished by its clarity in Chinese policy documents. Given the sensitivity of societal feedback, official statements appear to be intentionally open ended, leaving space for retraction or adjustment when needed.

What is made explicitly apparent in these statements as well as in interviews with officials[66] and scholars,[67] however, is that supervision by the media only works in so far as it is congruent with the agenda of the central state, and since this agenda is bound to shift, the media's supervision role is also inherently unstable. An excerpt from an interview with a scholar at the Government School at Nankai University, for instance, demonstrates how media supervision is only perceived as effective if it attracts the involvement of higher officials:

If higher authorities pay attention to a problem, then the supervision is effective. Top-down supervision is strong in China, whereas bottom-up is much weaker. If media supervision is combined with that by central authorities, it's more likely to bring about some results. *Yulun jiandu* is endorsed by authorities only as part of

China', paper presented at the American Annual Political Science Association Meeting, 4 September 2010.

[63] Stockmann, *Media Commercialization and Authoritarian Rule in China*.

[64] On 'backgrounding', see Thomas N. Huckin, 'Critical Discourse Analysis', in Tom Miller (ed.), *Functional Approaches to Written Text: Classroom Applications*, (1997), available at: http://eca.state.gov/education/engteaching/pubs/BR/functionalsec3_6.htm.

[65] Benjamin L. Liebman, 'The Media and the Courts': 833–850.

[66] Interviews COF01; COF02; COF03; COF05; COF06.

[67] Scholars from Nankai University's School of Government and Beida's Anti-Corruption Centre were interviewed about the importance of *yulun jiandu* as a supervision mechanism in the official discourse. Interviews CSE07; CSE08; CSE09; CSE10; CSE11; CSE12; CSE13.

a larger system driven by the party-state. It has never been envisioned as an entirely independent societal mechanism.[68]

The above interviewee, who has had extensive experience working with both local and central party officials on a variety of governance issues, including crises and media management, suggests that the only intrinsic characteristic of media supervision is its fusion with the party's agenda. Given the multilayered and at times non-transparent nature of the party's agenda, the role of the media as an oversight mechanism is inevitably bound to fluctuate. Similarly, an official from the Central Propaganda Department (CPD),[69] while praising media supervision as one of the important public oversight mechanisms, argues that media revelations alone are insufficient in affecting change, and the involvement of the party-state is instrumental for that to happen. The official further acknowledged that the nature of media supervision works on a case-by-case basis and does not follow a predictable institutionalised pattern. Another, former high-ranking official at the National People's Congress, and now an independent political consultant, gave a more cynical assessment of the workings of China's accountability system, including that of the media oversight: 'China could be described as an elitist consultative regime. The party-state, or rather individual officials only incorporate advice or criticism from below when it suits their core objectives in a given situation. It's a very selective idea of accountability'.[70] Media supervision as a mechanism of accountability, therefore, is cautiously endorsed by the party-state as potentially effective and significant, yet it constitutes a nascent, amorphous and state-led policy within the party's evolving thinking on checks and balances with Chinese characteristics. The fluid nature of media oversight as an accountability tool echoes the discussion in the previous chapter about consultative governance as only being tolerable in so far as it remains mouldable by the state.

Yulun Jiandu *and Media Policy*

The second key theme that features in the discussion of media supervision in the official discourse is that of media policy. In these articles and official statements, *yulun jiandu* is framed as an important element in the broader media policy of *yulun yindao* (輿論引导), translated as 'leading'[71] or 'channelling public opinion'.[72] This concept presents an

---

[68] Interview CSE10.   [69] Interview COF01.   [70] Interview COF04.
[71] Tong, *Investigative Journalism in China*: 64.
[72] China Media Project, 'How Officials Can Spin the Media', 19 June 2010, available at: http://cmp.hku.hk/2010/06/19/6238/.

upgraded version of the earlier-mentioned *yulun daoxiang* or guidance of public opinion by the media. Researchers from the China Media Project argue that 'channelling is less focused on suppressing negative news coverage and more concerned with spinning news in a direction favourable to the leadership'.[73] Since 'channelling' can be confused with conveying public opinion to authorities, however, *yulun yindao* is defined here as the media's role of directing or spinning public opinion in line with the party-state's priorities. This media role tends to be associated with the official directive of 'positive reporting' or *zhengmian baodao* (正面报道), discussed in detail in the next chapter. In the official discourse on media policy, the endorsement of *yulun jiandu* is either incorporated into the discussion on *yulun yindao* or vice versa. This framing grants authorities flexibility in their treatment of media oversight, as the line between the two media roles is kept blurry and critical journalism is to operate under the shadow of positive public opinion formation.

The following excerpt from an article on directing public opinion presents a typical example of the adjacency of *yulun jiandu* with *yulun yindao* in the official discourse:

> The correct treatment and conscious acceptance of on-line *yulun jiandu* is not only conducive to resolving conflicts or problems, and increasing productivity, but it can also improve the capacity of *yulun yindao*. Practice shows that the more effective *yulun jiandu* is, the more *yulun yindao* can win public confidence. [Written by the head of the Propaganda Department, Gansu Province, Pingliang Municipal Party Committee Standing Member.] [74]

This official stresses the interactive relationship between *yulun jiandu* and *yulun yindao*, with the former reinforcing the latter. By helping authorities address problems of concern to the public, media supervision raises official credibility and thereby facilitates the process of guiding public opinion. In another example of official analysis of media policy,[75] the discussion of *yulun jiandu* appears under the third point in a section titled 'being good at using news media' (*shanyong xinwen meiti*, 善用新闻媒体). The first point advocates pursuing the media's positive propaganda role, and the second focuses on the media's directing of public opinion on important issues – both characterised in the article as 'the sacred duty of news media' (*shensheng zhize*, 神圣职责). The discursive

---

[73] Ibid.

[74] Zhou Fengzhen, '"Maikefeng shidai" yulun yindao wenti' ('The Question of Guidance of Public Opinion in the Microphone Era'), *Qiushi* 4 (2010): 21–22.

[75] Tang Guozhong, 'Shanjie shandai shanyong shanguan xinwen meiti' ('Skilfully Understand, Treat, Use, and Manage News Media'), *Qiushi* 3 (2008).

pattern of positioning of the two concepts in this article implies the subordinate status of the former to the latter.

The invocation of *yulun jiandu* in discussions of *yulun yindao* in *Qiushi* directly reflects the top leadership's speeches on media policy, as exemplified by Hu Jintao's 2008 address at *Renmin Ribao*. This speech, proclaimed by some Chinese media scholars as Hu Jintao's only key statement on *yulun jiandu* during his time as general secretary,[76] contained one mention of the media supervision through public opinion, made in the wider context of *yulun yindao*:

> News propaganda work should hold high "flags", serve the people, reform and innovate, persist in correctly guiding public opinion ... and construct a good public opinion environment. It should also bring the following media roles into play: propagate the party's principles, enhance healthy societal atmosphere, report on social affairs and public opinion, lead on key societal issues, investigate public sentiment, and strengthen the important role of *yulun jiandu* ...[77]

The above statement clearly signals that *yulun jiandu* is an element of news propaganda work. This is achieved through the juxtaposition of the directive of channelling the party's principles to the public and media supervision functions, including 'investigating public sentiment' and 'reporting on social affairs and public opinion', as well as the direct mention of *yulun jiandu*. The mention of 'reporting on' and 'leading on' societal issues in the same sentence further alludes to the inherent fusion of *yulun jiandu* and *yulun yindao*.

The official discourse also underscores how journalists should perform the dual function of supervising and guiding public opinion by invoking the term 'constructive' (建设性) criticism, which signifies a productive critique aimed at solutions and hopeful sentiment. 'Actively launch *yulun jiandu* that is scientific, lawful and constructive ... Uncover and criticise illegal phenomena ... and problems that harm the interests of the people ... ' writes the head of the Propaganda Department of Fujian province.[78] A senior official at the General Administration for Propaganda and Press (GAPP) further extrapolates the official requirement for constructive criticism:

> In China, we encourage constructive supervision (建设性监督), this is a request from the Chinese government. The Chinese government calls for more constructive supervision. We request it as well. This means that while carrying out

---

[76] Interview CSE02.

[77] 'Hu Jintao zai Renmin Ribao kaocha gongzuo de jianghua' ('Hu Jintao's Speech While Investigating the Work of *People's Daily*'), *Xinhua News*, 26 June 2008, available at: http://news.xinhuanet.com/politics/2008–06/26/content_8442547.htm.

[78] Tang (2008).

supervision, you can't just merely curse the faults, cursing alone is useless, following the critique, you have to further explain what needs to be done about it.[79]

As evident in the two official statements above, investigative journalists are at once empowered by immense responsibility for coming up with solutions to the problems they expose, while limited to examining fixable issues. Beyond explicating solutions, it is evident that transmitting a hopeful sentiment is the cornerstone of constructive criticism. When exposing issues, journalists are encouraged to simultaneously signal to their readers that the party-state is capable of resolving them, or to use positive reports to offset the negative ones, as suggested by the editor-in-chief at the Xinhua News Agency.[80] As explained in detail in the following excerpt from the interview with a professor of journalism at Tsinghua University, reaching a careful balance between negative and positive phenomena is something expected of Chinese media professionals:

> If very negative and sensitive issues are reported in the press, then these reports should still ensure to include discussion of some positive aspects in society. If reports say that there is no hope and the society wouldn't change in a positive direction, then it's really not good ... Media should play the double role of watchdog and government's voice: it should supervise authorities, but also collaborate with them in achieving societal progress. Media should serve as an effective force in developing our society.[81]

The emphasis on the alignment of media oversight with guidance of public opinion, and on the importance of constructive criticism, designates the power with higher officials to adjudicate the boundaries of critical reporting in accordance to these principles. Given the open-ended meaning of the terms 'constructive', 'solutions' or 'positive sentiment', the party-state can patrol media supervision as it sees fit, and thereby continuously redefine the rules of the game in the name of political stability. An official at the Propaganda Ministry, for instance, emphasised the necessity of official oversight to mitigate the potentially negative effects of media's attempts at political oversight:

> The CCP considers the guidance of public opinion to be at the core of people's happiness. If it's guided correctly, it can bring many positive outcomes, whereas if it is being misled, it can be disastrous. In the past 30 years we have done a lot to improve the farsightedness of the media: We helped media to avoid many mistakes and tragedies, which could have resulted from its negative reports; preventing it from being weighed down by legal and societal disasters ...[82]

The above statement stresses the active role of propaganda authorities in rebalancing media oversight with the dominant objective of guiding

---

[79] Interview COF08.   [80] Ibid.   [81] Interview CSE01.   [82] Interview COF01.

public opinion.[83] Media is presumed to be prone to making mistakes, and thereby in need of official guidance. The constructive nature of criticism, therefore, as a vague ideal advocated by the party, and the convergence between propaganda and oversight, endow the authorities with flexibility and proactive control.

While analysed and presented separately here in order to distil the official thinking behind this policy, in practice media oversight constitutes both a supervision mechanism and a distinct media role. The analysis shows that while endorsed less overtly than in the 1990s, the official support for media supervision was still apparent in the past decade. Media investigations and channelling of public opinion have been envisioned as a useful oversight and a problem-solving mechanism, conducive to better performance of the party-state, which in turn fosters its capacity to wield stronger influence over public opinion. The official endorsements on the whole are ridden with ambiguity. The distinct features of *yulun jiandu* are left unspecified, as it is being loosely positioned within the supervision discourse and the broader discussions of media policy. The fluid nature of *yulun jiandu* is further evident in the officials' consistent resistance to clarifying and institutionalising this media role by substantiating the policy with practical legal protections for journalists.[84] As will be demonstrated in detail in the following chapters, the party-state is intent on making on-the-spot adjustments to its demands for media supervision. The red line for media critique, however, is apparent from the official discourse, as *yulun jiandu* is forcefully endorsed as a party-led mechanism serving the priorities of the leadership in maintaining the political status quo via appeasing the public demands for governance.

Part II: Journalists' Discourse on *Yulun Jiandu*

The analysis of interviews with top editors and journalists at China's nationally renowned publications for critical reporting,[85] as well as

---

[83] The author's interviews with several officials from the General Administration of Press and Publishing (GAPP) derived similar findings. According to these officials, *yulun jiandu* was welcomed so long as it would not threaten the CCP stability or violate any of its key principles and regulations (interviews were conducted in Beijing in December 2009): CSE02; CSE03.

[84] Some advocates have been pressing for a press law for years now. Sun Xupei is the most prominent one of these advocates. For his reflection on this process and the persisting obstacles, see Sun Xupei, 'Press Laws Save Media From Political Tangles', *Global Times*, 13 May 2010, available at: www.globaltimes.cn/opinion/commentary/2010–05/531580 .html; Sun Xupei and Elizabeth C. Michel, *An Orchestra of Voices: Making the Argument for Greater Speech and Press Freedom in the People's Republic of China* (Westport, CT: Praeger Publishers, 2001).

[85] As noted in the Introduction, the majority of interviews were conducted in Beijing but included journalists from media outlets based in other cities and regions.

participant observation at several annual *yulun jiandu* conferences during multiple trips to China from 2008 to 2012,[86] revealed that media practitioners actively engaged in supervising authorities tend to interpret their political roles largely in conjuncture with the official endorsement of *yulun jiandu*. Journalists aspire towards producing constructive criticism aimed at gradual progress, and envision their reporting as an important vertical accountability mechanism and a feedback channel for the party. At the same time, media practitioners appear to take advantage of the ambiguous nature of *yulun jiandu* policy to reinterpret their space within the system.

Mirroring the official emphasis on solutions-oriented journalism, media practitioners emphasise their aspirations to shape social change through reporting that goes beyond merely exposing official wrongdoing. The following excerpts from an interview with an investigative reporter at *Caijing* and an editor at *Caixin* magazines illustrate the journalists' complex interpretations of their political roles within the system:

> I think that *yulun jiandu* reporting does not just mean negative news . . . The best *yulun jiandu* reporting should be able to contribute to some progress. It is not just about exposing the problems, but about considering what happens after that. Do you continue reporting and carrying out rational analysis of the problem or do you just let it go immediately and move onto the next thing? When I report on a negative phenomenon I try to think about the aftermath of my report and to premeditate potential reactions from authorities. I try to be constructive in anticipating their reactions.[87]

> Beyond reporting facts, I think it is necessary to think through how to solve issues, how to move forward. I think Western understanding of journalism is often very focused on revealing facts and problems as the primary goal of journalism. In China, however, because it is now in a developing, transitioning phase, constructive and balanced criticism is much more valuable than merely reporting facts. I think by doing this we can avert multiple political pressures, and also have a stronger influence on societal development.[88]

Both interviewees confront the notion of negative reporting as the sole purpose of media supervision, and aspire to producing constructive

---

The interviewees include journalists and editors from *Caijing* magazine (most of them have now moved to *Caixin* magazine), *Nanfang Renwu Zhoukan*, *Nanfang Zhoumo*, *Nanfang Dushibao*, *Xinjing Bao*, *Bingdian*, *Zhongguo Qingnian Bao* and *Xinmin Bao*.

[86] The author attended two media supervision conferences, gathering media practitioners and scholars from across the country to discuss opportunities and challenges for investigative and in-depth reporting on sensitive issues in China. One of the conferences took place in Beijing, and the other in Hangzhou. The conferences tend to rotate from year to year depending on the academic institution willing to host them. In Hangzhou, the author was not allowed in the end to attend official proceedings of the conference, but obtained the materials distributed and participated in informal sessions.

[87] Interview CJ29.   [88] Interview CJ36.

coverage, which entails in-depth and thorough analysis of problems, engagement with solutions, as well as an expression of balanced critique. Whereas the aspiration for in-depth analysis appears straightforward, the notion of engaging with solutions is not clearly spelled out by the interviewees. Journalists are hesitant to differentiate between solving problems themselves and collaborating with officials in finding and publicising solutions. Chapters 5 and 6 demonstrate what solutions-oriented reports signify in practice, showing how they tend to include both journalists' individual attempts at solving problems and working with relevant authorities in finding and publicising solutions. As for 'balanced' reporting, journalist interviewees explain that they are careful about closely examining different sides of an issue and adhering to a neutral tone in their exposés.

Constructive reporting, as evident from the interviews, appears to be linked to both journalists' conception of social change in the Chinese context and to their pragmatic considerations for maintaining political space for critical reporting. Interviewees are generally convinced that measured, in-depth reports are most fitting for China's socio-political and economic context, while they also admit that constructive journalism is a survival tactic as it helps in shielding them from political pressures. The first interviewee quoted above shares that he attempts to 'anticipate' official reactions and tries to be 'constructive' in premeditating them, whereas the second interviewee suggests that such reporting can help 'avert political pressures'. Hu Shuli, one of the most renowned media personalities in China and the editor-in-chief of the outspoken *Caixin* magazine, is a prime example of someone who skilfully uses constructive reporting to both effect change and skirt political boundaries. Her colleagues describe her as a 'woodpecker'. 'Her purpose is to transform the system from within, to improve it, rather than to criticise for criticising's sake ... Hu Shuli is not a dissident, she is a fairly mainstream persona ...,' explained by one of her colleagues in an interview.[89] Other interviewees close to the editor have noted Hu's within-the-system disposition and her attribution of success in carving out some independent space in China's complex media landscape to adherence to constructive journalism.[90] On the whole, it is apparent from the interviews that media practitioners, driven by a mix of idealism and pragmatism, are partaking in the state-endorsed vision of societal progress as a gradual process, rather than embodying a disruptive force of rapid political change.

While the party's continuing ownership of the media makes journalists structurally predisposed to more cautious views about political and societal change, journalists working for web portals and blogs that are not

[89] Interview CJ19   [90] Interview CJ36.

directly owned by the party-state hold similar dispositions.[91] This is not to dismiss the presence of more explicit or politically engaged voices on the Chinese internet. Indeed, some recent studies of netizens found that they are more 'politically opinionated' and constitute a more 'critical citizenry', interested in democracy and dissatisfied with many facets of the party's rule.[92] When it comes to even the most critically minded journalists, however, the interview data suggests that their liberal views do not necessarily translate into aspirations towards regime change or into a radical break with the system. While some interviewees noted their dissatisfaction with the pace of reforms and political liberalisation, alluding to their hopes for a bigger space to practice media oversight, for instance, they had also expressed uncertainty about an adoption or transfusion of Western democratic models onto China. Some directly noted their concern with potential chaos and disorder, as well as their distrust for 'common people' (*laobaixing*) to elect officials and to shape the scope of China's transformation. Many interviewees were also critical of systemic failures in the party's governance, including corruption, nepotism and its rigidity in the course of bureaucratic reforms. Nonetheless, when asked about an alternative model for China, few jumped at the prospect of a Western-style democracy as an apt solution. And while journalists often actively share more direct criticisms of the regime on social media platforms, beyond these sporadic expressions, their political vision remains constrained to shaping moderate change.

This pragmatic perspective parallels an overarching intellectual concern with governance, rooted in the ancient tradition of helping improve the system, and further reaffirmed in light of recent failed experiences with wider political change. Journalists' emphasis on social change and improving governance from within echoes other studies on the notion of good governance (*shanzhi*, 善治) in China's intellectual discourses since the 1990s.[93] Yu Keping, one of China's most famous intellectuals and an advocate for promoting good governance, as distinct from Western-style democracy, is a prominent example of this school of thought. Good governance, which to him, as well as to Chinese journalists interviewed in this study, includes accountability, transparency and a better rule of law, amongst other features we typically associate with democracies, is

---

[91] Though most media practitioners interviewed for this study work for print media, the author also interviewed editors and journalists of online blogs and web portals, as well as freelance journalists solely publishing online. For more details, see Appendix.

[92] Ya-Wen Lei, 'The Political Consequences of the Rise of the Internet: Political Beliefs and Practices of Chinese Netizens', *Political Communication* 28 (2011): 291–322.

[93] Qinghua Wang and Gang Guo, 'Yu Keping and Chinese Intellectual Discourse on Good Governance', *The China Quarterly* 224 (2015): 985–1005.

something that can potentially develop under the leadership of the party-state.[94] Good governance, therefore, is not necessarily envisioned as an outcome of a democratic transition, but rather as a joint task of party officials, media and civil society. This vision of promoting good governance might be linked to the intellectual tradition of what Davies calls 'patriotic worrying' (*youhuan yishi*)[95] and what Link refers to as 'the worrying mentality'.[96] Davies notes that *youhouan* 'connotes but also confers a sense of personal responsibility about the nation's well-being'.[97] In a similar vein, other studies also highlight Chinese journalists' 'strong sense of social responsibility'.[98] The apparent parallels in political attitudes between Chinese critical journalists and liberal intellectuals is not surprising, as many journalists associate themselves with intellectuals in private, and express an interest in following and contributing to China's intellectual thought.

The within-the-system orientation for both groups, journalists and intellectuals, moreover, is likely a product of a historic circumstance, namely the tragic outcome of the attempt at effecting the wider political liberalisation as part of the Tiananmen protest. As noted in Chapter 2, many journalists supported students during the Tiananmen movement, or themselves were then students invigorated by the battle for more pluralistic governance.[99] While some activists and journalists have fled China in the aftermath of the brutal crackdown, those who have remained after 1989 have appeared to reconcile with silence about the past and more subtle modes of effecting policy change.[100] As Lagerkvist argues in his analysis of the legacy of the 1989 massacre, 'Effective state censorship has turned the vast majority of youth into "amnesiacs", while their parents and others of their generation keep silent about the recent

---

[94] Ibid.

[95] Gloria Davies, *Worrying about China: The Language of Chinese Critical Inquiry* (Cambridge: Harvard University Press, 2009).

[96] Perry Link, *Evening Chats in Beijing* (New York: Norton, 1992): 249.

[97] Davies, *Worrying about China:* 17.

[98] Zhao, 'Watchdogs on Party Leashes? Contexts and Implications of Investigative Journalism in Post-Deng China': 577–597; Jonathan Hassid, 'Four Models of the Fourth Estate: A Typology of Contemporary Chinese Journalists', *The China Quarterly* 208 (2011): 813–832.

[99] While many observers continue to refer to Tiananmen as a democracy movement, student grievances were diverse, but seemed to center on more participatory and accountable governance rather than strictly on democracy as the desired outcome. For a nuanced engagement with popular depictions of Tiananmen, see: Jeff Wasserstrom: 'Illuminating and Misleading Takes on China 20 Years Since Tiananmen', *The Huffington Post*, 5 July 2009, available at: www.huffingtonpost.com/jeffrey-wasserstrom/illuminating-and-misleadi_b_211610.html.

[100] A number of interviewees, especially those old enough to remember it, have noted that 1989 was a breaking point for their conception of political change.

past'.[101] Even some of the former Tiananmen activists now publicly express a moderate and almost a remorseful view about the movement. 'I really believe this kind of excitement in the streets is not constructive . . . If there is another choice other than this, I would choose it, rather than what happened in 1989', shares one of the former activists, cited in Lagerkvist's study.[102] This activist's invoking of the term 'constructive' echoes the pronouncements of the party discussed earlier, as well as the expressed commitments of critical journalists. Those who persist in publicly commemorating Tiananmen face harsh political repercussions, as evident in the recent jailing of China's famous civil rights lawyer, Pu Zhiqiang, shortly after his attendance at a Tiananmen memorial event.[103] The arrest of Pu, who is known as an avid defender of critical journalists and editors, has sent chills throughout the Chinese media community, serving as a reminder that even a modest manifestation of challenging the dominant narratives of the party-state gets quickly obstructed and manipulated by authorities. Pu has been released in 2015, but as of February 2017 remains under house arrest and cut off from public engagement domestically and internationally.[104] A more radical transformation, therefore, while it may be attractive in theory, is perceived as dangerous and chaotic by most media practitioners interviewed for this book, as they settle for more measured ways to influence change, especially in an increasingly politically volatile climate under Xi Jinping, as explained in detail in the Conclusion of the book.

The journalists' discussion of the influence of media supervision in enforcing top-down accountability and improving governance more broadly is aligned with the vision for *yulun jiandu* by the party-state.

---

[101] Johan Lagerkvist, 'The Legacy of the 1989 Beijing Massacre: Establishing Neo-Authoritarian Rule, Silencing Civil Society', *International Journal of China Studies* 5(2) (2014): 349–369. For a more in-depth analysis of state-produced amnesia when it comes to the Tiananmen massacre, see Louisa Lim, *The People's Republic of Amnesia* (Oxford: Oxford University Press: 2015).

[102] Lagerkvist, 'The Legacy of the 1989 Beijing Massacre: Establishing Neo-Authoritarian Rule, Silencing Civil Society': 356. 'Excitement' here appears to suggest disorderly behavior on behalf of the protesters. In reality, however, as documented by scholars and observers, movement proceeded peacefully and the label of 'disorder' (*luan*) came from the official side, as a way to frame protesters in a negative way. See, for instance: Joseph W. Esherick and Jeffrey N. Wasserstrom, 'Acting Out Democracy: Political Theater in Modern China', *The Journal of Asian Studies* 49(4) (1990): 835–865.

[103] See Verna Yu, 'Human Rights Lawyer among Four Detained over Tiananmen Commemoration Event', *South China Morning Post*, 6 May, 2014.

[104] Jane Perlez, 'Chinese Rights Lawyer, Pu Zhiqiang, Is Given Suspended Prison Sentence', *The New York Times*, 21 December 2015, available at: www.nytimes.com/2 015/12/22/world/asia/china-pu-zhiqiang-sentence.html.

The following excerpts from interviews showcase the journalists' perception of their reporting as conducive to addressing local-level failures:

Yulun jiandu provides the government with a small window into societal problems, which they otherwise might not be able to see. For instance, in a recent case of successful *yulun jiandu* reporting, our newspaper exposed a case of people coming to Beijing to complain about mistreatments by local officials (*shangfangzhe*, 上访者), and then being chased by local officials all the way to Beijing, brought home, and put into a mental hospital. Once such a case has been reported and uncovered, it should prevent such mistreatment by local officials from happening in the future.[105]

The key with *yulun jiandu* is that it forms a precedent, which is essential, especially with the lack of an independent judicial system. If it works in one case, it forces officials, namely those at the lower-levels, to restrain their corrupt activities, as well as fosters the public's engagement with the officials and the media ...[106]

Other than in interviews, journalists' focus on media oversight at the local level is also apparent in participant observations of conferences on media supervision, as well as of their day-to-day work. The key topics discussed at annual *yulun jiandu* conferences, emphasised local issues, ranging from media coverage of specific mining incidents to corruption cases, among other governance failures.[107] The use of the term 'case' (or *anjian*, 案件) by journalists in discussing their work further highlights the specificity of the issues they cover, as this term is deployed in discussing individual incidents, usually taking place at the provincial or sub-provincial level and often being named after a certain location or an individual. It is important to note here that the local nature of media investigations also resonates with citizen activism and reporting online. Famous cases of online shaming, such as the Deng Yujiao incident of a young woman's plight against a township official in Hebei[108] or the case of the unlawful conviction of Zhao Zuohai in a small village in Henan province,[109] tend to focus on injustice committed at the lower

---

[105] Interview CJ14.   [106] Interview CJ03.

[107] These insights were derived from attending and reading the materials from several annual *yulun jiandu huiyi*, as well as following the coverage of critical media outlets.

[108] For a detailed and rigorous analysis of the Deng Yujiao case, see Shiwen Wu, 'Contentious Discourse and Dynamic Frames: Interplay among Online Public Opinion, Media Reporting, and Government Discourse with Respect to Social Events', working paper presented at the Media Activism Research Collective, Annenberg School for Communication, University of Pennsylvania, 4 December 2015.

[109] For more details on this case, see Chin-Fu Hung, 'China's Changing State-Society Relations in the Internet Age: Case Study of Zhao Zuohai', *International Journal of China Studies* 3(3) (2012): 363–381.

levels of the system, rarely directly targeting or shaming central-level officials.

The local focus of journalists' investigations is a product of both their professional intent and the pressures from the bottom up, with citizens and activists directly approaching journalists with their stories of localised official mistreatment and corruption. In observing journalists' practices, the author has come across a number of cases of petitioners or civil society activists attempting to channel their stories to reporters. In one instance, while waiting for an interviewee at his office in the outskirts of Beijing, the author encountered a group of petitioners from southern China, who took a three-hour flight to meet this journalist in hope that he would pick up and disseminate their story. These petitioners, unjustly laid off from a state-owned enterprise, didn't get help from local officials, and arrived in Beijing to try to pressure them 'from the top down'. While this case – a vivid manifestation of rising social inequality and local-level corruption – may appear as newsworthy and significant to an outsider – the journalist interviewee shook his head and pulled out ten large binders filled with similar local-level cases, sent by common citizens from across the country. He admitted that he is often unable to cover these cases either due to the vast volume of his work, the repetitive nature of issues reported by citizens or political and editorial restrictions present at a given moment. This particular journalist is famous for covering human-interest stories of official injustice and therefore not surprisingly enjoys popularity amongst petitioners. Other interviewees who adhere to a more analytical style of professional reporting, however, also shared that they are often exposed to localised scandals directly or indirectly through social media and are also frequently contacted by victims and petitioners. Though unable to report on all the incidents, journalists take their mission of vertical accountability seriously, as confirmed by other media scholars, both in China and in the West.[110]

Beyond local-level oversight, media practitioners link their reporting to the party's better grasp on public opinion, which in turn facilitates its long-term adaptability:

Yulun jiandu is expanding in scope. One could say that after media has exposed various injustices, corruption, etc., there are more opportunities to enact change. Despite its deficiencies, there has been a huge increase in investigative reporting, which has led to better regulations by the government.[111]

---

[110] Interviews CSE01; CSE02; Tong, *Investigative Journalism in China*; Zhao and Wusan, 'Public Opinion Supervision'.
[111] Interview CJ22.

The media's supervision role has benefits for the public as well as for the government. It makes the government more efficient. Because China is a one-party system, there is little supervision of the government, other than through the media, which makes it quite influential and important. One of the latest examples of media supervision of the government was during the recent earthquake when the media investigated the reasons behind the earthquake's surprisingly strong effect on some housing constructions and found that these houses were not built adequately to begin with. This revelation benefits the government by exposing a serious problem, which can be effectively addressed by the government, leading to a prevention of such cases from reoccurring.[112]

Of course, *yulun jiandu* benefits the government. One of the defining characteristics of authoritarian societies is their simplification. The officials' information is not complete and they choose what they want to listen to. Moreover, the information tends to be tailored to the government, which makes it even more difficult for them to decipher facts from rumours. The more the media conveys the genuine public opinion to political authorities, the more the party-state can address the relevant issues, and adapt by improving itself ...[113]

The statements on local-level oversight and general governance improvements all highlight the journalists' expectations for authorities to respond to their reports, as they attribute the regime's responsiveness to its capacity for long-term survival. Rather than expecting public reactions to put pressure on authorities, as is the common practice in democratic systems, in China, journalists expect a direct response from authorities to pre-empt further public discontent. This expectation of the state to take note of and to incorporate media supervision in its policy agenda showcases the journalists' conception of their relations with the regime as that of a strategic partnership. Sharing the overarching aspiration towards better governance via incremental reform, journalists position themselves as consultants of central authorities and hope for their consultations to be taken on board.

At the same time, journalists' interviews reveal some improvisation on the official conceptualisation of media supervision, as they explicitly and implicitly take advantage of the ambiguity in the official discourse to amplify their influence within the system. First, while media professionals tend to invoke the official term *yulun jiandu* in discussing their work, they also reinterpret it in private and use it creatively to shield themselves from official pressures. Several interviewees, for instance, expressed that while they publicly use the term 'media supervision', they privately often invoke the concepts 'professional reporting' or 'in-depth journalism' that are more akin to Western descriptions of a media's watchdog role.[114] Public use of the *yulun jiandu* concept is in part

---

[112] Interview CJ54.   [113] Interview CJ02.   [114] Interviews CJ40; CJ30.

a strategic tactic for pushing the boundaries. One of the organisers of the annual *yulun jiandu* conference called the use of the official concept of media supervision a useful 'discourse strategy'. 'Everyone uses this concept, including officials ... Using this term provides for a safer way for us to hold such conferences and get published, while we often expand the meaning of this term in our actual discussions ... '[115] The author observed this discourse strategy in action when attending the annual *yulun jiandu* gathering at Zhejiang University in 2010. The term *yulun jiandu* was legitimate enough to get an official permission and a university agreement to host the event (though the conditions for hosting the conference vary depending on political circumstances). While much of the conference proceedings on the record engaged with successful cases of media supervision, in private, and during meals, the participants also discussed their challenges and frustrations with holding authorities accountable, in part critically reflecting on the official policy. On one occasion, a late night discussion even touched on a sensitive topic of the media's role in democratisation processes by focusing on the case of the collapse of the Soviet Union. Journalists and media scholars hovered around a small table with a professor of Russian media seated in the middle and cautiously explaining the significance of critical reporting during the Gorbachev era. Through this discussion at an officially sanctioned *yulun jiandu* conference, journalists were engaged in expanding the notion of media supervision from that of aiding the government to that of potentially helping facilitate its overthrow. Such attempts at playing with the official media concepts and using them to their advantage in partaking in more critical reflections on their role in the system extend to journalism classrooms and media training workshops, which the author has attended in the past six years. Chinese journalists thereby appear to adhere to what Yurchak referred to in the Soviet context as the 'hegemony of form', whereby they reproduce ideological forms but do not necessarily fully adopt its associated meanings.[116]

More implicit reinterpretation of the official policy is also notable in journalists' disassociation of media supervision from the soft propaganda role of guiding public opinion. While aspiring towards balanced and constructive reporting, journalists and editors do not envision incorporating positive messages into their reports or purposefully minimising their coverage of sensitive events as part of their mission.

---

[115] Interview CSE21.
[116] Alexey Yurchak, 'Soviet Hegemony of Form: Everything Was Forever, Until It Was No More', *Comparative Studies of Society and History* 45 (2003): 480–510.

When asked about the role of guiding public opinion, journalists tend to deny it and emphasise the difference between themselves and those media practitioners who are involved in carrying out official propaganda. Specifically, the interviewees tend to distance themselves from traditional roles of 'party mouthpieces', and emphasise their adherence to Western journalistic values such as 'objectivity' and 'professionalism'.[117] Many journalists share that they acquired these values in the West and also in journalism courses in China, which now incorporate such teachings in addition to traditional party-endorsed journalism theories. As we will discover in the following chapters, journalists perceive the 'positive reporting' directive as one of the political restrictions to grapple with rather than as an inherent duty. At the same time, constructive criticism tends to carry some positive undertones, as will be demonstrated in the case study chapters.

Finally, journalists' treatment of *yulun jiandu* as a local-level oversight mechanism is another manifestation of creative adaptation to ambiguity. Whereas the official discourse stresses the integration of different supervision systems and the capacity of media supervision to help solve a variety of problems, it does not explicitly assign the types of problems the media should be involved with nor the level of officials to be investigated. By aligning themselves with the centre and choosing to strike at the more politically accessible localised issues, therefore, journalists are acting as 'policy entrepreneurs'[118] and practise what O'Brien and Li refer to as 'rightful resistance', as noted in the previous chapter.[119] They are not passively complying with official policies, but are actively reinterpreting them to create a relatively safe space to practise media supervision. Moreover, beyond demarcating a niche for critical reporting, journalists and editors also frequently attempt to use local crises to highlight systemic problems and failures that are as much a responsibility of the central state as they are of local officials. Some interviewees directly underscored that their reporting of local issues is not isolated from

---

[117] Western journalism ideas were frequently invoked in interviews with Chinese media professionals. Professionalism, a contested concept in Chinese context, was discussed in some detail. For more details on the conflicting notions of professionalism in the Western sense and journalists' advocacy aspirations, see Hongyi Bai, 'Between Advocacy and Objectivity: New Role Models among Investigative Journalists', in *Chinese Investigative Journalists' Dreams: Autonomy, Agency, and Voice*: 75–91. More details on how journalists invoke professionalism to their advantage are discussed in the next chapter.

[118] Andrew Mertha, '"Fragmented Authoritarianism 2.0": Political Pluralization in the Chinese Policy Process,' *The China Quarterly* 200 (2009): 995–1012.

[119] Kevin J. O'Brien, *Rightful Resistance in Rural China* (New York: Cambridge University Press, 2006).

overseeing central problems, and they often use small incidents to point to the state's general lack of accountability or inefficiency. As demonstrated in the analysis of mining accidents in Chapter 6, for instance, journalists occasionally draw on multiple repetitive local crises to make an appeal to the public and to the central government for more systemic reform. At the same time, however, as we see in the following chapter, even localised issues frequently fluctuate in political sensitivity, which invites further creative improvisation by journalists.

Conclusion

This chapter mapped out the broader boundaries for collaboration between the party-state and China's critical journalists in the Hu-Wen era. It demonstrated how the two actors are tied together in a loose vision of improving governance within the system. The party-state has been cautiously endorsing limited critical reporting in the form of a policy of media supervision, or *yulun jiandu*, which is envisioned as both a useful oversight mechanism and a media role conducive to better guidance of public opinion. The journalists, in turn, have positioned themselves as change-makers within the system, striving to facilitate governance improvements and address societal crises as partners of the central state. Guarded improvisation is a notable feature in mutual negotiation

Image 1 'Zhejiang University Welcomes *Yulun Jiandu* Conference'; 27 November 2010 (photo by the author)

of this policy. The official conceptualisation and framing of the media supervision role is elusive, allowing for a reinvention of its specific dimensions. The journalists also engage in some moderate reinterpretation of the official policy by using the ambiguous terms to redefine or specify their role within the system. The party-state's endorsement of media supervision strictly as a party-led governance mechanism, however, sets out a strict limit on further evolution of and mutual improvisation with this policy. The authorities are not willing to trade independent oversight for potential political instability, and media practitioners submit to the roles vaguely ascribed to them by the party-state. In the following chapters, we will examine how the official and journalists' discourse on *yulun jiandu* plays out in practice, including the extent of their collaboration on specific governance processes. But first we shall investigate the routine limitations on critical journalism and how they are applied and negotiated.

4 Restrictions on Critical Journalism
How They Are Applied and Negotiated

Introduction

The previous chapter explained shared governance objectives that facilitate collaborative relations between critical journalists and the party-state. This chapter delves into routine constraints on their collaboration by examining restrictions on critical journalism through the bottom-up perspective of practising journalists and editors. It uncovers and categorises the political pressures on day-to-day reporting on sensitive topics, and delves into potential official motivations in applying these restrictions. The chapter starts out with a brief background of China's top-down mechanisms of media control, and then examines pre- and post-publication restrictions experienced by journalists. It shows how the process of containing and managing critical reporting is characterised by guarded improvisation. While the state outlaws coverage on the most sensitive topics, it maintains blurry boundaries for the media's supervision role, with pre- and post-publication restrictions often being applied arbitrarily. Beneath the inconsistency, however, the interviews with journalists unveil the adaptive, decentralised and dynamic nature of the state control over the media. Central authorities adjust restrictions to overcome their prevailing limitations: they adapt to the political environment, which, importantly, includes public opinion, and take into consideration the divergent interests of local officials and other influential actors. Moreover, local authorities embark on their own acts of improvisation in containing media investigations by restricting information access and deploying censorship and coercion. Journalists, in turn, negotiate the boundaries by using the inconsistencies in state control to their advantage.

From a Top-down to a Bottom-up Approach

Before engaging with limitations on critical journalism as experienced by media practitioners, it is important to briefly introduce top-down mechanisms of media control as depicted in the scholarship on Chinese media. The existing literature identifies a combination of institutional, commercial and other, indirect tactics of media management. As for media-regulating institutions, when it comes to print media the scholarship highlights the continuing importance of the party's Central Propaganda or Publicity Department (CPD)[1], and the state's General Administration for Press and Publication (GAPP)[2] in controlling and guiding journalists' coverage.[3] The CPD encompasses seventeen bureaus, including the Bureau of Publishing and the Bureau of Public Opinion,[4] and guides media content at a national level, whereas local propaganda departments preside over regional media. The overarching role of the CPD is that of shaping and guiding national ideological policy, which includes coordination across party units and state institutions, as well as management and oversight of cadres involved in diverse propaganda work, ranging from culture to education to the media.[5] The CPD's work in overseeing all media content and steering media policy is further assisted by the GAPP, which regulates Chinese media through licensing system, amongst other responsibilities.[6] The works on media management institutions highlight their capacity to adapt to the challenges of globalisation and commercialisation.[7] Some note an increase in status and responsibilities of the CPD and the GAPP in the reform era.[8] The GAPP, for

[1] The English translation has been changed to Central Publicity Department, but the Chinese term itself did not change. The word *xuanchuan* (宣传) can be interpreted as both propaganda and publicity. The alternation of the English name is part of an effort to modernize China's global image. In this book, both translations are used interchangeably in discussion of CPD and the officials who work there. Since propaganda is the original meaning embedded in the term, it appears more frequently in the text.

[2] In 2013, The GAPP has merged with the SARFT (The State Administration of Radio, Film and Television) in a new ministry called GAPPRFT (The General Administration of Press, Publication, Radio, Film and Television).

[3] Anne-Marie Brady, *Marketing Dictatorship: Propaganda and Thought Work in Contemporary China* (Lanham, MD: Rowman & Littlefield Publishers, Inc., 2008).

[4] Ibid.: 21.

[5] Brady, *Marketing Dictatorship: Propaganda and Thought Work in Contemporary China*.

[6] The General Administration for Press and Publication (GAPP) grew out of the Central People's Government Publishing Administration. Formerly under the Ministry of Culture, since 1986 it has been directly responsible to the State Council. For more details on historic evolution of the GAPP, see Andrew Mertha, *The Politics of Piracy: Intellectual Property in Contemporary China* (Cornell University Press, 2005).

[7] Brady, *Marketing Dictatorship: Propaganda and Thought Work in Contemporary China*; Ashley Esarey, 'Cornering the Market: State Strategies for Controlling China's Commercial Media', *Asian Perspective* 29 (2005): 37–83; David Shambaugh, 'China's Propaganda System: Institutions, Processes, and Efficacy', *China Journal* 57 (2007), 25–58. Yuezhi Zhao, *Communication in China: Political Economy, Power, and Conflict* (Lanham, MD: Rowman & Littlefield, 2008).

[8] Brady, *Marketing Dictatorship: Propaganda and Thought Work in Contemporary China*; Shambaugh, 'China's Propaganda System: Institutions, Processes, and Efficacy'.

instance, was upgraded from deputy ministry to full ministry level, adding an annual review of all newspapers and magazines to its list of responsibilities. To complement the GAPP's work, in 1993 the CPD established news groups of party cadres who previously worked in the media to monitor news content, reporting back to the CPD.[9] Personnel control, a responsibility added to the CPD in 1982, is highlighted as another key tool for keeping press coverage in check, as propaganda authorities can appoint and dismiss senior editors and producers.[10] Esarey's analysis of this control mechanism finds that the CPD appoints top media managers and creates financial incentives for them to make publications profitable while remaining loyal to the party.[11] In addition to the transformations of the CPD and the GAPP, it is important to note here that the internet management institutions have also undergone structural changes, especially since 2011, and most recently, under Xi Jinping. The biggest change has been the official attempt to centralise the internet management through the establishment of the Cyberspace Administration of China (CAC) – a joint party-state organisation that combines the General Office of the Central Leadership Group for Internet Security and Informatisation (*zhongyang wangluo anquan de xinxihua lingdao xiaozu bangongshi*) and the State Internet Information Office.[12] The responsibilities of CAC are far reaching, including 'regulating internet content, e-commerce, e-finance, cyber security and encryption, and combating online crime, rumors, and pornography'.[13] Given that much of the critical coverage is posted and read online, the new internet management also has direct repercussions for the practice of critical journalism. In addition to these structural transformations of the regulating agencies, some scholars note the parallel trends of decentralization or delegation of control as an important adaptation that the party-state undertook in managing the media in the reform era.[14] By forcing different actors to hold responsibility for their own territory (i.e., editors and online content providers), Zhao argues that the party-state has succeeded in expanding the practice of self-censorship that in turn reduces the impetus for constant official intervention.[15]

Other works also point to state-initiated commercialisation of the media as a means of exerting top-down control. Zhao, for instance, argues

[9] Brady, *Marketing Dictatorship: Propaganda and Thought Work in Contemporary China.*
[10] Esarey, 'Cornering the Market: State Strategies for Controlling China's Commercial Media'.
[11] Ibid.
[12] Christopher Cairns, 'Prerequisites for Selective Censorship: Leaders' Evolving Beliefs and Bureaucratic Re-centralization', Dissertation chapter 3 (Cornell University, 2016).
[13] Ibid.: 23.
[14] Zhao, *Communication in China: Political Economy, Power, and Conflict.*   [15] Ibid.

that the interlinks between business and political actors in China have produced new constraints on the media, with the newly emerged press conglomerates being subject to market pressures while remaining subordinate to local propaganda departments.[16] Other scholars, including Lagerkvist and MacKinnon, apply a similar logic to social media content, arguing that the nexus between internet companies and the party-state is critical to pervasive censorship over political discourse online.[17] Stockmann further shows how market mechanisms can induce uniformity in news content, thus decreasing the need for the state to censor as frequently.[18] Finally, as already noted in Chapter 2, some works argue that it is not merely the institutional or the commercial control itself that restrains journalists and social media contributors, but the party-state's deployment of vagueness and uncertainty in managing the media. Hassid, for instance, contends that uncertainty is at the core of the party's success in containing media coverage,[19] and Brady suggests that intentionally vague media regulations issued by the CPD and the GAPP tend to facilitate more caution among journalists.[20]

On the whole, the literature on top-down mechanisms of media control adapts a state-centric perspective and presents control as deliberate and monolithic. Even the mechanism of uncertainty is portrayed as a strategic tactic of the state rather than as an element in its improvisational approach to policy-making. With the exception of some works that delve into the decentralisation of media control,[21] the existing literature depicts it as a largely cohesive and powerful system, capable of consistently and effectively responding to political and economic challenges facing the media sector. While these works illuminate the dominant mechanisms at play and explain an overarching capacity of the party-state to contain outspoken journalists, they tell us little about the process of managing critical reporting on a routine basis. Specifically, we still

---

[16] Ibid.

[17] Johan Lagerkvist, 'New Media Entrepreneurs in China: Allies of the Party-State or Civil Society?' *Journal of International Affairs* 65(1) (2011): 169–182; Rebecca MacKinnon, 'China's Censorship 2.0: How Companies Censor Bloggers', *First Monday* 13(2) (2009).

[18] Daniela Stockmann, *Media Commercialization and Authoritarian Rule in China* (New York: Cambridge University Press, 2012).

[19] Jonathan Hassid, 'Controlling the Chinese Media: An Uncertain Business', *Asian Survey* 48 (2008): 414–430.

[20] Brady, *Marketing Dictatorship: Propaganda and Thought Work in Contemporary China.*

[21] Jingrong Tong is one of the exceptions. She presents the opposite argument that the centralised media control theory is outdated, and local officials are the ones most actively restraining the media, often in opposition to the centre's objectives. See Tong Jingrong, 'The Crisis of the Centralized Media Control Theory: How Local Power Controls Media in China', *Media, Culture & Society* 32 (2010): 925–942. Zhao also discusses decentralisation of control in her analysis of media management. See Zhao, *Communication in China: Political Economy, Power, and Conflict.*

know little about the dynamism of media regulation[22] and the intricate pressures both officials and journalists are operating under when man-oeuvring in the grey zone of semi-sensitive, contentious issues.

This chapter intentionally employs a bottom-up approach in analysing limitations on critical journalism, as it seeks to illuminate and differentiate between specific processes at play in journalist-state relations when it comes to negotiating these restrictions. Unlike the deliberate imagery of the party's propaganda apparatus, it depicts the state's improvisational implementation of restrictions over the media, which is underlined by its adaptiveness to public opinion and to diverse agendas of other political actors, especially local officials. The bottom-up approach also highlights the interactivity of improvisation with media restrictions, as journalists use various tactics to mediate and at times successfully negotiate them. This chapter, therefore, contributes to the existing literature on media control by delving deeper into how it is applied on sensitive content and showcasing that restrictions themselves are very much a product of the fusion of societal and journalists' activism. The following discussion starts out by differentiating politically sensitive topics, and then goes on to examine the process whereby these restrictions are applied and contested.

Political Pressures on Critical Reporting: The Journalists' Perspective

Interviews with Chinese media practitioners, experts and officials demon-strate that the party-state explicitly outlaws the most politically sensitive subjects, while upholding blurry boundaries when it comes to contentious issues of societal significance that do not directly or immediately provoke the party's leadership. Specifically, according to the interviewees, sensi-tive subjects fall into two broad categories: those completely inaccessible and those in the grey zone. The former include topics that explicitly challenge the party-state, such as the writings on separatist claims in Tibet, Taiwan, or Xinjiang, pro-democracy movements and any groups that strive to discredit the party's legitimacy. While Western

---

[22] Lorentzen's work is a notable exception as he argues that dynamism in media censorship as manifested in frequent adjustment of the boundaries for investigative reporting is essential for the regime to maintain control yet still benefit from bottom-up feedback. See Peter Lorentzen, 'China's Strategic Censorship', *American Journal of Political Science* 58(2) (2014): 402–414. King and his co-authors also demonstrate the selective modes of media censorship online, with criticism being tolerated so long as it doesn't yield social mobilization. See Gary King, Jennifer Pan, and Molly Roberts, 'How Censorship in China Allows Government Criticism but Silences Collective Expression', *American Political Science Review* 107 (2014): 1–18. Both scholars, however, still portray uncer-tainty as a deliberate mechanism of media control.

commentators often focus on these issues,[23] Chinese journalists note them only in passing. The following excerpts from the interviews are representative of the resigned attitudes China's critical journalists hold about these impervious topics:

In China, we have to practise journalism with Chinese characteristics (*zhongguo tese*, 中国特色). This means completely avoiding some clearly outlawed topics, such as Taiwan's claims to independence, the alternatives to the present political system, Falun Gong, the Tiananmen incident, some religious topics, and the issues concerning contentious minorities, like Tibetans and Uyghurs. Journalists do not have such restrictions in Western countries, but we are accustomed to avoiding the most obviously sensitive topics. It is simply part of our work.[24]

If you were to start working at our magazine today, very quickly you would grasp which topics are not to be touched at all. The list of the completely inaccessible topics is pretty clear and stable, and it is not difficult to get used to.[25]

Some Chinese dissidents, including cyber dissidents,[26] do break into these taboo areas and strike at the core of the political system. The imprisoned Nobel Peace Prize winner, Liu Xiaobo, for instance, openly questions the basis for the party's legitimacy through literary writings and essays.[27] In one of his famous essays, he discusses and comments on the interviews with family members of Tiananmen massacre victims, including, primarily, mothers of murdered sons who together formed a group called the Tiananmen Mothers.[28] Other high-profile dissidents like China's famous critic and artist, Ai Weiwei, channel their systemic critique through a fusion of artwork and active social commentary online.[29] On his popular blog, Ai Weiwei has continuously

---

[23] See, for instance, Roy Greenslade, 'China Launches Attack on Tibet Coverage', *The Guardian*, 25 March 2008. The Freedom House reports on China also tend to highlight the restrictions on reporting on Tibet and Xinjiang, including that carried out by domestic and foreign correspondents. See, for instance, 'China Media Bulletin', 88 (2013), available at: www.freedomhouse.org/cmb/88_061313.

[24] Interview CJ04.   [25] Interview CJ10.

[26] This term is used to describe dissidents who are using the internet as the key platform for expressing dissent.

[27] In December 2008, Liu Xiaobo and 303 other Chinese intellectuals put forward the 'Charter 08', which called for human rights and democratisation in China. This manifesto has in part led to Liu's subsequent imprisonment. For more details about the manifesto, see the translated version, 'Charter 08', *Foreign Policy*, 8 October 2010, available at: www.foreignpolicy.com/articles/2010/10/08/charter_08.

[28] Liu Xiabo, 'Listen Carefully to the Voices of the Tiananmen Mothers', in Perry Link, Tienchi Martin-Liao, and Liu Xia (eds.), *No Enemies, No Hatred* (Harvard University Press, 2013): 3–13.

[29] Most of Ai Weiwei's comments appear on his blog or on Twitter, as he gets repeatedly censored on Weibo. For more on Ai Weiwei's online expression, see Ai Weiwei and Lee Ambrozy, *Ai Weiwei's Blog: Writings, Interviews, and Digital Rants, 2006–2009*

crossed the red line by discussing high-level party corruption or the destruction of Tibetan culture with China's construction of a railroad into Tibet.[30] These dissidents, however, are the exceptions to the rule. Journalists from traditional media, including critical outlets, abstain from crossing the red line in their professional writing,[31] generally not reporting on issues that would get them immediately in trouble. This highlights the journalists' adherence to a state-sanctioned framework for improvisation with political restrictions, as they do not broach the subjects consistently outlawed by authorities. In this respect, critical journalists are not very distinct from average citizen journalists and politically engaged netizens, as much of the social media activism also appears to skirt the red line, or only probe it through creative satire and indirect commentaries.[32] 'Online activism rarely demands radical political change. The struggles are about social justice, citizenship rights, cultural values, and personal identity', writes Guobin Yang in his seminal work on the Chinese internet.[33] The observations of citizen journalism, as part of the research for this book, also found netizens' cautiousness in pre-empting censorship by abstaining from the most contentious subjects or only invoking them indirectly through symbols and imagery accessible to a minority of like-minded netizens.

When it comes to the grey zone, the boundaries for permissible reporting frequently fluctuate. The grey zone contains stories that media regulators don't ban from the outset, but perceive as potentially politically sensitive, including those on official corruption, environmental degradation, local protests, societal incidents, income inequality, and crisis events, amongst others. The state's flexible attitude on these topics on

(Cambridge, MA: MIT Press, 2011). Also, for more on Ai Weiwei's stance against the system, see Evan Osnos, 'It's Not Beautiful: An Artist Takes on the System', *The New Yorker*, 24 May 2010.

[30] Evan Osnos, 'It's Not Beautiful: An Artist Takes on the System'.

[31] Some journalists break into the taboo subjects with Weibo postings and commentaries. More on this appears later in this chapter. For more details on journalists' use of the internet, see also Jonathan Hassid and Maria Repnikova, 'Why Chinese Print Journalists Embrace the Internet', *Journalism* 17(7) (2016): 882–898.

[32] The criticisms of the party-state that appear on Weibo are often indirect, in the form of satire. For more details on netizens' critical expression online, see Ashley Esarey and Xiao Qiang, 'Political Expression in the Chinese Blogosphere: Below the Radar', *Asian Survey* 48(5) (2008): 752–777; Guobin Yang, *The Power of the Internet in China: Citizen Activism Online* (New York: Columbia University Press, 2011); Jonathan Hassid, 'Safety Valve or Pressure Cooker? Blogs in Chinese Political Life', *Journal of Communication* 62 (2) (2012): 212–230; and Xin Xin, 'The Impact of "Citizen Journalism" on Chinese Media and Society', *Journalism Practice* 4(3) (2010): 333–344. For a nuanced discussion on the existing literature on China's microblogging, including its challenges to the party-state, as well as the state's adaptation to new media, see Jonathan Sullivan, 'China's Weibo: Is Faster Different?' *New Media & Society* 16(1) (2014): 24–37.

[33] Guobin Yang, *The Power of the Internet in China*, 33.

the one hand induces widespread self-censorship across media outlets,[34] while on the other provokes some journalists to take advantage of blurry boundaries and engage in watchdog reporting. Media-regulating authorities, in turn, try to contain investigative and in-depth reporting on the spot by applying pre- and post-publication restrictions, including pre-publication censorship and limited access to official information, as well as post-publication censorship and coercive measures. These interactions between the party-state and critical journalists can be characterised as a game of cat and mouse, with the two actors constantly trying to outrun each other, as the state keeps placing traps to guard its territory and the journalists find loopholes around them.

Pre-Publication Restrictions: Censorship and Limited Information Access

The interview analysis finds that pre-publication censorship and limited access to official information present the most common and intrusive restrictions on daily practice of watchdog reporting. The former bans media coverage and the latter complicates it. Their improvisational implementation, however, leaves space for journalists to negotiate the restrictions, as will be explained below.

Pre-Publication Censorship

Interviews with journalists and editors illuminate four types of pre-publication censorship, or restrictive orders (*jinling*, 禁令): an order to carry positive coverage (*zhengmian baodao*, 正面报道); an order to carry a version produced by the Xinhua News Agency[35] but still allowing for an independent selection of opinion pieces; an order to carry only the Xinhua's version, including its editorial pieces; and, finally, a ban on all media coverage and discussion. According to the interviewees, despite the party-state's emphasis on guiding (*yindao*, 引导) rather than suppressing media coverage, the first order tends to primarily concern coverage of national policies or issues of wide interest to the public, such as food safety. The Xinhua

---

[34] As already discussed, some scholars, including Hassid, Brady and Link, note the importance of 'uncertainty' and 'ambiguity' in facilitating self-censorship among journalists. See also Jingrong Tong, 'Press Self-Censorship in China: A Case Study in the Transformation of Discourse', *Discourse & Society* 20(5) (2009):593–612; For commercialisation of the media and self-censorship, see also Daniela Stockmann and Mary E. Gallagher, 'Remote Control: How the Media Sustain Authoritarian Rule in China', *Comparative Political Studies* 44(4) (2011): 436–467.

[35] The Xinhua News Agency is China's official and largest news agency. It reports to the Central Propaganda Department and is subordinate to the State Council.

restriction appears as more commonly applied, followed by the ban on all coverage, according to the interviewees. Although the Xinhua-only coverage is supposed to primarily concern national crises or breaking news,[36] authorities seem to apply this restriction arbitrarily to a wide range of stories. Interviewees note that even when they are allowed to publish their own editorials, editors tend to be reluctant to do so, cautious of making unfounded claims that could put their publications at risk.[37]

Pre-emptive censorship primarily targets specific incidents, events or cases (*shijian*, 事件 or *anjian*, 案件), including regular news stories, as well as unforeseen incidents or breaking news (*tufa shijian*, 突发事件), and is often applied on an ad hoc basis, with orders arriving when reporting is already in progress, bringing ongoing investigations to a halt.[38] The frustration expressed by an investigative journalist at *Caixin* magazine about losing a story due to an abrupt censorship order echoes in most of the interviews:

The most challenging part of my work is that I am often forced to give up on a story I would spend a long time working on because of an abrupt directive from the Central Propaganda Department. The unpredictable nature of my work can be very exhausting. A topic accessible a few days ago can quickly shift into the restricted territory. I would say that on the whole about half of the stories I investigate don't make it into print . . .[39]

The 'loss' of stories is so widespread that the national annual conference on *yulun jiandu* devotes a separate section to discussing them, as observed by the author and confirmed by conference organisers and regular participants.[40] Interviewees attribute the arbitrariness of pre-publication censorship to the growing importance of online public opinion and the influence of local officials in containing critical coverage. As for the former, the censorship apparatus appears to rapidly adapt to

---

[36] Brady, *Marketing Dictatorship: Propaganda and Thought Work in Contemporary China.*

[37] Since the Xinhua restriction tends to come with bans on independent interviews, editors often lack the information to write in-depth and balanced editorials.

[38] This targeted approach to managing potential dissent has also been observed by other scholars. Nara Dillon, for instance, argues that the control of non-governmental organizations (NGOs) and voluntary associations has also been characterised by targeted isolation of specific elements, something she traces back to the Mao period. See Nara Dillon, 'Governing Civil Society: Adapting Revolutionary Methods to Serve Post-Communist Goals', in Sebastian Heilmann and Elizabeth J. Perry (eds.), *Mao's Invisible Hand* (Cambridge, MA: Harvard University Press, 2011): 138–165.

[39] Interview CJ34.

[40] Interviews with a professor of journalism at Beiwai University and one of the organisers of the annual *yulun jiandu* conference (CSE02; CSE21), and a number of conference attendants took place in Beijing in December 2009, 2010, and again in the summer of 2012.

online public opinion currents, namely Weibo posts, as the number of active microblog users has gone up to 198 million by the first quarter of 2015.[41] Interviews with Chinese officials from the CPD and GAPP reveal that they closely follow Weibo, assigning responsibility to individual cadres to alert them to important discussion trends, which, in turn, inform their decisions vis-à-vis the media.[42] Other studies on official management of social media further confirm the party's concern with the linkages between social media and stability, especially when it comes to breaking events online.[43] Journalist interviewees note that the capacity of microblogging platforms (Weibo) to rapidly transform isolated incidents into national events also indirectly facilitates more state censorship over traditional news media. An example of Weibo magnifying a local event into a national one and influencing the process of media censorship that featured in a number of interviews is that of the 2012 environmental protest that took place in Shifang, Sichuan (*shifang shijian*, 什放事件).[44] This large-scale anti-pollution protest was initially uncovered on Weibo, sparking wide public interest. While online discussions were still proceeding, the authorities abruptly stopped traditional media from covering and investigating this story.[45] Journalist interviewees expressed surprise at online postings being less censored than regular news reporting. 'Everyone knows about the issue, so by banning media coverage authorities look ridiculous', remarked one of the former editors of *Nanfang Zhoumo*.[46] The authorities, however, quickly resolved the issue in favour of the protesters,[47] pre-empting traditional media from exaggerating the problem and using it to channel the image of the party's responsiveness instead. During the July 2012 fatal rainstorms in Beijing,[48] at the height of

---

[41] Paul Bischoff, 'Weibo Kicks Off 2015 with Renewed Growth, Now Has 198M Monthly Active Users', *TechInAsia*, 14 May2015.

[42] Interviews COF02; COF05; COF08. The awareness and adaptation of Chinese higher officials to new media have also been noted by other scholars. See, for instance, Patricia M. Thornton, 'Censorship and Surveillance in Chinese Cyberspace: Beyond the Great Firewall', in Peter Hays Gries and Stanley Rosen (eds.), *Chinese Politics: State, Society and the Market* (London and New York: Routledge, 2010): 179–198; Rebecca MacKinnon, 'China's "Networked Authoritarianism" ', *Journal of Democracy* 22(2) (2011): 32–46; On interviews with officials about their use of Weibo, see Gao Mingyong, 'Weibo wen zheng de 30 tangke' ('30 Lessons from Interviews with Officials about Weibo') (Zhejiang: Zhejiang People's Publishing House, 2012).

[43] Christopher Cairns (2016).

[44] Thousands of people in Shifang, Sichuan province staged a three-day protest against the building of a large copper plant. See: Tania Branigan, 'Anti-Pollution Protesters Halt Construction of Copper Plant in China', *The Guardian*, 3 July 2012, available at: www .theguardian.com/world/2012/jul/03/china-anti-pollution-protest-copper.

[45] *Caijing*'s report was one of the exceptions.   [46] Interview CJ26.

[47] 'Anti-Pollution Protesters Halt Construction of Copper Plant in China'.

[48] The storm killed seventy people and was followed by widespread public criticism of the state's management of the crisis, including insufficient preparation for it. For more details

public criticism on Weibo, traditional media was similarly abruptly banned from investigating the issue, as authorities were working to address public concerns.[49] Most recently, in the Xi era, we are seeing similar patterns, with major incidents like the 2015 Kunming terrorist attack and the 2015 Shenzhen landslide silenced in traditional media, but initially widely discussed online.[50]

The correlation of online popularity of a certain incident or an issue and tighter censorship over traditional media investigations has also been demonstrated in other studies. Lorentzen, in his formal model of Chinese censorship, for instance, finds that as the internet penetration has spread, the Chinese party-state has resorted to containing traditional media coverage of contentious issues discussed online as a balancing act to give mixed signals to the public about the political atmosphere.[51] He writes that the regime can 'maintain uncertainty about the true state of affairs by giving the traditional media less leeway to cover new stories when more bad news is likely to come out via channels it cannot control'.[52] As the majority of breaking news stories and events are now appearing on Weibo before being covered by traditional media,[53] these censorship dynamics are likely to become only more prevalent. This is not to argue that Weibo discussions are generally less censored. There are sophisticated mechanisms in place to weed out sensitive keywords and monitor online debates, especially when they touch on social mobilisation,[54] and Weibo censorship has become more pervasive in the last several years under Xi Jinping's rule. While presenting a serious challenge to authorities, however, Weibo, like some traditional media, has also served as a feedback mechanism, facilitating the party-state's management of public opinion (with the help of the media), which has been its key priority in the reform era.[55]

---

on media coverage, see Maria Repnikova, 'Information Management during Crisis Events: A Case Study of Beijing Floods of 2012', *Journal of Contemporary China* 26 (105) (2017): 1–15.

[49] According to the interviewees from both critical and official media, most traditional media were told to only explain the official achievements in managing the crisis.

[50] The new examples were shared via online correspondence by two Chinese journalists at *Caixin*, previously interviewed in Beijing, and who have remained active in investigative reporting in the past several years.

[51] Lorentzen, 'China's Strategic Censorship', 402–414.   [52] Ibid.: 403.

[53] Xie Yungeng, Zhongguo shehui yuqing yu weiji guanli baogao (Report on Chinese Social Opinion and Crisis Management) (Beijing: Social Sciences Academic Press, 2012).

[54] King, Pan, and Roberts, 'How Censorship in China Allows Government Criticism but Silences Collective Expression'; Rebecca MacKinnon, 'Flatter World and Thicker Walls? Blogs, Censorship and Civic Discourse in China', *Public Choice* 134(1–2) (2008): 31–46; Thornton, 'Censorship and Surveillance in Chinese Cyberspace: Beyond the Great Firewall'.

[55] Patricia M. Thornton, 'Retrofitting the Steel Frame: From Mobilizing the Masses to Surveying the Public', in Sebastian Heilmann and Elizabeth J. Perry (eds.), *Mao's*

Other than being influenced by online public opinion, pre-publication restrictive orders can represent the interests of powerful actors outside the media-regulating apparatus. According to the interviewees, officials interested in limiting media coverage can exert pressure on the media through their connections at the CPD, as well as at local propaganda departments and the GAPP. Interviewees shared that they were often capable of drawing linkages between banning orders and the driving interests behind them. Some even alluded to the corrupt nature of the propaganda authorities, accepting bribes in return for media bans. 'The Propaganda Department is increasingly a commercial entity . . .', argued one of the interviewees.[56] 'The work of the CPD mainly involves coordination among other bureaus and interests', noted another reporter.[57] While the claim of corruption is difficult to attest through journalists' interviews, other actors do appear to influence some of the censorship decisions.

According to the media professionals, interests of local officials, in particular, feed into the media bans on specific events and incidents. Interviewees explain that local authorities would frequently lobby propaganda officials to contain negative media coverage. The following excerpt from an interview with a *Caijing* journalist explains local officials' use of personal networks to limit media reports in their regions:

In many instances, the key local officials use their special networks to explain the situation (*fanying qingkuang*, 反映情况) to higher officials, asking them to "support" (*zhi'ai*, 支爱) them in leading media coverage, to eliminate the negative media reports that could have a harmful influence on local stability. Depending on multiple factors, propaganda authorities might choose to issue a ban.[58]

Some interviewees even admitted to avoiding local officials when conducting their investigations out of fear for jeopardising their reports:

There have been times when I would approach local officials and instead of accepting or declining my interview, they would report about my presence to local propaganda authorities, who in turn would complain to central authorities. A number of times my report was cut off as a result. Therefore, what I do now is I avoid interviewing local officials while in their area, and try to get a phone interview when I am back in Beijing instead. This way, there are less chances they can block my article.[59]

When dealing with local media outlets, officials can contain reporting through local propaganda departments. Since many critical journalists

---

Invisible Hand: The Political Foundations of Adaptive Governance in China (Cambridge, MA: Harvard University Press, 2011): 237–269; Sullivan (2014).
[56] Interview CJ52.   [57] Interview CJ53.   [58] Interview CJ05.   [59] Interview CJ29.

engage in cross-territorial supervision or *yidi jiandu* (异地监督), whereby they report on sensitive issues outside their jurisdiction, local propaganda departments have to complain to central propaganda officials to issue censorship orders. A ban on coverage of the Yunnan earthquake (*yunnan yiliang dizhen shijian*, 云南彝良地震期间) exemplified the complex linkages between local and central propaganda authorities. An investigative journalist from *Jingji Guanchabao* was already at the scene of the disaster when, according to him, 'the director of the Yunnan Provincial Propaganda Department immediately contacted the head of the Central Propaganda Department and urged him to issue a ban to guard local stability'.[60] This journalist's report never made it into the newspaper.

The web of interests behind media bans can also include local commercial interests, when media investigations threaten to expose their corrupt operations, as demonstrated by the following example from another journalist at *Jingji Guanchabao*:

In April of this year I was investigating a scandal concerning a large enterprise in Qinghai province. The head of the enterprise sought out the provincial leaders, who in turn contacted the CPD authorities, requesting a banning order. I was still conducting my investigations when the CPD issued a ban to my newspaper, telling me to stop all interviewing immediately. This would not have happened if not for some shared commercial interests between the large enterprise and the propaganda authorities.[61]

Many other interviewees also noted the persisting pressures from enterprises to cover up negative stories.[62] These revelations are not surprising, considering the interdependency of official and commercial interests at the local level, with local officials often depending on large enterprises for economic growth, with many entrepreneurs also being party members[63] and with corruption becoming an apparent feature of the Chinese political reality.[64]

Local officials' improvisation with pre-empting media coverage is further manifested in their occasional use of non-media legislation or even physical

---

[60] This journalist managed to obtain internal documents issued by Yunnan propaganda authorities to the CPD, which confirmed his account and which he shared with the author.

[61] Interview CJ51.

[62] This pattern has also been documented by other scholars. Tong, for instance, argues that local officials' intrusion into media coverage on behalf of local business interests is increasingly common. See Jingrong Tong, 'The Crisis of the Centralized Media Control Theory'.

[63] Bruce J. Dickson, *Red Capitalists in China: The Party, Private Entrepreneurs, and Prospects for Political Change* (New York: Cambridge University Press, 2003).

[64] Ting Gong, 'Dangerous Collusion: Corruption as a Collective Venture in Contemporary China', *Communist and Post-Communist Studies* 35 (2002): 85–103; Melanie Manion, *Corruption by Design: Building Clean Government in Mainland China and Hong Kong* (Cambridge, MA: Harvard University Press, 2004).

retaliation, if connections with propaganda authorities fail to stop journalists. An investigative journalist from *Nanfang Renwu Zhoukan*, for instance, shared a story about local officials bringing false corruption charges against his colleagues to halt threatening investigations:

Even if an editor supports a certain investigative story, and there are no notable negative signs from media regulating authorities, one could still experience unexpected coercion from local officials. For example, my colleagues were recently reporting on corruption of some local officials. The annoyed authorities inquired where these journalists were staying and secretly left envelopes with cash outside the doors of their hotel rooms. This happened at night, so the journalists did not notice. The next morning authorities requested an investigation against these journalists on corruption charges, accusing them of accepting bribes.[65]

Some interviewees have also experienced physical assaults by local officials. While coercion seems less frequent in contrast to censorship bans, it highlights the extreme measures local officials are willing to undertake to silence the media.[66] This treatment is not unique to journalists. Studies of Chinese lawyers, for instance, indicate that they often face allegations on trumped-up charges at the local level, and some even fear for their safety when involved in sensitive cases outside their jurisdictions.[67]

Although the influences of online public opinion and other powerful interests have been discussed separately here, they tend to work together in producing ad hoc bans on media coverage. If an incident that is of concern to local officials or enterprises is also a popular topic on weibo, central propaganda authorities would have a higher incentive to issue a banning order, and vice versa. At the same time, if one element is missing, especially online public opinion, it might diminish the bargaining power of local officials.

While presenting a constant challenge to critical journalists, the inconsistent nature of pre-publication censorship also creates some opportunities for them to negotiate it. Specifically, with a combination of microblogging, cross-media collaboration and the waiting-out strategy, journalists often succeed in outrunning or averting pre-publication pressures. As for microblogging, journalists, like officials, also use Weibo and, most recently, Weixin to learn about public opinion trends. At times, they are capable of spotting a trend or an incident and reporting on it before

---

[65] Interview CJ10.

[66] Some interviewees also experienced physical assaults by local officials.

[67] John W. Givens and Maria Repnikova, 'Advocates of Change in Authoritarian Regimes: How Chinese Lawyers, Chinese Journalists, and Russian Journalists Stay out of Trouble', paper presented at the annual meeting of the American Political Science Association, Seattle, 3 September 2011.

the officials take notice. In their drive to meet public demands for more accurate information, journalists and editors at traditional media are highly attuned to online activism and critical expression, as they try to cater to issues of immediate interest to social media users.[68] Moreover, if a ban reaches journalists prior to publication, social media can serve as a channel for publicising censored reports.[69] Journalists use either their real or fake names to post unpublished articles on Weibo. An example is *Nanfang Zhoumo*'s coverage of the fatal Beijing floods of July 2012. As a result of internal self-censorship most likely following editorial shifts within the newspaper,[70] an in-depth article investigating the individual deaths of all the victims of the storm was not published.[71] One of the journalists, however, uploaded a photograph of the article on Weibo, including editorial markings.[72] This posting was widely circulated and discussed in the journalistic community. Though the censors quickly deleted the post, by that time it had already managed to attract wide public attention. While journalists' online sharing of editorial censorship markings is relatively infrequent, the leaking of unpublished stories with the help of netizens is more common, according to the interviewees, which poses a direct challenge to the effectiveness of pre-publication censorship.

Other than outrunning censors through social media, journalists also embark on cross-media and cross-regional collaboration that takes advantage of the highly decentralised censorship apparatus.[73] A journalist providing information is often based at a small local media outlet, collaborating with colleagues at larger, more influential news outlets, such as *Nanfang Zhoumo* or *Caijing*.[74] 'While conducting my reporting, I established

---

[68] These observations are also confirmed by other scholars. See H. Christoph Steinhardt, 'From Blind Spot to Media Spotlight: Propaganda Policy, Media Activism and the Emergence of Protest Events in the Chinese Public Sphere', *Asian Studies Review* (39) (1) (2015): 119–137.

[69] This practice was also observed in other studies. See Jonathan Hassid and Maria Repnikova, 'Why Chinese Print Journalists Embrace the Internet', *Journalism* (17)(7) (2016): 882–898.

[70] This information was gathered from personal interviews with former journalists from *Nanfang Zhoumo*.

[71] See, for instance, 'Beijing Flood Stories Cut from *Southern Weekend*', *China Digital Times*, 26 July 2012; available at: http://chinadigitaltimes.net/2012/07/beijing-flood-stories-cut-southern-weekend/.

[72] Ibid. The author also confirmed this through participant observation on Weibo, as well as through interviews with critical journalists immediately following these developments.

[73] At times, this collaboration takes place within the same newspaper group. Some papers establish their own local branches, while others collaborate with papers within the same conglomerate. See Jingrong Tong, 'The Crisis of the Centralized Media Control Theory'.

[74] Other scholars note similar dynamics about local journalists getting in touch with those at more influential media electronically and sharing sensitive stories. See Benjamin L. Liebman, 'Changing Media, Changing Courts', in Susan Shirk (ed.), *Changing*

connections with journalists across China. Sometimes when a story breaks that they are banned from covering, they would get in touch and ask if I would be interested in it', explains a journalist at *Nanfang Zhoumo*.[75] Cross-regional collaboration combined with new media can also help in dealing with arbitrary retaliation from local officials. Journalists admit that they rarely use official structures, such as legal institutions, journalist associations or government bureaus, in dealing with troublesome officials. They prefer to resort to personal and professional networks, reinforced by new media. The following example shared by a journalist at *Nanfang Dushibao* reveals the powerful fusion of professional networks and new media in escaping official assault:

Journalists at commercial, and especially at more critical newspapers know each other quite well and have a 'QQ group'[76] to keep in touch and discuss their work. Once a journalist is in trouble, others usually try to support him or her. For instance, a few months ago, my colleague went to Hubei with a reporter from Beijing's popular daily, Xinjing Bao to investigate a local corruption case, and got assaulted by local authorities. My colleague immediately informed me and asked me to publicise this on Weibo. I did. I could not imagine that messages from concerned journalists would flood my inbox and chat rooms so quickly. As a result, my colleague and the other reporter were released. As for official organs ... there is no point in trying to use them because the journalist victims were trying to report on something already forbidden by the Propaganda Department.[77]

The QQ groups have now largely been replaced by Weixin groups or circles, but the practice of cross-regional sharing in closed online

Media, Changing China (Oxford, New York: Oxford University Press, 2011): 150–175. The latest interviews in China, however, also suggest that collaboration between local journalists and investigative reporters from national media outlets has been less prominent in recent years. Interviewees from *Caijing* and investigative publications in Guangzhou reveal that local journalists are increasingly more concerned with their personal safety and less idealistic about the societal role of the media than they used to be in the past. Instead of helping journalists from these famous outlets to either learn about censored topics or access specific information, local journalists at times can even report the activities of the investigative reporters to local authorities and thus compromise their investigations. Those local journalists still willing to help are driven either by admiration for specific journalists or their media outlets or by personal relationships.

[75] Interview CJ46.

[76] QQ is an instant-messaging application that is very popular in China. For more on the use of QQ by China's investigative and critical journalists, see Ju Jing, 'Shendu baodao shengchan fangshi de xin bianhua – Shendu baodao jizhe QQ qun chutan' ('A New Change in the Mode of Production of In-Depth Reporting: A First Exploration of QQ Groups among In-Depth Journalists'), *Xinwen Jizhe* 1 (2012), available at: http://xwjz.eastday.com/eastday/xwjz/node595770/; Marina Svensson, 'Media and Civil Society in China: Community Building and Networking Among Investigative Journalists and Beyond', *China Perspectives* 3 (2012). Most recently, Weixin has become another platform for journalists' networking as it allows for real-time communication and chats across small groups that require an invitation and approval of entry.

[77] Interview CJ18.

communities has remained the same. *Yidi jiandu* has recently also become apparent in online social movements, whereby microblogging platforms have allowed for a development of issue publics across regions. Huang and Sun's study of China's homeowners' associations, for instance, found that social media enables linkages and collaboration otherwise inhibited by geographic distance.[78] Cross-regional supervision and activism, therefore, is another facet of convergence between new and traditional media when it comes to bottom-up contestation of political pressures.

If outpacing censors and other pre-emptive pressures is not possible, journalists can at times wait out censorship. The following comment by a journalist at *Nandu Zhoukan* explains how censorship bans can abate over time and make previously outlawed stories feasible to publish:

Censorship bans do not have official expiration dates; they are meant to be effective for extended periods of time. But their control capacity can slowly diminish, as time passes and the incident becomes less relevant. For instance, my piece on the explosion in Yunnan was banned from publication at the end of May, but in August the Yunnan police had already uncovered this incident, and the reports on this subject became completely open. Since the issue appeared resolved, at that point the propaganda authorities did not enforce new bans on the media. By then, media coverage was actually helpful to the propaganda mission of guiding public opinion ...[79]

This comment reflects the official discourse on *yulun jiandu*, discussed in the previous chapter, specifically the idea that *yulun jiandu* should be conducive to the party-state's guidance of public opinion. While investigative coverage appeared threatening to propaganda authorities in the immediate aftermath of the incident, once the issue was publicly acknowledged with a police investigation, media reports may have been conducive to public opinion management. This journalist's comment indicates his awareness of the official logic, which he tries to use to his advantage. He is also exploiting the decentralised control system by playing to the interests of the central state. His report might still aggravate local officials, but it is likely to benefit central authorities by signalling the regime's efficiency and reinforcing public trust.

While central authorities can reap some definite gains from journalists' contestation of pre-publication censorship, they also actively attempt to contain their use of social media and cross-territorial investigations. The practice of sharing unpublished stories or post-publication pressures on Weibo has been restricted in recent years. Weibo users are now

---

[78] Ronggui Huang and Xiaoyi Sun, 'Weibo Network, Information Diffusion and Implications for Collective Action in China', *Information, Communication & Society* (17)(1) (2014): 86–104.
[79] Interview CJ50.

required to register with their real names and identity card numbers.[80] Though many still find ways around it, if one's postings are continuously provocative, censors can delete a user account – a tactic that has become especially prominent in the past two years, under Xi Jinping, as will be explained further in the concluding part of the book.[81] While it is possible to register again under a different user name, it requires extensive time and effort to re-establish an online network and to resume influencing public opinion. Moreover, the GAPP has imposed new restrictions on the media about sharing professional content, including unpublished stories and grievances.[82] According to the deputy director of the GAPP, such regulations are likely to intensify.[83] A number of media professionals have also confirmed that they are increasingly more careful about the way they use social media so as not to compromise their professional standing.[84] One of the veteran reporters at *Caijing* and *Caixin* revealed that she mostly posts personal things and tries to avoid political discussions.[85] As for cross-territorial collaboration, central authorities restricted *yidi jiandu* in 2004 because of complaints from provincial officials. Specifically, they limited it to reporting at the county level and below.[86] Despite the new restrictions, journalists persist in using social media as well as cross-regional reporting to bypass pre-publication censorship, even if less openly and extensively than in the past, according to the latest observations in the field. This further underlines the interactive and improvisational nature of the state's restrictions on the media: the party and state officials and critical journalists continuously engage in mutual adjustments in response to one another.

We now proceed to discussing another form of pre-publication limitation on critical journalism: limited access to official information.

---

[80] Kathrin Hille, 'Real Name Rule to Add to Sina Weibo's Woes', *The Financial Times*, 29 February 2012, available at: www.ft.com/intl/cms/s/0/e995b7aa-6201-11e1-807f-00144feabdc0.html#axzz2cRu2f1qm.

[81] In the past two years, a new campaign against 'false rumours' has gained momentum, with many Weibo accounts deleted. See Chris Buckley, 'Crackdown on Bloggers Is Mounted by China', *The New York Times*, 10 September, 2013, available at: www.nytimes.com/2013/09/11/world/asia/china-cracks-down-on-online-opinion-makers.html?_r=0.

[82] The deputy director of the GAPP said in a personal interview that he sends out official instructions to media outlets warning them about not publicising official instructions received and editorial dynamics behind their stories on Weibo. Interview COF08.

[83] Ibid.

[84] Investigative journalists at *Caixin* even shared that there are new internal rules at the magazine about the use of Weibo, including restrictions on posting professional content.

[85] Interview CJ29.

[86] Susan L. Shirk, *Changing Media, Changing China* (New York: Oxford University Press, 2011).

Limited Access to Official Information

While pre-publication censorship presents the most pervasive pressure on journalists, limited access to official information also inhibits media investigations. Despite the new Open Government Information Regulation (*xinxi gongkai tiaoli*, 信息公开条例) on official information openness,[87] journalists note the challenge of getting officials to participate in their investigations. Both central and local officials improvise with restricting information access. Whereas central authorities, having partially incorporated Western public relations norms, deploy ambiguity in responding to journalists, local officials align information sharing with their strategic interests, most often using various tactics to stop information from reaching the media. Journalists, in turn, negotiate information access, especially at the local level, by building personal relationships with officials, insisting upon their professional norms and using new media as an alternative information source.

Media professionals shared that central officials tend to be more open to journalists' requests, while growing increasingly skilful at producing a general response devoid of facts. Specifically, interviews with high-level officials have started to resemble public relations briefings, often administered by media spokespeople. Crisis management experts further explain that many high-ranking officials have studied government and crisis communication at top Western universities, such as Harvard, and adapt the newly acquired skills and tactics to the local context.[88] Ironically, by learning Western-style strategies, Chinese authorities have appeared to find new ways of hiding information. In response to the question on whether central authorities are easier to work with than local officials, an investigative journalist at *Nanfang Dushibao* explained the downsides of high-level 'responsiveness':

Central officials are definitely more knowledgeable about the media. Instead of ignoring our requests, they would accept them. However, they have learned to speak vaguely and eloquently on many issues without giving any concrete information. So unless these interviews are arranged through personal contacts, sometimes they are not so helpful to us.[89]

---

[87] The first nationwide regulations on open government information were enacted in 2008. For more details on the regulations, see Jamie P. Horsley, 'China Adopts First Nationwide Open Government Information Regulations', Freedominfo.org, May 2007, available at: www.law.yale.edu/documents/pdf/Intellectual_Life/CL-OGI-China_Adopts_JPH-English.pdf.

[88] In the summer of 2012, the author interviewed crisis management scholars at Tsinghua, Renda and Beida, as well as private public relations consultants. All of them confirmed that central officials are intensively adopting Western public relations tools into their communication practices.

[89] Interview CJ43.

In contrast to central officials, local officials tend to limit journalists' information access by either refusing interviews or offering bribes, while sharing information only when it is to their immediate advantage. As for refusals, interviewees note a general reluctance of local officials to agree to interviews. 'When it comes to local officials, their primary goal tends to be to hide the problem at any cost. Getting them to speak openly to us and to give us reliable information is very difficult', shared a journalist at *Nanfang Zhoumo*.[90] Interviews with media experts who have trained local officials in media communication techniques similarly confirm an overarching perception held by local officials about media being primarily a threat to their careers and reputations. A professor from Beijing University, who has worked extensively with local officials, observed that they are fearful of negative coverage:

> Local officials frequently voice their concerns to me about being negatively portrayed by the media. They worry about being presented as incapable and being misunderstood by journalists. I train them to face the media and to share information as openly as possible, but I think it will take a long time for local officials to change their mindset . . .[91]

According to journalist interviewees, other than simply declining interviews, local officials frequently attempt to bribe journalists into silence or positive coverage by giving them a 'sealed fee' or a 'shut up fee' (*feng koufei*, 封口费). The following comment by a former journalist of *Nanfang Zhoumo* illustrates the corrupt webs of interactions initiated by local officials:

> On many occasions in investigating local-level incidents, I have witnessed local officials trying to bribe journalists. Many journalists accept bribes, and even arrive to 'cover' the accident with the purpose of getting the money. Therefore, journalists and media are also at the core of this problem. The most professional outlets, like *Nanfang Zhoumo*, have rules about not accepting bribes, but editors of smaller commercial media can even encourage journalists to take the money.[92]

While intensification of corruption in the Chinese media industry has also been documented in other studies,[93] journalists from more professional outlets examined here appear to successfully resist the pressures of accepting official bribes, as evident from the comment above and as we discover more in Chapter 6. Some news outlets explicitly prohibit journalists from taking any payments from officials. A former editor of *Caijing*

---

[90] Interview CJ46.   [91] Interview CSE05.   [92] Interview CJ41.
[93] See, for instance, Liu Xiaobo, 'Corruption Lingers in the Shadows of the Chinese Media', *China Perspectives* 54 (2004), available at: http://chinaperspectives.revues.org /3012; Yuezhi Zhao, *Media, Market, and Democracy: Between the Party Line and the Bottom Line* (Urbana and Chicago: University of Illinois Press, 1998).

(now at *Caixin*), for instance, shared that his magazine has adopted an ethics code from the *New York Times*, which strictly outlaws any forms of journalistic corruption.[94] When asked about bribes, most interviewees would deny ever taking them. Despite this resilience by journalists from a few professional publications, official bribery narrows the scope for a media watchdog role as it co-opts many other journalists who could otherwise potentially embark on in-depth reporting on sensitive issues. Interviews with journalists and editors at mainstream news outlets, such as Beijing's popular newspaper *Xinjing Bao*, and especially at official news outlets like *Xinhua*, for instance, underscore journalists' difficulties in declining official payments.[95] Press conferences tend to provide meals, transport and even accommodation in order to induce positive coverage. Most reporters find it close to impossible to abstain from this treatment if they are to complete their reporting.

Occasionally, however, local officials are willing to share information with journalists when it is in their strategic interest. *Caijing*'s editor explains local officials' rationale when dealing with investigative reporters, arguing that officials are responsive to journalists when it complements their agenda:

Local officials' willingness to speak to us really depends on their stakes in the issue we are investigating. Most times I would find them completely unapproachable, while on certain occasions they would contact me themselves wanting to share information. Sometimes they are dissatisfied with a certain central policy and want to channel it through the media. On other occasions they might need central government's investment in their area, and might see our report as a way to get it.[96]

Local officials, therefore, can take advantage of journalists and partner with them to leverage their interests vis-à-vis the centre. If journalists' reporting can help garner necessary attention from high-level authorities, officials may be more open to sharing information and even facilitating journalists' investigations. Just like central officials, local authorities can use journalists as allies in their efforts to navigate and take advantage of the fragmented political system.

On the whole, however, working with both central and local officials presents a continuous challenge to China's critical journalists and their editors. This difficulty is not unique to China, of course, as journalists in democratic countries similarly face officials' reluctance to share information. Charles Lewis, a former producer at *60 Minutes* and the founder of an investigative journalism NGO, The Center for Public Integrity, shared that the difficulty of accessing official data is a normal part of his job.

---

[94] Interview CJ13.   [95] Interviews CJ14; CJ07; CJ23.   [96] Interview CJ25.

'The officials' response can range from avoiding my questions to directly threatening me', he stated.[97] In China, a weak rule of law and one-party rule further exacerbate these dynamics, creating more room for officials, especially at the local level, to improvise with restricting information access.

Chinese journalists, however, rise to the challenge and negotiate information access by working to build trust with officials as well as by using social media to complement or to bypass interactions with local authorities. As for building trust, journalists do so by forming personal bonds with officials and by projecting themselves as professionals who aspire towards balanced reporting. In explaining the process of fostering relationships, a former journalist at *Nanfang Zhoumo* described it as a search for a compromise:

Local officials tend to be quite rude to journalists' requests (*cubao de duidai*, 粗暴的对待), and hide information. One way to deal with this is to establish close personal relations with some officials in that town or region. The relationship-based information sharing only happens if our interests intersect (*liyi goutong*, 利益沟通). It is often about a compromise. An official might agree to tell me something if I protect his interests and reputation. It is always a tricky balance to maintain between remaining professional and getting the information you need. It takes some experience to get used to it . . .[98]

In the above excerpt, the interviewee appears to indirectly imply that in order to win officials' trust and persuade them to collaborate, journalists may have to censor themselves. Some interviewees are more explicit about protecting officials in exchange for information. 'If a local official tells me not to include something in my report, I will oblige him. I would not expose him and try to ruin his reputation. Once this report comes out, we might even become good friends', comments a journalist at *Caijing*.[99] In addition to accommodating officials' demands, journalists also appeal to a common background in building a personal rapport. Specifically, a shared geographic and societal upbringing appears to facilitate a formation of personal bonds between journalists and officials. An editor at *Caijing*, who comes from a small town in Hubei province, for instance, admits that he finds it easier to relate to and cooperate with local officials than his colleagues with an urban background, and he uses his personal experience to his professional advantage.[100] Building personal relationships with officials, of course, is common across political contexts.

---

[97] Conversation with Charles Lewis, Washington, DC, 11 September 2012.
[98] Interview CJ41.   [99] Interview CJ38.
[100] Interview CJ25. Similar observations were shared by other reporters and editors with a rural background. Interviews CJ57; CJ60; CJ51; CJ38; CJ28; CJ20, among others.

Like Chinese reporters, Western journalists build relationships with officials as a way to mitigate information challenges and to deepen their access to the political establishment. Some scholars have subsequently referred to Western (namely US) media as 'the uncertain guardians', struggling to balance out their quest for objectivity with their need for maintaining relationships with politicians.[101] Given the more acute information constraints, this balance is even more fragile in the Chinese context.

Other than attempting to befriend and co-opt officials, China's critical journalists also use professionalism rhetoric to their advantage in attempting to alleviate officials' fears of negative and sensationalist reporting. The following excerpts from interviews with journalists at two different media outlets show how they can use the discourse of media professionalism as a tactic for winning officials' trust:

In order to make an official agree to accept an interview, it is important to make him understand that my mission is to provide objective reporting. Many officials, especially at the local level, worry that journalists would misunderstand them and misrepresent them (*wujie tamen*, 误解他们). Many journalists, when interviewing an official accused of some wrongdoing, start out the interview by blaming him. This has nothing to do with professional reporting.[102]

Someone will still cover the story, so we try to explain to official interviewees that it is better if the more professional media like ours would channel their perspectives. Otherwise, they might face more criticism from public opinion. We just try to reason with them calmly and explain that the very purpose of the interview is to publish a more balanced story. Sometimes we manage to convince them.[103]

Considering that media commercialisation has indirectly facilitated the emergence of many sensationalist and unprofessional media outlets, critical journalists try to distinguish themselves as ethical and professional. Investigative reporters at reputable official outlets, however, tend to make use of this tactic more successfully than their counterparts at commercialised news outlets. A former anchor at a popular China Central Television (CCTV) programme, *Mian Dui Mian*, which has frequently probed into governance failures, for instance, shared that most local officials she interviewed would know of and respect the programme, and would tend to accept her interviews in part out of fear of hurting their reputations.[104] This appears to be less the case for journalists from the commercial

---

[101] Bartholomew H. Sparrow, *Uncertain Guardians: The News Media as a Political Institution* (Baltimore, MD: Johns Hopkins University Press, 1999).
[102] Interview CJ01.   [103] Interview CJ51.
[104] Interview CJ01; Similar revelations came out in an interview with a producer at *Xinwen Diaocha*; Interview CJ33.

Caijing or *Nanfang Zhoumo*, which are well known but less immediately recognisable and intimidating to local officials than central television programmes. Nonetheless, regardless of their media affiliation, journalists attempt to persuade officials to trust their professional credentials.

Finally, interviewees share that they make the best use of official Weibo pages and online discussions in their investigations, which can offer some clues for the stories, as well as reveal official positions on the issues, at times replacing the interviews. Journalists, for instance, find official Weibo pages useful in disaster coverage, as they update the number of victims and the areas most in need of media investigations. In their Weibo pages, similarly to the interviews, however, officials tend to hide details and employ ambiguous statements highlighting their accomplishments. Moreover, according to journalist interviewees, many local officials still do not have Weibo accounts.[105] Information leaked either through officials' accidental postings on Weibo or through netizens' investigations appears to be more relevant, but needs to be carefully verified, according to the interviewees:

> Weibo embodies citizen journalism. It contains a lot of information leaked by insiders, which can provide clues for our reports. Moreover, it is often the content that officials are not willing to reveal. But this content is merely an information thread and needs to be carefully discerned and checked before being used as journalistic evidence. Weibo contains a lot of false information and rumours, and therefore cannot be taken for granted . . .[106]

The mix of opportunism and caution that journalists exhibit towards Weibo as an information source highlights the complexity of social media as a force for critical reporting. On the one hand, it presents a wealth of information previously inaccessible to media professionals. 'Internet is a public forum that the government struggles to control', noted a journalist at *Caijing*.[107] 'Internet is a sort of manna, an irreversible progress for public discourse and openness', argued another reporter at *Caijing*.[108] 'Internet allows for unprecedented information leaks', shared an online editor of the same magazine.[109] At the same time, the internet creates new challenges of verifying the credibility of sources and sorting through immense data pools to piece a story together. Some journalists noted that the internet 'exaggerates the voices of the grassroot movements'[110] and that it 'elevates voices of some individuals above

---

[105] Journalists' opinions were further substantiated by interviews with crisis management experts who train local officials.

[106] Interview CJ35. The need for cautiousness in accessing information on Weibo came up in many interviews, particularly in 2012, when Weibo rumours were widely discussed in societal and official circles.

[107] Interview CJ04.   [108] Interview CJ05.   [109] Interview CJ19.   [110] Interview CJ05.

others'.[111] While presenting a double-edged sword for battling information constraints, social media creates an opportunity for critical journalists to distinguish themselves from citizen journalists as information guardians. Whereas the latter are primarily preoccupied with exposing the truth or leaking information to the public, the former work to deliver a reliable, objective story for the public and authorities. As noted by an editor at *Bingdian*, 'we need to provide quality reports and added value to the new media news and reporting coverage'.[112] In making sense of social media as a strategy for mitigating official information access, therefore, journalists are also delineating their space and role in a complex shifting media environment.

To conclude the discussion of information access, as with bypassing pre-publication censorship, journalists attempt to contest this pressure by employing the inconsistencies in official information control to their advantage. They play to the interests of the local state by appealing to help local officials gain the appropriate recognition from the centre: journalists create incentives for local officials to share information by presenting it as being in their strategic interest, which allows them to promote a less damaging version of events and attempt to secure their reputations. Moreover, journalists are aware of the officials' inconsistency in sharing information in offline versus online domains, and thereby try to avoid interview refusals by carefully following official online discussions. As with battling pre-publication censorship, journalists closely follow netizen leaks as a form of investigating a story, while carefully verifying the sources and critically examining the biases of this information sharing.

We now proceed to the discussion of post-publication pressures: how they are applied by authorities and negotiated by critical journalists.

Post-Publication Censorship and Repressive Measures

Other than dealing with pre-publication restrictions in the form of censorship and limited access to official information, an additional challenge to critical journalism comes in the form of post-publication censorship and repressive measures. The former includes deletion of online content and removal of unwanted articles from published editions, while the latter constitutes official warnings and personnel replacements. As with pre-publication restrictions, these measures are characterised by guarded improvisation. The improvisation in both directions, however, is more limited in the case of post-publication restrictions, as official actions are more deliberate, leaving journalists with less space to negotiate.

[111] Interview CJ10.   [112] Interview CJ22.

Post-publication censorship applies to cases when pre-publication bans either fail or are outpaced by journalists. The most frequent measure, according to the interviewees, is a deletion of online content. Interviews with editors reveal that they receive frequent phone calls and messages on a daily basis from propaganda authorities, instructing them to delete or alter content.[113] 'Every day I face an instruction of either "must release" or "cannot release" an article, or demands to take out certain words or sentences without any justifiable reason … it is much easier to delete content in online editions than in traditional media …', shared an online editor at *Jingji Guanchabao*.[114] Here again, it is apparent that the expansion of the internet and the digitalisation of traditional media carry mixed implications for critical journalists. On the one hand, as explained earlier, the internet is a channel for resisting censorship. On the other, it propels a quicker, more intensive oversight from authorities. As the majority of readership of critical publications is now online, digital editions have turned into the most contested spaces for journalists and officials. Other than digital censorship, however, journalists shared examples of removal of printed articles. 'I recall once being forced to reprint the entire edition of our newspaper because one of the stories was deemed as too sensitive', noted a former journalist at *Nanfang Dushibao*.[115] Others mentioned cases of newspapers being pulled off the market.[116] A case of post-publication removal of sensitive articles that attracted international attention is that of President Obama's interview with *Nanfang Zhoumo* being ripped out of some of the Beijing editions of the paper, allegedly by local propaganda authorities.[117] Such incidents, however, are rare, manifesting a desperate attempt by some officials to contain the influence of the media.

Similarly to pre-publication bans, arbitrary post-publication censorship appears to reflect trends in online public opinion, as well as the interests of local officials. When it comes to digital deletions, they tend to follow escalating public interest in an event, according to the editors and journalists. Local officials also play a role in post-publication censorship, especially when it comes to removal of printed articles and online deletions. A journalist at *Jingji Guanchabao*, for instance, shared a story about propaganda authorities deleting his investigative article about

---

[113] Interviews were conducted with the online editor of *Jingji Guanchabao* (Interview CJ09) and *Caijing* (Interview CJ19). Print editors who are in part responsible for online content at *Nanfang Zhoumo*, *Nanfang Dushibao* and *Bingdian* have confirmed similar trends.
[114] Interview CJ09.   [115] Interview CJ43.   [116] Interview CJ47.
[117] Malcolm Moore, 'Barack Obama's Exclusive Interview with the Chinese Media', *The Telegraph*, 19 November 2009, available at: http://blogs.telegraph.co.uk/news/mal colmmoore/100017310/barack-obamase-exclusive-interview-with-the-chinese-media/.

a financial crisis in Ordos, Inner Mongolia, following pleas by local officials that the article would compromise social stability.[118] Journalists, however, at times manage to bypass post-publication censorship directly by sharing deleted articles online or indirectly by having their readers repost the articles. Weibo users are also increasingly skilful at photographing and sharing sensitive articles to pre-empt post-publication deletion of online content.

As for other repressive measures, the most frequent one, according to editors, is an official warning (*huangpai jinggao*, 黄牌警告) that criticises media conduct and forces re-examination and self-criticism, while the most damaging coercive measure is that of dismissal and replacement of media personnel. As for the former, media professionals note that they do not perceive individual warnings as threatening, but political risk for news outlets increases if the warnings are to accumulate over time. A following comment by a journalist at *Nanfang Zhoumo* explains a long-term threat of continuous official warnings:

We can easily withstand being criticized by the propaganda authorities and having to pass their examinations. At times we even welcome criticism, as it shows that we achieved a breakthrough in our watchdog reporting. So long as the post-publication measures do not reach the level of personnel dismissal, we usually treat them as a routine activity. Of course, if you receive many official warnings, they can accumulate to the level of disobedience (*bu tinghua zhishu*, 不听话指数). The risk then progressively magnifies. It is like a continuous stress on the earth's crust eventually triggering a large earthquake …[119]

Other than a long-term risk of harsher political repercussions from propaganda authorities, journalists also note the self-censorship effect that these warnings can produce. Since warnings are issued to entire media outlets rather than to individual editors or journalists, they can foster a risk-averse professional environment. As stated by a journalist at *Caijing* magazine, referring to the official warnings, 'they can even change the culture and the value system of the magazine in the long-run'.[120]

The more dangerous measure compromising editorial culture, however, is replacement of editors and party secretaries of media groups and dismissals of media professionals. As already noted earlier in this chapter, personnel control has long constituted an important mechanism of media control,[121] and it has occasionally been used to rein in critical outlets. An important example of this from the late Hu-Wen era is the replacement of the liberal-minded, Yang Xinfeng, by a conservative former

---

[118] Interview CJ51.   [119] Interview CJ55.   [120] Interview CJ52.
[121] Esarey, 'Cornering the Market: State Strategies for Controlling China's Commercial Media'.

deputy minister of Guangdong's propaganda department, Yang Jian, as the party secretary of the Nanfang Daily Media Group, which contains some of China's most outspoken publications.[122] An investigation into the Nanfang Daily Media Group reveals a tightening of the editorial freedom of its critical publications in the aftermath of this appointment, as manifested by the formation of a new internal 'examination office' (*shendu shi*, 深度室) to closely monitor journalists' operations.[123] There are also multiple cases of editors and journalists being dismissed from critical publications on orders from propaganda authorities.[124] While considering dismissal to be one of the most drastic outcomes of their critical articles,[125] most journalists shared that they have not experienced this threat in their careers. When a personnel reshuffling does take place, however, its repercussions can have long-term destabilising effects. *Bingdian*, a critical feature supplement of the *China Youth Daily*, has never fully recovered its critical edge since its temporary shutdown in 2006 and the dismissal of its top editors, according to one of these editors.[126] And the pressures on the Nanfang Media Group have already resulted in some of its editors and journalists quitting. In late 2012, two of the former *Nanfang Zhoumo* journalists interviewed for this book, for instance, have left to start a new magazine, *Yidu*, which would abstain from sharp political criticism.[127] Most recently, a number of *Nanfang*

---

[122] Chen Baocheng, 'Guangdong sheng-wei xuanchuanbu fubuzhang zhuanren nanfang baoye dangwei shuji' ('Vice-Minister of the Guangdong's Department of Propaganda Was Transferred to the Position of the Party Secretary of the Nanfang Press Group'), *Caixin*, 3 May 2012, available at: http://news.sohu.com/20120503/n342262531.shtml.

[123] Hou Fangyu, 'Nanfang Shibian' ('Southern Incident'), *Yangguang Shiwu*, 9 August 2012, available at: www.isunaffairs.com/?p=10133. Interviews with former journalists of these publications as well as media scholars further verified the new political pressures. See also David Bandurski, 'China's Boldest Media: Losing Battle?' *China Media Project*, 14 August 2012, available at: http://cmp.hku.hk/2012/08/14/25926/. Most recently, under Xi, this tightening has become more prominent. See Maria Repnikova and Kecheng Fang, 'Behind the Fall of China's Greatest Newspaper', *Foreign Policy*, 29 January 2015, available at: http://foreignpolicy.com/2015/01/29/southern-weekly-china-media-censorship/.

[124] A prominent example is that of the dismissal of a popular commentator, Chang Ping, available at: www.nybooks.com/blogs/nyrblog/2012/jan/27/is-democracy-chinese-chang-ping-interview/. A number of other examples are noted in the annual Human Rights Watch reports on China.

[125] Detentions and imprisonment present the most coercive measures, but they have not been brought up by media professionals, as they generally shared that losing their job and reputation was something they feared most in their professional lives. In the Xi period detentions have been discussed more frequently, as noted in the concluding chapter.

[126] Interview CJ31. This opinion was also held by media scholars interviewed for this study. The general perception of other journalists was also that of *Bingdian* being more subdued following the editorial reshuffling.

[127] Interviews with two former *Nanfang Zhoumo* journalists (CJ40 and CJ41).

Zhoumo journalists have followed a similar path, and quit either to join new ventures, go to graduate school or start a new career altogether.[128]

As with other restrictions, coercive measures fluctuate depending on the political environment, with warnings and personnel removal being more likely during politically sensitive periods, including the weeks (and sometimes months) prior to major political events, anniversaries and international spectacles, such as the Beijing Olympics of 2008 and the Party Congress sessions, according to the interviewees and the author's observations on the ground. The above-mentioned pressures on *Nanfang Zhoumo*, for instance, started months before the Eighteenth Party Congress. Moreover, there is often, once again, a distinction to be made between the interests of local and central officials. Following the Beijing flooding referred to earlier, Beijing officials temporarily shut down *Jingji Guanchabao* for its article criticising an official cover-up of victim numbers. Central authorities, however, soon ordered the newspaper to reopen, not perceiving the article as a threat and, in fact, seeing the paper's closure as potentially more harmful to the party's image leading up to the Eighteenth Party Congress, according to a well-known media scholar and a former editor at the paper.[129] Also, personnel removal can equally be a result of pressures from local or central officials, according to the interviewees. In comparison to other restrictions, however, post-publication coercion tends to be more deliberate and centralised, leaving less space for journalists to renegotiate their space. Journalists and editors nonetheless try to anticipate these measures by adhering to constructive criticism. Interviewees admit to using official and expert opinions and suggestions in investigative reports in part as a self-protection tactic and in part as a professional objective. The following comment from an editor at *Caijing* magazine explains the importance of objective and constructive reporting to maintain 'space' (*kongjian*, 空间) for publishing sensitive stories:

In comparison to other media, we have maintained continuous relative independence even before the Eighteenth Party Congress. We have been able to cover the big fire in Tianjin and other sensitive topics. But our reporting is very sound (*zhashi*, 扎实); it does not contain insults just for the sake of insulting. This is very common on Weibo. Many Weibo users just throw insults at each other, without providing any specific suggestions. When we provide opinions and suggestions, we do so in an objective manner, including perspectives of scholars and officials. Authorities then might also take our criticisms on board. If you just criticise for the

---

[128] Maria Repnikova and Kecheng Fang, 'Behind the Fall of China's Greatest Newspaper', *The Foreign Policy*, 29 January 2015.
[129] Interviews CSE21; CJ28.

sake of criticising, then of course they will get very angry, and there is a higher risk for getting into trouble.[130]

As with the use of professionalism rhetoric to target local officials, critical journalists distinguish themselves from citizen journalists in their quest for constructive and grounded critique. In a way, media professionals are positioning themselves as watchdogs of online content – a goal that is aligned with the official interest in containing social media activism. Journalists' perception of their role as that of contributing to finding solutions to problems was already discussed in the previous chapter. The encouragement of constructive criticism was also noted in the analysis of the official discourse on the media's supervision role. Moreover, interviews with CPD and GAPP officials highlight the importance of fostering constructive criticism as part of the official media policy. 'We demand the media do more constructive supervision, not simply criticise for the sake of criticising', commented the deputy director of the GAPP in a personal interview.[131] Interviews with crisis management experts further reveal officials' frequent blaming of media for exaggerating crises through their reporting, which emphasises personal and emotional stories at the expense of balanced and constructive analysis.[132] To determine the degree to which critical journalists are actually carrying out constructive criticism, it is necessary to examine their reports, to which we will turn in the following chapters.

Finally, it is worth noting that while direct resistance to personnel reshuffling and coercive measures is rare, there are instances of journalists' organised strikes against them. In 2005, for instance, the staff at *Xinjing Bao* went on strike after their editor's removal following publication of a sensitive corruption case.[133] And in January 2013, *Nanfang Zhoumo* journalists publicly spoke out against local censor, Tuo Zhen, which triggered a protest in support of the journalists' cause.[134] Although this case is most immediately linked to pre-publication censorship of the New Year editorial, it reflects an enduring frustration of journalists with continuous coercion and personnel reshuffling. Here again, the internet has played a role in galvanising the movement. Namely, a number of celebrity microbloggers spoke up for *Southern Weekly* through their Weibo posts. 'One word of truth outweighs the whole world', wrote an

---

[130] Interview CJ25.   [131] Interview COF08.   [132] Interview CSE15.

[133] Chris Gill, 'Beijing Paper's Staff Strike after Editor's Removal', *The Guardian*, 30 December 2005, available at: www.theguardian.com/media/2005/dec/31/pressand publishing.china.

[134] Maria Repnikova, 'China's Journalists are No Revolutionaries', *The Wall Street Journal*, 15 January 2013, available at: http://online.wsj.com/article/S B10001424127887324235104578244203546122918.html.

actress Yao Chen, one of the most popular celebrities on Weibo, quoting the Russian dissident, Solzhenitsyn.[135] Citizens who came out to protest in Guangzhou have also organised and spread information through social media, thereby empowering and activating journalists' resistance from the bottom up. At the same time, while Western media has laid much hope on this anti-censorship movement as the seed for a larger wave of resistance,[136] this effort still resembled improvisation within the boundaries of the permissible. Namely, *Southern Weekly* journalists have appealed to central authorities, have abstained from resisting the censorship system at large and have disassociated from citizen activists in their negotiations with local propaganda authorities.[137] On the whole, even the most daring form of resistance still takes place under the shadow of the party.

Conclusion

This chapter examined the limitations on critical reporting through the perspectives of critical journalists. While some subjects are outlawed, when it comes to topics that are sensitive but not strictly off limits, interviews with journalists illuminate the adaptive, decentralised and negotiable forms of political restrictions that apply to the media's supervision role. Officials and journalists, therefore, are capable of managing the limitations on their cooperation by engaging in improvisation within the domains set out by the party-state.

The authorities adapt their restrictions according to their perceptions of the changing political environment, and especially of public opinion on sensitive issues. Restrictions can also reflect the adjustments to pressures from local officials and other actors at risk from media investigations. Other than lobbying higher officials to issue media bans, local officials engage in other forms of improvisation with media restrictions, including posing direct threats to journalists, restricting their information access and deleting published reports. The fact that pre-publication censorship, which is characterised by the highest degree of improvisation, is the most intrusive restriction for journalists, suggests that this fluid approach to containing watchdog journalism is working.

---

[135] Eric Harwit, 'The Rise and Influence of *Weibo* (Microblogs) in China', *Asian Survey* 54 (6) (2015): 1072.

[136] Western coverage of this incident has referred to it as 'a press renaissance' (see Jason Lee, 'A Press Renaissance? The Legacy of China's "Southern Weekend" ', *The Atlantic*, 11 January2013); and have generally referred to it as 'censorship protest' (see: 'Censorship Protest Gains Support in China', *The Wall Street Journal*, 8 January 2013).

[137] Ibid.

The very inconsistencies in implementation of political restrictions, however, leave space for journalists to creatively renegotiate the boundaries. Like officials, they are attentive to public opinion and central-local divisions. When bypassing pre-publication censorship, they closely monitor public opinion through social media, collaborate across media outlets, especially cross-regionally, and wait out censorship until what they wish to report would no longer be perceived as sensitive or threatening by central authorities. In negotiating information access with local officials, journalists try to play into officials' strategic interests vis-à-vis the centre. In resisting post-publication censorship, which is typically conducted by local authorities, journalists or their readers can share banned reports online. And, finally, journalists try to avert repressive post-publication measures by framing their criticism in constructive terms, and thereby aligning themselves with the central state.

While the interactions between officials attempting to contain watchdog reporting and the outspoken journalists can be characterised as a cat and mouse game, it is important to stress that the very contestation journalists are engaged in takes place within the political boundaries dictated by the centre. Journalists do not attempt to publicly breach the taboo subjects or confront the central state, but rather engage in bargaining for more space to undertake the supervision role in accordance with the official interpretation of media oversight. As such, their ways of adjusting to media restrictions do not appear to threaten the party's legitimacy, which underscores the guarded nature of these improvised practices.

Part III

Crisis Events

5 Critical Journalists, the Party-state and the Wenchuan Earthquake

The two preceding chapters illustrated the shared agenda between critical journalists and the party-state when it comes to the conception of media oversight, as well as the routine pressures on their relationship, as experienced by practising journalists. This chapter demonstrates how these dynamics play out in the aftermath of a major national crisis: the Wenchuan earthquake of 2008, the deadliest natural disaster of the Hu-Wen era and one of the worst calamities in recent Chinese history. It begins by examining the state's management of the media after the earthquake, followed by analysis of critical reports and the policy response to media investigations. The chapter draws on in-depth interviews with critical journalists and editors involved in the Wenchuan coverage, crisis management experts and media regulating officials, as well as a textual analysis of critical reporting on sensitive governance issues that emerged from the crisis.

The following discussion demonstrates how the journalists and the party-state cautiously and creatively uphold their cooperative arrangement when they are both faced with significant and unexpected pressure. In the immediate aftermath of the disaster, after an initial reluctance to publicise the event, the party-state opened up some space for media supervision by engaging it in a furious campaign of crisis management. Critical journalists, in turn, carefully positioned themselves as supervision agents of the central state, and reported on deep-seated governance failures exposed by the earthquake. The official reaction to media supervision was that of a creative compromise: on the one hand, the central authorities acknowledged the reports by enacting immediate policy measures, while, on the other, they outlawed further investigation by the media and strayed from addressing accountability failures at the heart of the crisis. The case of the Sichuan earthquake, therefore, shows that a fluid and unequal collaboration between journalists and officials can also result in superficial improvements in governance, as authorities straddle the treacherous line of showcasing responsiveness to public concerns while keeping political instability at bay.

Let the Media Help: From Evasion to Partnership

On 12 May 2008, a 7.9-magnitude quake hit China's Sichuan province, with shocks reverberating as far away as Beijing.[1] 'I ran out onto the street. Then I heard the earth was roaring, and the roads under my feet were waving like a sea', recalls one of the survivors.[2] The deadliest earthquake since the 1976 Tangshan calamity, it left nearly 70,000 dead and thousands more missing,[3] destroyed major infrastructure, including hospitals, schools and water systems, and wiped out villages, townships and even entire counties, like Beichuan.

Effective handling of the crisis was critical to the party-state's domestic and international legitimacy. Domestically, the leadership faced the largest disaster in decades at a time of a growing social unrest and increasing public pressures on official performance.[4] The pressure was especially acute in light of recent crises. In March 2008, the Chinese party-state faced violent unrest in Tibet,[5] and just months prior, China was paralysed by a snowstorm that crippled the transport system, affecting nearly sixty-seven million people.[6] Internationally, the earthquake also struck at a politically sensitive time, with the party-state finalising its preparations for the opening of the Beijing Olympics, scheduled to take place three months later. With global attention already directed at China following the violent Tibet riots, even a slight mishandling of the post-earthquake management could overshadow the sustained Olympic effort and strain China's unfolding soft-power campaign, carefully constructed over the years.[7]

---

[1] James Daniell, 'Sichuan 2008: A Disaster on an Immense Scale', *BBC News*, 9 May 2013, available at: www.bbc.co.uk/news/science-environment-22398684.

[2] Bin Xu, 'Durkheim in Sichuan: The Earthquake, National Solidarity, and the Politics of Small Things', *Social Psychology Quarterly* 72(1) (2009): 5.

[3] The account of numbers still varies. Chinese official media reports, including Xinhua News, noted in July after the quake that the number of dead was about 69,196. See: Zhu Liyi and Tan Hao, 'Wenchuan dizhen yijing zaocheng 69196ren yunan 18379 ren shizong' (Wenchuan Earthquake Already Incurred 69196 Deaths and 18379 Missing), *Xinwen Zhongxin* (Sina Web), 6 July 2008, available at: http://news.sina.com.cn/c/2008-07-06/162615881691.shtml. BBC News anniversary report on the quake notes 87,150 number of deaths. See: James Daniell, 'Sichuan 2008: A Disaster on an Immense Scale'.

[4] According to a report produced by the Chinese Academy of Governance, the number of protests in China doubled between 2006 and 2010. See Alan Taylor, 'Rising Protests in China', *The Atlantic*, 12 February 2012, available at: www.theatlantic.com/infocus/2012/02/rising-protests-in-china/100247.

[5] Jim Yardley, 'Violence in Tibet as Monks Clash with the Police', *The New York Times*, 15 March 2008.

[6] Tania Branigan, 'Snowstorms Cause Havoc in China', *The Guardian*, 28 January 2008.

[7] Anne-Marie Brady, 'The Beijing Olympics as a Campaign of Mass Distraction', *The China Quarterly* 197 (2009): 1–24. Domestic and international legitimacy is also interlinked, as eloquently explained by Sorace in his analysis of the party's management of the earthquake. See Christian Sorace, 'The Communist Party Miracle? The Alchemy of Turning

The media presented a critical instrument for, but also a potential threat to the state's capacity to rally public support and uphold legitimacy. The initial tension in the official approach to the media was apparent at the very outbreak of the crisis. Breaking the usual procedure of having to wait for official instructions before embarking on crisis coverage, journalists, including those at official news outlets like China Central Television (CCTV), reacted immediately and began reporting without state approval, in what was described by some scholars as a media-led 'breakthrough' in disaster coverage.[8] While critical journalists, as discussed in Chapter 4, regularly strive to 'outrun' censorship bans, those working for official media usually tend to adopt a more conservative stance towards negotiating political pressures, and wait for directives in times of crises. The decision of CCTV and other state media journalists to abide by professional and market logic at the risk of official criticism, therefore, was a daring, improvised move that caught propaganda authorities off guard.

The immediate reaction of party officials was a conservative one. Specifically, the authorities banned most reporting on the scene, requiring journalists to channel only the official, CCTV or the *Xinhua News Agency*, version of events.[9] This meant that these news agencies were made gatekeepers of information that went out to the public, and disaster coverage was to be heavily and narrowly managed by propaganda authorities. Many journalists, however, were already en route to the disaster zone, some receiving restrictive orders only upon arrival.[10] About fifty minutes after the earthquake, the CCTV stopped its normal programming, and started a live broadcast of 'Focusing on the Wenchuan Earthquake' (关注汶川地震), a programme dedicated to the disaster.[11] Moreover, as with many breaking events in late 2000s, citizen journalists outpaced traditional media in relaying first news about the earthquake.

Post-Disaster Reconstruction into Great Leap Development', *Comparative Politics* 208 (2014): 404–427.

[8] Pi Chuanrong, 'Wenchuan dizhen meiti baodao zhi fansi' ('Reflections on the Media Reporting of the Wenchuan Earthquake'), *Xinan Mingzu Daxue Xuebao* 8 (2008): 149–204; Xiaoling Zhang, 'From Totalitarianism to Hegemony: The Reconfiguration of the Party-State and the Transformation of Chinese Communication', *Journal of Contemporary China* 20 (2011): 103–115; Junfei Du, 'The Road to Openness: the Communication Legacy of the Wenchuan Earthquake', in Xiaotao Liang (ed.) *Convulsion: Media Reflections* (Beijing: China Democracy and Legal System Publishing House, 2008): 116–125. Some even argue that it was a turning point for media freedom: Li Zixin, *Zainan ruhe baodao* (*How Disasters are Reported*) (Guangzhou Nanfang Ribao Chubanshe, 2009).

[9] Xiaoling Zhang, 'From Totalitarianism to Hegemony'.

[10] Ibid. This was also confirmed in my interviews.

[11] Jian Xu, *Media Events in Web 2.0 China: Interventions of Online Activism* (Eastbourne: Sussex Academic Press, 2016).

Youku[12] video of the quake, for instance, appeared online sixteen minutes prior to the official announcement by Xinhua, and blog posts documenting the first signs of disaster preceded all official broadcasts.[13] With the presence of 253 million netizens by 2008,[14] the posts and videos spread quickly across the nation escalating pressure on the media and officials. Propaganda authorities thereby faced a risk of being accused of a disaster cover-up on the one hand, and harmful media and online coverage on the other. In this tense situation they decided to act in an opportunistic manner, overturning their initially conservative stance towards the media and fiercely engaging it in a shared battle of crisis management.[15] Specifically, propaganda officials facilitated media presence in the earthquake zone and encouraged positive publicity of the official response. This was manifested in the relatively mild restrictions sent down to news outlets in the immediate aftermath of the disaster. The authorities issued a general directive of positive coverage and assisted journalists in their reporting, while engaging in selective and covert guidance of some news outlets.

In the first two weeks there were no censorship bans, only directives promoting positive reporting (*zhengmian baodao*, 正面报道), according to the interviewees. As explained in Chapter 4, this type of directive is the most lenient one, as it constitutes neither a ban nor an enforcement of a strictly official, *Xinhua News* version of events. The official interviewees, including those from the General Administration for Press and Publication (GAPP) and the Central Propaganda Department (CPD), stressed that guiding public opinion was the key role assigned to the media in the aftermath of the earthquake, as authorities wanted to project unity and confidence in the party's rescue initiatives.[16] Journalists from critical news outlets and official outlets alike shared that in the first phase of the disaster they faced minimal political restrictions and even received assistance in conducting their reporting.[17] Interviewing officials and accessing official information was manageable for journalists, in part due to the chaotic nature of the event, bringing government representatives and journalists together in a shared struggle against the disaster. 'In the beginning everyone was present at the scene,

---

[12] Youku is one of China's largest video sites.
[13] Jian Xu, *Media Events in Web 2.0 China: Interventions of Online Activism.*   [14] Ibid.
[15] Pierre F. Landry and Daniela Stockmann, 'Crisis Management in an Authoritarian Regime: Media Effects during the Sichuan Earthquake', paper delivered at the American Political Science Association annual meeting, September, 2009, available at: http://papers.ssrn.com/sol3/papers.cfm?abstract_id=1463796.
[16] Interview COF09.
[17] Chuanrong, 'Wenchuan dizhen meiti baodao zhi fansi' ('Reflections on the Media Reporting of the Wenchuan Earthquake').

coping with the crisis. The officials' cautiousness about journalists was somewhat reduced, and cooperation was more feasible', commented a reporter involved in the coverage.[18] Even local propaganda representatives were cooperative, providing travel permits, interview arrangements and official data about the impact of the earthquake.[19] This collaborative attitude extended beyond traditional media, to civil society. As Shieh and Deng write in their analysis of the relationship between non-governmental organisations (NGOs) and the state in the aftermath of the disaster, 'the earthquake forced local authorities to work with NGOs often for the first time'.[20] They further note that while the official attitude was not uniform, many were willing to enable NGO participation, especially during the first week, when the state needed all possible resources to cope with the crisis. Other scholars categorise the earthquake as a case of a 'consensus crisis', which brought a 'situational opening' for civil associations to partake in crisis response.[21] On the national level, unity and solidarity across all layers of society, media and the state, was further reinforced through the staging of a major national spectacle or a media event in the form of an unprecedented nationwide public mourning for disaster victims, held one week after the earthquake. For the first time, the Chinese state sanctioned a public mourning for ordinary citizens rather than for high-level officials and soldiers. 'Construction workers, shopkeepers and bureaucrats across the bustling nation of 1.3 billion people paused for three minutes at 2:28pm', reported foreign journalists.[22] The phrase 'unprecedented solidarity' (*kongqian tuanjie*) marked public expression of their feelings about the event, widely televised and reported by the Chinese media.[23]

Amidst the spirit of unity and cooperation permeating state-media relations, and state-society interactions at large, however, the authorities still selectively applied more extensive oversight over some news outlets. While commercial print outlets like *Nanfang Zhoumo* received few initial instructions beyond that of positive coverage, the producers and

[18] Interview CJ30.

[19] This was further confirmed in other works on journalists' reporting of the earthquake. See, for instance, Zixin, *Zainan ruhe baodao* (*How are Disasters Reported*).

[20] Shawn Shieh and Guosheng Deng, 'An Emerging Civil Society: The Impact of the 2008 Sichuan Earthquake on Grass-Roots Associations in China', *The China Journal* 65 (2011): 192.

[21] Bin Xu, 'Consensus Crisis and Civil Society: The Sichuan Earthquake Response and State-Society Relations', *The China Journal* 71 (2014): 91–108.

[22] 'China Mourns as Quake Claims More Victims', *CBSNews*, 19 May 2008.

[23] Bin Xu, 'For Whom the Bell Tolls: State-Society Relations and the Sichuan Earthquake Mourning in China', *Theory &Society* 42 (2013): 509–542.

journalists at CCTV's investigative *Xinwen Diaocha* programme were advised in detail about specific features to emphasise and to understate in their coverage.[24] Exercising a close watch over official news outlets, of course, is a common feature of the Chinese control apparatus, and is therefore not surprising to be found following a large crisis event. Critical outlets, however, were not immune to implicit oversight. Some interviewees report that their writings were monitored by state-sponsored online commentators, otherwise known as 'the 50-cent army' (*wu mao dang*, 五毛党) in the aftermath of the earthquake.[25] These commentators are hired by the party to spread official views and to battle online critical discourse. While not carrying the enforcement capacity of the official directives, online commentators tried to discipline journalists by reminding them of their role as voices of the party. 'Once we reported on challenges concerning rescue operations, including coordination issues across different agencies, we encountered pressures from official online commentators, rather than directly from propaganda authorities . . . They scolded us for writing critical reports at a time when people are still struggling with basic survival', revealed a journalist at *Nanfang Zhoumo*.[26] Online commentators, therefore, complemented the party's efforts by actively drawing the line between coverage that was acceptable and that which hurt the official and public interests. Journalists, however, pushed back against these pressures, in part through the use of social media, as it provided a plethora of useful information for their reporting and inspired them to expand their coverage. As already noted earlier, citizen journalists 'broke' the crisis, and online reports have been subsequently incorporated into traditional media, in the first powerful manifestation of convergence between new and traditional media in China.[27] CCTV News, for instance, used snapshots from QQ chat groups and video clips recorded by local residents in Sichuan.[28] Studies of the popular online forum, Tianya, have further uncovered that the key function

---

[24] Interview CJ33.

[25] For a detailed discussion of China's '50-cent army', see Rongbin Han, 'Manufacturing Consent in Cyberspace: China's "Fifty-Cent Army" ', *Journal of Current Chinese Affairs* 44 (2)(2015).

[26] Interview CJ40. Though some of these commentators were likely directly hired by the propaganda department, others may have commented voluntarily. According to a recent study by Rongbin Han, there is a growing movement of 'voluntary 50-centers' who form online communities and attack critical journalists and thinkers for being unpatriotic. See Rongbin Han, 'Defending Authoritarian Regime Online: China's "Voluntary Fifty-cent Army" ', *The China Quarterly* 224 (2015): 1006–1025.

[27] Jian Xu, *Media Events in Web 2.0 China*.

[28] J. Nip, 'Citizen Journalism in China's Wenchuan Earthquake', in S. Allan and E. Thorsen (eds.), *Citizen Journalism: Global Perspectives* (New York: Peter Lang, 2009): 95–106.

of this chat platform following the earthquake was information sharing and validation, which undoubtedly has also aided journalists' reporting of the crisis.[29]

On the whole, the Wenchuan earthquake played an important role in further transforming the official approach to crisis communication in the direction of managed transparency and public relations – a process that started after the 2003 SARS (severe acute respiratory syndrome) epidemic.[30] Interviews with crisis management experts suggest that the earthquake marked another milestone in official transparency. 'I think after the SARS incident, the approach of the Chinese government towards crisis management has gradually resembled that of the West. Although information management in the aftermath of the earthquake was not perfect, it was another significant improvement from previous crises', commented a crisis management expert involved in training Chinese officials in effective communication.[31] Some scholars go so far as to argue that the earthquake marked the institutionalisation of public relations as an official approach to crisis communication.[32] 'The Wenchuan earthquake demonstrated the efficiency of the government's spokesmen system. Whatever information authorities had concerning the disaster, they quickly transmitted it to the public', remarked a senior crisis expert at the Chinese Academy of Social Sciences.[33] Some argue that the upcoming Beijing Olympics served as a key catalyst for the party-state's proactive engagement with the media and the public. 'If the government could not handle Sichuan earthquake well, China's international image would be damaged', argued a TV journalist, cited in one of the studies.[34] The Sichuan disaster further facilitated more transparency

---

[29] Yan Qu, Philip Fei Wu, and Xiaoqing Wang, 'Online Community Response to Major Disaster: A Study of Tianya Forum in the 2008 Sichuan Earthquake', *System Sciences* (2009): 1–11.

[30] On how audience members contested state's restricted information flows and pushed for more openness, see: Zixue Tai and Tao Sun, 'Media Dependencies in a Changing Media Environment: The Case of the 2003 SARS Epidemic in China', *New Media & Society* 9 (6) (2007):987–1009.

[31] Interview CSE18.

[32] Ni Chen, 'Institutionalizing Public Relations: A Case Study of Chinese Government Crisis Communication on the 2008 Sichuan Earthquake', *Public Relations Review* 35 (2009): 187–198. For a detailed discussion on the state's transparency following the earthquake, see also Dennis Lai and Hang Hui, 'Politics of Sichuan Earthquake, 2008', *Journal of Contingencies and Crisis Management* 17(2) (2009): 137–140.

[33] Interview CSE19. See also Wang Fengxiang, 'Dizhen zaihai de weiji baodao – yi 2008 nian sichuan wenchuan dizhen, 2010 nian qinghai baoshu dizhen de weiji baodao weilie' ('Reporting of Earthquake Disasters – Case Studies of 2008 Sichuan Wenchuan Earthquake and the 2010 Qinghai Baoshu Earthquake'), in *Zhongguo weiji guanli baogao* (*Blue Book on Crisis Management*) (Beijing: Social Sciences Academic Press, 2011): 130–149.

[34] Jian Xu, *Media Events in Web 2.0 China*: 61.

at the local level, as officials were eager to demonstrate their compliance with recently passed transparency legislation,[35] as well as to attract attention and resources from central authorities.[36] The Regulation of the People's Republic of China on the Disclosure of Government Information, passed on 1 May 2008, had two articles dedicated specifically to disaster situations (Articles 4 and 10), obliging authorities to release information about the 'nature' and the 'threat' of the crisis.[37] At the same time, as the above analysis demonstrates, the transparency efforts were aimed strategically at boosting the party's image, and the authorities actively worked with media outlets in ensuring that they contributed to this objective.

The party-state's partnership with the media in managing the crisis had initially paid off, as most coverage concerning crisis management positively portrayed the state's rescue efforts, only pointing to weaknesses indirectly. The analysis of official media coverage found the emphasis on the party-state as a 'competent leader',[38] guided by the primary objective of serving the people.[39] Official news outlets channelled the message of effective 'people-centered' relief efforts, whereby people's lives stood above all else in the official agenda.[40] ' ... Life, either an individual life or the life of every Chinese citizen, is elevated to a place of paramount importance. It is essential to show the respect and solicitude for and the understanding of people, to protect them and be at their service, and to explain the connotation of the concept of "putting people first"', read a segment from *Renmin Ribao*, cited in scholarly analysis of official disaster discourse.[41] Textual representation was complemented by compelling videos of tearful Premier Wen at the scene of the disaster, symbolising the leadership's unwavering commitment to the people.[42]

Critical outlets also struck a favourable tone in their coverage of the state's response. The analysis of reports in *Nanfang Zhoumo* and *Caijing* found that some mildly critical or reflective content was published concerning China's Red Cross,[43] insufficient coordination in rescue

[35] Ibid.   [36] Ibid.
[37] Dennis Lai and Hang Hui, 'Research Note: Politics of Sichuan Earthquake', *Journal of Contingencies and Crisis Management* 17(2) (2009): 138.
[38] Xiaoling Zhang, 'From Totalitarianism to Hegemony'.
[39] Liangen Yin and Haiyan Wang, 'People-Centred Myth: Representation of the Wenchuan Earthquake in *China Daily*', *Discourse & Communication* 4 (2010): 383–398.
[40] Florian Schneider and Yin-Jye Hwang, 'The Sichuan Earthquake and the Heavenly Mandate: Legitimizing Chinese Rule through Disaster Discourse', *Journal of Contemporary China* 23(88) (2014): 636–656.
[41] Ibid.: 645.
[42] Charlene Makley, 'Spectacular Compassion', *Critical Asian Studies* 46(3) (2014): 371–404.
[43] Shen Liang and Yang Ruichun, 'Zhongguo hongshizihui zhi mian xinren fengbo' (China's Red Cross Faces Crisis of Public Confidence'), *Nanfang Zhoumo*, 6 June 2008.

operations,[44] inadequacy of some financial mechanisms[45] and weak preventative measures.[46] The criticisms, however, were generally expressed indirectly, buried in hopeful feature stories and editorials, merged with suggestions and presented as lessons and warnings rather than as negative judgements. A *Nanfang Zhoumo* editorial titled 'How to Rejuvenate a Country from Many Disasters', for instance, argued that it was critical to take lessons from Wenchuan as the country moved forward and faced new crises.[47] When touching on weaknesses in disaster response, the articles also tended to obfuscate agency in favour of describing processes. While explaining certain failures in the crisis response, they did not refer to officials or even official bureaus to be held responsible for the implied misconduct. In a few instances, when specific actors were blamed, as in the case of the telecommunication companies and the Red Cross, the journalists drew a clear distinction between these actors and the central state, attributing responsibility to the former. For instance, in discussing the telecommunication companies, the journalist overlooked the fact that they were state owned, praising the central authorities for having taken the appropriate measures to reorganise the industry.[48] In examining the state's disaster response, therefore, critical journalists encouraged some future rethinking of certain areas, while carefully distancing specific problems away from the political system, or even from local authorities.

[44] For more details on weak coordination between non-governmental organisations (NGOs) and state agencies, see Cao Haili, Chang Hongxiao, Wu Yan, and Li Jing, 'Zhenhan Zhongguo: jiuyuan pian: juguo jiuzai' ('China Shocked: The Rescue Edition: The Whole Nation Provides Disaster Relief'), *Caijing*, 26 May 2008; On weak coordination between different rescue units, see Xia Yu, 'Jiuyuan de liliang bu zai renshu, zai zhuanye nengli' ('The Strength of Rescue Operations Is Not in Numbers, But in Professionalism'), *Nanfang Zhoumo*, 29 May 2008; On financial coordination, see Cao Haili, Chang Hongxiao, Wu Yan, and Li Jing, 'Zhenhan Zhongguo: jiuyuan pian: juguo jiuzai' ('China Shocked: The Rescue Edition: The Whole Nation Provides Disaster Relief'); On coordination between telecommunication companies, see Ming Shuliang, 'Dianxin: cuiruo de yinji tongxin' ('Telecommunications: Weak Disaster Response'), *Caijing*, 26 May 2008.

[45] The reports note the weaknesses of loan-granting and insurance schemes, as well as the inadequate bankruptcy legislation: Wen Xiu, Zhang Yuzhe, and Li Zhigang, 'Yinhang: duochong fengxian' (Banks: Multiple Risks'), *Caijing*, 26 May 2008; Chen Huiying, 'Baoxian: buneng chengshou zhi qing' (Insurance: Cannot Bear It'), *Caijing*, 26 May 2008; Shu Mei, 'Zaihou jinrong: xuqiu bi congqian geng poqie' (Post-Disaster Finance: The Demand is More Pressing Than Before'), *Nanfang Zhoumo*, 5 June 2008;'Duonan heyi xingbang' ('How to Rejuvenate a Country from Many Disasters'), *Nanfang Zhoumo*, 5 June 2008.

[46] Wang Yichao, Wang Heyan, and Li Hujun, 'Zhenhan zhongguo: keji pian: kan bu jian de zhan xian' ('China Shocked: The Science Section: The Invisible Battle Front'), *Caijing*, 26 May 2008.

[47] 'Duonan heyi xingbang'.

[48] Shuliang, 'Dianxin: cuiruo de yinji tongxin' ('Telecommunications: Weak Disaster Response').

On the whole, when it came to assessing the initial disaster management, both official and mainstream media as well as critical outlets largely played the role of directing public opinion by channelling and affirming the message of state capacity, as instructed by propaganda authorities. The media were also in unison in their emotional projection of national unity in solidarity for earthquake victims. As argued in Lan Yuxun's comprehensive analysis of post-earthquake media coverage, an overwhelming proportion of writing was emotional, with phrases such as 'We are all Wenchuan people' or 'China hold on!' featured in the reports.[49] This patriotic discourse was also adopted and reinvented by social media users. One of the striking manifestations of this creative online solidarity is the publication of 'Quake Poetry' – poems produced by netizens and disseminated and readapted by other media platforms.[50] Many of the popular 'Quake Poems' featured a stark nationalistic spark, as evident in the following excerpt from a poem dedicated to earthquake solidarity: 'China! Don't Cry! Chinese People! Don't Cry! When the Olympic Torch met with humiliation we pursued justice with no turning back! When wind and snow cut off the roads we protected each other! .... China! Don't Cry!'[51] Many of these poems, not surprisingly, were appropriated by the media and the government, as they fuelled the overarching imagery of national resilience. The largely positive and emotional discourse in traditional and social media appears to have been effective in shaping public perceptions in favour of the state's response. Landry and Stockmann's analysis of public opinion surveys following the earthquake, for instance, demonstrates the initially high public trust in the party-state and satisfaction with official rescue operations.[52] Alongside the positive reporting on the state's response, however, some sensitive content began to emerge in the media concerning the underlying governance failures that amplified the effects of the earthquake, as explained below.

Pushing the Boundaries: *Yulun Jiandu* in the Wenchuan Earthquake

Amid the stories of successful official response, the heart of the Wenchuan tragedy began to crystallise in the media coverage: the collapse

---

[49] Yuxin Lan, 'Coverage of the Wenchuan Earthquake: An Overview', *The China Nonprofit Review* 1(2) (2009): 221–245. Initially found in Schneider and Hwang (2014).

[50] Heather Inwood, 'Multimedia Quake Poetry: Convergence Culture after the Sichuan Earthquake', *The China Quarterly* 208 (2011): 932–950.

[51] Ibid.: 936.

[52] Landry and Stockmann, 'Crisis Management in an Authoritarian Regime'.

of school buildings in the disaster zone, killing over 5,000 students,[53] emerged as the most tragic story of the earthquake. According to media observers and insiders, once the first reports came out drawing attention to the high number of student deaths, the authorities attempted to downplay the story by asking journalists to avoid the coverage of rescue efforts at the schools as part of the wider 'positive reporting' directive introduced earlier.[54] Since this instruction did not completely ban media reporting of the schools but restrained coverage of rescue efforts, it ended up only encouraging the media, including official outlets, to continue digging into the startling images of school buildings turned into rubble.

The official media mainly portrayed the school tragedy as an unfortunate outcome of the natural disaster, abstaining from serious investigations and stopping its coverage about a week after the earthquake struck.[55] The most hard-hitting, in-depth and investigative reports came out later (21 and 25 May and 9 June) and were published by commercial critical outlets, including *Nanfang Dushibao*, *Nanfang Zhoumo* and *Caijing* (see Table 5.1).[56] The series of reports by *Nanfang Dushibao*, titled 'Premature Deaths of Students', sparked a wave of intensive coverage, documenting in vivid and emotional detail the deaths of students, as well as parents' and officials' reactions to the tragedy. 'The most fragile lives are those of children ... the collapse of hundreds of schools and the resulting deaths of thousands of students present the most violent act of the disaster, the deepest-rooted pain of the entire nation', read the opening sentence of the first part of the series.[57] The supervision role of the media, with more emphasis on official accountability, was manifested in later reports by *Nanfang Zhoumo* and *Caijing*. To demonstrate the scope of media oversight, the following analysis draws on reporting by these two news outlets.

The key themes of investigative and in-depth articles are the proximate and long-standing factors behind the school tragedy. As for the former, the reports allege that, beyond the natural forces of the earthquake, it was

---

[53] This is the official statistic, but some sources argue that it could be as high as 10,000. See Andrew Jacobs and Edward Wong, 'China Reports Student Toll for Quake', *The New York Times*, 7 May 2009, available at: www.nytimes.com/2009/05/08/world/asia/08china.html.

[54] Qian Gang, 'Looking Back on Chinese Media Reporting of School Collapses', *China Media Project*, 7 May 2009 available at: http://cmp.hku.hk/2009/05/07/1599/ (accessed 2 August 2013). Interviews with editors and journalists involved in the coverage confirmed the analysis in this report.

[55] Ibid.

[56] Ibid. The author also conducted additional searches for investigative reports on the schools' collapse via Baidu and China National Knowledge Infrastructure (CNKI).

[57] 'Xue shang (shang) yongyuan xiaoshi de banji' ('The Premature Death of Our Students: Forever Disappeared Classes'), *Nanfang Dushibao*, 19 May 2008.

Table 5.1 *Investigative coverage of the schools scandal*

Date	Media outlet	Article title
19 May	*Nanfang Dushibao*	'Xue shang (shang) yongyuan xiaoshi de banji' ('The Premature Death of Our Students: Forever Disappeared Classes')
20 May		'Xue shang (zhong) zou de qi cheng shi haizi' ('The Premature Death of Our Students: Those Who Left Qicheng are Children')
22 May		'Xueshang (xia) xiang women zemme xinyun de hen shao=' ('The Premature Death of Our Students: Very Few Turned Out As Lucky As Us')
29 May	*Nanfang Zhoumo*	'Mianzhu fuxin er xiao: daota jiaoshe she zenmeyang jiancheng de?' ('Mianzhu Fuxin Number 2 School: How was the Collapsed School Building Constructed?')
		'Duo ming de shi jianzhuwu er bu shi dizhen bei hushi de kanzheng shifang wenti' ('The Loss of Life is from the Constructions Not from the Earthquake – The Ignored Question of Quake-Proof Fortifications')
		'Jianshe bu zhuanjia rending ju yuan zhongxueshi wenti jianzhu – ju yuan zhongxue daota beiju diaocha' ('The Experts from the Construction Department Firmly Believe that the Construction of the Ju Yuan Middle School has a Problem – The Investigation into the Ju Yuan Middle School Tragic Collapse')
		'Dongqi zhongxue: canju huoke bimian' ('Dongqi Middle School: Could Tragedy Have Been Averted?')
		'Kangzhen shefang biaozhun xu chongxin zhiding-zhuanjia pingjie wenchuan dizhen daliang fangwu daota yanjiu' ('Standards for Quake-Proof Protection Need to be Redrafted – Experts Criticise the Reasons behind the Large Number of Buildings' Collapse during the Wenchuan Earthquake')
6 June	*Xinwen Guanchabao*	(An Investigation into Schools' Collapse in the Quake Zone: Why Did Old Residential Structures Survive?')
9 June	*Caijing*	'Jiaoshe yousi lu' ('The Worrisome Record of School Buildings')
		'Gongjian jianzhu hechu bu lao' ('How to Make Public Constructions Sturdy')

the low-quality materials used as well as the faulty designs of the buildings that led to their dramatic collapse. A *Nanfang Zhoumo* report points to the problematic use of prefabricated boards (as opposed to safer but more costly steel boards) in school construction, calling them 'coffin boards' and arguing that their danger had been known since the Tangshan earthquake.[58] Other articles further uncovered the low or non-existent quake-proof protection present in the initial designs of school buildings. '"A birth defect" is not an excuse', stressed one article, disclaiming some official allegations that school buildings are inherently more vulnerable during earthquakes.[59] By presenting these proximate factors, the reporters already challenged the explanations offered by authorities.

Some reports went so far as to accuse specific officials for their failure to oversee school safety. The articles argued that local education officials in charge of monitoring and supervising the quality of school buildings were aware of the problem but avoided addressing it. The reports revealed persisting bottom-up pressures on local education authorities to deal with poorly built schools, which were not taken on board by officials. For instance, according to a *Nanfang Zhoumo* report, in 1998, in response to concerns about school infrastructure, the principal of one of the schools that collapsed in the earthquake was instructed by education officials to add extra support to the building but to leave the existing core infrastructure in place.[60] Other articles also highlighted top-down pressures on local authorities to address the problem years before the earthquake struck.[61] Journalists further unravelled the reasons for local officials' neglect, arguing that their dual role of supervising and financing school construction disincentivised them from addressing the issue. Without making explicit claims about corruption, journalists alluded to the collusion of interests of local education bureaus and construction companies. According to interviewees involved in construction projects, cited in the articles, education authorities hired companies they had connections with without carefully checking their qualifications.[62] To summarise, while local officials and state media mostly presented the schools tragedy as an unfortunate yet inevitable outcome of the magnitude of the earthquake, in-depth and investigative articles engaged with contentious man-made

---

[58] Yuan Wan, 'Duo ming de shi jianzhuwu er bu shi dizhen – bei hushi de kanzheng shifang wenti' ('The Loss of Life is from the Constructions Not from the Earthquake – The Ignored Question of Quake-Proof Fortifications'), *Nanfang Zhoumo*, 29 May 2008.

[59] Ibid.

[60] Fu Jianfeng and Yao Yijiang, 'Jianshe bu zhuanjia rending ju yuan zhongxue shi wenti jianzhu – ju yuan zhongxue daota beiju diaocha' ('The Experts from the Construction Department Firmly Believe That the Construction of the Ju Yuan Middle School Has a Problem – The Investigation into the Ju Yuan Middle School's Tragic Collapse'), *Nanfang Zhoumo*, 29 May 2008.

[61] Yang Binbin, Zhao Hejuan, Li Zhigang, Chang Hongxiao, Zhang Yingguang, and Chenzhong Xiaolu, 'Jiaoshe yousi lu' ('The Worrisome Record about the School Buildings'), *Caijing*, 9 June 2012.

[62] Fu Jianfeng and Yao Yijiang, 'Jianshe bu zhuanjia rending ju yuan zhongxue shi wenti jianzhu – ju yuan zhongxue daota beiju diaocha' ('The Experts from the Construction Department Firmly Believe That the Construction of the Ju Yuan Middle School Has a Problem – The Investigation into the Ju Yuan Middle School's Tragic Collapse').

governance failures behind it, presenting an alternative explanation to officials and the wider public.

At the same time, these articles still managed to project a collaborative stance of critical journalists vis-à-vis the central state. This was achieved by localising the tragedy and complementing critique with constructive suggestions. The framing of official responsibility was overwhelmingly focused on local officials. The articles either avoided discussing the involvement of central authorities entirely or portrayed them as attentive to the problem. The *Nanfang Zhoumo* articles devoted their analysis solely to specific cases of local-level failures without linking them to top-down supervision by central authorities. *Caijing* reports drew a contrast between proactive central authorities, who foresaw the disaster, and inefficient local officials, who ignored central directives. The 9 June report, the last and perhaps the most serious investigation into the school crisis, devoted a separate section to pre-emptive central initiatives undertaken to address the problem. 'In reality central government has long been aware of the situation concerning the quality of some middle and elementary schools . . . .' reads the opening of this section. It continues to explain that central authorities have instructed local officials about addressing this problem. 'There were repeated orders given and documents issued by the Ministry of Education to education departments at all levels . . .', it proceeds,[63] further documenting the investments into school infrastructure poured in by the centre across the provinces, including Sichuan. By arguing that local officials obstructed well-intentioned directives from the centre, this report rhetorically relieves central authorities of all responsibility.[64]

Another way in which journalists projected a collaborative stance was through adopting a constructive tone when discussing failures, which was achieved with three discursive devices: by appealing to expert testimonies, by drawing parallels to successful cases and by proposing solutions. In addition to substantiating a critical stance, references to experts were also employed to create some distance between journalists' opinions and 'objective' expertise. Interviews with experts from Taiwan and the United

---

[63] Yang Binbin, Zhao Hejuan, Li Zhigang, Chang Hongxiao, Zhang Yingguang, and Chenzhong Xiaolu, 'Jiaoshe yousi lu' ('The Worrisome Record about the School Buildings').

[64] The only exception to the sole focus on local failures is one *Caijing* report, which notes the problematic features of the current supervision arrangement. It argues that the centre-led system for monitoring public construction safety endows different departments under the State Council with responsibility for managing the safety of their own construction projects, thus giving rise to conflicts of interest. Beyond noting the questionable 'central arrangement', however, this article does not disclose the authorities in charge of creating it or the reasoning behind it. See Zhang Yingguang, Cheng Zhongxiaolu, and Yang Binbin, 'Gongjian jianzhu hechu bu lao' ('Where to Mend Strong Public Construction'), *Caijing*, 9 June 2008.

States, for instance, served to illustrate the construction faults, as exemplified by the following comment in a *Caijing* report: 'An Atlanta-based architect ... who worked for seven years in a safety inspection organisation ... expressed that based on his many years of experience with construction and design, even by looking at the photographs it is clear that many of the collapsed school buildings had construction quality issues'.[65] This interview with a Western professional helped amplify the journalist's argument about construction quality being at the heart of the matter. When discussing systemic supervision failures, a *Caijing* report channelled the most critical comments through official interviewees. A former leader of Beijing's Municipal Commission for Housing and Urban Reform (北京市建委), for instance, was cited in one of the articles as cautiously denouncing the effectiveness of the current oversight mechanisms:

> So long as there are no apparent problems found during the final check-up of the engineering project, the quality control system is typically unlikely to create difficulties for the construction project. At this stage, it is not realistic for the quality control system to overturn the entire project. In the game of power, the quality control system is at a strong disadvantage.[66]

In this interview, the former official signalled the existing weaknesses in the current oversight mechanisms over construction safety. He implied that monitoring was superficial and not backed by sufficient institutional power to challenge officials managing the construction projects. While not directly accusing anyone, the official's comment was important as it hinted at systemic failure linked to the crisis. An appeal to official expert authority by the journalist, therefore, was used to construct a critical stance within the state-allocated boundaries.

In addition to expert interviews, criticisms were also conveyed through illustrative comparative examples that implied potential solutions. Both *Caijing* and *Nanfang Zhoumo*, for instance, drew parallels to privately funded schools, which withstood the earthquake, arguing that strict supervision as opposed to particular building materials determined their survival, and thereby indirectly calling for more independent oversight in public construction projects.[67] Comparisons to other cases of school

---

[65] Yang Binbin, Zhao Hejuan, Li Zhigang, Chang Hongxiao, Zhang Yingguang, and Chenzhong Xiaolu, 'Jiaoshe yousi lu' ('The Worrisome Record about the School Buildings').

[66] Zhang Yingguang, Cheng Zhongxiaolu, and Yang Binbin, 'Gongjian jianzhu hechu bu lao' ('Where to Mend Strong Public Construction').

[67] *Nanfang Zhoumo* included interviews with directors for these school projects alongside investigative articles, whereas *Caijing* incorporated comparisons directly into the investigative articles. See Wu Bingqing, ' "Miaopu xingdong" de xuexiao weihe yili bu dao –

destruction during earthquakes, such as that during the Taiwan earthquake of 1999, were also used to indirectly advocate for higher quake-proof standards and thorough investigation of school buildings:

Other than implementing quake-proof design and construction, the degree to which the government prioritises school safety can also influence quake-proof capacity. In that respect, Taiwan has already travelled a long and treacherous route. During Taiwan's 9.21 earthquake in 1991, 800 schools on Dao Island were seriously damaged . . . After the earthquake, the standards for quake-proof construction in school buildings significantly improved. At present time, Taiwan authorities are actively carrying out comprehensive evaluations of the anti-quake capacity in school buildings, and continuously promoting quake-proof reinforcement in all school buildings. According to Taiwan regulations, quake-proof capacity of school buildings should be about 25 per cent higher than that of average buildings in the same area. Prior to the Wenchuan earthquake, the quake-proof capacity of kindergartens and schools in the mainland was not granted higher priority.[68]

In the above excerpt, a journalist emphasised the successful example of Taiwan, only alluding to China indirectly. By explaining how the Taiwanese authorities had dealt with a similar crisis, a journalist provided a model for mainland officials to follow, including specific suggestions, such as raising quake-proof standards of the schools, and regularly evaluating school infrastructure for potential faults.[69] At the same time, by spelling out similarities between the Taiwanese and Chinese cases, including the lack of preparedness for the disaster and the initial slow response, the report indirectly explained and excused the reaction of Chinese authorities. The earthquake was presented here as a wake-up call, as the journalist urged authorities to treat the crisis as an opportunity to enact positive change.

Finally, some reports explicitly advised that comprehensive measures should be taken in response to the school scandal. A *Caijing* report, for

miaopu xingdong yiwu zongganshi liang jianha zhuanfang' ('Why Didn't the Miaopu Xingdong Schools Collapse – Interview with the Secretary-General of the Miaopu Xingdong Philanthropic Organisation'), *Nanfang Zhoumo*, 29 May 2008; Shen Liang, '"Qing ji hui" 169 suo xiwang xiaoxue jiben wanhao – zhuanfang nan dou gongyi jijinhui fu lishizhang jian mishuzhang, zhongguo qing-shaonian fazhan jijin qian chuangbanren xu yong guang' ('Qing Ji Hui 169 Primary Schools Are Basically Intact – Report Based on Interviews with the Vice-Chair of the Nan Dou Public Goods/Welfare Foundation, Secretary Jian, and the Founder of China's Young People Development Fund, Xu Yong Guang'), *Nanfang Zhoumo*, 29 May 2008; Zhang Yingguang, Cheng Zhongxiaolu, and Yang Binbin, 'Gongjian jianzhu hechu bu lao' ('Where to Mend Strong Public Construction').

[68] Yuan Wan, 'Duo ming de shi jianzhuwu er bu shi dizhen – bei hushi de kanzheng shifang wenti' ('The Loss of Life is from the Constructions Not from the Earthquake – The Ignored Question of Quake-Proof Fortifications').

[69] Ibid.

instance, concluded by advocating for systemic change in the supervision system of public construction, including that of the schools:

Many experts interviewed by *Caijing* believe that the top priority besides incorporating more market mechanisms is to establish a strong supervision and accountability link. On the one hand, construction companies and government officials have to undertake responsibility of quality supervision. On the other hand, when it concerns public engineering projects, the public should be endowed with the right to information access and supervision authority. That way there would be multiple levels of supervision in place to effectively monitor the quality of construction. As soon as a problem is discovered, one can promptly deploy the accountability mechanisms – this is the only way to solve China's construction crisis.[70]

In this excerpt, the journalist argued in favour of establishing more external oversight channels over public construction projects. Given the deficiency of top-down and horizontal supervision in the case of the Sichuan school scandal, the journalist suggested that engaging the public in monitoring efforts is the way forward. Rather than leaving citizens to fruitlessly complain to local officials, as they had done in Sichuan, new channels should be established for the public to voice their concerns independently of official channels. This argument presented a sharp contrast to the status quo, which was a supervision system driven by local officials and weakly overseen by the centre. It also challenged the mainstream discourse on the school scandal as an isolated incident, by treating it as part of a wider systemic problem of public construction safety that needed to be addressed at the highest levels.

Although discussed separately here, the three discursive strategies are interconnected and can be combined by journalists in fortifying a constructive stance vis-à-vis the central state. The solutions are often presented by experts, or alluded to with comparative examples. In the segment above, for instance, the argument for a better supervision system initially draws on the opinions of experts, as noted in the opening of the paragraph. Another investigative report by *Nanfang Zhoumo* similarly appealed to expert authority in both confirming the failure and offering solutions. It argued that, according to experts, 'the most important thing is to use simple economic methods to effectively raise the quake-proof capacity in the engineering designs', further outlining the necessary prerequisites for this to take place, including 'rigorous planning/design, standardised construction, and halting all "tofu

---

[70] Zhang Yingguang, Cheng Zhongxiaolu, and Yang Binbin, 'Gongjian jianzhu hechu bu lao' ('Where to Mend Strong Public Construction').

constructions".[71,72] Comparisons also go hand in hand with providing solutions to problems, as exemplified by the contrasts drawn with private schools in Sichuan and to the official response in Taiwan following the 1999 earthquake.

In conclusion, the investigation into the school scandal constituted a creative negotiation of political boundaries by critical journalists, as they stretched the limits of 'positive reporting' directives and pursued an issue perceived as sensitive by officials. Journalists' behaviour confirmed a pattern of 'outrunning' the censors, as demonstrated throughout the book. The journalists who took part in the investigative reporting admitted that they had been aware of the potential political repercussions of their reports, but had chosen to focus on getting the story and worry about the consequences later.[73] They had also tried to stave off potentially harsh official reactions by carefully aligning their arguments with the interests of the central state. Placing the responsibility primarily on local education officials, framing the reports in a constructive tone and presenting a balanced explanation and solutions to problems, critical journalists positioned themselves as fair critics as well as responsible advisers to the party-state. The authorities, however, were reluctant to extensively incorporate journalists' suggestions, as we find out below.

The Authorities React: A Creative Compromise

The official reaction to media investigations of the school scandal was that of a creative compromise between managing the risk of political instability by restricting further media investigations and using media supervision as a governance mechanism by addressing the immediate issues raised in the reports and projecting an image of responsive government. The discussion below highlights the fluid, unequal nature of the

---

[71] The term 'tofu construction' or 'tofu-dreg projects' (*doufuzha gongcheng*, 豆腐渣工程) has been used frequently to describe hasty, low-quality constructions in China.

[72] Yuan Wan, 'Duo ming de shi jianzhuwu er bu shi dizhen – bei hushi de kanzheng shifang wenti' ('The Loss of Life is from the Constructions Not from the Earthquake – The Ignored Question of Quake-Proof Fortifications').

[73] The journalists would likely have managed to report more before receiving the censorship order, if not for the professional challenges they faced in the crisis. The editors of *Nanfang Dushibao*, *Nanfang Zhoumo* and *Caijing* shared that this was the most difficult assignment for most of their staff, and they found themselves unprepared in dealing with the chaotic situation, including broken communication systems and other infrastructure problems. The journalists also experienced significant psychological torment during this assignment, as they witnessed unprecedented suffering. Interviews CJ30; CJ29. For more details on professional challenges of journalistic coverage of the earthquake, see also Nan Xianghong, *Juzai shidai de meiti caozuo* (*Media Operations in the Disaster Era*) (Guangzhou: Nanfang Daily Press, 2009); Zixin, *Zainan ruhe baodao* (*How Disasters are Reported*).

relationship between critical journalists and the party-state, as the latter quickly drew a strict line on further negotiation of the boundaries and only selectively addressed the exposed oversight failures.

Once the hard-hitting school investigations came out, the authorities showed little tolerance for further media supervision and enacted restrictive orders, including censorship, limits on information access and coercion, according to journalists interviewed.[74] Censorship bans (central and provincial) outlawing reporting and debating of the school scandal followed *Nanfang Zhoumo*'s 29 May investigations.[75] The bans cut short future and ongoing investigations, with a number of articles never making it into print.[76] An increasing resistance on the part of local officials also made accessing school sites more challenging.[77] Other than banning coverage and restricting information access, propaganda authorities issued reprimands to some media outlets, with *Nanfang Zhoumo* and *Nanfang Dushibao*, for instance, receiving official warnings (警告), according to their editors and journalists.[78]

The timing of these restrictions appears to parallel a growing public concern with the scandal, as well as the interlinked pressure from local officials. Fitting the general pattern unfolding throughout this book, an increasing public interest in the school scandal facilitated more censorship from the state. Journalist interviewees reveal that the restrictions came down shortly after their reports had spread online[79] and garnered a wide public interest. 'Our reports were reposted online across the country. The attitude of higher authorities then began to shift dramatically, away from openness and tolerance of the earlier phase of the disaster, and towards impatience and coercion . . .',[80] shared a journalist at *Caijing*. As already noted earlier, the internet was already a significant force in China by 2008, and netizens documented and discussed the earthquake on popular chat platforms, such as Tianya, which by the time of the quake already had twenty million registered users.[81] If in the previous disasters, the reach of critical articles would extend only to

---

[74] All interviewees who participated in the coverage directly or indirectly confirmed this trend, including editors of *Nanfang Dushibao, Nanfang Zhoumo* and *Caijing*.

[75] Interviews CJ25; CJ26; CJ36.   [76] Interviews CJ30; CJ29; CJ41.

[77] Interviews CJ30; CJ45; CJ25.

[78] Interviews CJ40; CJ30; CJ39; Some reports suggest that editorial purges took place following these publications (see Qian Gang, 'Looking Back on Chinese Media Reporting of School Collapses'), but the interviewees denied that.

[79] Although microblogging platforms (Weibo) were in the nascent phases of development at the time of the earthquake, the internet still spread the news about the scandal, as readers shared the story widely across their networks with the help of QQ chats, blogs and online news platforms.

[80] Interview CJ29.

[81] Qu, Wu, and Wang, 'Online Community Response to Major Disaster'.

newspaper readers, by the time of the Sichuan calamity, it encompassed all social media users. 'Once both local and central officials realised that the school scandal could grow into a wide public indignation of authorities, they moved to clamp down on media coverage', commented a former *Nanfang Dushibao* reporter, who was involved in reporting on the scandal from the very beginning.[82] Studies of public attitudes towards the party-state immediately after the revelations of the school scandal suggest that the official concerns with public indignation were justified. The analysis by Landry and Stockmann, for instance, reveals a drop in public support for the party-state following the publication of media investigations.[83]

The pressure from local officials, intertwined with growing public interest in the scandal, may also have influenced the timing of the censorship bans, as local officials attempted to persuade central and regional propaganda authorities to halt media investigations. Qian Gang, a former editor-in-chief at *Nanfang Zhoumo* and now a scholar at Hong Kong University, for instance, argued that Sichuan officials lobbied the central propaganda authorities to impose restrictions on all media in investigating the school scandal. The implication of high-ranking provincial officials in the scandal, including the Sichuan propaganda chief, and the presence of Sichuan officials in central ministries in Beijing, bolstered their lobbying efforts, according to Qian Gang.[84] Sichuan authorities also indirectly influenced Guangzhou propaganda officials, who enacted limitations on media reporting by issuing warnings to *Nanfang Zhoumo* and *Nanfang Dushibao*, the primary publications involved in investigative coverage, according to editors of the outlets.[85] Interviewees shared that Guangzhou propaganda officials, who had close ties with Sichuan officials, wanted to play down the crisis in the media.[86] The Sichuan officials, therefore, creatively navigated both vertical and horizontal networks in pushing for media censorship bans. The fact that the school scandal was already becoming a national issue made their pleas more convincing in the eyes of propaganda authorities at different levels of the system.

Censorship bans and other official restrictions were largely effective in stopping critical journalists from further negotiating the boundaries and most journalists and editors retreated from tackling the issue. *Caijing* magazine, however, was the one exception, which managed to take advantage of the inconsistencies in localised pressures. Unrestrained

[82] Interview CJ39.
[83] Landry and Stockmann, 'Crisis Management in an Authoritarian Regime'.
[84] Qian Gang, 'Looking Back on Chinese Media Reporting of School Collapses'.
[85] Interviews CJ30; CJ26; CJ22.   [86] Interview CJ40.

by Sichuan officials, and protected by central party contacts,[87] the magazine published its key 12-page investigative report on 9 June, more than a week after the first censorship ban came out. While infuriating some officials, the magazine's daring improvisation went largely unpunished.[88] The investigations, however, have stopped with the 9 June article, as the magazine feared to endanger its relationship with authorities. Specifically, interviews with *Caijing* editorial staff overseeing the Sichuan coverage indicated that the decision to halt reporting had been a strategic one, as the editors were aware that further investigations could jeopardise their space for future reporting on other sensitive issues.[89] Outside the traditional media sphere, more creative resistance to state censorship came from some citizen activists, who have persisted in investigating the scandal after June 9. A civil rights advocate, Tan Zuoren, for instance, kept travelling to the disaster areas and interviewing the families of victims to create a publicly accessible archive. A famous documentary filmmaker and professor, Ai Xiaoming, recorded the aftermath of the school scandal in July and August 2008, which culminated in a documentary, 'Our Children' (*Women de wawa*, 我们的娃娃).[90] 'Ai Xiaoming's role in documentary production resembled that of an investigative journalist ... However, her non-journalist identity enabled her to investigate the issue more freely than investigative journalists, who were imposed with institutional restrictions', notes a study of citizen journalism in Wenchuan.[91] At the same time, as explained later in this chapter, the efforts of these citizen journalists had limited public reach as a result of strong reactions from authorities. As demonstrated throughout the book, therefore, publicly accessible critical journalism can only proceed in so far as journalists carefully manage their improvisation within the system, even when it comes to social media activism.

The official restrictions on the media in late May and early June 2008 went hand in hand with some policy responses to journalists' investigations, which were in turn widely publicised in the media. Specifically, the party-state engaged with the problems feasible to address in the short term, such as faulty constructions of schools in Sichuan, and enacted preemptive measures for raising school safety standards at the national level. The party's responsiveness to the school crisis was highlighted in interviews with officials and critical journalists, as well as in expert assessments. The official interviewees stressed the unmatchable efficiency of

---

[87] *Caijing* magazine, financed by the Stock Exchange Executive Council as opposed to local authorities, has enjoyed greater latitude in its reporting, according to its editors and journalists.

[88] Evan Osnos, 'The Forbidden Zone', *The New Yorker*, 13 July 2009, available at: www .newyorker.com/magazine/2009/07/20/the-forbidden-zone.

[89] Interview CJ36.   [90] Jian Xu, *Media Events in Web 2.0 China*.   [91] Ibid.: 70.

the Chinese state in rebuilding the schools in Wenchuan, as demonstrated in the following excerpt from an interview with a high-ranking propaganda official in Beijing:

In China, the post-disaster relief and reconstruction work is very fast and efficient. You should go and see for yourself! They really reconstructed everything well, including the schools and other public infrastructure. So many resources were poured into the Wenchuan area. This would be unimaginable in other countries! I think local residents now enjoy a much better quality of life than before the earthquake. The schools there are incomparable to those in the past ...[92]

This official described how the government outdid itself in disaster relief, especially with regard to the schools. He portrayed China's official effort as uniquely effective. China, in his eyes, might serve as a model for other countries in dealing with future calamities. Moreover, he implied that the earthquake, despite its tragic outcome, had ultimately improved residents' lives as it attracted vast resources to the region from all over the country. The notion of turning reconstruction into a 'development miracle' went far beyond the schools and concerned the rebuilding of the province more broadly. 'The development imagined was not marginal improvement over pre-earthquake but a "great leap [in] development" that would catapult Sichuan's rural economy by twenty to thirty years after two years of fervent reconstruction activity', argued an in-depth scholarly account of official reconstruction plans that drew on reports by the Sichuan Academy of Social Sciences.[93] The school reconstruction was one manifestation of this ambitious project implemented from the top.

The perceptions of critical journalists on official rebuilding of damaged schools echoed that of propaganda officials. A former journalist at *Nanfang Zhoumo* involved in post-earthquake investigations, for instance, argued that authorities had enacted some positive change in response to critical coverage: 'I travelled there a year after the earthquake and found that most schools there were rebuilt very well. I think officials were forced to do so in response to media revelations and the subsequent public pressure'.[94] 'In terms of the actual reconstruction, it has all been resolved. The school in the village where I come from in Sichuan has been rebuilt beautifully. They put new furniture and other brand-new equipment inside the school as well. It is really first class! I think other schools in the earthquake zone are now first class too ... ',[95] commented a former

---

[92] Interview COF05.
[93] Sorace, 'The Communist Party Miracle? The Alchemy of Turning Post-Disaster Reconstruction into Great Leap Development'.
[94] Interview CJ41.   [95] Interview CJ31.

editor of *Bingdian*, now an activist, involved in monitoring this issue and collaborating with local NGOs.

Crisis management experts similarly concur that authorities 'faced the media's supervision role' and addressed the controversial revelations by rebuilding the schools to the highest standard.[96] Several Chinese studies called it a 'reconstruction miracle', arguing that the state performed exceptionally well given the magnitude of the disaster and the global financial crisis at the time.[97] 'It turned hardship into opportunity, pressure into force, and bad things into good things', argues one article, referring to 3,002 schools rebuilt in Sichuan within two years after the earthquake.[98] According to a 2012 World Bank study, the state spent $16.6 billion on rebuilding public infrastructure, including schools, with the highest anti-quake protection.[99] In addition to the reconstruction efforts, experts point to the central government's preventative measures. In July 2008, for instance, the standards for anti-quake protection in public infrastructure, including schools, were raised by one degree.[100] In November of the same year, the Ministry of Education and the Construction Bureau jointly announced new standards for construction of schools in rural areas, which included more explicit regulations about anti-quake protection.[101] Based on the official press release, central

[96] Interviews CSE14; CSE05.

[97] 'Sichuan zaihou chongjian moshi: fazhanxing chongjian' ('The Model of Sichuan's Post-Disaster Reconstruction: The Development Type of Reconstruction'), in Xueguo Wen and Zhengqing Fan (eds.), *Zhongguo weiji guanli baogao* (*The Blue Book on China's Crisis Management*) (Beijing: Social Sciences Academic Press, 2011): 103–130; *Chongjian wenchuan – renlei kangzheng, jiuzai shi de qiji* (*Rebuilding Wenchuan – A Miracle in Quake Proof Provision of Disaster Relief in Human History*) (Beijing: Dizhen chubanshe, Earthquake Publishing House, 2012).

[98] 'Sichuan zaihou chongjian moshi: fazhanxing chongjian' ('The Model of Sichuan's Post-Disaster Reconstruction: The Development Type of Reconstruction'): 109.

[99] Vivian Argueta Bernal and Paul Grocee, 'Four Years on: What China Got Right When Rebuilding after the Sichuan Earthquake', 5 November 2012, available at: http://blogs.worldbank.org/eastasiapacific/four-years-on-what-china-got-right-when-rebuilding-after-the-sichuan-earthquake.

[100] Zhou Hai, 'Zhenhai diaocha zu pilu wenchuan dizhen xiaoshe sunhui yanzhong yuanyin' ('The Group That Investigated the Earthquake Uncovered the Key Reasons behind the Schools' Ruins'), *Zhongguo Jingji Zhoukan*, 25 May 2009. For the original report, see 'Jianzhu gongcheng kangzhen shefang fenlei biaozhun' ('Standard for Classification of Seismic Protection of Building Constructions'), zhonghua renmin gonghe he guo zhufang he chengxiang jianzhu bu; guojia zhiliang jiandu jianyan jianyi zongju (People's Republic Housing and Town and County Construction Bureau; the state's quality supervision and quarantine inspection central headquarters), 30 May 2008, available at: http://wenku.baidu.com/view/8f818f2e3169a4517723a3e1.html.

[101] 'Jiaoyubu jianshebu xiuding nongcun xuexiao jianshe biaozhun 12 yue qi shishi' ('Department of Education and Construction Revise the Standards for Construction of Schools in Rural Areas, to be Taking Effect at the Start of December'), *Zhongguo Wang*, 24 November 2008, available at: www.china.com.cn/news/2008–11/24/content_16

authorities would train provincial leaders in implementing these standards. According to some expert interviewees, in 2013, for instance, the central authorities demanded Beijing officials oversee the reinforcement of all elementary and middle schools in the capital.[102]

It appears, therefore, that the party-state took active steps to use the Sichuan school scandal as a platform for projecting effective responsiveness to public concerns. This responsiveness was further amplified through the media and state-sanctioned cultural products that were projected to the public during mass media events that took place long after the earthquake. The theme of the earthquake, for instance, was resurrected at the 2010 Shanghai World Expo. An eight-minute film, titled 'Process' (*Licheng*, 历程), shown at the China's National Pavilion, fused the Wenchuan reconstruction theme into the larger narrative of China's successful development and modernization in the past thirty years.[103] Journalist interviewees further mentioned museum exhibits, TV programmes and film series dedicated to the Wenchuan success story.

Despite these widely applauded and documented measures, however, the party-state, both at the central and local levels, did not publicly address the heart of the issue raised in critical reports: the accountability failures and the faulty supervision system in place that facilitated the crisis in the first place. As for assigning responsibility, Sichuan authorities denied their role in the scandal, and central officials played down the issue. The local authorities publicly acknowledged the faulty construction of the schools but primarily attributed the disaster to external circumstances. Around the time of the publication of media investigations, Sichuan authorities published a press release outlining key reasons for the collapse of the schools. The primary reason they identified was the strength of the earthquake, followed by the unfortunate timing of the disaster (it hit when students were in school), the general disposition of school buildings, and finally the outmoded construction of some schools, including their insufficient anti-quake protection.[104] Central authorities (the education ministry) launched their own investigation into the scandal in June 2008,[105] but never released the results to the

817976.htm. These standards, however, appear to deal with the scope and quality of construction more broadly, as opposed to anti-quake protection in particular.
[102] Interview CSE09.
[103] Schneider and Hwang, 'The Sichuan Earthquake and the Heavenly Mandate'.
[104] Xie Maofang and Hu Yazhu,, 'Sichuan sheng jiaoyuting guina xiaoshe daota wu dian yuanyin' ('Sichuan Province Department of Education Gives Five Reasons Why the Schools Collapsed'), *Nanfang Ribao*, 28 May 2008, available at: http://news.qq.com/a/ 20080528/000849.htm.
[105] 'Jiaoyubu guanyu chengli jiaoyubu wenchuan dizhen zaihou xuexiao huifu chongjian gongzuo lingdao xiaozu de tongzhi' ('The Ministry of Education Notice about the

public[106] nor to the scholarly community.[107] Even the total number of student deaths was shared only a year after the earthquake,[108] with victims' identities still hidden despite requests by the media to release this information to the public.[109]

As well as refusing to carry out a public investigation into the scandal, the authorities silenced and punished those who did. Even six years after the disaster, the bans on media investigation of the issue remained active, according to the interviewees (both journalists and media experts). When asked whether it might be possible to investigate the aftermath of the scandal in the near future, an editor of *Nanfang Dushibao* offered no hopeful answers: 'This issue is still too sensitive for now ... we have not probed into it'.[110] When some media outlets delicately attempted to look into this matter, the authorities had quickly halted their efforts. In 2009, an article in *Zhongguo Jingji Zhoukan* presented the results of an academic investigation into the schools' collapse.[111] While arguing that there are multiple reasons behind the disaster, the scholars cited in the report stressed that the problem was not in insufficient regulations but in their weak implementation at the local level. Though this report merely cautiously reinstated earlier findings, it was quickly censored and removed from online platforms.[112] Interviewed four years after the earthquake,

---

Establishment of the Ministry of Education's Leadership Group Concerning the Work on the Recovery and Reconstruction of Schools Following the Wenchuan Earthquake'), Zhonghua renmin gonghe guo jiaoyubu (Ministry of Education of the People's Republic of China), 11 June 2008, available at: http://www.moe.gov.cn/publicfiles/business/htmlfiles/moe/moe_2083/200806/xxgk_62880.html.

[106] The author has checked the official sites of the Ministry of Education as well as the Construction Bureau and found no public announcements there. A journalist contact has attempted to get information regarding this from the education ministry but was told that they were unaware of a public investigation. Interviews with crisis management experts also revealed that they were not aware of the results of the investigation.

[107] Interviews CSE16; CSE15.

[108] 'Sichuan sheng nei gongji 5335 ming xuesheng zai wenchuan dizhen zhong yunan huo shizong' ('5,335 Students were Killed or Went Missing in Sichuan Province during the Wenchuan Earthquake'), *Xinhuashe*, 7 May 2009, available at: http://news.xinhuanet.com/newscenter/2009–05/07/content_11328503.htm.

[109] *Nanfang Dushibao* published an editorial one year after the disaster, pleading with authorities to reveal the identities to the public as a gesture to commemorate the victims, according to its editor. Interview CJ30.

[110] Interview CJ30.

[111] Zhou Haibin, 'Dizhen diaocha zu pilu wenchuan dizhen xiaoshe sunhui yanzhong yuanyin' ('The Group That Investigated the Earthquake Uncovered the Key Reasons Behind the Schools' Ruins'), *Zhongguo Jingji Zhoukan*, 25 May 2009, available at: http://news.ifeng.com/mainland/special/512dizhenyizhounian/zuixinbaodao/200905/0525_6415_1172036.shtml.

[112] David Bandurski, 'A News Story on School Collapses Tantalizes, Then Disappears', *The China Beat*, 27 May 2009, available at: www.thechinabeat.org/?tag=2008-earthquake.

critical journalists still lamented their inability to investigate further, arguing that it would benefit the party-state and society:

In reality, I believe that if there were no censorship bans stopping the coverage of the school scandal and other sensitive issues, critical reports could be done in more depth and detail. You cannot find the real causes of problems so quickly after a major disaster. In the United States following the 9/11 disaster, media incessantly reported and investigated, and only after a long time they were able to come out with clearer answers. Same thing with the recent earthquake in Japan. Only a year later the media was able to reveal partial truths to the public. They will probably continue investigating it next year and the year after, and will keep enlightening the authorities and society. But we have been reigned in (被管制) ... we have no way of doing more. If I had a way to do it, I certainly would, but for now I do not see an opening ... this situation is very particular to China ...[113]

By drawing contrasts to the United States and Japan, this journalist presented a critique of China's political system, hindering journalists from playing a more thorough supervision role. Her comment highlights journalists' intention of striving to improve the system through their investigations and their frustration with the official unwillingness to allow them to do so over a more extended period of time.

The authorities not only consistently restrained the media but also took strong measures against other actors, including victims' relatives and citizen journalists. Shortly after the publication of investigative articles, victims' parents were forbidden from protesting and speaking to the media. Failing to silence the victims' relatives through financial compensation, local officials resorted to coercion.[114] 'Instead of providing victims with a channel for expressing their grievances, authorities treated them as perpetrators of societal disturbances', remarked an editor at *Caijing*.[115] Activists who publicly pursued official accountability were also dealt with harshly. Huang Qi, an activist who helped victims' parents to press their grievances, was given a three-year jail sentence.[116] Ai Weiwei, China's famous artist and social media activist, who collected the identities of students perished in the earthquake, suffered physical reprisals from authorities.[117] Tan Zuoren, who researched the schools' collapse, never

---

[113] Interview CJ30.
[114] 'Quake Parents Protest in Sichuan', *Radio Free Asia*, 11 January 2012, available at: www.rfa.org/english/news/china/parents-01112012151815.html.
[115] Interview CJ25.
[116] Sharon LaFraniere, 'School Construction Critic Gets Prison Term in China', *The New York Times*, 23 November 2009, available at: www.nytimes.com/2009/11/24/world/asia/24quake.html.
[117] Roberta Smith, 'The Message over the Medium', *The New York Times*, 11 October 2012, available at: www.nytimes.com/2012/10/12/arts/design/ai-weiwei-survey-in-washington.html?pagewanted=all.

managed to launch his database, and was sentenced to five years in prison in 2010 for revealing state secrets – a charge linked to his alleged activism in 1989.[118] Ai Xiaoming's film was never officially released, and she was blacklisted for her investigation.[119] Even those responsible for supervising the construction of the few schools that withstood the earthquake were punished rather than rewarded. One such unfortunate hero, Gou Yandong, who successfully supervised the construction of the schools for the Hong Kong Project Hope in Sichuan, not only did not get any official recognition for his efforts but was driven out of Sichuan as the authorities did not want him to attract the attention of the public and activists.[120] More recently, in February 2016, Huang Qi, a Chengdu-based activist, was detained, along with two Japanese journalists investigating post-earthquake reconstruction.[121]

The party-state's ongoing sensitivity about the school scandal is linked to its perceived risks of political instability. According to crisis management experts who followed the developments of this case, the authorities, including those at the highest levels, wanted not only to ensure local-level stability in the short term but also to prevent the public from drawing connections between the school scandal and larger systemic failures in the long term. As for local dynamics, openly addressing accountability matters would interfere with the immediate goal of effective reconstruction, which is contingent upon cooperation with local officials.[122] Some experts also pointed to the official concern for inviting public scrutiny of the system. 'The central authorities do not want to touch this issue because it concerns them as well. They realise they cannot completely shake off the responsibility. They did not supervise well, and failed to pre-empt this crisis. The central state itself has a problem and has tried to handle this crisis in the gentlest way possible to avoid blowing it out even more',[123] explained a scholar at Beijing University. While some experts

---

[118] Edward Wong, 'Editor Reviewing China Quake Deaths is Sentenced', 9 February 2010, available at: www.nytimes.com/2010/02/10/world/asia/10quake.html. He was released in 2014.

[119] Jian Xu, *Media Events in Web 2.0 China*.

[120] Li Chengpeng, 'Patriotism with Chinese Characteristics', *The New York Times*, 25 May 2012, available at: www.nytimes.com/2012/05/26/opinion/patriotism-with-chinese-characteristics.html?pagewanted=all&_r=0.

[121] 'Interview: "The Authorities Fear We Will Expose the Scandal of Post-Quake Reconstruction"', *Radio Free Asia*, 4 March 2016, available at: www.rfa.org/english/ne ws/china/china-huang-03042016153923.html

[122] Interview CSE07. This point was also made by a China Central Television (CCTV) anchor who suggested that tackling accountability has to be done gradually and carefully, as local officials were important in completing reconstruction successfully. See Li Chengpeng, 'Patriotism with Chinese Characteristics'.

[123] Interview CSE08.

were less explicit about central-level vulnerabilities, they still alluded to official worry 'at all levels' about reigniting the scandal if investigations into accountability failures were publicly carried out.[124]

The official reluctance to address accountability in the Sichuan school scandal further calls into question the effectiveness of its reconstruction efforts, as well as that of its wider pre-emptive measures, according to journalist and expert interviewees. Journalists who managed to investigate the reconstructed schools in Sichuan found that there were some apparent flaws in the rushed reconstruction process, including unequal funding allocation and potential hidden quality defects. An editor at *Nanfang Zhoumo* and *Caijing*, for instance, pointed to the disproportionate funding being allocated to a few schools while the condition of other schools was uncertain.[125] Another journalist from a Hong Kong publication further argued in his report that the quality and safety of some newly reconstructed school buildings remained questionable:

I went back two years after the earthquake and found that there were still some quality issues with the new buildings and there was corruption involved in the reconstruction process. The buildings tend to look beautiful from the outside, but have problems on the inside. For instance, in some of the new schools the toilets were not working and some basic equipment was missing. Some parents were also not confident about their kids' safety. 'They look great, but who knows what's on the inside', they told me.[126]

Other than the drawbacks in the reconstruction response demonstrated in some media reports, the interviewees also suggested that there might be a gap between official rhetoric and action when it came to future

---

[124] Interviews CSE09; CSE10; CSE11.

[125] Interviews CJ40; CJ25. The investigation this editor was referring to was published last year, right around the time when Sichuan authorities announced that reconstruction work had been completed. See Li Weiao, Gao Shengke, and Dong Yuxiao, 'Chuan zhen chongjian de zhangdan' ('Sichuan Earthquake Reconstruction Bill'), *Caijing*, 7 May 2012.

[126] Interview CJ38. This journalist investigated the post-disaster reconstruction for *Fenghuang Zhoukan*. The magazine belongs to Fenghuang TV, based in Hong Kong, and therefore enjoys more political freedom to report and publish on sensitive issues in China. According to this journalist, a number of his reports came out in 2010 but were later censored in China and are difficult to locate on China's online platforms. The magazine itself practised self-censorship by burying the stories in less visible parts of the publication. The journalist shared the original texts of the articles with the author, which confirms the corruption and quality issues he described in the interview. For more details on larger problems with reconstruction and the notion of so-called 'celebrity zones' not being representative of the larger results, see Sorace, 'The Communist Party Miracle? The Alchemy of Turning Post-Disaster Reconstruction into Great Leap Development'. For more details on public dissatisfied reactions to Sichuan reconstruction efforts, see Christian Sorace, ' China's Vision for Developing Sichuan's Post-Earthquake Countryside: Turning Unruly Peasants into Grateful Urban Citizens', *The China Quarterly* 218 (2014): 404–424.

enforcement of quake-proof construction standards. Crisis management scholars expressed doubts over the willingness and capacity of local officials to seriously implement these measures.[127] Investigative journalists, who followed this issue over the years, similarly demonstrated little confidence in the school safety issue being addressed nationwide.[128] A former *Nanfang Zhoumo* journalist, for instance, argued that this problem remained unresolved in many places outside Wenchuan:

There has been no systemic change as a result of our reports. By this I mean addressing the issue of poor quality of schools buildings across the country, not just in Wenchuan. The poorly built buildings are a product of the 1990s, when the central state didn't have much money and local authorities were on a very tight budget, trying to promote fast development at the expense of quality. This problem is everywhere in China . . .

He further went on to explain why the state had not implemented wider reform, arguing that it was not in its immediate interest:

When I discussed this issue with high-ranking authorities in Beijing I could tell that they have been thinking about it, but are not ready to act upon it. First, though the central government has more money now, it does not mean it wants to invest in this area. It prefers more "visible" projects, those that could bring quick results and bolster its public image. Moreover, there is a problem with controlling local officials. Because of frequent rotations of officials at the local level, few local officials would be willing to undertake such a difficult task. They are mostly short-term oriented. So the approach of central authorities is to deal with the problem once it arises, and leave the rest for later . . . and local officials would not bring up the problems themselves.[129]

This journalist's remark alluded to the parallels between the official reasoning behind its reluctance to tackle the systemic problem of school safety and its avoidance of public investigation into the Sichuan scandal. The regime's fixation with its public image means that policies not directly promoting or even potentially hurting it in the short run are to remain of low priority. Interviews with crisis management experts similarly highlighted the short-term orientation of the Chinese state in dealing with many crisis management issues, beyond the case of the school scandal.[130] 'There is still a lack of macro approach to these problems', commented the director of the Tsinghua Crisis Management Centre, 'and too much focus on changes in appearance (*biaomian de bianhua*, 表面的变化), as opposed to systemic reform (*tizhi de bianhua*, 体制的变化)', he added.[131] The journalist's comment above similarly points to the

---

[127] Interviews CSE15; CSE14; CSE16.   [128] Interviews CJ26; CJ22; CJ31.
[129] Interview CJ41.   [130] Interviews CSE11; CSE 14; CSE15; CSE16.
[131] Interview CSE15.

direct link between the faulty supervision over local authorities and the weak potential for a wider systemic reform. Without addressing the vertical accountability issue, central authorities are unlikely to ensure that their initiatives are effectively implemented at the local level. Other journalists expressed distrust with respect to local implementation of central directives and alluded to the possibility of school destruction in future disasters. If local education authorities were still responsible for both financing and supervising the construction of schools, similar problems to those in Wenchuan were bound to arise, according to the interviewees. The 2010 Qinghai earthquake is another, more recent example. Though the number of student victims was relatively small (the official statistic was between 103 and 207),[132] domestic media could not extensively investigate the disaster due to heavy censorship,[133] and critical comments on microblogs drew similarities between the man-made factors behind the school collapse in Qinghai and in Wenchuan.[134]

The state's reaction to journalists' investigations points to the official prioritising of political stability when it comes to incorporating *yulun jiandu* into its governance apparatus. While the authorities have notably reacted to media reports with different measures aimed at improving the situation on the ground, they quickly closed the window for journalists to further supervise them on this matter and bypassed the more sensitive issues concerning accountability and systemic reform. The analysis illuminates the state-guided process of journalists' interactions with authorities. Despite the initial openings for investigative coverage, there was little room for journalists to further question the policy response and to negotiate restrictions in the aftermath of their courageous reporting.

Conclusion

The analysis of the interactions between critical journalists and the party-state presented in this chapter shows how the fluid unequal partnership between the state and the media works following a major national-level crisis. This chapter demonstrated how the authorities backtracked on

---

[132] Gordon Fairclough, 'Eleven Schools Collapsed in Quake: China Faces Renewed Scrutiny over Building Safety Two Years after Sichuan Disaster Killed Thousands of Students', *The Wall Street Journal* 15 April 2010, available at: http://online.wsj.com/article/S B10001424052702304628704575185431052701868.html; 'China Quake Killed 207 Schoolchildren: State Media', *China Digital Times*, 22 April 2010, available at: http://chi nadigitaltimes.net/2010/04/china-quake-killed-207-schoolchildren-state-media/.

[133] Evan Osnos, 'Letter from China: Qinghai Earthquake', *The New Yorker*, 14 April 2010, available at: www.newyorker.com/online/blogs/evanosnos/2010/04/qinghai-earthquake .html.

[134] Fairclough, 'Eleven Schools Collapsed in Quake'.

their initially restrictive approach towards the media and invited journal-ists to partake in crisis management, which eventually facilitated critical journalists' negotiation of the boundaries and publication of carefully constructed critical reports on a sensitive issue of the school scandal. It further showed how journalists 'outran' pre-publication censorship and pre-empted the harshest post-publication measures by aligning their arguments closely with the interests of the central state. The official reaction to the media investigations was that of creative ambiguity. Ad hoc restrictions on the media followed along with a limited and largely short-term-oriented governance response to media investigations. The perceived effects on substantive policy-making, how-ever, remain ambivalent, echoing the official discourse on media super-vision presented in Chapter 3. In addition to illustrating the dynamics of state-journalist relations, the case of the Wenchuan earthquake also showcased some of the drawbacks of the loose collaboration between journalists and the state. In this case, the notion of effective governance was determined by the party-state and involved only its superficial dimen-sions of on-the-spot improvements, but less so the more complex issues concerning accountability and systemic change that journalists had hoped for. We now continue to examine another case of a national-level crisis: the repeated coal-mining accidents of the Hu-Wen era.

Image 2 Rescue Scene at the Newly Built Dujiangyan Elementary School; 13 May 2008

6   The Battle over Coal-Mining Safety

The previous chapter illustrated the interactions between critical journalists and the party-state following a major natural disaster – an exogenous shock to the system that unearthed some pre-existing oversight flaws. This chapter engages with a national-level crisis that represents an accumulation of continuous governance failures: major coal-mining disasters. Drawing on interviews with journalists, experts, media and mining safety-regulating officials, as well as on analysis of investigative and in-depth reports of major mining disasters, the following discussion examines the party-state's approach to media coverage of this issue, the nature of media oversight and the official policy response.

The analysis shows how the dynamics of a fluid collaboration between journalists and central officials are reaffirmed in the aftermath of repetitive disasters. The official approach to managing mining media coverage in the past decade features a combination of an overall loosening of restrictions with selective censorship and persistent local-level attempts at blocking media investigations. Journalists' behaviour demonstrates creativity in navigating political pressures and in exploiting the gaps between local- and central-level objectives with regard to media oversight of coal-mining safety. In the past decade, critical journalists have cautiously investigated complex governance failures behind mining disasters, positioning themselves as consultants to the central state. The authorities reacted to extensive media reports and investigations by taking comprehensive measures to improve the coal-mining safety record, but enacted a more guarded response to media revelations of endemic corruption and weak oversight implicated in major disasters.

Official Approach to the Media: Openness with Chinese Characteristics

Nearly a century ago, the Anyuan coal mine on the Jiangxi-Henan provincial border served as the historic base for Mao's party

142

mobilisation, which culminated in the famous Anyuan Great Strike of 1922.[1] Throughout the reform era, the coal-mining industry served as an engine for the party's unprecedented transformation of China into a global economic powerhouse. Facing a shortage of other natural resources, China has continuously relied on coal for most energy needs.[2] In 2013, coal accounted for 66 per cent of total energy consumption.[3] While the past two years have witnessed a slight decrease in coal reliance,[4] new revelations about Chinese government underreporting of coal consumption by up to 17 per cent have put this shift into question. 'It is quite a lot more than previously reported – it is basically equivalent to the whole national consumption of Germany, and Germany is a large-coal consumption country in Europe', noted Li Shuo, the senior climate and energy policy officer for Greenpeace East Asia, in an interview with *The Guardian*.[5] The enormous consumption of coal has in turn translated into significant environmental costs for China and for the world, featuring in global negotiations on climate change and environmental governance.[6]

Coal mining has also been notoriously one of China's most dangerous industries, incurring 5–7,000 deaths annually in the past decade.[7] The hazards have long captured global attention, with Western media continuously reporting on miners trapped in the deep concave of China's hinterland. China's mining fatalities remain the highest in the world,

---

[1] Elizabeth Perry, *Anyuan: Mining China's Revolutionary Tradition* (Berkeley: University of California Press, 2012).

[2] Some experts note that China's resource shortage is its 'default setting', which is why it has kept reverting to the use of coal: see: 'How Resource Scarcity Constrains China', *China Digital Times*, 7 October 2013, available at: http://chinadigitaltimes.net/2013/10/resource-scarcity-constrains-china/. Others point to resource scarcity as one of its key challenges in becoming a global power. See: Zheng Bijian, 'China's "Peaceful Rise" to Great-Power Status', *Foreign Affairs* 84(5) (2005): 18–24. On China's coal consumption data, see: 'China: International Energy Data and Analysis', *US Energy Information Administration*, available at: www.eia.gov/beta/international/analysis.cfm?iso=CHN.

[3] 'China Plans to Slow Energy Consumption Increase to 28% by 2020', *Bloomberg*, 11 May 2015, available at: www.bloomberg.com/news/articles/2014–11–19/china-plans-to-slow-energy-consumption-increase-to-28-by-2020.

[4] 'China's Coal Consumption Drops Again', *The Guardian*, 29 February 2016, available at: www.theguardian.com/environment/2016/feb/29/china-coal-consumption-drops-again.

[5] Tom Phillips, 'China Underreporting Coal Consumption By up to 17%, Data Suggests', *The Guardian*, 4 November 2015, available at: www.theguardian.com/world/2015/nov/04/china-underreporting-coal-consumption-by-up-to-17-data-suggests.

[6] Lucy Hornby and Christian Shepherd, 'China Learns Lessons of Past Failures ahead of Paris Climate Talks', *Financial Times*, 29 November 2015, available at: www.ft.com/cms/s/0/480e813a-8f81-11e5-a549-b89a1dfede9b.html#axzz4FFuyRm5T.

[7] Jiajun Tu, 'Safety Challenges in China's Coal Mining Industry', *The Jamestown Foundation, China Brief*, 15 March 2006, available at: www.asianresearch.org/articles/2997.html.

Table 6.1 *Major mining accidents (30-plus victims) and investigative coverage*

Year	Major mining accidents	Number of fatalities
2003	Luliang, Shanxi	72
	Huaibei, Anhui	86
	Fengcheng, Jianxi	51
2004	Daping, Zhengzhou, Henan	148
	Tongchuan, Shaanxi	166
2005	Fuxin, Liaoning	214
	Shuozhou, Shanxi	72
	Chengde, Hebei	50
	Fukang, Xinjiang	83
	Meizhou, Guangdong	121
	Qitaihe, Heilongjiang	171
	Tangshan, Hebei	108
2006	Zuoyun, Shanxi	56
2007	Huayuan, Shandong	172
	Linfen, Shanxi	105
2008	Xiaoyi, Shanxi	34
	Weixian, Hebei	34
2009	Gujiao, Shanxi	78
	Pingdingshan, Henan	76
	Qijiang, Shanxi	30
	Hegang, Heilongjiang	108
2010	Xiangtan, Hunan	34
	Jihai, Neimengu	32
	Linfen, Shanxi	38
	Pingdingshan, Henan	47
	Yuzhou, Henan	37
2011	Shizong, Yunnan	43
2012	Xiaojawan, Sichuan	44

comprising 80 per cent of the total.[8] From 2003 through 2012, China witnessed 28 major mining disasters, with the number of victims ranging from 30 to 172 (see Table 6.1). Most of these accidents are man-made, ridden with oversight flaws that question the party's capacity to uphold minimal work safety standards and to protect one of the most socially disadvantaged groups – miners, who come from poor rural backgrounds. From the very outset of the Hu-Wen leadership, the top party officials have expressed symbolic

[8] Tim Wright, *The Political Economy of the Chinese Coal Industry: Black Gold and Blood-Stained Coal* (London: Routledge, 2011).

concern for the mining crisis. Premier Wen, for instance, went down a shaft for a meal of dumplings with workers as early as in 2003 (an occasion widely televised in China).[9] In managing the media coverage of this thorny issue in the past decade, the party-state has generally moved away from containing media exposure to inviting selective reporting of the accidents and showcasing high-level responsiveness.

Interviews with officials, journalists and scholars all pointed to a trajectory of the state's diminishing control over media reporting on coal-mining disasters, as manifested in milder pre-publication restrictions and post-publication pressures. As for the former, the general official tendency has been that of engaging journalists in effective crisis response by implicitly facilitating their coverage of mining disasters. Official interviewees argued that reporting on mining accidents has been 'pretty open (*gongkai*, 公开) in recent years',[10] and that journalists have contributed to successful rescue operations.[11]

Journalist interviewees noted that official openness carried a mix of general tolerance with persisting guidance over the tone of media coverage. An investigative reporter at *Caixin*, who has frequently covered mining accidents during the past twelve years, explained the official move away from bans and complete blackouts towards guiding public opinion in the past decade:

Whereas in the early 2000s we would receive censorship bans outlawing any coverage or opinion pieces on mining accidents, in the past eight years or so central propaganda authorities have allowed for publishing on this subject. They reinvented their directives towards the media by either asking us to construct a positive narrative or to primarily publish the official, *Xinhua News*, version of events. I think they realised that it is impossible to completely cover up major accidents, and just try to conceal some details or reasons behind them, channelling their own version of events instead.[12]

The shift from outlawing media coverage to shaping public opinion through the media is further evident in smoother official information access. Journalist interviewees pointed to the typically accommodating attitudes of high-level officials present at the scene of an accident. A senior reporter at *Zhongguo Qingnian Bao*, for

---

[9] 'Shaft of Light: The Coal That Fuels China's Boom is Becoming Less Deadly to Extract', *The Economist*, July 18, 2015, available at: www.economist.com/news/china/21657824-coal-fuels-chinas-boom-becoming-less-deadly-extract-shaft-light.
[10] Interview COF08.
[11] Interviews COF05; COF06.   [12] Interview CJ39.

instance, noted that he has not faced substantial difficulties in accessing central officials when conducting reports on mining disasters in recent years:

I found that interviewing officials, especially central ones, in the immediate aftermath of an accident is relatively easy. In that period even the highest leaders, including the Premier, appear at the scene of big accidents and dispatch investigative teams. This allows us to not only interview officials but to quickly collect the information available about an accident.[13]

Other interviewees similarly shared that high-level authorities present at disaster sites are generally responsive to media requests for comments and information.[14] In recent years, officials (both central and local) have also used social media to update the public on rescue efforts – information that comes handy to investigative journalists.

In addition to relaxing pre-publication censorship and control over information access, the authorities have eased post-publication pressures. In the aftermath of critical reports on mining safety, central propaganda authorities would direct criticisms at specific media outlets but forgo harsher measures, such as issuing official warnings or ordering personnel reshuffling – the two strategies introduced in Chapter 4. After publishing a series of critical reports investigating large-scale mining accidents in 2005, for instance, a *Caijing* editor was privately scolded by authorities and cautioned to exercise restraint in further coverage of mining accidents, but no coercive measures followed these verbal condemnations.[15] Post-publication deletion or adjustment of online reports has also been less pervasive in contrast to that concerning other sensitive issues, such as protests and large-scale natural disasters, according to media professionals.

Experts suggest that the official tendency to open up media reporting on mining accidents reflects the evolving approach towards crisis management. They note that tolerance of media coverage is just one manifestation of official attempts at revamping crisis communication in direction of controlled transparency. Specifically, as already explained in the previous chapter, after the damaging cover-up of the SARS outbreak in 2003, the authorities have opted for inviting some media coverage, while carefully guiding

[13] Interview CJ24.
[14] The notion of 'official responsiveness' featured in most interviews concerning coal-mining reporting.
[15] Interview CJ36.

the media message to ensure that the imagery of responsiveness and effective crisis management is transmitted to the public.[16] As with other disasters, moreover, the spread of social media has escalated the risks of a cover-up, as information quickly moves from online platforms to news outlets and the general public.

At the same time, inviting more media reporting on mining accidents may also have been a low-risk strategy for the party-state considering a relatively mild public reaction to these disasters, according to journalist interviewees. An editor at *Caijing*, who has repeatedly overseen articles on mining accidents, for instance, argued that they represent small-scale corruption for the public, in contrast to other disasters directly affecting their day-to-day life:

When people hear about a mining accident they want those behind it dismissed and punished, but an accident itself does not directly involve them, and thereby does not provoke a deeper reflection about the systemic failures behind it. After the 2011 train accident (*dongche shijian* 动车事件),[17] a new term appeared in the online discourse: 'corruption terrorism' (*fubai kongbuzhuyi*, 腐败恐怖主义), which refers to the type of corrupt activity that inhibits most people's lives. No matter if you are a white-collar worker, a member of the elite, or a government official, you still have to take a train. Same thing goes for food-safety scandals. No matter how protected, you are directly affected by toxic food ingredients. This is not the case with mining accidents ...[18]

The interviewee cited above suggested that unlike incidents that fall under the category of 'corruption terrorism' and can quickly shake up public trust in the regime, mining disasters are more removed from the daily bearings of average citizens, and are thereby less likely to spark immediate political discontent. The general public – by which the interviewee means his readers – middle-class urban residents – associates mining accidents with localised failures, expecting the central state to step in and punish the offenders. The low technological connectivity of miners and their families[19] further marginalises them in the wider web of online communication and inhibits them from generating public support

---

[16] Interviews CSE14; CSE15; CSE18; CSE19.

[17] This editor referred to the 2011 Wenzhou train collision. On 23 July 2011, two high-speed trains collided in the suburbs of Wenzhou, Zhejiang province, killing forty people and injuring many others. Local authorities tried to cover up the accident, which led to wide public outrage. For more details about the accident and the corruption uncovered behind it, see Evan Osnos, 'Boss Rail: The Disaster That Exposed the Underside of the Boom', *The New Yorker*, 22 October 2012, available at: www.newyorker.com/reporting/2012/10/22/121022fa_fact_osnos.

[18] Interview CJ25.   [19] Interviews CSE06; CSE17.

for their cause.[20] Unlike the tech-savvy victims of the 2011 Shanghai train wreck,[21] for instance, miners rarely take advantage of social media to build a wider activist network and to put pressure on the state. Higher authorities, therefore, may view mining disasters as opportunities for projecting leadership and responsiveness, rather than as imminent threats to political stability.

The general tendency of official openness, however, is also paralleled by some countertendencies of persisting irregular pressures on mining investigations. Specifically, higher authorities exercise selective restraint, while local officials regularly deploy enterprising measures to silence journalists in order to avoid penalties from the centre. As with other politically sensitive cases, journalist interviewees recounted that central propaganda authorities bolster restrictions following large-scale accidents at state-owned mines. An excerpt below from an interview with a former journalist at *Nanfang Dushibao*, who covered many major mining disasters, details the process of official regulations in these types of incidents:

In the aftermath of major disasters at state mines, we would receive more numerous and more detailed restrictions from propaganda officials. The adherence to *Xinhua News* version of events would be more strictly enforced than following other accidents, and getting officials to provide alternative comments would also be more challenging. This selective enforcement of restrictions comes as no surprise. It is consistent with the propaganda department's driving objective to pre-empt public discontent and to shield state-owned enterprises . . .[22]

The journalist's comment, echoed in interviews with media experts and observers,[23] highlights a distinction in official treatment of general media reporting of disasters at private mines as opposed to those at large state mines. The journalist suggested that propaganda authorities are motivated by the core objective of pre-empting public discontent, as well as protecting certain interests at stake, including those of mine managers. Considering that state mines are known for better working conditions

---

[20] This marginalization might shift over time. In 2011, there was an increase in 11.13 million rural internet users from 2010, with rural internet users making up 26.5 per cent of the total. See 'Statistical Report on the Internet Development in China', no. 29, China Internet Network Information Centre (CNNIC), January 2012.

[21] On the role of technology in facilitating criticism of official management of the 2011 Shanghai train crash, see: David Bandurski, 'Chatter Heats Up Over High-Speed Rail Glitch', *China Media Project*, 7 November 2011, available at: http://cmp.hku.hk/2011/07/11/13686/.

[22] Interview CJ39.   [23] Interviews CSE11; CSE08; CSE16.

than private mines,[24] and are directly under the oversight of the party-state, state mine accidents are also more likely to provoke public indignation of official policies, brewing a wider sentiment of discontent that authorities are keen to suppress.

When it comes to imposing restraint, higher authorities may also come under direct influence of local actors, namely state mine managers and local officials, in issuing censorship bans. An experienced reporter at *Caixin*, for instance, argued that restrictive directives from the centre are often a reflection of local-level attempts to halt investigations:

If a major accident either has not yet been widely publicised, or if the reasons behind it are sensitive, local officials often try to exert pressure on the centre to pre-empt or halt media investigations. Therefore, we have to be very careful in balancing our need for official information with protecting our freedom to report on the accident while at the scene of the disaster.[25]

The above comment is indicative of a widespread trend of higher officials shielding local officials by restraining the media – a phenomenon explained in detail in Chapter 4. Since local propaganda authorities can face difficulty in halting investigations by media outlets outside their own jurisdiction, networking with high-level officials remains an important mechanism for blocking and mitigating negative coverage. Even after an investigation is published, local officials often attempt to use their contacts to deter further media enquiries or to censor media reports, according to the interviewees.[26]

Local officials can also serve as important intermediaries between the journalists and the central state by applying independent restrictive measures on the media. Specifically, they have repeatedly persisted in obstructing journalists' work through a combination of bribes, threats and refusals to provide information. A senior reporter at *Zhongguo Qingnian Bao* explained the fusion of carrot and stick approaches by local officials in intimidating journalists pursuing investigations:

Since the reasons behind mining accidents are always complex, usually involving managers, local officials and different forms of corruption, multiple local officials (together with managers) try to pressure us after an accident, some threatening our physical safety. But I think the most disturbing fact is that they try to bribe us. This is extremely widespread and is the biggest challenge facing Chinese media in covering and investigating mining accidents. Although central authorities have taken some measures to address the problem, I remain pessimistic, and think it will persist for a long time . . .[27]

---

[24] Wright, *The Political Economy of the Chinese Coal Industry.*   [25] Interview CJ34.
[26] Interviews CJ40; CJ35; CJ34.   [27] Interview CJ24.

A journalist at *Caixin* further revealed the dynamics of local-level bribing attempts and his negotiation of official pressures:

> I witnessed with my own eyes local officials bribing journalists at almost every accident I covered. The officials often acted on behalf of managers of the mines. I also regularly get text messages from other journalist friends who witnessed accident cover-ups. Very few journalists refuse bribes. When I would decline them, officials and managers would get extremely nervous and uncomfortable. If it were not for my journalist identification card, and the fact that I come from a major media outlet, I think they would probably beat me or hurt me in some way.[28]

The comment above underscores the effectiveness of bribes in facilitating cover-ups – a tactic frequently deployed at the local level following many incidents perceived as sensitive by local officials, as explained in Chapter 4. While critical journalists appear to effectively negotiate bribes with a combination of professionalism and a display of powerful credentials, these journalists are still affected by local co-optation pressures as they struggle to solicit official cooperation in their investigations. Other than attempting to silence journalists, some interviewees shared that local officials bribe victims' families and survivors to prevent them from speaking out, thereby further denying journalists access to valuable information.[29] These bribing attempts were confirmed in interviews with central-level media-regulating officials. According to the deputy director of the General Administration of Publication and Press (GAPP), for instance, local officials offer up to 10,000 yuan (about $1,530) to victims' relatives in exchange for their silence.[30] Official interviewees at the Central Propaganda Department (CPD) and the GAPP shared that they work to curb these corrupt practices. Their measures, however, not limited to mining accidents, tend to target journalists rather than local officials, and threaten to revoke journalists' licences and expose them to a wider public scrutiny.[31] In the meantime, local officials remain difficult to trace and to restrain as they continue to aggressively suppress media coverage, according to official and expert interviewees.[32]

In deploying a mix of on-the-spot pressures on the media, local officials appear to fear for their professional interests at stake. An editor at *Jingji Guanchabao* explained how the official attempts at cover-ups are directly connected to their perception of mining disasters as threatening to their promotion prospects:

---

[28] Interview CJ39.   [29] Interviews CJ24; CJ25; CJ28.   [30] Interview COF08.

[31] According to interviewees at the General Administration for Press and Publication (GAPP), in the past several years new initiatives were undertaken to facilitate transparency in the journalism profession whereby any citizen approached by the media can look up a journalist's permit number and ensure that he or she is indeed a representative of the media.

[32] Interviews COF08; COF05; COF06.

Every time the number of victims is not openly declared or remains uncertain, it is closely linked to officials' promotion aspirations. In many localities when local officials discuss politics they discuss stability, but in reality what they are talking about are their future career prospects. Depending on the number of victims, mining accidents can lead to the dismissals of county and city officials. Therefore, they consider it the biggest issue in local politics.[33]

A senior scholar specialising in media and crisis management at the China Academy of Social Science (CASS) further argued that mining accidents expose not only local officials' inability to oversee mining safety but also their long-term pursuit of improper policies, which explains their intent to downplay the disasters by pressuring the media:

Why do local officials often try to cover up accidents? It is because they know that accidents would reveal their long-term governance failures. Their approach to economic development has largely been centred on pursuing GDP growth. Their management style was often messy. One can say that the majority of China's mining accidents are due to local officials' negligence. They contract mines out to people who only want to make money at the expense of safety. On many levels, local officials have to be held accountable. Here I especially stress that this is the problem of local officials (as opposed to central)![34]

The interviewee directly blamed local officials for attempting to conceal disasters, as well as for prioritising economic growth at the expense of safety. Reaching higher growth standards, of course, is a major part of the political promotion criteria endorsed by the centre,[35] which suggests that the behaviour of local officials vis-à-vis the media ensues in part from the inherent contradictions of China's political system.

The shift towards increasing state tolerance of media coverage of coal-mining accidents, therefore, has also carried undercurrents of erratic restrictions, especially at the local level. On the one hand, as with other crises, including the Wenchuan earthquake, the party-state invited media to partake in crisis management and to favourably shape public opinion; on the other, the space for media reporting has been repeatedly narrowed in response to specific events. The above analysis also points to some disconnect between local- and central-level objectives when it comes to media management in the aftermath of mining accidents. Whereas higher authorities are most sensitive about major disasters at state-owned mines, local officials are sensitive about media investigations of most incidents, as manifested in their incessant pursuits to restrict or purge the media.

---

[33] Interview CJ28.   [34] Interview CSE19.
[35] Fubing Su, Ran Tao, Lu Xu and Ming Li, 'Local Officials' Incentives and China's Economic Growth: Tournament Thesis Reexamined and Alternative Explanatory Framework', *China & World Economy* 20(4) (1 July 2012): 1–18.

The overall management of media reporting of mining disasters is far from uniform. The apparent contradictions and ambiguity in official approaches, however, leave room for critical journalists to negotiate restrictions and to probe deeper into governance failures behind repetitive disasters, as explained below.

Journalist Investigations: *Yulun Jiandu* and Coal-Mining Accidents

The party-state's shift towards relaxing restrictions on the media and engaging it in guiding public opinion has facilitated a significant increase in media coverage of mining accidents in the past decade, with official news outlets, including *Renmin Ribao* and *Xinhua*, even devoting special sections to the issue in their online editions.[36] The focus of most media reports has been primarily on rescue operations, highlighting the capacity of the state in managing the disasters.[37] Some news outlets, however, including *Caijing, Nanfang Zhoumo, Zhongguo Xinwen Zhoukan, Sanlian Shenhuo Zhoukan* and *Zhongguo Qingnian Bao*,[38] have pushed the envelope further by critically examining repetitive major disasters, including the ones at state-owned mines.

Interviews with investigative journalists who reported on mining disasters revealed how they have creatively navigated the timing of their investigations and publications, as well as skilfully minimised their interactions with local officials. As for timing, journalists would attempt to either outrun or wait out censorship. The period between an official

[36] Shaoguang Wang, 'Regulating Death at Coalmines: Changing Mode of Governance in China', *Journal of Contemporary China* 15 (2007): 1–30.

[37] Tu Jianjun, 'Coal Mining Safety: China's Achilles' Heel', *China Security* 3 (2007): 36–53.

[38] The author searched for critical reports in several ways to optimise the results: first by locating and sorting through all reports on specific major mining accidents via a Baidu search, then looking for investigative reports by using the name of the accident and the word 'investigation' (*diaocha baodao*, 调查) and 'in-depth reporting' (*shendu baodao* 深度 报道) as search terms. Finally, the author searched for individual media outlets in conjunction with a name of a major accident accident. The outlets searched for include *Caijing, Nanfang Zhoumo, Nanfang Dushibao, Nanfang Zhoukan, Zhongguo Xinwen Zhoukan, Sanlian Shenghuo, Zhongguo Qingnian Bao, Renmin Ribao* and *Zhongguo Ribao*. Reports by local and small-scale media outlets are not included in the analysis. While there were many more in-depth reports, which focused solely on the human interest angle of coal-mining stories, this chapter does not include those in the analysis, as the search was focused on coverage that examines responsibility and the underlying governance failures. These reports are primarily of investigative genre but also include in-depth and editorial pieces that draw on journalists' investigations. I group them together under 'investigative' bracket in Tables 6.2 to 6.3. Reports focusing on minor accidents and illegal mining, which is widespread in China, were also not included in the analysis, given the focus on major recurrent disasters.

issuance of a positive-coverage directive and that of a censorship ban presents a limited window of opportunity for journalists to investigate and analyse a mining disaster. If investigation is completed but not published by the time a censorship ban strikes, there is still an option to 'wait out' the ban and publish reports at a later date, sometimes in connection with another mining accident. An experienced *Caijing* reporter who has long investigated mining accidents explained the timing dynamics, as part of his negotiation of the boundaries:

We always try to get the reporting done before receiving a censorship order, but even if we get one, we do not stop straight away. We try to continue researching the subject and get more information, but then wait out for an appropriate moment to publish the report. For instance, once a bit of time passes after an accident, it often becomes possible to publish a story that includes official information, but also our own investigation.[39]

The interviewee above highlighted the skilful practice of waiting out censorship, which includes both letting the sensitivity of the subject subside and incorporating the official investigations into an updated analysis – a tactic discussed in more detail further in this section. While the authorities persisted in issuing censorship bans over the years following the Sichuan school scandal, they did not follow up with new restrictions on individual mining accidents, making 'waiting out' a feasible strategy. The repetitive nature of mining disasters has also made the stories less time sensitive, as they could be aggregated or updated in light of the latest accident, as has been done by *Caijing* magazine in 2004 and 2005, when mining safety was selected as the magazine's investigative topic of the year.

In negotiating local-level restrictions on mining coverage, journalists strategically limited their engagement with local officials and actively sought out alternative sources of information for their reports. A journalist at *Caixin* (previously at *Caijing*) explained the use of all possible channels of information prior to turning to local officials:

When I conduct investigations on mining accidents, I typically use my personal network of contacts to gain reliable evidence before seeking information from local officials. Thereby by the time they might try to restrain my investigation, my piece would have already been relatively complete and hopefully published. The less time you give to officials to react, the more you minimise the chances of being pressured by them. New media or new communication technologies have been useful for information access. I also privately collaborate with journalist colleagues from other media in exchanging information, including interview content.[40]

---

[39] Interview CJ29.   [40] Interview CJ54.

This interviewee points to the importance of social media use and cross-media collaboration in bypassing local official pressures. As with other incidents, social media has become an important source of information on mining accidents. While miners and their families tend to be less active online, citizen journalists' posts about an accident on chat or microblog platforms, as well as official updates on disaster response can replace the in-person meetings with local officials. This trend is likely to expand as more rural residents gain access to the internet, and local officials come under more pressure to publicise their crisis response online. The expansion of the internet is further closely intertwined with the effectiveness of the strategy of cross-media collaboration, as critical journalists from large news outlets use microblogging platforms to locate potential colleagues present at the scene of an accident, who are restricted from publishing a story but may be willing to leak it to other media. Though as noted in Chapter 4, this form of cross-regional supervision has been recently restricted, this analysis indicates that journalists have continued to test this limitation in investigating mining accidents, with the help of social media platforms.

In managing official assaults, journalists have also resorted to social media by applying collective pressure on local officials. Some interviewees explained, for instance, that they would share local official efforts at co-opting them on social media and thereby mobilise colleagues and the wider public to shame corrupt local officials. Finally, the internet has served as a channel for carefully leaking censored reports, as well as for fuelling media activism on the mining issue. While rarely sharing uncensored reports through their social media accounts, journalists' articles are often picked up and spread on social media by netizens, before they get censored or amended by authorities. In addition, some individual journalists have used the internet to raise public awareness of miners' struggles through non-governmental organisation (NGO) initiatives, such as the Love Save Pneumoconiosis, started by an investigative journalist, Wang Keqin, which raises funds for miners to cure lung cancer.[41] Wang Keqin's interest in helping miners was awakened during his investigations of mining disasters and poor working conditions at coal mines across China. Social media, therefore, has been deployed by some journalists as a tool for expanding into the wider domain of societal activism and combining that with media reporting.

To examine how journalists' negotiation of restrictions translated into their supervision of authorities and to illuminate journalists' linguistic

---

[41] 'Helping Them Breathing', *China Daily*, 12 September 2014, available at: www.chinadaily.com.cn/2014–09/12/content_18585768.htm.

strategies used to mitigate pressures, the following discussion engages with selective analysis of in-depth media reports on major mining disasters. Major disasters – where the number of victims ranges between 30 and 200 – carry the highest political sensitivity in the eyes of the state and thereby underscore journalists' capacity to negotiate restrictions and provide oversight. The peaks in investigative coverage were in 2004, 2005 and 2009, which corresponded to the occurrence of several big accidents (see Table 6.1). The majority of serious in-depth investigative and analytical coverage was carried by *Nanfang Zhoumo* and *Caijing* (see Tables 6.2 and 6.3). The analysis of these articles, including the identification of prominent themes, frames and discourse devices, shows that critical journalists provided significant oversight on the issue of coal-mining safety while carefully guarding their space within the system.

The examination of the reports found three prominent governance themes dominating the coverage: the negligence of mining managers, weak oversight by local officials and ineffective regulation from the centre. The first and most prominent theme concerns mine managers and their ignorance of urgent and ongoing safety risks due to their prioritising production targets at the expense of occupational safety. In most cases, the reports reveal that managers consciously overlooked the inherent defects leading up to the accidents, including the high gas levels and water leaks in the mines. *Nanfang Zhoumo*, for instance, writes that prior to the 2005 Daxing flood disaster, the management knew about dangerous water levels but only took light precautions,[42] and in the case of the 2009 Hegang explosion, managers were informed about dangerous gas levels in the mine forty-three minutes prior to the calamity.[43] The reports further reveal that, in some cases, the managers also tried to conceal or downplay an accident and provided slow emergency relief, which further exacerbated the disasters. Following the 2009 Tunlan mining disaster, which killed seventy-four people, for instance, *Caijing* notes that it took an hour and a half after the initial miners' notification about the accident for the rescue team to arrive,[44] and following the 2006 flood disaster at the Zuoyun mine, the manager fled and underreported the number of victims.[45] Other than ignoring immediate safety hazards,

---

[42] Yu Jing, 'Yi ge kuangzhu de facai shi' ('A Story of How One Mining Manager Became Wealthy'), *Nanfang Zhoumo*, 18 August 2005.

[43] Chen Jiang, 'Zhiming 43 fenzhong' ('Fatal 43 Minutes'), *Nanfang Zhoumo*, 26 November 2009.

[44] Zhu Tao and Wang Heyan, 'Tunlan kuangnan nan ciren ze' ('Tunlan Mining Accident: Difficult to Brush off Responsibility'), *Caijing*, 2 March 2009.

[45] *Caijing*, 'Zuoyun kuangnan zhi sheng yiji' ('Zuoyun Mine Disaster Only Saved by Miracle'), 29 May 2006.

Table 6.2 *Investigative reports on mining accidents by media outlets:* Caijing *and* Nanfang Zhoumo

Date	Caijing	Date	Nanfang Zhoumo
5 April 2003	'Xuese xiao meiyao' ('Blood-Coloured Small-Scale Mining Operations')	2 December 2004	Li Liang, 'Zhi ji tongchuan kuagnan' ('Directly Beat Tongchuan Mining Disaster')
20 June2004	'Haizhoulijing beiju' ('Haizhoulijing Tragedy')	18 August 2005	'Xinning kuangnan fasheng zhihou' ('After the Xinning Mine Disaster')
27 December 2004	Shi Dong, Li Weinuo, 'Kuangnan shen yuan' ('Deep Reasons behind the Mining Accidents')		Yu Jing, 'Yi ge kuangzhu de fajiashi' ('A Story of How One Mine Manager Got Wealthy')
21 February 2005	'Zhuixin kuangnan beiju' ('Zhuixin Mine Accident Disaster')	27 October 2005	Guan Jun, 'Daping kaishi zouchu yangxing' ('Daping is Beginning to Come Out of the Shadow')
3 October 2005	'Guan mei tou jie zhengjue' ('Resolving the Corrupt Links between Managers and Officials')	26 November 2009	Chen Jiang, 'Zhimin 43 fenzhong' ('Fatal 43 Minutes')
29 December 2005	Wang Haiming, '2005 de kuangnan' ('Mine Disasters of 2005')	1 April 2010	Piang Xiang, 'Shisi feng hexin yu yi ci kuangnan' ('Fourteen Congratulatory Letters and One Mining Disaster')
			Ma Changbo, 'Weixian "feng kou fei" an: jiu jizhe quan bei panxing' ('Weixian's "Shut Up Fee" Case: Nine Journalists Completely Sentenced')

29 May 2006	'Zuoyun kuangnan zhi sheng yiji' ('Zuoyun Mine Disaster Only Saved by a Miracle')
17 September 2010	Huang Xiuli, 'Zhongzui zhikong yizai zuji kuangnan' ('The Meaning of Felony Accusations in Blocking Mining Accidents')
22 February 2009	'Weixian kuangnan "miehuo zhan"' ('The Struggle to Put Out a Fire After the Weixian Mining Accident')
5 January 2011	Zong He, 'Jia renshu, jia shijian, jia tuzhi: henan "tuoshengmen" kuangnan pu jianghuan loudong' ('Fake Number of People, Fake Time, Fake Drawing: Henan "tuoshengmen" Mine Accident Exposure of Managerial Leaks')
2 May 2009	Zhu Tao, Wang Heyan, 'Tunlan kuangnan nan ciren ze' ('Tunlan Mining Accident: Difficult to Brush Off Responsibility')
7 June 2009	'Qijiang 5.30 kuangnan huo cong helai' ('Where did the 5.30 Qijiang Mining Disaster Come from')
6 December 2009	'Hegang renwei kuangnan' ('Hegang Man-Made Mining Accident')
11 April 2010	'Kuangnan shenghuan wu yiji' ('No Miracle in Returning to Life After the Mining Disaster')

Table 6.3 *Investigative reports by media outlets*

Media outlet	Number of reports
Caijing	12
Nanfang Zhoumo	9
Zhongguo Xinwen Zhoukan	7
Sanlian Shenghuo Zhoukan	3
Zhongguo Qingnian Bao	2

the articles uncover ongoing mismanagement of the mines facilitating the accidents. Managers often failed to implement basic safety measures, such as putting in place an appropriate technology and enacting safety training procedures. Drawing on central state investigations, the media reports list weak ventilation systems and overcrowded mines, among other inherent management failures. The articles also show that the payment incentive structure at some of the mines induced miners to ignore their own safety. Miners interviewed by *Nanfang Zhoumo* following the deadly 2005 Xinning disaster, for instance, reveal that the cost of their safety equipment was deducted from their salaries and only reimbursed if no accidents took place during the year.[46] 'This is equivalent to miners' providing their own safety insurance', argues the journalist. *Caijing*'s investigation into the Zuoyun disaster finds that managers threatened miners with being fined one hundred yuan each time they failed to show up for work.[47] And the *Nanfang Zhoumo* investigation into the Hegang mine disaster finds that miners were only reimbursed for the work accomplished.[48] 'Even though we are a state-owned mine, we have no fixed salaries', commented one of the miners cited in the report. Overcapacity (often illegal) in coal production was uncovered following many major accidents by official investigators, cited in media reports. Overall, the investigations show that management of the mines focused overwhelmingly on production targets, overlooking urgent and ongoing safety risks, and indirectly encouraging risky mining activity.

The second key theme is the prevalence of corrupt ties between mine managers and local officials (*guan mei goujie*, 官煤勾结), which have allegedly enabled managers' irresponsible behaviour. While some articles note weak enforcement capacity of the local Work Safety and Coal

---

[46] Yu Jing, 'Yi ge kuangzhu de facai shi' ('A Story of How One Mining Manager Became Wealthy').

[47] *Caijing*, 'Zuoyun kuangnan zhi sheng yiji' ('Zuoyun Mine Disaster Only Saved by Miracle').

[48] Chen Jiang, 'Zhiming 43 fenzhong' ('Fatal 43 Minutes').

Mining Safety Bureaus[49] due to their insufficient resources and coordination,[50] most point to local officials' corruption as the primary culprit for managers' persisting violation of regulations. The reports show that local officials have been reluctant to enforce safety regulations because they have either received bribes from mining managers, held shares in the mines, or both, according to the reports.[51] Moreover, local officials benefit from high production of coal, as it is conducive to economic growth and to their subsequent promotion. The *Nanfang Zhoumo* investigation of Ceng Yung Gao, the manager behind the Xinning mine disaster, found that he donated large sums to local authorities, which allowed him to annex small mines illegally, overlooking safety hazards.[52] An investigation into the same mine disaster by *Caijing* found that local officials were also major shareholders in the mine and were concerned about slowing economic growth in case of mine closure.[53] The collusion of local officials and mining managers is further exposed in reports about officials bribing journalists to cover up disasters – a trend already discussed in the previous section. Following the 2008 Weixian accident, for instance, local propaganda officials gave 'shut up fees' (*feng kou fei*, 封口费) to journalists from ten different media, including national outlets.[54] *Caijing* argues that while journalists are also implicated in the cover-up, local officials initiated it and accepted bribes from mining managers to silence the media.[55]

Finally, the third theme, more apparent in *Caijing* than in *Nanfang Zhoumo*, is the failure of central policies in reducing mining accidents. Specifically, the articles criticise the state's policy of consolidating small-scale mines in favour of state-owned enterprises, arguing that it has not fixed the safety problem, as demonstrated by persisting major disasters at state-owned mines (*da kuang da nan*, 大矿大难). In investigating the 2011

---

[49] The national bureaus are called 国家生产安全监督管理总局 and 国家煤矿安全监察局. For more information, see the official website: www.chinasafety.gov.cn/newpage/.

[50] *Caijing*, 'Xuese xiao meiyao' ('Blood coloured small-scale mining operations'), 5 April 2003.

[51] *Caijing*, ' "Guanmei goujie" zheng jie' (Correctly Separating the Collision Between Officials and Mining Managers), 22 October 2005.

[52] Yu Jing, 'Yi ge kuangzhu de facai shi' ('A Story of How One Mining Manager Became Wealthy'), *Nanfang Zhoumo*, 18 August 2005.

[53] *Caijing*, 'Zhuiwen xinning kuangnan' ('Examining Xinning Mining Accident'), 22 August 2005.

[54] Wang Heyan, 'Weixian kuangnan "miehuo zhan"' ('The Struggle to "Put Out a Fire" After Weixian Kuangnan'), *Caijing*, 22 February 2009; Ma Changbo, 'Weixian "feng kou fei" an: jiu jizhe quan bei panxing' ('Weixian's Case of "feng kou fei": Nine Journalists Have Been Completely Sentenced'), *Nanfang Zhoumo*, 1 April 2010.

[55] Wang Heyan, 'Weixian kuangnan "miehuo zhan"' ('The Struggle to "Put Out a Fire" After Weixian Kuangnan').

Henan accident, *Nanfang Zhoumo* finds that the mine had recently been annexed by a state-owned company, yet did not improve its safety record.[56] 'Large state-owned mines cannot fix the root of the problem in China's coal mining safety', commented an expert cited in that report. The 2004 *Caijing* report into recurrent major accidents at state-owned mines argues that the current vertical system of supervising mining safety via the newly established Mining Safety Supervision Bureau is a 'toothless dragon', as the state is trying to 'manage coal production with one hand, while guarding safety with the other'.[57] In the 2005 end-of-year investigation into mining accidents, *Caijing* continues to argue that the state's consolidation of the mining sector cannot break the corrupt symbiotic ties between local officials and mining managers.[58] And a *Nanfang Zhoumo* report about the 2010 Wangjialing accident further implies that consolidation of mines could lead to the acquittal of local officials, as responsibility for mining safety would shift to provincial authorities.[59]

In contrast to the Wenchuan school scandal, journalists investigated and analysed mining disasters in more depth and over a longer time frame, unravelling multiple layers of oversight and policy failures behind the repetitive accidents. At the same time, the analysis of discourse and framing strategies used in the reports, shows how journalists exercised significant caution in carrying out oversight, especially on the third theme of central-level failures. This is manifested in the notable abstraction of the immediately sensitive content, as well as in diffusing and obscuring responsibility, and in expressing criticisms in a constructive way by veiling them as solutions and appeals to expert authority. As for abstracting critical content, an obvious tendency in the articles is that of either veiling the immediately sensitive content concerning individual disasters in broader discussions of mining accidents or hiding them in human interest stories. *Caijing* favoured the former, settling for an analytical style and often aggregating discussions of multiple accidents into single reports, whereas *Nanfang Zhoumo* embraced the latter, presenting mining accidents largely from the perspective of a specific victim or another character involved in the disaster, thereby shifting the focus from an event to an individual. This discourse technique likely helped journalists negotiate

---

[56] Zong He, 'Jia renshu, jia shijian, jia tuzhi: henan 'luoshengmen' kuangnan pu jianguan loudong,' ('Fake Number of People, Fake Time, Fake Drawing: Henan 'Luoshengmen' Mine Accident Exposure of Management Leaks'), *Nanfang Zhoumo*, 5 January 2011.

[57] *Caijing*, 'Kuangnan tanyuan' ('Extensive Investigation into the Roots of the Mining Accidents'), 27 December 2004.

[58] *Caijing*, '2005 de kuangnan' ('2005 Coal Mining Accidents'), 29 December 2005.

[59] Ping Xiang, 'Shisi feng hexin yu yi ci kuangnan' ('Fourteen Congratulatory Letters and One Mining Disaster'), *Nanfang Zhoumo*, 1 April 2010.

the *Xinhua*-only official regulation, as they did not directly report on censored events but referred to them implicitly or in passing.

As for journalists' assigning of responsibility, the reports on mining accidents diffuse responsibility among several actors, including central authorities. The most precise attribution of accountability, however, is laid on mine managers, followed by local officials, and only then central officials. The investigative reports portray managers as solely profit-driven individuals, consciously compromising miners' safety for personal gain. In discussing the appropriate punishment for those complicit in coal-mining accidents, media reports only focus on managers. One of the *Nanfang Zhoumo* articles, for instance, debates the appropriate prison term for managers, with some critics cited advocating for extending the current average term of seven years.[60] When it comes to attributing responsibility to local officials, the discussion turns more ambiguous. While some reports point to specific individuals accused of corruption, others feature generic actors, such as 'local officials' (*difang guanyuan*, 地方官员), which could range from county to provincial authorities. Within this loose category of 'local officials', however, the reports imply that the lowest-ranking ones, such as county and city officials, are most responsible, by describing provincial authorities as concerned and responsive to the issue of mining safety.[61] The responsibility is further obscured when it comes to central failure. One clearly observed pattern here is that criticism is aimed at policies rather than at individuals. Some articles directly point to the deficiency of the Coal Mining Safety Supervision Bureau, while others critique the central policy of favouring the state-owned mining sector. The reports refrain from naming specific officials behind these policies. Moreover, while criticising some central policies, journalists also portray central authorities as immediately responsive in the aftermath of mining disasters. Most reports incorporate a brief description of the central state's follow-up to the accidents, including plans for or results of initial investigations and the punishments of the culprits. A *Caijing* report into the 2009 Hegang accident, for instance, includes the following discussion of the centre's reaction:

On November 21, the day of the accident, following the instructions from our nation's General Secretary, Hu Jintao, and the State Council's Premier, Wen Jiabao, the State Council's vice-Premier, Zhang Dejiang, urgently rushed to the

---

[60] Huang Xiuli, 'Zhongzui zhikong yizai zuji kuangnan?' ('The Meaning of Felony Accusation Lies In Blocking Mining Accidents?'), *Nanfang Zhoumo*, 17 September 2010.
[61] Ma Changbo, 'Tunlan Kuangnan: "an jian shengzhang" de lei yu tong' ('Tunlan Mining Accident: The Tiredness and Pain of the Provincial Governor'), *Nanfang Zhoumo*, 26 February 2009.

scene. On the third day after the accident an investigation team of sixty people was formed, led by the director of the nation's Safety Supervision Bureau, Luo Lin...[62]

The above excerpt is just one example of how the responsiveness of the central state is portrayed in an engaging narrative. By using phrases such as 'urgently rushed to the scene' and 'investigation team formed' in either the concluding or the introductory parts of many articles, as well as by detailing the results of official investigations, journalists produced a per-suasive emotional narrative with high-ranking officials positioned at the centre of the crisis management effort on the ground. Some reports also emphasise systemic changes undertaken by central authorities to halt repeated disasters. The follow-up investigations on several accidents by *Nanfang Zhoumo* highlight the state's capacity to implement preventative measures. A 2005 report about the 2004 Daping accident, for instance, starts out by presenting new central regulations requiring local officials to withdraw shares from coal-mining companies.[63] And a 2008 report about local officials' bribery of journalists following the Weixian accident notes the regulations implemented by the GAPP to curb the corrupt ties between journalists and local officials.[64] The responsibility of central authorities, therefore, is not only diffused and obscured but also under-played with positive accounts of official proactive policies aimed at improving coal-mining safety.

Another important tendency found in the analysis of media reports on mining disasters is the framing of criticism in terms of suggestions. Journalists express their concerns about the safety repercussions of the state's consolidation of the mining industry in the form of suggestions for marketising the mining sector or prioritising safety management as opposed to ownership models. In fact, *Caijing* reports often resemble in-depth policy briefings, with most space devoted to convincing authorities of adopting their suggestions.[65] In 2004 and 2005, the *Caijing* editorial board selected mining disasters as an investigative topic of the year, with in-depth reports analysing failed mechanisms behind this growing crisis in

---

[62] Li Weiao, 'Hegang "renwei" kuangnan' ('Hegang "Man-Made" Mining Accident'), *Caijing*, 6 December 2009.

[63] Guan Jun, 'Daping kaishi zouchu yangxing' ('Daping is Beginning to Come Out of the Shadow'), *Nanfang Zhoumo*, 27 October 2005.

[64] Wang Heyan, 'Weixian kuangnan "miehuo zhan" ' ('The Struggle to "Put Out a Fire" After Weixian Kuangnan').

[65] In some issues, the op-eds appear either right before or immediately after the investigative article, further outlining and defending marketisation strategy. Some op-eds are written by Hu Shuli, the former editor-in-chief of *Caijing*. Hu Shuli, 'Fuxin kuangnan zai bi meikuang gaige' ('Fuxin Mining Disaster is Again Forcing the Reform of the Mining Industry'), *Caijing*, 21 February 2005.

occupational safety. In the introductory paragraphs, the articles briefly describe the tragic incidents, but then attempt to answer the question of why the state thus far had been unable to fix the problem, arguing that it is unwilling to let the industry marketise. The reports then persist in advocating for marketisation by invoking the rhetorical device of 'appealing to authority' or presenting critical comments through 'expert testimony'. A 2004 in-depth article arguing in favour of marketisation, for instance, concludes with the following comment:

> Experts point out, 'the safety issue is not an isolated problem, the key lies in the government's performing its own duty in the coal production sphere', there is no doubt that 'its own duty' is supervision. Only once many coal enterprises turn into genuine market companies, no longer under government responsibility . . . can the monitoring bureaus genuinely achieve the wanted supervision over large state-owned enterprises.[66]

As apparent in this excerpt, the journalist defers a key critical comment to experts, thereby distancing oneself from potential controversy. This rhetorical device is frequently employed by journalists in their discussion of potential solutions to the mining crisis. One scholar often cited in *Caijing* in connection with the pro-marketisation argument, for instance, is Qian Pinfang, a research associate at the State Council's Development Research Centre. 'China currently has over ten thousand coal enterprises. It appears as a competitive industry, but in practice, that is not at all the case . . . it is still a state monopoly . . . ', he comments in a 2004 *Caijing* report.[67] 'The corrupt links between officials and mining managers are not a result of marketisation, but precisely because market reforms are progressing too slow . . . . ', he is cited again in a 2005 *Caijing* report.[68] His comments here implicitly suggest that the state's reversal of marketisation is endangering mining safety. *Nanfang Zhoumo* does not explicitly include pro-marketisation arguments but still relies on expert opinions when arguing in favour of the state's strict enforcement of national safety regulations as opposed to its emphasis on industry consolidation as a way of avoiding disasters.[69] The paper also appeals to expert authority in implicitly advocating for further commercialisation of the media as a way to reassert its capacity to hold local officials accountable and to break

---

[66] *Caijing*, 'Kuangnan tanyuan' ('Extensive Investigation into the Roots of the Mining Accidents').

[67] Ibid.

[68] *Caijing*, 'Niandu huati zhuizong 2005 nian de kuangnan' ('End of the Year Topic Pursues 2005 Mining Accidents'), 26 December 2012.

[69] Zong He, 'Jia renshu, jia shijian, jia tuzhi: henan 'luoshengmen' kuangnan pu jianguan loudong,' ('Fake Number of People, Fake Time, Fake Drawing: Henan 'Luoshengmen' Mine Accident Exposure of Management Leaks').

corrupt ties between journalists and local officials. The report on the Weixian mining disaster, for instance, critiques the GAPP decision to enforce harsher penalties on journalists by citing Zhou Ze, a media lawyer, and Sun Xupei, a renowned media scholar, both stressing the importance of reforming the media system as a way forward.[70]

The reporting tactics and their actual coverage of major mining disasters highlight journalists' strategic creativity vis-à-vis both central and local authorities. Journalists managed to bend the fluid official restrictions to their advantage and to carry out some reporting that critically delves into multifaceted governance failures behind the disasters. The published reports feature journalists' attempts at providing oversight, while upholding their space within the system. This is manifested in their occasional dulling of immediately sensitive events, as well as in the careful framing of official responsibility, and in constructive formulation of the most critical comments. The following section now proceeds to the analysis of the official policy response to the mining safety issue in the past decade, and examines whether it has reflected the issues found in journalists' investigations.

The Official Policy Response: Reduce Deaths and Centralise Supervision

The analysis of the party-state's management of the mining safety crisis under the Hu-Wen leadership underscores its complexity and fluidity. On the one hand, the authorities have prioritised and successfully reduced mining deaths in the second half of the decade, suggesting that there may be a link between media reporting and the actual improvements on this issue. On the other, the official approach to battling systemic corruption exposed in media investigations only featured some modest policy shifts. Journalists' suggestions for separating the state's role as a regulator of safety from that of a manager of production were also ignored by authorities, with the idea of instituting more independent oversight being further sidelined by centralised supervision.

According to expert interviews and secondary sources, the Hu-Wen administration started to prioritise coal-mining safety following the major outbreak of accidents in 2004 and 2005, which were widely reported and investigated by the media. The authorities approached the issue by enhancing the measures undertaken by the previous administration. Specifically, they continued to close small-scale private mines, notorious

---

[70] Ma Changbo, 'Tunlan Kuangnan: "an jian shengzhang" de lei yu tong' ('Tunlan Mining Accident: The Tiredness and Pain of the Provincial Governor').

for their low safety standards,[71] while increasing investments in safety technology and management training at large state-owned mines, and fortifying the existing regulations on mining safety.[72] Under the Eleventh Five Year Plan (2006–2011), all mines producing less than 300,000 tonnes per year were ordered to shut down.[73] Some were closed permanently while others were annexed by state-owned mines. The closure of small mines is still proceeding, as the State Administration of Work Safety (SAWS) plans to shut 600 more mines in the coming years.[74] The authorities (both local and central) have also invested in gas extraction technology to prevent gas explosions[75] and poured money into safety technology and training at state-owned mines, according to official sources.[76] Some management training, including that on safety procedures, has involved international collaborations with Germany, the United States, and New Zealand, among other countries, according to experts and secondary sources.[77] The authorities also worked to strengthen their regulatory capacity by promoting the SAWS to a full ministerial level in 2005,[78] and tried to break corrupt ties between managers and local officials by intensifying post-accident punishment for managers,[79] ordering local officials to withdraw their shares in coal mines,[80] and requiring managers to spend twenty-four hours in a mine to experience and inspect safety conditions.[81] A combination of the above measures, but especially the closure of private mines and improvements

---

[71] China's Township and Village Coal Mine (TVM) have registered much higher fatalities in mine accidents than state mines, with some scholars citing a statistic of TVM fatalities being 'seven to eight times higher than the large SOEs'. See Wright, *The Political Economy of the Chinese Coal Industry.*

[72] The authorities began consolidating the mining industry in the late 1990s, resulting in the closure of about 50,000 private mines between 1997 and 2001. The investment in safety technology at state mines has also increased during that period. Most of the key regulations concerning mining safety, as well as institutional supervision arrangements, were implemented in the 1990s. In fact, Shaoguang Wang argues that by 2004 a new regulatory system emerged to deal with China's coal-mining safety problem: Shaoguang Wang, 'Regulating Death at Coalmines'.

[73] Tu Jianjun, 'Coal Mining Safety'.

[74] Associated Press, 'China Mine Blast That Killed 43 Blamed on Management', 1 September 2012, available at: www.cbc.ca/news/world/story/2012/09/01/china-mine.html.

[75] Wright, *The Political Economy of the Chinese Coal Industry.*

[76] Qian Pinfang and Zhou Jianyi, 'Wo guo tigao meikuang anquan shengchan shuiping de cuoshi yu jingyan' ('My Country's Policies and Experiences in Improving Mining Safety Level'), Guowuyuan fazhan yanjiu zhongxin diaocha yanjiu baogao (Development Research Centre of the State Council, research report 226 (2011)).

[77] Ibid.; Interviews CSE20; CSE11.

[78] Wright, *The Political Economy of the Chinese Coal Industry.*   [79] Ibid.; Interview CSE11.

[80] Tu Jianjun, 'Coal Mining Safety'; Interview CSE08.

[81] Wright, *The Political Economy of the Chinese Coal Industry.*

in safety technology,[82] has notably reduced the fatality rates in mining accidents starting in 2006, according to scholars and experts.[83] A recent study by China University of Mining and Technology shows that the death rate in mining accidents, as well as the total number of accidents, dropped significantly in the second half of the last decade (they claim an 85.01 per cent drop in death rate per million people and a 57.09 per cent decrease in the overall death rate since 2001).[84] The 2011 report from the Development Research Centre at the State Council finds a general trend of decline in mining fatalities since 2000, with the rate of decline intensifying since 2005.[85] In 2014, the number of deaths in mining accidents has for the first time fallen below 1,000.[86] Even taking into account the high rate of concealment of mining accidents, mining scholars argue that there has still been 'a dramatic improvement in the safety record'.[87]

Experts and journalists interviewed drew some linkages between the official response and extensive media reporting and investigations of mining accidents in the mid-2000s. An associate researcher at the Development Research Centre at the State Council, who has closely followed mining safety in the past decade, argued that the media's in-depth coverage has been one of the triggers for further reform.[88] A professor at the China Geological University who has extensively researched coal-mining safety also praised the media's watchdog role in exposing accidents and inciting support and action from authorities.[89] A scholar at Beijing University's Anti-Corruption Centre further claimed that the media outstripped both courts and official institutions in supervising mining safety.[90] Studies on coal-mining accidents confirm the importance of the media in highlighting the severity of the problem to the public and the state,[91] and journalists themselves who were involved in mining investigations admitted that there have been some

---

[82] I did not come across a study that convincingly argues that one specific factor was most responsible for safety improvements, but experts interviewed overwhelmingly argue that the reduction of small mines and better technology are at the core of it.

[83] The improvements are likely the result of cumulative efforts, including the measures adopted by the previous administration.

[84] Hong Chen, Hui Qi, Ruyin Long, and Maolong Zhang, 'Research on 10-Year Tendency of China Coal Mine Accidents and Characteristics of Human Factors', *Safety Science* 50 (2012): 745–750.

[85] Qian Pinfang and Zhou Jianyi, 'Wo guo tigao meikuang anquan shengchan shuiping de cuoshi yu jingyan' ('My Country's Policies and Experiences in Improving Mining Safety Level').

[86] 'Shaft of Light' (2015).

[87] Wright, *The Political Economy of the Chinese Coal Industry.*   [88] Interview COF09.

[89] Interview CSE20.   [90] Interview CSE08.

[91] Wright, *The Political Economy of the Chinese Coal Industry.* Nicholas Martin, 'Safety, Media Coverage and Provincial SOEs: Explaining Ownership Variation in Chinese Coal-Industry Restructuring', Working Paper 2013-39 (2013); available at: https://papers.ssrn.com/sol3/papers.cfm?abstract_id=2351473.

improvements in recent years, and that their reports as well as the wider media coverage of the problem have had some influence on state policy.[92]

While there is a correlation between media coverage and the general improvements in coal-mining safety, when it comes to tracing the official approaches to systemic issues behind the disasters, highlighted in media investigations, such as pervasive corruption at the local level, the connections become less apparent. The occurrence of mining accidents, including cover-ups, late into the Hu-Wen's leadership (see Table 6.1) and at the outset of the Xi leadership[93] suggests that the ties between local officials and managers are far from eliminated. As noted earlier, Chinese authorities have toughened their punishment of mine managers – the prime culprit of disasters, as framed in investigative reports – but the effectiveness of these measures is uncertain as they can also serve to reinforce managers' incentives for a cover-up once an accident has taken place, especially in the absence of additional economic retribution (i.e., confiscation of assets).[94] The lighter penalties placed on local officials further mean that officials could provoke and encourage mine managers to conceal disasters or to overlook safety concerns.[95] The attempt at cutting official ties to the mines by forcing them to withdraw their shares has also been only partially effective, as many ended up transferring their shares to relatives or even refusing to withdraw them.[96]

Moreover, the party's approach to safety oversight carries contradictions in pre-empting corrupt behaviour at the local level. The official reinforcement of the existing oversight channels has only produced moderate changes on the ground. Although the SAWS official status has been elevated, it still lacks enough inspectors at the local level to oversee all mining operations appropriately.[97] In Yulin (Shaanxi), for instance, 'only twenty staff was responsible for more than four hundred mines'.[98] Most notably, the authorities have ignored journalists' plea for enacting more independent oversight by further commercialising the industry and facilitating a separation between the party-state's responsibility for coal production and safety management – two often conflicting priorities. On the contrary, by strengthening the state-mining sector, the party-state has further fused these two roles together and upheld the top-down oversight

---

[92] Interviews CJ24, CJ28, CJ37; CJ41.
[93] A number of accidents occurred in the past several years (2013–2016). A recent accident at a state-mine took place this January (2017) at the Danshuigou mine in Shanxi. The alleged cause is illegal over-production. See: 'China Safety Agency Says "Illegal" Output Led to Fatalities at State Coal Mine', Reuters, 24 January 2017, available at: www.reut ers.com/article/china-coal-mining-idusl4n1fe1jp.
[94] Wright, *The Political Economy of the Chinese Coal Industry*.   [95] Ibid.
[96] Tu Jianjun, 'Coal Mining Safety'.   [97] Ibid.
[98] Wright, *The Political Economy of the Chinese Coal Industry*.

system. This approach has had mixed reviews, with some – the official experts – praising its effectiveness in monitoring occupational safety, and others – including external observers and critical journalists – pointing to its underlying drawbacks for eradicating local corruption. Mining safety experts argue that consolidation of the industry has been effective in improving accountability of mining managers and officials. A research associate at the Development Research Centre, for instance, explained that the integration of private mines into the vertical system of the party's oversight raises the stakes for mine managers to uphold safety standards:

The key mechanism for supervising mining safety is directly linked to the principles of China's political system. The heads of state-owned mines are officials, responsible to higher officials. As they are integrated into the party system, their career development is directly linked to it. If an official is found guilty of causing a mining accident, he will immediately drop out of the system. There is no way he could find a job at another party bureau, and definitely not at a state mine. It is not like in the United States, where a guilty manager might later end up working at another mine. In China, his political, societal and economic influence would completely evaporate. Moreover, everyone under this official would lose their jobs as well. This puts enormous pressure on everyone to take their job seriously. Therefore, such post-accident punishment remains the strongest incentive for managers, and is directly linked to the party's decision to expand state-owned mines in recent years. Unlike dealing with smaller mines that are harder to regulate, higher officials can directly oversee state mines and enforce accountability. China is not a law-ruled, but a party-ruled system. Strengthening state mines is the key to safety.[99]

In this excerpt, the interviewee suggests that by virtue of being a party official, a manager at a state mine is incentivised to uphold a good safety record, as the risks he faces go beyond a prison term and involve a permanent termination of a party career. This argument echoes that expressed by other mining and crisis management scholars in Beijing, who suggested that mine managers will be better at self-regulation at large state mines than at private enterprises, praising the official choice of reasserting the top-down supervision system.[100] These experts, however, as manifested in the above quote, did not elaborate on how higher authorities would monitor and enforce accountability at state-owned mines beyond relying on managers' self-interest in compliance.

A contrasting perspective expressed by crisis experts and journalists is that tighter top-down integration might facilitate more large-scale cover-ups of future disasters. Some crisis management experts interviewed in Beijing argued that by being ranked as superior or as equal to local

[99] Interview COF09.   [100] Interviews CSE20; CSE10; CSE08.

officials, state mine managers have additional leverage vis-à-vis local officials, and managers' connections with higher officials can further help them in administering a cover-up.[101] As discussed earlier, cover-ups involving corrupt ties between managers and local officials were exposed by the media in a number of major disasters at state mines. The 2008 Weixian accident, for instance, even involved local propaganda officials. Some Chinese provincial officials recently admitted to foreign media the potential dangers of state mine managers evading responsibility via powerful networks.[102] And a recent study of China's hazardous industries, including coal mining, by Fisman and Wang, found a strong correlation between a company's degree of political connectivity and the rate of work deaths.[103] Scepticism of the official approach to mining safety also echoed in interviews with critical journalists. Editors at *Caijing* expressed disappointment at the state's decision to ignore a pro-marketisation path, arguing that the state's interest in managing and expanding coal production will continue to conflict with its objective of supervising mining safety. 'We were hoping the government would serve as a watchdog not a direct participant in [the] coal-mining industry', commented an editor at *Caijing*.[104] Another former editor at *Caijing* also indirectly criticised the state's approach: 'They chose a different path, thinking that consolidating private mines into state mines will resolve the root of the problem. However, I am still confident that our opinion on this matter was correct. I have not changed my mind about it'.[105]

Another important implication of the state's centralisation of supervision is the ensuing narrowing of space for the media to provide continuing oversight on mining safety. Specifically, by assuming the dominant role in enforcing accountability over mine managers, the authorities have also favoured internal party oversight mechanisms to external supervision. In discussing the repercussions of the official response on their future investigations of mining accidents, journalist interviewees pointed to the potentially diminishing opportunities for them to navigate political pressures. A former journalist at *Nanfang Dushibao* (most recently at *Caixin*), for instance, explained how media supervision over state mines is bound to become more limited in the

---

[101] Interviews CSE15; CSE11.
[102] Christina Larson, 'In China, Politically Connected Firms Have Higher Worker Death Rates', *Bloomberg Businessweek*, 28 January 2013, available at: www.businessweek.com/articles/2013-01-28/in-china-corrupt-officials-and-worker-deaths#p1.
[103] Raymond Fisman and Yongxiang Wang, 'The Unsafe Side of Chinese Crony Capitalism', *Harvard Business Review*, January–February 2013.
[104] Interview CJ25.   [105] Interview CJ36.

years to come, as journalists will face more difficulties in investigating the state-owned sector:

I think that while the total number of fatalities in mining accidents decreased in recent years, the state's appropriation of private mines exacerbated systemic problems, namely the issue of external supervision. It is more challenging for the media to investigate state-owned mines. First of all, we receive more censorship bans when it comes to state-owned enterprises. And since the coal mining industry is increasingly state-owned, our limits on playing the supervision role are bound to increase. But even if we are able to bypass censorship, there are other challenges. The managers of state mines can engage other bureaus to help them cover up the accidents, as they are more influential than private mines. It is also challenging for us to attribute responsibility in the case of state mines, as it's often blurred since the companies all belong to the state. It is also hard to achieve some systemic change following these investigations . . .[106]

Though as demonstrated in this chapter, some critical journalists have managed to conduct independent in-depth reporting on state mine accidents, propaganda authorities are more prone to limiting these investigations due to their perceived political sensitivity. While complete cover-ups will be unlikely with the spread of social media, in-depth investigations will still be a challenge. Overall, the official response to mining disasters underscores the conception of *yulun jiandu* as an ambiguous governance mechanism. The party-state has appeared to take advantage of media reports in publicly demonstrating its capacity to handle an important governance issue, while burying the criticisms over the management of state-owned mines and the practice of external oversight under the veil of official responsiveness.

Conclusion

This chapter underscored the dynamics of a fluid partnership between critical journalists and the party-state in the case of repeated coal-mining accidents. The collaborative framework is evident in the party-state's gradual expansion of space for media coverage of coal-mining disasters, in journalists' constructive in-depth investigations and in the high-level official response to media revelations. Both journalists and central authorities have worked strenuously to resolve the coal-mining safety crisis in the past decade. At the same time, ambiguity was present at multiple levels of journalist-state interactions, as different actors, including central authorities, local officials and critical journalists, exploited it to their advantage. Although the party-state generally invited media coverage, it

---

[106] Interview CJ39.

favoured positive reporting on official crisis management to in-depth investigations, and selectively restricted journalists' involvement in the aftermath of more sensitive large-scale accidents at state-owned mines or disasters that could undermine certain official interests at the local level. Local officials, in turn, have regularly bypassed central-level interests in applying mixed pressures on journalists. A minority of media professionals succeeded in negotiating restrictions and publishing in-depth investigations and analytical pieces on recurring major disasters in the past decade, delving far beyond the immediate crisis management response into pre-existing governance failures at the root of the crisis. While cautious about implicating central officials, investigative reports highlighted a weak oversight and questionable top-down regulations on mining safety. The official reaction to the media, particularly to intensive investigations carried out in the mid-2000s, has also featured some fluidity, as the authorities have effectively reduced fatality rates but left the same oversight mechanisms in place and further tightened top-down supervision, which implicitly narrowed the opportunities for the media to further investigate major incidents. The improvised nature of interactions between critical journalists and the party-state following mining disasters, therefore, has remained consistently guarded.

Image 3 Hebei Shahe Mining Disaster: Already Forty-Eight Dead, Rushing to Save Forty-Five People; 21 November 2004 (photo by Ma Hailin)

Part IV

Comparisons

7   Beyond China

Critical Journalists and the State under Gorbachev and Putin

With the reader by now well versed in the multifaceted dynamics of journalist-state relations in China, this chapter offers a unique comparison to two other cases of media openings under authoritarianism. Specifically, this chapter employs the analytical framework of a fluid cooperation featuring shared objectives and guarded improvisation to examine the dynamics between critical journalists and the state in the Soviet Union under Gorbachev (1985–1991) and in Russia under Putin (2000–present).[1] The former represents a case of failed or short-lived cooperation between journalists and party reformers, which culminated in a surge of democratisation, whereas the latter manifests a disengaged relationship, with journalists indefinitely coexisting with the regime but being kept isolated from governance agenda. Drawing on a combination of secondary sources and interviews,[2] the following discussion engages with political objectives of high-level officials and critical journalists with regard to the role of the media, and explains the modes of the state's management of limited media openings. The application of the proposed framework illuminates that, in contrast to China, the objectives between journalists and officials were less aligned in the two Russia cases, and the state's management of media openings carried a less interactive engagement, which contributed to the evolution of distinct relations between journalists and the state. The chapter further highlights some additional contextual factors at play in facilitating the fluid collaboration between China's critical journalists and the party.

---

[1] While Medvedev was President from 2008 to 2012, Putin remained very influential in his role as a Prime Minister. The empirical analysis in this chapter is primarily centered on the years up to 2012, but includes some references to the latest developments in media-state relations from 2012 to 2017.

[2] Twenty-five interviews were conducted with critical journalists at Russia's prominent critical outlets including *Novaya Gazeta*, *The New Times*, *Kommersant*, *Vedomosti*, *Russian Newsweek* and *Vlast'*. Interviews were also conducted with former editors of critical outlets, media scholars at the Carnegie Centre and Moscow State University, as well as the current and former directors of non-governmental organizations (NGOs) advocating for media freedom, including the Glasnost Foundation and Internews.

Critical Journalists and the State: The Soviet Union under Gorbachev

In 1985, upon his election as a general secretary of the Communist Party of the Soviet Union (CPSU), Gorbachev faced a stagnating economic and political system in need of urgent reform. The eighteen-year Brezhnev rule that preceded that of Gorbachev was marked by ineffective, ageing leadership, the overturn of the Khrushchev Thaw[3] in favour of neo-Stalinism and political conservatism, and economic decline, including widespread corruption and decaying infrastructure.[4] Gorbachev surprised most international and domestic observers by embarking on far-reaching economic and political reform aimed at revitalising the Soviet system. The opening up of new channels for public expression, including the media, constituted an important element in Gorbachev's reform agenda. These top-down initiatives, however, soon took on a life of their own, with journalists and intellectuals mobilising in favour of a complete overhaul of the communist system. The following analysis proceeds with explaining the motivations driving Gorbachev and his advisers to open up the media, as well as the political aspirations of liberal journalists. It demonstrates that in contrast to China, where journalists and central authorities have been unified by a shared, albeit a fluid, agenda of improving governance within the existing political framework, in the Soviet Union under Gorbachev, the motivations quickly diverged between the party reformers and the journalists. The discussion further examines the process of media liberalisation reform, arguing that the dramatic opening-up initiated by Gorbachev did not allow for sustainable guarded improvisation, but rather proceeded in consequential phases of state-initiated liberalisation and a journalist-driven expansion and takeover of the media sphere.

Party reformers: Liberalise the Media, Reform the Soviet System

At the outset, Gorbachev's policy of media liberalisation, *glasnost* (openness), was advocated as part of the wider political and economic reform initiative or *perestroika* (restructuring). The media was envisioned as a channel for conveying the reform agenda to the public, as well as for gauging public preferences and concerns. As for the former, by opening

---

[3] 'Khrushchev Thaw' refers to the period of political and societal liberalisation under Khrushchev from the mid-1950s to the early 1960s.
[4] Richard Sakwa, *Gorbachev and His Reforms, 1985–1990* (Hertfordshire: Philip Allan, 1990); Archie Brown, *The Gorbachev Factor* (Oxford: Oxford University Press, 1996).

up the media, Gorbachev strove to mobilise the public in support of official reforms, which involved such new controversial measures as multi-candidate elections at the regional and local levels and limited private ownership.[5] 'The main task of the press is to help the nation understand and assimilate the ideas of restructuring, to mobilise the masses to struggle for successful implementation of party plans', read Gorbachev's official statement in 1987.[6] The media, therefore, was meant to publicise reform agenda and align the public in support of these initiatives. This was especially critical for Gorbachev given the strong resistance he faced from within the party. 'The chief problem of [Gorbachev's] launching of *perestroika* was that he was practically alone, surrounded by authors and impresarios of Brezhnev's "era of stagnation", who were determined to ensure the indestructibility of the old order of things', argued Yeltsin, a later opponent and successor of Gorbachev.[7] Yakovlev, a close adviser of Gorbachev, similarly affirmed the minority position that Gorbachev and his supporters were occupying in the party apparatus at the outset of the reform.[8] By aligning with the media and liberal intellectuals, Gorbachev was creating a momentum for the reform, putting pressure on party leaders to comply. According to Brown's analysis, Gorbachev saw *glasnost* as an 'instrument in his struggle against conservative forces within the party-state bureaucracy [...] a way of establishing contact with the society and of winning their support in his battle with the party conservatives'.[9] Gorbachev made use of his powerful position in the party by holding press conferences and feeding liberal agenda to the editors. Ligachev, Gorbachev's key opponent at the time, for instance, recalls that Gorbachev used to dominate press meetings by blocking conservative members from speaking up.[10] Gibbs, in his analysis of Gorbachev's interactions with the media, notes that 'Gorbachev recognised the potential power of having a "media presence"', referring to his use of media as a channel to gain popularity in contrast to his less media-savvy conservative opponents.[11]

Other than garnering public momentum through the media, Gorbachev's promotion of *glasnost* also endowed journalists with an oversight role or that of a feedback mechanism. Zaslavskaya, one of

[5] Stephen White, *After Gorbachev* (Cambridge: Cambridge University Press, 1993).
[6] *Krasnaya Zvezda*, 14 February 1987, quoted in Natalie Gross, 'Glasnost: Roots and Practice', *Problems of Communism* (November–December 1987): 73.
[7] Brown, *The Gorbachev Factor* : 93.   [8] Ibid.   [9] Ibid.: 162.
[10] Yegor Ligachev, *Inside Gorbachev's Kremlin* (New York: Random House, 1993): 100, 101.
[11] Joseph Gibbs, *Gorbachev's Glasnost: The Soviet Media in the First Phase of Perestroika* (College Station, TX: Texas A&M University Press, 1999): 16.

Gorbachev's closest advisers, argued in the official newspaper, *Pravda*, that societal feedback was instrumental for policy improvements, something overlooked in the decades of the Soviet rule.[12] In referring to *glasnost* in his volume on *perestroika*, Gorbachev similarly highlighted the importance of the public ability to spot problems and contribute to making improvements: 'People should know what is good, and what is bad, too, in order to multiply the good and combat the bad ... As never before we need no dark corners where mould can reappear ... That's why there must be more light'.[13] *Glasnost*, often referred to as 'criticism and self-criticism', opened up a number of subjects considered taboo throughout the Soviet period, including intensive examination of the Soviet past, particularly mass repressions under Stalin, party privileges, economic problems, crises, and dissidents, among other issues.[14] Journalists were invited to investigate and expose societal ills to the party, which would in turn be addressed as part of the reform initiative.

Media liberalisation reform, therefore, was aimed at creating both a mobilisation and a feedback channel for authorities to effectively align and respond to public opinion.[15] Not surprisingly, this reform met intense resistance from within the party, as opponents had anticipated its potential to destabilise the system. Gorbachev later recalled that 'there was practically never a single session of the Politburo without debate over *glasnost*'.[16] In his memoirs, Ligachev confirms the persistent opposition from other Politburo members towards the growing influence of liberal media. 'I think that Gorbachev at first underestimated the social consequences of the destructive work of the press, television, and radio', Ligachev writes.[17] 'It's hard to recall a Politburo meeting at which media questions did not appear ... They were raised by almost all the members of the Politburo [...] and the secretaries of the Central Committee'.[18] Gorbachev, therefore, was stuck in a precarious cycle of having to open up the media to carry out *perestroika*, while facing party resistance in implementing these openings. The constraints likely pushed him to expedite media liberalisation by directly encouraging journalists to

---

[12] White, *After Gorbachev*: 77.
[13] Mikhail Gorbachev, *Perestroika* (London: Collins, 1987).
[14] Brian McNair, *Glasnost, Perestroika, and the Soviet Media* (London; New York: Routledge, 1991); Seweryn Bailer (ed.), *Politics, Society, and Nationality inside Gorbachev's Russia* (Boulder, CO; London: Westview Press, 1989).
[15] Bailer, *Politics, Society, and Nationality Inside Gorbachev's Russia*.
[16] Mikhail Gorbachev and Zdeněk Mlynář, *Conversations with Gorbachev: On Perestroika, the Prague Spring, and the Crossroads of Socialism* (New York: Columbia University Press, 1993): 71.
[17] Ligachev, *Inside Gorbachev's Kremlin*.   [18] Ibid.

promote and expand glasnost, as will be explained in the next section of
this chapter.

The objectives for endorsing some limited openings in the media in the
Soviet case feature some similarities and distinctions from those guiding
Chinese officials. On the one hand, Gorbachev's interest in using the
media to engage the public in governance initiatives resonates with the
Chinese logic explained in Chapter 3. Like their Soviet counterparts,
Chinese authorities have used the media to guide and mobilise public
opinion, as well as to improve top-down oversight. At the same time, the
actual responsibility granted to journalists in the late Soviet period by far
outstripped that delegated to their Chinese counterparts. Whereas in the
Soviet case, the media was meant to drive the political and economic
reform process and help overcome the institutional gridlock, in China it
was to help address the problems resonating from economic reform,
which was under way long before the official endorsements of media
supervision. The institutional challenge that facilitated limited political
openings in Chinese media was not that of overcoming internal opposition to reform but that of ineffective oversight over local officials.
The official-journalist collaboration, therefore, carried smaller risks in
China than in Gorbachev's Soviet Union. Whereas in the former, the
regime was using it as an additional tool for managing specific governance
issues, in the latter, the reformers were relying on the media to enact
unprecedented political and economic transformation on a national scale.
We now turn to the discussion of Soviet journalists and their objectives
vis-à-vis party reformers.

Critical Journalists under Gorbachev: From Partners to Enemies

While liberal-minded editors and journalists initially embraced cooperation with the party reformers by carrying out *glasnost* and publicising
perestroika reform initiatives, they ended up turning against Gorbachev's
agenda and supporting radical democratisation (the Yeltsin camp).[19]
Like party reformers, critical journalists were in favour of liberalising
the media and public discourse, but transformed these openings into
opportunities for not solely reforming the system from within but for
overhauling it entirely.[20] 'Not only were the Democratic Russia movement and its member parties at that time professing their faith in anti-

---

[19] Minxin Pei, *From Reform to Revolution: The Demise of Communism in China and the Soviet Union* (Cambridge, MA; London: Harvard University Press, 1994).
[20] Ibid.

communism and liberalism, so too were the most influential mass media', writes Sogrin in his analysis of Russia's political transformation from Gorbachev to Yeltsin.[21] By the late 1980s, liberal journalists became increasingly in favour of the concept of the 'fourth estate', or the press as an independent institution overseeing other branches of government. Their political objectives, accordingly, evolved from those of carrying out *glasnost* and facilitating Gorbachev's initiatives, to enlightening and organising the public in support of liberal and democratic values, as practised in the West, and as distinct from those envisioned by the party reformers.[22]

While it is challenging to isolate specific factors behind journalists' shifting agenda, the combination of historic legacies of journalist-state relations and the presence of strong public and political support for a systemic change in the late 1980s, undoubtedly contributed to journalists' radicalised stance. As for the former, the partnership between Gorbachev and critical journalists and intellectuals was largely a novel experiment, which contributed to the opportunistic attitudes of Soviet journalists in the final years of the Soviet Union. With the exception of the Khrushchev Thaw, a period from the early 1950s to the early 1960s, known for the loosening up of restrictions on the media and public expression, Soviet intellectuals were isolated from the party apparatus. Shlapentokh's detailed study of Soviet intellectuals argues that 'for the most part the intelligentsia has been excluded from participation or even substantive consultation in the policy-making process ... '[23] Prior to being placed into influential positions in the mid-1980s, critical journalists, therefore, not surprisingly, held a long-standing predisposition against the regime.[24] Some of the leaders of the journalists' movement, had even advocated for political change as early as during the Khrushchev Thaw.[25] Gorbachev's granting of amnesty to many dissidents, in addition, indirectly radicalised the liberal media discourse, as many of the dissident writings were published by critical press.[26]

Journalists' explicitly radical political aspirations were also emboldened by vast public support on their side, including the emergence of

[21] V. Sogrin, *Politicheskaya istoriya sovremennoi Rossii 1985–1994: ot Gorbacheva do Yeltsina* (The Political History of Modern Russia 1985–1994: From Gorbachev to Yeltsin) (Moscow: Progress-Akademia, 1994): 68–69.

[22] Ivan Zassoursky, *Media and Power in Post-Soviet Russia* (Armonk, NY: M.E. Sharpe, 2004).

[23] Vladimir Shlapentokh, *Soviet Intellectuals and Political Power: The Post-Stalin Era* (London; New York: I.B. Tauris, 1990): 21.

[24] Gibbs, *Gorbachev's Glasnost*: 90–91.   [25] Pei, *From Reform to Revolution*.

[26] The number of these publications increased from less than twenty in 1987 to over five hundred in 1989 (Pei, *From Reform to Revolution*).

a dissenting, pro-democratisation faction in the top leadership. 'Supported by intense public interest, the politicization of the mass public, and an unprecedented increase in readership, the press – that unconditional ally of the Soviet leader – turned against Gorbachev', writes Zassoursky in his analysis of the media transition from the Soviet period into the 1990s.[27] Whereas in the past, outspoken journalists had been isolated critics, by the late 1980s, they enjoyed unprecedented popularity. In the late 1980s, the readership of liberal publications by far outpaced that of official party papers. Between 1987 and 1990, for instance, the circulation of the most official Soviet paper, *Pravda*, dropped from 11.1 to 6.5 million, while that of the liberal *Argumenty I Fakty* jumped from 3.5 to 31.5 million.[28] Public opinion polls also reflect the skyrocketing popularity of liberal publications, with 60 per cent of respondents in one survey favouring liberal *Ogoniok*, followed by two other critical publications, *Noviy Mir* and *Znamya*.[29] Public enthusiasm for *glasnost* was also manifested in the numerous letters sent to the editors of these publications. The number of letters received by *Ogoniok*, for instance, increased from twenty a day in 1986 to one thousand a day in 1988, according to Korotich, the magazine editor.[30] 'People are hurrying to have their say, like a stutterer who has just been cured and is hastening to prove to himself that he can talk as well as everyone else', Korotich remarked about letters from the public in the late 1980s.[31]

An overview of a selection of published letters reveals a fervent public sentiment in support of more freedom of expression. 'In and of itself, glasnost will not feed people, give them drink or build homes for them, but if glasnost ends, then we will certainly have no food [. . .] we will not have anything at all, except for the omnipotence of the authorities and the old, familiar stagnant swamp . . . Glasnost, so far, is perestroika's only REAL achievement . . . ', read one letter to the editor of *Ogoniok*.[32] Some letters directly advocated for more democracy and the end of one-party rule. 'There seems to be no end to our intoxication with glasnost. Oh, how marvellous it is that you can say what you think! [. . .] But isn't it time to move on? [. . .] We must climb higher. Glasnost should become a genuine institution of democracy and a guarantor of perestroika', read another letter from Voroshilovgrad oblast.[33] 'We must reject the Stalinist stereotype of the benefit of a one-party system and move toward creating a multiparty state . . . ', read another letter from Moscow.[34] These

---

[27] Zassoursky, *Media and Power in Post-Soviet Russia*: 10.
[28] Shlapentokh, *Soviet Intellectuals and Political Power*.   [29] Ibid.   [30] Ibid.
[31] Christopher Cerf and Marina Albee, *Voices of Glasnost* (London: Kyle Cathie Limited, 1990).
[32] Ibid.: 75.   [33] Ibid.: 87.   [34] Ibid.: 110.

comments showcase public enthusiasm for *glasnost* and support for further democratisation. In creating a channel for public discussion of wider political reform, journalists were also likely influenced by their readers' backing of a more critical stance against the system. The emergence of support for radical democratisation among some party leaders by the end of the 1980s further aggravated the growing disconnect between critical journalists and the establishment. Yeltsin, elected as the chairman of the Supreme Soviet in 1990, became the primary opponent of Gorbachev, and rallied many liberal journalists around his democratisation agenda.[35] The split in top leadership and the presence of an alternative reformer to cooperate with undoubtedly played a role in further mobilising journalists in favour of systemic change.

By the end of the Gorbachev period, the political objectives of Soviet critical journalists were distinct from those of their Chinese counterparts in the past decade. Whereas the former turned against the system they were initially working to transform, the latter have thus far persisted in identifying themselves as change-makers *within* the system. The above analysis highlights the importance of historic legacies and public attitudes in moulding the objectives of critical journalists in non-democratic contexts. While a long-standing legacy of confronting the system has contributed to journalists' radicalisation in the Soviet case, the historically constructive stance of Chinese intellectuals has facilitated the collaborative attitudes of China's contemporary critical journalists vis-à-vis the regime, as explained in Chapter 3. These distinctions may date to even before the communist period. In drawing comparisons between pre-revolutionary Russian and Chinese intellectuals, Wright argues that unlike Russian intellectuals who protested against the state and were generally hostile towards the establishment, Chinese intellectuals appeared 'politically nationalistic' and did not hold a similar hostility.[36] The communist revolution led to a repression of intellectuals in both countries, but Chinese leadership in the reform era has managed to co-opt them into the governance apparatus, especially in the aftermath of the Tiananmen incident, as explained in Chapter 2.

Other than historic legacies, the analysis of Soviet journalists during the Gorbachev period demonstrates the importance of public support, including that among top elites, in shifting journalists' objectives in the anti-regime direction. Although China's critical publications are popular

---

[35] Brown, *The Gorbachev Factor*; Pei, *From Reform to Revolution*.
[36] Mary C. Wright, 'A Review Article: The Pre-Revolutionary Intellectuals of China and Russia', *The China Quarterly* 6 (1961).

among some strands of the public, there has been no wider movement for further media liberalisation since 1989. A stark manifestation of subdued public opinion with regard to media freedom is the 2013 case of *Nanfang Zhoumo*'s public resistance to local censorship. The paper struck a critical stance against provincial propaganda authorities following unprecedented intrusion into its editorial policy. Although some intellectuals and netizens voiced support online and even physically protested outside the newspaper's building, the movement failed in mobilising other media outlets (with the exception of *Xinjing Bao*) or the wider public against the state censorship apparatus – not to mention the party-system.[37] This incident is illustrative of ambivalent attitudes held by the Chinese public about censorship and media freedom.

Resistance to political liberalisation, and especially, democratisation among the top leadership in China is also an important factor deterring critical journalists from openly expressing alternative views about the political system. Leaders who favoured a more liberal agenda, such as Hu Yaobang and Zhao Ziyang, got mercilessly struck down by the establishment, and no new prominent official voices promoting wider political change have emerged in China's political arena ever since. On the contrary, in recent years, the system has produced more conservative voices when it comes to media freedom, as explained in the concluding chapter of this book.

The Process of Liberalisation: Open-ended Improvisation

Echoing Gorbachev's approach to political and economic liberalisation, the implementation of *glasnost* policy featured a rapid and far-reaching reform, leaving little room for retreat and adjustment, and granting journalists an unprecedented space to improvise with political restrictions.[38] Specifically, the open-ended high-level endorsements via official statements and editorial appointments, as well as slow official reactions to journalists' improvisation, facilitated an expansion of media openings outside the boundaries envisioned by party reformers.

As for high-level discourse, Gorbachev's initial endorsements of *glasnost* symbolised an open-ended opening. Whereas the term *glasnost*, translated as 'openness' or 'transparency', had been invoked by Russia's statesmen prior to and during the Soviet era, generally as a call for more official transparency,[39] Gorbachev expanded the scope of this concept to

---

[37] Maria Repnikova, 'China's Journalists Are No Revolutionaries', *The Wall Street Journal*, 15 January 2013.
[38] Pei, *From Reform to Revolution*.   [39] Gibbs, *Gorbachev's Glasnost*: 12.

include the cultural sphere and mass media. Explaining *glasnost* at the
Central Committee Plenum in 1986 as 'freedom of the spoken and
printed word [...] a real socialist pluralism of opinions [...] the open
exchange of ideas and interests', Gorbachev directly endorsed significant
media liberalisation.[40] He further emphasised that *glasnost* was a long-
term systematic reform at the heart of the transformation of the Soviet
Union: '*Glasnost,* criticism and self-criticism are not just a new campaign
[...] they must become the norm in the Soviet way of life'.[41] While
Gorbachev noted the importance of 'constructive'[42] and 'responsible'
criticism, as well as an adherence to the 'party spirit' and 'socialist values',
he left these terms largely open to interpretation.[43] This ambiguity
appears to resonate with the official discourse on media supervision in
China, introduced in Chapter 3, but its scope was much wider in the
Soviet case. In his volume on *perestroika,* for instance, Gorbachev writes:
'Criticism is, first and foremost, responsibility, and the sharper the criticism, the more responsible it should be ... [C]riticism should always be
based on truth, and this depends on the conscience of the author and
editor, on his sense of responsibility to the people ... '[44] While on the one
hand, this statement may imply responsibility to the party, on the other, it
can be interpreted as journalists' responsibility solely to the people, giving
free rein to the media to expose public grievances. Some explicit restrictions and expectations with regard to *glasnost* were publicised only years
later when critical reporting was already in full swing. In his analysis,
McNair notes that 'firmer guidelines as to what constituted *glasnost* did
not begin to appear until the summer of 1988, after a major political
reorganization was well under way'.[45] The clarification of *glasnost*
appeared in *Pravda,* the official newspaper, right before the Nineteenth
All Union CPSU Conference in 1988.[46] On the whole, therefore, *glasnost*
served as a 'facilitating concept', empowering journalists to push the
boundaries.[47]

Other than endorsing an open-ended conception of media freedom in
his speeches, Gorbachev consolidated media openings through the
appointment of gatekeepers or media policy advisors and editors.
Specifically, in 1985, Gorbachev nominated Alexander Yakovlev, his
liberal advisor, as the head of the propaganda department of the CPSU
Central Committee, who in turn (with Gorbachev's direct involvement)

---

[40] McNair, *Glasnost, Perestroika, and the Soviet Media*: 53.   [41] Ibid.: 79.
[42] 'Constructive glasnost' was particularly stressed by Ligachev in 1987, in response to
Korotich's critical exposé of Soviet youth. See Gibbs, *Gorbachev's Glasnost*: 50.
[43] Sakwa, *Gorbachev and His Reforms, 1985–1990.*   [44] Gorbachev, *Perestroika*: 78.
[45] McNair, *Glasnost, Perestroika, and the Soviet Media.*
[46] Gibbs, *Gorbachev's Glasnost*: 76.   [47] Brown, *The Gorbachev Factor*: 125.

appointed liberal intellectuals in charge of major publications.[48] The following year, for instance, Grigory Baklanov, a well-known Russian writer, was in charge of *Znamya*, Sergei Zalygin headed *Noviy Mir*, and Vitaly Korotich, a liberal Ukrainian writer, was the editor of *Ogoniok*. While editorial appointments were frequently used for controlling the media in the Soviet Union and in China, Gorbachev-era reformers entrusted critically minded gatekeepers with facilitating media liberalisation. Ligachev, the conservative critic of Gorbachev's policies, recalls in his memoirs that Yakovlev put the most outspoken editors in charge of major media outlets.[49] Moreover, the newly appointed editors were granted substantial discretion over editorial agenda, at times outpacing that of the chief censor, Glavlit.[50] By the end of the 1980s, not surprisingly, most topics were accessible to Soviet journalists.

Finally, the Soviet reformers minimised or largely obliterated post-factum punishments for publication of critical articles,[51] once again, signalling to journalists the indefinite weakening of the state control apparatus. 'When it became clear that [when you overstepped the boundaries of glasnost] Gorbachev would shout at you and do nothing more, they [journalists and editors] started to do what they liked', remarked Korotich, the editor-in-chief of *Ogoniok*, in 1990.[52] When the authorities reigned in the media coverage, they did so in a clumsy manner, as demonstrated by the case of the Chernobyl disaster. The biggest nuclear disaster in human history was only noted by the official news agency, TASS (*informatsionnoe agenstvo Rossii*), sixty-five hours after the incident, followed by brief coverage in *Pravda*, an official newspaper, and an extensive propaganda campaign diverting public attention to other problems.[53] This return to old tactics of information control in the midst of the *glasnost* campaign likely weakened public and, especially, intellectuals' trust in the regime, and emboldened them to push forward media liberalisation to secure their gains. But it also may have paradoxically motivated Gorbachev to accelerate *glasnost* reforms and mobilise support for *perestroika*, according to some scholars.[54] Towards the end of

[48] Pei, *From Reform to Revolution*; Brown, *The Gorbachev Factor*; Gibbs, *Gorbachev's Glasnost*.
[49] Ligachev, *Inside Gorbachev's Kremlin*.   [50] Gibbs, *Gorbachev's Glasnost*: 7.
[51] Pei, *From Reform to Revolution*; McNair, *Glasnost, Perestroika, and the Soviet Media*; Gibbs, *Gorbachev's Glasnost*.
[52] Gibbs, *Gorbachev's Glasnost*: 63.
[53] Ibid.; Brown writes that 'in a paradoxical way, the disastrous accident at the Chernobyl nuclear power station [...] was a stimulus to the further development of glasnost'. See Brown, *The Gorbachev Factor*: 163.
[54] Brown, *The Gorbachev Factor*; Grigori Medvedev, *No Breathing Room: The Aftermath of Chernobyl* (New York, NY: Basic Books, 1993); Bialer, *Politics, Society, and Nationality Inside Gorbachev's Russia*.

his rule, however, Gorbachev attempted to regain control and reverse the side effects of *glasnost* through personnel replacements[55] and threats to suspend the press law.[56] These efforts came too late, and despite his reluctance, Gorbachev ended up sanctioning the press law, which institutionalised press freedom and 'effectively legitimised the expression of anti-communist opinions'.[57] Gorbachev and his advisers, therefore, eventually gave into journalists' demands and granted them legal empowerment, further erasing boundaries on freedom of expression.

The unguarded media liberalisation under Gorbachev comes into stark contrast with the cautiously improvisational process of endorsing limited media oversight undertaken by the Chinese leadership. Although both *glasnost* and *yulun jiandu* are fluid concepts, the latter is more restrictive as it grants journalists a specific function of limited supervision, as opposed to freedom of expression more broadly. Moreover, unlike Gorbachev's prioritising of media liberalisation in the reform agenda, the Chinese official discourse on the media supervision role is overshadowed by other more prominent policies of top-down supervision and guidance of public opinion. In contrast to Gorbachev, who gave journalists significant leverage in determining the course of media liberalisation reform, the Chinese authorities ensured that they themselves remain the drivers of media policy, capable of making continuous adjustments in response to their diverse objectives and unforeseen political pressures and sensitivities. The practical endorsement of media openings in China was also more subdued and implicit in contrast to that in the Soviet Union under Gorbachev, with Chinese authorities consistently acting as gatekeepers of media content. Unlike Soviet reformers, Chinese authorities have never explicitly promoted any liberal editors, but on the contrary have occasionally favoured conservative voices to keep the lid on critical outlets. The state's delayed reaction to journalists' improvisation under Gorbachev further differs from the highly adaptive approach of Chinese authorities who have been attentive and reactive to media criticism by improvising with restrictions and policy responses. And, finally, the party-state has consistently resisted institutionalising media freedoms by abstaining from passing a media law, advocated by some intellectuals and critical journalists in the reform era.

To conclude the discussion of the Soviet case, the distinct political visions of Soviet journalists and Gorbachev, combined with Gorbachev's

---

[55] Gorbachev appointed Kravchenko as the head of central Soviet television, who agreed to take off the air the popular programme, *Vzgliad* (Viewpoint). Brown, *The Gorbachev Factor.*
[56] Ibid.   [57] Ibid.: 284.

open-ended liberalisation of the media help explain the short-lived coexistence of the two actors. In contrast to the loosely aligned objectives with regard to limited media oversight in the China case, in the Soviet Union under Gorbachev, the objectives quickly diverged between the Gorbachev circle wanting to use more media freedom as a mechanism for reforming the system, and critical journalists, using it as a platform for a more radical change. The process of media liberalisation undertaken by Gorbachev was also not conducive to upholding collaboration. The dramatic opening enacted by Soviet reformers left them with little leverage to contain the journalists and incentivise them to persist working within the system. Not surprisingly, therefore, the Gorbachev case has consistently remained an anti-model for Chinese political leaders in the reform era and a cautionary tale for how not to carry out political liberalisation.[58] Most recently, under the leadership of Xi Jinping, the study of the Soviet collapse has been revived once again, with party cadres forced to watch state-produced documentaries contrasting the success of the Soviet system with its dramatic, mismanaged dismantling.[59] Gorbachev's rule is deemed a failure in the eyes of the Chinese Communist Party – one that can at once invoke fear but also an opportunity to enforce creative compliance and maintain political status quo.

Critical Journalists and the State in Putin's Russia

The Yeltsin era (1991–1999), which followed the collapse of the Soviet Union, was characterised not only by market liberalisation and democratisation but also by economic stagnation, deterioration of security and law enforcement, corruption and the rise of oligarchy, including that in the media sector.[60] When Vladimir Putin, a former intelligence officer directly appointed by Yeltsin, came to power in 1999, he rapidly began to reverse the course of his predecessor, steering Russia away from a path of democracy and free market, towards state consolidation of the political system, the economy and society.[61] These changes directly touched on the development of the media, as the state has taken over major television

[58] Anne-Marie Brady, *Marketing Dictatorship: Propaganda and Thought Work in Contemporary China* (Lanham, MD; Plymouth: Rowman & Littlefield, 2008).

[59] Maria Repnikova, 'China Learns from the Soviet Union: Contrasting Glasnost with *Yulun Jiandu*', *Problems of Post-Communism* (forthcoming).

[60] David Winston, 'From Yeltsin to Putin', *Hoover Policy Review* 100 (2000), available at: www.hoover.org/publications/policy-review/article/7127.

[61] Sakwa terms Putin's regime as that of 'consolidation' and contrasts it with Yeltsin's regime of 'transition'. See Richard Sakwa, 'Regime Change from Yeltsin to Putin: Normality, Normalcy or Normalisation?' in Cameron Ross (ed.), *Russian Politics under Putin* (Manchester; New York: Manchester University Press, 2004): 17–39.

networks and publishing houses, ousting competing oligarchs who dominated the media landscape in the 1990s.[62] Amidst this state capture of the media, some critical and independent voices, however, were left untouched so long as they didn't appear to threaten the political status quo.[63] Even in the past few years with Western outlets claiming the death of Russia's independent media,[64] pockets of critical reporting continue to survive and challenge the status quo.[65] Critical journalists, highly influential in the late 1980s and still prominent in the 1990s, found themselves isolated from the governance apparatus, engaged in confronting the regime, but achieving little substantive governance change under Putin. The following discussion proceeds to explain the objectives for Putin's regime in tolerating critical voices, as well as for critical journalists in continuing to test the boundaries of the permissible. The analysis shows that critical journalists and the state have adhered to distinct visions with respect to the political role of the media and the notion of media oversight. The discussion further engages with the modes of the state's management of critical voices, showing how it has featured arbitrary coercion rather than guarded improvisation, which has further exacerbated the disengaged relationship between journalists and ruling elites.

The Putin Leadership: Strategic Tolerance of Critical Voices

In contrast to Gorbachev and Chinese party officials, Putin's leadership did not engage critical journalists in substantive governance agenda, but rather treated them as ineffectual, marginal actors. Russian media experts argue that in Russia under Putin, there has been no policy equivalent to China's *yulun jiandu* and no publicly notable high-level intent at

---

[62] Putin's confrontation with and the eventual ousting of Gussinsky, the owner and founder of Media Most company, which contained the critical NTV channel, was the most dramatic blow to media freedom. In 2001, the channel was forcefully taken over by Gazprom, a major state-owned oil company. For a more detailed discussion of the confrontation between Putin and Gussinsky, see Masha Lipman and Michael McFaul, '"Managed Democracy" in Russia: Putin and the Press', *The Harvard International Journal of Press/Politics* 6(3) (2001): 116–127. For a rich account of the appropriation of major media outlets by the regime, see Laura Belin, 'The Russian Media in the 1990s', *Communist Studies and Transition Politics* 18(1) (2002): 139–160.

[63] Maria Lipman, 'Freedom of Expression without Freedom of the Press', *Journal of International Affairs* 63(2) (2010): 153–169.

[64] Konstantin Benyumov, 'How Russia's Independent Media Was Dismantled Piece by Piece', *The Guardian*, 25 May 2016, available at: www.theguardian.com/world/2016/m ay/25/how-russia-independent-media-was-dismantled-piece-by-piece.

[65] Maria Lipman, 'Independent Media Live On in Putin's Russia', Russian Analytical Digest 197 (2017), available at: www.css.ethz.ch/content/dam/ethz/special-interest/ges s/cis/center-for-securities-studies/pdfs/RAD197.pdf.

endorsing media oversight or the media's role as a feedback mechanism.[66] On the contrary, in the past decade, critical media have been isolated from the policy-making apparatus, left to survive on the margins of the political system. Some scholars refer to limited openings in the media sphere as 'islands of press freedom' or 'liberal ghettos' symbolising their disconnectedness from mainstream media and politics.[67] Specifically, the few remaining Moscow-based liberal news outlets have been cut off from access to top public officials and television appearances (television has been mostly brought under control of the state under Putin), left to cater to like-minded audiences of liberal thinkers and intellectuals.

The leadership has exhibited a degree of tolerance towards critical voices, but has used them primarily for image construction purposes rather than for any meaningful policy-making agenda. As argued by Balzer in his analysis of Putin's regime, the goal of maintaining some spaces for political contestation, including those in the media, has been to avoid rather than to enhance accountability. Media observers and scholars note that maintaining these 'islands' poses little political threat and helps authorities construct a more democratic image domestically and internationally.[68] Putin's reaction to the 2006 assassination of Anna Politkovskaya,[69] one of the most famous journalists who covered the war in Chechnya and exposed systemic governance failures of the Putin regime at Russia's primary investigative newspaper, *Novaya Gazeta*, illustrates the combination of the state's indifference towards journalists' criticism and a modest concern for its international image: 'Politkovskaya's ability to influence life in Russia was extremely insignificant, and her murder caused greater danger to Russia than her writings'.[70] This statement points to the official outright dismissal of critical investigations, as well as to their discomfort with an image of 'journalist murderers' projected by the international community.

In another widely cited international statement delivered by Putin about the media, he has fought off Western criticisms of dwindling press freedoms in Russia by pointing to the existing pluralism in the

---

[66] Interviews RSE06; RSE04; RSE03; RSE02; RSE09.

[67] Interview RSE04; See also Lipman, 'Freedom of Expression Without Freedom of the Press'; Adam Federman, 'Moscow's New Rules', *Columbia Journalism Review*, 17 April 2012, available at: www.cjr.org/feature/moscows_new_rules.php.

[68] Interviews RSE04; RSE03.

[69] In 2006, Anna Politkovskaya, a persistent critic of Putin's policy in Chechnya, was murdered outside the elevator in her home. Her murderers have still not been convicted.

[70] 'Putin's Comments on Politkovskaya Anger Activists', *Radio Free Europe/Radio Liberty*, 11 October 2006, available at: www.rferl.org/content/article/1071942.html.

media sphere, especially in print media.[71] While not explicitly referring to critical media, he suggested that given the large number of newspapers, the government couldn't possibly control all of them even if it had intended to do so. Some Russian media practitioners and experts further point to the regime's use of critical outlets, such as the investigative *Novaya Gazeta* as a symbol of media freedom (*vizitnaya kartochka*). 'Someone might be imprisoned in Russia for their articles, but *Novaya Gazeta* will continue to exist and showcase to the outside world that we do have freedom of speech in Russia. If someone criticises the lack of freedom of the press, authorities can point to *Novaya Gazeta* as a counter-example', commented a long-time media practitioner and observer in Moscow.[72]

The pseudo-democratic, yet isolated positioning of critical media in Russia's political system echoes that of other democratic institutions and civil society groups. The regime's superficial engagement with critical media parallels that of its management of elections, judiciary and parliament – all treated as nominal democratic mechanisms, fostering an appearance of political and societal pluralism, while being largely ignored in practice.[73] The political objectives of the regime with regard to critical voices and societal input more broadly are linked to the key characteristics of governance under Putin, including its personalistic and top-down features, as well as the overriding emphasis on maintaining political stability. The combination of the personalistic nature of Putin's regime[74] with an increasing power of the secret services[75] has diminished the regime's need for responding to public opinion and thereby for the feedback role of the media and society. On the one hand, the legitimacy of the Russian regime is tied to Putin's personal popularity, while, on the other, Putin is accountable to specific bureaucracies, less so to a wider public opinion. Moreover, Putin's weakening of institutions, such as the

---

[71] 'President Vladimir Putin Took Part in the 59th World Newspaper Congress', the official site of the Ministry of Foreign Affairs of the Russian Federation, 5 June 2006, available at: www.mid.ru/bdomp/brp_4.nsf/e78a48070f128a7b43256999005bcbb3/715106ca4d6 f2911c32571850043f9af!OpenDocument.

[72] Interview RJ08.

[73] Lilia Fedorovna Shevtsova, 'The Limits of Bureaucratic Authoritarianism', *Journal of Democracy* 15(3) (2004): 67–77; Harley Balzer, 'Managed Pluralism: Vladimir Putin's Emerging Regime', *Post-Soviet Affairs* 19(3) (1 January 2003): 189–227.

[74] Lilia Shevtsova, 'The Return of Personalized Power', *Journal of Democracy* 20(2) (2009): 61–65.

[75] Stephen White, *Understanding Russian Politics* (Cambridge: Cambridge University Press, 2011); Stephen Holmes, 'Conclusion: The State of the State in Putin's Russia', in Timothy J. Colton and Stephen Holmes (eds.), *The State After Communism* (Lanham, MD; Oxford: Rowman & Littlefield, 2006): 299–311; Andrei Illarionov, 'The *Siloviki* in Charge', *Journal of Democracy* 20(2) (2009): 69–72.

courts and the Parliament (Duma), and his centralisation of power enabled him to implement a largely top-down approach (*power vertikal*) in most spheres of policy-making.[76] Directly in charge of approving many political and economic appointments, Putin has had few incentives for inviting bottom-up oversight. In his comprehensive study of state building under Putin, for instance, Taylor writes that the state has 'actively worked to disable mechanisms of popular accountability, favouring internal "police patrols" over external "fire alarms" as a way to monitor state law enforcement'.[77] Finally, Putin has conceived of minimizing public participation in policy-making as conductive to maintaining stability – one of the key premises of his leadership after the turbulent period under Yeltsin.[78] Some scholars refer to state-society relations under Putin as a 'non-participation pact', whereby the regime delivers economic and political stability and the public abstains from political participation.[79] 'The contemporary Russian state does not engage society at large ... Indeed, it actively works to exclude the public from the processes of government, not so much to control the public as to prevent uncontrollable elements—such as a mass-based movement—from entering the political arena ... ' argues Greene in his analysis of protest movements in Russia.[80] Granting media and society a more substantial role in policy-making, therefore, was never on the agenda of the Putin's regime, as it would be deemed politically destabilising.

As evident from the above analysis, the objectives with regard to critical media differ between Russian and Chinese authorities. While both regimes have been motivated by the higher goal of upholding political stability, the former have primarily tolerated critical voices to recreate a façade of democracy, and the latter have encouraged some media oversight to assist in the party's governance. Unlike Putin's rhetoric playing into the Western conceptions of media freedom, the Chinese party's discourse on media supervision does not invoke nor react to Western

---

[76] For a critical assessment of weak institutions and centralisation of power under Putin, see Kathryn Stoner-Weiss, 'Russia: Authoritarianism Without Authority', *Journal of Democracy* 17(1) (2006): 104–118.

[77] Brian D. Taylor, *State Building in Putin's Russia: Policing and Coercion after Communism*, Reprint edition (Cambridge: Cambridge University Press, 2013).

[78] For further discussion of Putin's emphasis on political stability from the very beginning of his rule, see Richard Rose, William Mishler, and Neil Munro, *Popular Support for an Undemocratic Regime* (Cambridge; New York: Cambridge University Press, 2011): 45–46.

[79] Maria Lipman, 'Russia's No-Participation Pact', *Carnegie Endowment for International Peace*, 30 March 2011, available at: http://carnegieendowment.org/2011/03/30/russia-s-no-participation pact/bmkg.

[80] Samuel Greene, *Moscow in Movement: Power and Opposition in Putin's Russia* (Stanford: Stanford University Press, 2014): 7.

ideals, but rather speaks to the internal governance challenges, including vertical accountability and public opinion management. While the actual impact critical journalists have on policy-making in China remains ambiguous, the party's loose incorporation of media supervision into its accountability toolkit assigns journalists more meaning in contrast to their Russian counterparts. These distinct approaches towards critical media are rooted in varieties of authoritarianism, namely the variation in the degree of political fragmentation and in institutional arrangements of the one-party rule versus personalistic governance. As for the former, unlike Putin's centralised or top-down mode of policy-making, which leaves little space for societal accountability channels, China's decentralised apparatus calls for more bottom-up feedback. Whereas in Russia, the top-down or *power vertical* approach to governance might make internal oversight a more fitting strategy in the eyes of the state, China's fragmented authoritarian system, featuring significant variation in local-level implementation of central policy, especially when it comes to economic issues, creates significant oversight loopholes that can be ameliorated with more external supervision. Moreover, while Russia's personalistic regime, intertwined with the security apparatus, is under limited pressure to respond to public opinion, China's one-party state needs to secure broader bases for its legitimacy, as it vows to represent diverse societal interests, and higher officials are directly accountable to the party, rather than to specific interest groups. Responding to public opinion, therefore, remains one of the priorities of the Chinese party-state, which has thus far been in part achieved by creating more feedback loops, including that of the media, as explained in detail in Chapter 3. The endorsement of *yulun jiandu*, therefore, stems from the constraints of China's political system, which differ from those present under another authoritarian model embodied by Putin's regime. As we see in recent years, under Xi's rule, however, the Chinese model might be starting to feature some of Putin's characteristics including a more centralised management of vertical accountability, as explained in the next chapter. Nonetheless, the emphasis on understanding and reacting to public opinion remains more present in contemporary China than it does in Russia, which carries implications for the media's oversight role. We now turn to perspectives of Russia's critical journalists on their relationship with the state, which also diverge from those held by their Chinese counterparts.

Critical Journalists under Putin: Vocal Outsiders

Not surprisingly, in contrast to their Chinese counterparts, Russian critical journalists have adopted a stance of more overt resistance to authority. Specifically, interviews with a wide range of Russia's critical journalists reveal that they are driven to confront and change the system rather than to collaborate with the regime on reforming governance from within. When discussing their political aspirations, Russian journalists allude to contributing to systemic political transformation. These aspirations are reflected indirectly in their critiques of the current political system, as well as in their explicit statements about having to confront the regime as part of their daily work. The following excerpt from an interview with a journalist at *Novaya Gazeta* highlights the broad political agenda aspired to by these journalists:

We want to help people to live freely, so that government changes and becomes more transparent, more dynamic. We wish for the judicial system to work more professionally, we want to help eradicate corruption, stop terrorism against our own citizens, not only on the public level but also on a personal level.[81]

In the above excerpt, the journalist gets at a number of thorny governance issues frequently highlighted by domestic opposition and Western media. They include an opaque decision-making apparatus, a weak rule of law, widespread corruption and violent military operations endorsed by the state both within Russia and in its near abroad, on the grounds of fighting extremism and upholding stability. The journalist's interest in reversing these alleged practices through her reporting alludes to a long-term systemic political vision driving her work. Other interviewees are more forceful about their ambition to stir up the status quo, as exemplified by an excerpt from an interview with an op-ed editor at *Vedomosti* newspaper, Russia's most reputable business daily and the only national-level liberal publication still carrying an editorial page:

It was very hard to come to terms with the fact that while we are living in the 21st century, our political role is now similar to that in the 1970s – fighting against the regime. I still feel it's unproductive, and I find it stupid. This should be done by the political parties, and they should fight for power and authority, not against the regime. But we are forced to be doing this because of the changing circumstances.[82]

By drawing parallels to the 1970s – the period known for political tightening and a shrinking space for public discourse – the editor points to a setback experienced by critical journalists and intellectuals under Putin. His comment also showcases journalists' frustration with acting as opposition rather than solely as media professionals. The interviewee suggests that journalists are in part replacing the functions of other

---

[81] Interview RJ02.   [82] Interview RJ03.

institutions in attempting to keep checks on power and balancing the dominance of the executive, or the personalistic rule of Vladimir Putin.

Some journalists even refer to themselves as 'opposition',[83] while others admit that while they do not act as dissidents in public, in private they hold anti-regime views.[84] The links between critical journalists and opposition have become more prominent in recent years (especially between 2011 and 2013), with many journalists partaking in anti-government demonstrations and some even becoming leaders of the infamous 'white ribbon' movement'.[85] Parkhomenko, for instance, a former editor of a number of popular liberal magazines, including *Itogi*, and Parfionov, a former journalist at state television who later turned into a prominent critic of the regime, have both been leading figures in the protest movement, speaking out at large gatherings and mobilising the public online.[86] The links between critical journalists and opposition are also notable in critical outlets consistently providing platforms for opposition voices cut off from mainstream media. *Ekho Moskvi*, Russia's famous liberal radio station, for instance, has served as a channel for opposition thinkers and leaders, as has the *TVRain*, the remaining independent Russian TV channel, now available only online.[87]

Journalists' anti-regime sentiments and radicalised political motivations appear to be directly linked to their isolated positioning in the political system. Unlike their Chinese counterparts who expect authorities to take notice of their reports and potentially respond with some policy adjustments, albeit at the local level, Russian journalists do not anticipate the state to intervene. When asked whether their investigative and critical reports contribute to policy-making, Russian journalists are dismissive, stressing the regime's indifference towards critical voices.

[83] Interviews RJ03; RJ09.   [84] Interviews RJ06; RJ08; RJ02; RJ13.

[85] The white ribbon movement is associated with the protests that started in the aftermath of the 2011 legislative elections and continued into 2012 and 2013. Protesters attached white ribbons to their clothes and cars in support of fair elections. Xenia Grubstein, 'Should Journalists Participate in Protests?' *Russia Beyond the Headlines*, 12 April 2012, available at: http://rbth.ru/articles/2012/04/12/should_journalists_participate_in_the_protests_15304.html.

[86] The author has followed Parkomenko's posts on social media since the protests erupted in 2011. He has continuously mobilised the public to participate in protests, and also helped with logistical organisation of protests and the opposition movement more broadly. Parkhomenko is featured in a number of Western media accounts of Russian protests. See, for instance, Christian Neef and Matthias Schepp, 'The Battle for Moscow: Russian Opposition at Odds over Path for Future', *Spiegel International*, 14 March 2012, available at: www.spiegel.de/international/europe/anti-putin-protests-continue-in-moscow-a-820900.html. Parfionov made a number of moving speeches at the protests, and also continued to present his position in a talk show he was hosting for *TVRain*.

[87] The author has been a frequent observer of both of these outlets for the past five years.

The former editor of the op-ed page of *Kommersant*, and a well-known political commentator for a number of critical news outlets, expressed frustration and hopelessness at journalists' attempts to influence governance: 'When you tell the government what to do, you feel stupid because they are not listening. Everybody knows that they are not. Nobody's pretending that they are. You cannot reach out to the other side'.[88] The very use of the phrase 'the other side' underscores a vast rupture between critical journalists and decision-makers. A senior investigative journalist at *Novaya Gazeta* similarly stresses the scant impact of media criticism on official decisions:

The main problem is that Russian press, and critical media more broadly, can barely influence anything. In every edition of our newspaper you can find plenty of opportunities for initiating small governance reforms, but nothing happens. At times we do influence policy, when our report is used in some political intrigue or as a justification for someone's opposing opinion.[89]

The above excerpt depicts a political atmosphere whereby media reports are either ignored or used as political capital to tackle an opponent or to gain political favours. The journalist's comment suggests that whereas reports may appeal for some governance reforms, these appeals tend to be generally dismissed by authorities.

Some interviewees further question the importance of reaching out to policy-makers, arguing that shaping individual perceptions is a more realistic pursuit:

Other than the reports on the Vesti TV programme, when some individuals get something changed through a phone call to the Kremlin, I don't know of such cases of direct influence of our reporting. I care about changing people's perceptions [...] that we write an article that helps people understand something and maybe make some changes in their own way. What the Kremlin says, I guess, I don't care about.[90]

This prominent editor at *Vlast'* magazine points not only at the apparent rupture between critical media and official decision-making apparatus but also at journalists' ambivalence about bridging this gap. The interviewee sets an individual, or a reader as her target of influence, keeping expectations for any substantive change in the socio-political landscape to the minimum.

Journalists' marginalisation in the political arena is especially striking in contrast to their dramatic influence on political processes in the 1980s

---

[88] Cited in Lipman, 'Freedom of Expression Without Freedom of the Press'. He conveyed similar views in a personal interview with the author: RJ10.
[89] Interview RJ08.   [90] Interview RJ13.

and 1990s. A long-time investigative journalist who has worked in the media for the past three decades compares the current political climate to that under Yeltsin and Gorbachev: 'During the Yeltsin and Gorbachev era it was a fascinating time for political reporting. Now there is less political reporting, less freedom, and fewer political events ... '[91] Many journalists share this editor's disappointment with the Putin period, reminiscing about the recent past when they were capable of shaping governance and public opinion.

Other than being isolated by the regime, however, critical journalists under Putin also face a public largely indifferent to their cause.[92] According to one of the leading Russian sociologists at Levada Centre, the trust in mass media, and especially in critical outlets was very high during the *perestroika* period but has been crumbling ever since.[93] National public opinion polls about trust in media confirm this general trend of decline, with only 26 per cent of respondents saying that they trusted the media in 2012. Moreover, when asked about whether the government should increase, relax or keep the same level of control over the media, only 16 per cent favoured loosening of restrictions, suggesting that the majority of the public is either ambivalent to or in support of stronger government oversight over the media – a stark change from the euphoric *glasnost* era.[94] A 2016 public opinion poll by Levada that included questions on public perceptions of independent news outlets, such as *TVRain* found that the majority of respondents never consume *TVRain* or *Ekho Moskvi* content, alluding to public apathy towards critical outlets.[95] Some journalists, such as the former editor of *Itogi*, a famous publication of the *perestroika* era, link public indifference towards freedom of speech to disillusionment with democracy in the

---

[91] Interview RJ14.

[92] Michael McFaul and Maria Lipman, 'Putin and the Media', in Dale Herspring (ed.), *The Putin Russia: Past Imperfect, Future Uncertain* (New York: M.E. Sharpe, 2003): 63–84.

[93] Interview RSE02. Other studies on Russian media have reached similar conclusions. See, for example, Floriana Fossato, 'The Russian Media: From Popularity to Distrust', *Current History* 100(648) (2001): 343–347.

[94] The majority of respondents to the media trust question swayed from "incomplete" (*ne vpolne*) trust in the media to complete mistrust (*sovsem net*). *Obshestvennoe Mnenie-2012* (*Public Opinion-2012*) (Moscow: Levada Center, 2013): 152; available: www.levada.ru /cp/wp-content/uploads/2015/09/OM2012.pdf.

[95] *Obshestvennoe Mnenie: 2016* (Public Opinion: 2016)(Moscow Levada Center, 2017): 153, available at: www.levada.ru/cp/wp-content/uploads/2017/02/OM-2016.pdf. Public opinion data from this Levada poll also shows that Russians are aware of censorship in mainstream TV and government interference into media content. This notion of skeptical and critical Russian audiences was eloquently presented in the work by Mickiewicz on Russian television. See: Ellen Mickiewicz, *Television, Power and the Public in Russia* (Cambridge, UK; New York: Cambridge University Press, 2008).

1990s: 'The public thinks we already had democracy and freedom of speech, and it didn't lead to anything good ... [T]he public associates economic stagnation of the 1990s with free press and democracy'.[96] Scholarship on public attitudes towards Putin's rule more broadly has found a generally high support for a stable, centralised, non-democratic regime that emerged in the past decade.[97] Some studies further demonstrate that even those segments of the public partaking in recent anti-Putin protests are still more likely to favour an authoritarian leadership, as opposed to a democratic transition.[98] Public apathy towards critical journalists, therefore, is connected to its disregard for the turbulent democratisation period in the 1990s and its continuing preference for a stable leadership despite the recent signs of growing discontent. Disengaged from both the political system and the wider society, Russia's critical journalists struggle to shift the balance of power.

The motivations for pushing the boundaries of the permissible diverge for critical journalists in Russia and in China. Whereas Russian journalists conceive of themselves as independent critics, and harbour radical aspirations for changing the political status quo, Chinese journalists position themselves as pseudo-partners of the central state and aim for revitalising or at least slightly amending the current system. While Russian critical journalists either explicitly label themselves as 'opposition' or implicitly assume this role by aligning with and stirring anti-regime movements, Chinese journalists assume the function of change-makers within the system, distinguishing themselves from dissidents, at least in public.

The contrast highlights the importance of top-down policies, public attitudes and historical legacies in shaping critical journalists' political objectives in authoritarian contexts. While the regime's disregard for journalists' investigations in Putin's Russia has arguably exacerbated journalists' non-conformist dispositions, the party-state's notable interest in media supervision in China has likely helped keep journalists in the official orbit. Public attitudes towards critical media, featuring aversion in Russia and respect in China, have further served to isolate journalists in the former and to integrate them into the socio-political system in the latter. Finally, the recent experiences with effecting democratic change in Russia, and failing to do so in China, have inspired nostalgia and grand political motives in Russian journalists, and a search for political

---

[96] Interview RJ09.
[97] Rose, Mishler, and Munro, *Popular Support for an Undemocratic Regime*.
[98] Paul Chaisty and Stephen Whitefield, 'Forward to Democracy or Back to Authoritarianism? The Attitudinal Bases of Mass Support for the Russian Election Protests of 2011–2012', *Post-Soviet Affairs* (June 2013).

compromise in their Chinese counterparts. While both Russian and Chinese journalists test the limits of official tolerance, therefore, their motivations for doing so are distinct, and are a product of a combination of factors, including current political context and historic experiences, which in turn shape journalists' relationship with the state. We now turn to examining the process of the regime's management of critical journalists in Russia, which has worked to further alienate them from the political apparatus, marking yet another distinction with the case of China.

Maintaining Coexistence: Freedom of Expression with Arbitrary Coercion

In managing the 'islands of press freedom' within the state-dominated media landscape, Russian authorities under Putin have adhered to a reactive approach. They have rarely resorted to pre-emptive tactics in shaping the content of these marginal outlets, but have occasionally deployed arbitrary coercive punishments against individual journalists or news outlets. While the state's treatment of critical voices has featured a high degree of unpredictability, the way in which it has been deployed, has worked to deter rather than to facilitate interactive improvisation or a closer engagement between journalists and authorities.

Outlets operating on the 'islands of press freedom' have generally not faced the routine political pressures experienced by state media. Unlike Chinese journalists who have juggled with uncertainty over restricted topics on daily bases along with a list of issues that are permanently censored, Russian journalists have struggled to name subjects they are unable to cover. In the past decade, Russia's critical journalists tackled many high-level politically sensitive issues, including corruption, organized crime, separatism and political protests, and even repeatedly expressed direct mockery of the Putin leadership style, according to journalist interviews and the author's media observations. The issues journalists tend to be cautious about are relatively predictable, as they directly concern the interests of their media owners or investors. For instance, journalists and editors at *Novaya Gazeta* are careful about compromising the agenda of their newspaper's main investor, Lebedev, a former intelligence officer turned businessman and Putin critic.[99] Journalists and editors at *Kommersant* and *Ekho Moskvi* are wary of the linkages between Usmanov, the media group's owner and one of Russia's wealthiest businessmen, and the Kremlin.[100] Interviewees also note their

---

[99] Interviews RJ02; RJ08; RJ11.   [100] Interviews RJ04; RJ01; RJ10; RJ13.

concern with potential libel suits and with protecting their sources –
a common consideration for journalists across political contexts. While
Russia's critical journalists undoubtedly practice a degree of self-
censorship, therefore, they are not explicitly told what to downplay in
advance, with editors routinely making careful decisions on the potential
risks of sensitive disclosures and investigations.

These risks include harsh post-facto punishments and pressures, as the
authorities regularly ensure the separation between the 'islands' of press
freedom and the 'continent' of state-controlled media and politics.
As Balzer writes in his discussion of Putin's regime, which he conceptua-
lises as 'managed pluralism': 'The press is free to criticise, but can be
brought to heel at specific times and on important issues ... '[101]
The state's post-factum coercive acts appear to reflect its accumulated
dissatisfaction with a specific outlet or a journalist, aiming to intimidate
critical voices and pre-empt them from expanding and spilling over into
mainstream society. The state applies targeted coercion through personal
relationships with media owners, ambiguous legislation, as well as
indirectly, by condoning violent acts against critical journalists. As for
economic pressures, the authorities have leverage over most media
owners,[102] and can use it to pressure editors of critical publications.
A common tactic has been the replacement of editors, or pressures that
would yield journalists' voluntary resignations. A prominent editor at
Kommersant Vlast', for instance, was forced to leave by the magazine's
owner, Usmanov, after openly supporting anti-Putin protesters in
December 2011.[103] In May 2016, the top editorial team of RBC Media
Group resigned following official pressures applied on the group's owner,
Prokhorov – a billionaire and a 2012 presidential contestant.[104] Other
than directly intimidating media owners, news outlets can also be
squeezed via landlords and advertisers. Interviewees recounted experiences with both. *TVRain* was forced to move its production studio into
a private apartment when its lease was abruptly cut following the

---

[101] Balzer, 'Managed Pluralism'.

[102] Some of the exceptions include Lebedev, the co-owner of *Novaya Gazeta*, and
Lesnevskaya, the owner of *The New Times*. Even these less susceptible owners, however,
have experienced personalised attacks from the Kremlin.

[103] Maxim Kovalsky, the editor of *Vlast'–Kommersant*, was fired by Usmanov after
printing photographs of graffiti with obscene language about Putin. See William
Mauldin and Alexander Kolyandr, 'Moscow Editor Fired over Coverage of Putin',
Wall Street Journal, 14 December 2011, available at: http://online.wsj.com/article/S
B10001424052970203518404577096083626131686.html.

[104] Roy Greenslade, 'Three Russian Editors Resign Amid Threats to Press Freedom',
The Guardian, 17 May 2016, available at: www.theguardian.com/media/greenslade/20
16/may/17/three-russian-editors-resign-amid-threats-to-press-freedom.

channel's forced removal from the cable networks.[105] *Novaya Gazeta* was cautious about criticising Moscow mayor Luzhkov since the newspaper's centrally located office was housed in a building owned by the city government. A senior journalist at the newspaper noted that they were renting the space at a subsidised price, and finding an equally central location at this cost would be nearly impossible.[106] Advertising companies can also be signalled by the state to withdraw from or to minimize their ads in critical news outlets. A *Novaya Gazeta* editor, for instance, recounted an incident of a big commercial enterprise initially agreeing to place adverts but then quickly cancelling the contract after being forewarned by top officials in the Kremlin administration about the political and business risks that such ads would entail.[107]

As for legal pressures, the state has often used vaguely phrased anti-terrorism and especially anti-extremism provisions on the media to punish critical journalists.[108] 'Officials can use the extremism excuse to accuse journalists of unfair depictions of political leaders and biased coverage of social protests, amongst other issues ... [I]n reality, anti-extremism works as a censorship regime [...] but not in terms of permitting but in terms of punishment (post-facto)', remarked a senior journalist, who worked for most of Russia's critical outlets in the past three decades.[109] If a news outlet is found to be breaking the law, it gets a warning, two of which can lead to a closure of an outlet. A number of editors interviewed admit that while closures are rare, vague legislation and official warnings can deter them from investigating certain sensitive issues, thereby alluding to the practice of self-censorship. Journalists appear to struggle with anticipating the topics that would fall under the anti-extremism clause, and are often struck by the peculiarity of official sensitivities. In June 2014, the authorities have extended the anti-extremism provisions to social media content, increasing penalties (up to five years in prison) for spreading information related to 'extremism'.[110] This means that political bloggers, previously little inhibited by the Russian state, now face similar repercussions to those of professional news outlets in writing on contentious topics. The new

---

[105] Jill Dougherty, 'How the Media Became One of Putin's Most Powerful Weapons', *The Atlantic*, 21 April, 2015, available at: www.theatlantic.com/international/archive/2015/04/how-the-media-became-putins-most-powerful-weapon/391062/.

[106] Interview RJ08.   [107] Interview RJ02.

[108] Interview RSE08; See also Laura Belin, 'Politics and the Mass Media under Putin', in Cameron Ross (ed.), *Russian Politics under Putin* (Manchester; New York: Manchester University Press, 2004): 133–155.

[109] Interview RJ11.

[110] Freedom House Russia Report, 2015, available at: https://freedomhouse.org/report/freedom-net/2015/russia.

media provisions have already been dramatically deployed vis-à-vis online only outlets. In 2014, authorities have used anti-extremism legislation as an excuse to block *Grani.ru*, an opposition online media outlet. The outlet was accused of provoking unsanctioned political activities.[111] In the same year, the managing shareholder of the company that owns *Lenta. ru* – another liberal online outlet – fired the chief editor after receiving an official warning of extremism charges.[112] The majority of editors and journalists of the news outlet have quit in protest, leaving *Lenta.ru* to be reappropriated by pro-Kremlin media personnel.

The Russian state has further used other, non-media legislation as an excuse for targeted coercion against individual journalists. For instance, in 2007, Natalia Morar, a Bulgarian journalist working for *The New Times* magazine, was refused entrance into Russia at a Moscow airport under the pretext of her posing a national security threat. This retaliation measure was taken following Morar's publication of an investigative piece about security services and the funding of pro-Kremlin political parties.[113] Such coercive measures have also been deployed against media activists and outspoken political critics. Manana Aslamazian, the former head of Internews Russia,[114] for instance, faced arbitrary corruption charges, leading to her subsequent departure from Russia.[115] Corruption charges have also been levelled against the politically outspoken businessman, Mikhail Khodorkovsky,[116] and most recently against Russia's popular anti-corruption blogger, Aleksey Navalny.[117] Finally, physical retribution remains a real threat for

[111] Konstantin Benyumov, 'How Russia's Independent Media was Dismantled Piece by Piece', *The Guardian*, 25 May 2016, available at: www.theguardian.com/world/2016/may/25/how-russia-independent-media-was-dismantled-piece-by-piece.

[112] Ibid.

[113] 'Reporter Who Wrote about Kremlin Slush Fund Banned from Reentering Russia', *Reporters Without Borders*, 18 December 2008, available at: http://archives.rsf.org/article.php3?id_article=24793.

[114] Internews is a US-based international NGO involved in supporting independent media. See www.internews.org/.

[115] 'Successor of Internews Suspends Activity After Police Search', report by the Committee to Protect Journalists, April 2007, available at: http://cpj.org/2007/04/successor-of-internews-russia-suspends-activity-af.php.

[116] Khodorkovsky, once one of Russia's richest men and the head of oil company, Yukos, was arrested and jailed on corruption charges. The charges against him came in the wake of his open support for liberal opposition and criticism against the Putin's regime. See 'Profile: Mikhail Khodorkovsky', *BBC News*, 30 December 2010, available at: www.bbc.co.uk/news/world-europe-12082222. He was released from jail in December 2013.

[117] Navalny became known for his anti-corruption campaigns, which then expanded into wider political activism. He is now charged with embezzling $500,000 from a timber company and faces a ten-year jail sentence. See Ellen Barry, 'Putin Nemesis Stays Defiant Ahead of Trial', *The New York Times*, 16 April 2013, available at:

Russia's critical journalists, with fifty-six journalists murdered since 1992, according to the Committee to Protect Journalists.[118] 'It was difficult to come to terms with [the fact] that every two to three years someone from our team gets murdered ... Of course, we try not to think of who is next ... ', shared a young journalist from *Novaya Gazeta*,[119] a paper that lost four journalists since 2001, including the internationally renowned Anna Politkovskaya. The 2015 murder of Boris Nemtsov, Russia's outspoken opposition politician who was investigating the government's atrocities in Ukraine, has sparked a new wave of panic amongst Russia's critical voices.[120] While there is no proof that the central authorities are behind these murders, the general climate of fear and the lack of official retribution for the murders keep critical journalists and opposition voices on the margins.[121]

The different tactics often used in conjunction with one another are not easily negotiable for journalists. When it comes to an editorial reshuffling or a closure of an outlet, for instance, other than collectively quitting as an act of protest or attempting to move a media platform elsewhere, individual journalists have little room to push back on the state. The state's coercive acts against journalists under a legal pretext similarly leave journalists largely in retreat especially in cases of selective individual targeting, such as that applied against Morar and Manana. Finally, physical violence is something impossible to push back on. The arbitrariness of these targeted measures is reinforced by their non-institutionalised nature. Interviewees reveal that while they might occasionally guess the reason for an attack, they have difficulty in tracking the source of it, which further limits the opportunities for negotiation. Beyond being difficult to negotiate, these arbitrary acts, especially physical repression, may serve to further galvanise media critics in the direction of opposition to the regime. Following Nemtsov's murder, for instance, the editor-in-chief of *The New Times* magazine proclaimed in an interview with foreign media 'we are at war now'. 'Those who are believers in democracy, those who for some reason, back in the late 1980s, got on board this train, and had all these hopes and aspirations', she said, 'they are at war today'.[122]

www.nytimes.com/2013/04/17/world/europe/trial-of-russian-activist-aleksei-navalny-to-begin.html?pagewanted=all.

[118] www.cpj.org/killed/europe/russia/.   [119] Interview RJ05.

[120] Andrew E. Kramer, 'Fear Envelops Russia After Killing of Putin Critic Boris Nemtsov', *The New York Times*, 28 February 2015, available at:www.nytimes.com/2015/03/01/world/europe/killing-of-boris-nemtsov-putin-critic-breeds-fear-in-russia.html.

[121] 'Media Watchdog Ranks Russia 9th in Unsolved Journalist Killings', *The Moscow Times*, 3 May 2013, available at: www.themoscowtimes.com/news/article/media-watchdog-ranks-russia-9th-in-unsolved-journalist-killings/479543.html.

[122] Kramer, 'Fear Envelops Russia After Killing of Putin Critic Boris Nemtsov'.

While both Russian and Chinese regimes deploy ambiguity to their advantage in dealing with critical journalists, the reactive mode of punishment in Putin's Russia contrasts with that of China's pre-emptive signalling featuring intensive guarded improvisation. Unlike Chinese authorities who create mutual improvisation by actively shaping the space for critical journalism and resorting to more negotiable pressure tactics, Russian authorities under Putin combine a hands-off approach towards critical outlets with arbitrary acts of repression that leaves little space for critical journalists to negotiate. Ironically, while Russian journalists enjoy more freedom of expression, they also operate in the shadow of a more arbitrary state than their Chinese counterparts, for whom constant negotiation remains a daily reality. Whereas in Russia, post-factum management contributes to a more estranged positioning of journalists in the political system, in China, the constant mutual improvisation pulls journalists closer to officials, in a dynamic cat and mouse game that defines their interactions.

To summarise the discussion of the Putin case, the conflicting objectives when it comes to the role of critical media, as well as the mode of the state's containment of critical voices, appears to facilitate a disengaged coexistence between critical journalists and the state in Russia. Unlike Chinese authorities, the Russian leadership has not endorsed media oversight, but has rather tolerated some critical voices for cosmetic purposes of liberal image making. Russian journalists exist on 'islands of press freedom', driven by a political agenda disconnected or opposed to that of the state, and oriented towards democratization of Russian politics. The state's handling of critical voices, featuring a combination of *laissez-faire* attitude with post-facto punishments, in contrast to China's mode of guarded improvisation, further works to minimize the engagement between Russian journalists and officials. Such disconnected relationship appears to have radicalised many liberal journalists who have eagerly joined larger opposition movements against the regime in recent years, and continue to construct their identity as vocal outsiders, opposed to the state's neo-authoritarian agenda. The comparison between the Russian and the Chinese cases demonstrates that while on the surface two similar authoritarian contexts would expect to produce parallel relationships between critical journalists and the state, in reality, their modes of engagement are strikingly different, highlighting varieties of authoritarianism when it comes to participatory mechanisms and the functions of critical press.

Conclusion

This chapter applied the analytical framework of a fluid improvisational collaboration in analysing the relations between critical journalists and the state in other cases, beyond China. The discussion featured two contrasting scenarios of political liberalisation under authoritarian rule: a fleeting and (for the regime) failed cooperation between critical journalists and reformers under Gorbachev and a disengaged coexistence between critical journalists and the Putin regime. The analysis examined the political objectives of authorities and journalists, as well as the modes of the official engagement with critical voices. In the Gorbachev case, while the short-term objectives were congruent between journalists and reformers, their long-term aspirations diverged, with journalists shifting in favour of systemic change. Other than the anti-regime predisposition of critical journalists and the presence of public support for their cause, the rapid open-ended process of media liberalisation shaped this short-lived partnership. Gorbachev adopted an unguarded improvisational approach, with journalists given nearly unlimited scope to negotiate and take advantage of media openings. In the Putin case, the objectives of journalists and the state diverged from the very beginning, with the former pursuing a democratic agenda and the latter using isolated critical media to cover up authoritarian governance. The regime's successful isolation of critical voices from the governance apparatus, combined with the declining public trust in liberal media, forced critical journalists into an uncomfortable coexistence. The state's combination of an indifferent attitude towards marginal critics with arbitrary coercion has further exacerbated the divide between the two actors.

This comparative analysis highlights the advantages of examining the process of limited political liberalisation from both the top-down and the bottom-up perspectives. In particular, it demonstrates that the modes of coexistence between critical journalists and the state can be helpful for understanding the outcomes of partial liberalisation in authoritarian regimes. As the Soviet and Russian examples show, limited liberalisation is just one contingent result. While Gorbachev's reforms have often been used to reassert the links between liberalisation and democratisation, this analysis shows that it is not the liberalisation alone but the objectives of different actors and the process of reform that made it particularly risky, and eventually unsustainable. The analysis of the Putin case contributes to theories on mixed regimes by affirming the findings of other scholars about limited political openings in these regimes mainly serving a nominal role. At the same time, the analysis suggests that isolating critical actors can lead to sharp tensions between state and society, and increase the risks of political instability. As this chapter drew careful comparisons to the China case, it also illuminated important contextual factors that can be conducive to improvisational collaboration. They include historic legacies, as well as institutional opportunities and constraints that not only allow the party-state to incorporate limited political openings but also to create pressures for authorities to respond to public opinion. Finally, the nature of public support, a factor that played an important role in empowering critical journalists under Gorbachev and in undermining them under Putin, might be significant in contributing to collaborative ties between Chinese journalists and the state.

Beyond their comparative significance, the two cases of media management under Gorbachev and Putin have interactive effects with the China case. Whereas Gorbachev's leadership has consistently served as an anti-model for the party-state, Putin's leadership, especially in the Xi era, has in some ways presented itself as a potential model for media and civil society management. These interactive effects across the three cases are something to watch closely as Xi's leadership unfolds.

8 From Hu to Xi
Shifts and Continuities

Drawing on in-depth fieldwork and unique access to Chinese media professionals, experts and officials, this book has set out to investigate the interactions between the party-state and Chinese critical journalists who operate on the fringes of the political system, continuously probing its limits through their reporting. The analysis engaged with exceptional rather than mainstream practices of Chinese media as a way to uncover the pockets of dynamism in what otherwise may appear as a black box of state domination. It sought to explain the role allocated to critical voices in the system renowned for pervasive control, the objectives of journalists vis-à-vis the party, and most of all, the process whereby officials and journalists have managed their thorny coexistence in the past decade.

Challenging the popular antagonistic depictions of the party-state versus its critics, this book presented the subtle dynamics of a fluid collaboration underpinning their relationship. When it comes to invoking and practicing media oversight, journalists and central officials work within the bounds of a shared agenda – that of improving or at least creating an imagery of improvement of the party's governance. Party officials have endorsed media supervision as part of a higher objective of fostering top-down accountability and responding to and guiding public opinion, while journalists, in turn, have largely aligned their vision of political change within the parameters laid down by the central state. These actors have been capable of maintaining their partnership in part due to the flexible nature of this arrangement, or the process of 'guarded improvisation'. The party-state has adopted significant flexibility in its endorsements, restrictions and responses to media supervision, whereas journalists have employed the state's ambiguity to their advantage in pushing the boundaries of the permissible. The central state has remained the dominant party in this assymetrical relationship, guiding its dynamic interactions with journalists by setting out and reinventing boundaries for creative manoeuvring. Journalists, while demonstrating a deep awareness of their state-sanctioned space and generally not venturing outside the grey zone, nonetheless possess professional skills and resources that the state is unable to match or replicate. In the past decade, therefore, critical journalists and higher authorities have improvised with one another, but it is the Chinese Communist Party (CCP) that is the 'band leader', which consistently and uncompromisingly sets the tune.

This concluding chapter reassesses these arguments and the relationship between critical journalists and the party in the context of the latest shifts in media policy and political governance under President Xi Jinping. It further revisits the implications that the constantly evolving journalist-state collaboration holds for China's consultative authoritarianism, as well as for our understanding of participatory channels under authoritarianism and media oversight in the global context. The chapter argues that despite the apparent changes in media politics in the Xi era, the framework for conceptualising the dynamics between critical journalists and the state introduced in this book still holds and will continue to do so into the foreseeable future. What we see are shifts of degree – not of the fundamental nature – of engagement between journalists and officials. The discussion that follows starts with an analysis of Xi's distinctive management of media and civil society, and continues to examine continuities and shifts in journalist-state relations, and concludes by drawing out implications of this study for our thinking on Chinese politics, comparative authoritarianism and media supervision across political spectrums.

Like previous leaders, President Xi has thus far consistently prioritised political stability as the key objective in media and society management. His approach in achieving that, however, has featured a more intensive deployment of repressive tools, combined with enhanced ideology-based propaganda work, and a more centralised mode of upholding vertical accountability. These strategies are a continuation of the previous era, but they have been intensified and expanded under his leadership. As for repression, while it has always constituted an important tactic in the regime's repertoire of manipulation, its magnitude and reach has escalated in recent years. The regime in some ways appears to have retracted from the process of 'civilising'[1] punishment and embraced more violent and deliberate means of control, reminiscent of the Mao period. Commentators and scholars alike have characterised Xi's approach to civil society as that of a crackdown, with some arguing that it marks a fundamental shift not only from the Hu-Wen period but also from

---

[1] The notion of civilising punishment is borrowed from Foucault's analysis of the birth of the prison system and the transition from violent public spectacles and torture to more disciplinary forms of punishment. See Michel Foucault, *Discipline & Punish: The Birth of the Prison* (New York: Vintage Books, 1995).

that of the leadership in the reform era more broadly.[2] Indeed, the number of activists, including journalists, jailed in the past several years is as remarkable[3] as the regime's use of far-reaching coercive threats to induce self-censorship. In the realm of social media, for instance, a campaign against 'false rumours', threatening to delete the accounts of and to detain those allegedly spreading them, has already silenced many contentious users.[4] Whereas in the past it has presented a dynamic space for political discussions, Weibo now appears to be on the decline, with more users, including public opinion leaders, willingly quitting out of fear for political repercussions and even their physical safety.[5] Access to the global internet has also been significantly curtailed with a renewed crackdown on Virtual Private Network (VPN) services that allow for circumventing the Great Firewall.[6] The central leadership has further taken internet control agenda onto the international arena by promoting a model of internet sovereignty and justifying control over cyberspace as part of effective socio-political management.[7]

Beyond the intensity of repression, another striking shift is the scope of its targets, encompassing a wider group of critics than has been the case in the past. While Western media tends to blur together all types of Chinese activists into a recognised category of dissidents, in reality, as underscored in this book, the two have held distinct political visions, with dissidents posing a greater threat to political stability in the eyes of the party. In the

[2] See, for instance, Tom Mitchell, 'Xi's China: Smothering Dissent', *The Financial Times*, 27 July 2016, available at: www.ft.com/content/ccd94b46-4db5-11e6-88c5-db83e98a590a; David Shambaugh, 'The Coming Chinese Crackup', *Wall Street Journal*, 6 March 2015, available at: www.wsj.com/articles/the-coming-chinese-crack-up-1425659198.

[3] The exact numbers are difficult to gauge, as many arrests are not publicly documented. Some human rights organisations, however, argue that already in the first year of Xi's presidency the number of forced detentions has tripled from the previous year. 'Detentions of Chinese Activists Tripled Last Year: Report', *Radio Free Asia*, 3 March 2014, available at: www.rfa.org/english/news/china/detentions-03032014182151.html. Specifically on journalist detentions, see: 'China, Egypt Imprison Record Numbers of Journalists', *Committee to Protect Journalists*, 15 December 2015, available: www.cpj.org /reports/2015/12/china-egypt-imprison-record-numbers-of-journalists-jail.php.

[4] Jonathan Kaiman, 'China Cracks down on Social Media with Threat of Jail for "Online Rumours,"' *The Guardian*, 10 September 2013, available at: www.theguardian.com/wor ld/2013/sep/10/china-social-media-jail-rumours.

[5] 'Censorship, Prosecution Drive Exodus of Opinion Leaders from China's Sina Weibo', *Global Voices Advocacy*, 6 January 2015, available at: http://advocacy.globalvoicesonline .org/2014/01/06/censorship-prosecution-drive-exodus-of-opinion-leaders-from-chinas-si na-weibo/.

[6] Charles Clover, 'China Intensifies VPN Services Crackdown', *The Financial Times*, 23 January 2015, available at: www.ft.com/intl/cms/s/0/46ad9e26-a2b9-11e4-9630-001 44feab7de.html.

[7] 'Xi Defends China's Great Firewall in Push for "Cybersovereignty"', *Bloomberg*, 15 December 2015, available at: www.bloomberg.com/news/articles/2015-12-16/china-s-xi-defends-web-controls-in-call-for-cybersovereignty-.

past, detentions and overt coercion were deployed more readily against dissidents, like the Nobel Prize winner, Liu Xiaobo, but much less so against critics pushing for governance changes within the system, like critical journalists and non-governmental organisation (NGO) activists. In the last three years, however, the two categories have somewhat blurred, with a number of mainstream or within-the-system change-makers, including netizens, NGO activists, lawyers and journalists, arrested to the surprise of external and internal observers alike. Many of the targets, such as feminist NGO activists[8] and labour activists[9] have been carrying out issue-specific campaigns, which did not overtly challenge the legitimacy of the party. In the journalists' circle, a prime example is the arrest of Shen Hao, a former editor at Shanghai's popular *21 Shiji Jingji Baodao*, and an inspiration to many Chinese journalists striving to carry out professional investigative reporting.[10] Shen was arrested on corruption charges, and made a forced confession on China Central Television (CCTV) – a popular ritual under Xi's leadership.[11] While the extent to which this journalist is guilty of the charges is difficult to evaluate, the fact that he was singled out from a media ecosystem rife with corruption, suggests that it may have been a selective attack on more critical voices, according to some Chinese journalists.[12] This wider net of repression signals the state's attempt at redrawing the red line of political sensitivity, and thereby at implicitly curbing or narrowing the grey zone for guarded improvisation.

The repressive-coercive strategies towards critical voices have paralleled a renewed wave of ideological pronouncements and a more forceful and explicit resurrection of the media propaganda role. As with Hu's leadership, Xi's key media speech has emphasised the mouthpiece role of the media. Unlike Hu Jintao's single visit to *Renmin Ribao*, in 2008, however, Xi Jinping has made a more forceful demonstration of his expectation for the media to support the party's interests. In late February 2016, President Xi has carried out a high-profile tour

---

[8] 'Concern for Women's Rights Activists Detained in China', *BBC News*, 9 March 2015, available at: www.bbc.com/news/world-asia-china-31792608.

[9] Mitchell, 'Xi's China: Smothering Dissent'.

[10] Simon Denyer, 'Arrest of Inspirational Editor Shen Hao Marks End of an Era for Chinese Journalism', *The Washington Post*, 9 January 2015, available at: www .washingtonpost.com/world/asia_pacific/arrest-of-inspirational-editor-shen-hao-marks-end-of-an-era-for-chinese-journalism/2015/01/09/4e7e9ece-8924-11e4-ace9- 47de1af4 c3eb_story.html.

[11] Tania Branigan, 'Televised Confessions on State-Run TV Consolidate China's Social Control', *The Guardian*, 11 August 2014, available at: www.theguardian.com/world/20 14/aug/11/televised-confessions-state-tv-china-social-control.

[12] Denyer, 'Arrest of Inspirational Editor Shen Hao Marks End of an Era for Chinese Journalism'.

of the key official media, including CCTV, Xinhua News and *Renmin Ribao*, demanding 'absolute loyalty' from journalists and stressing the key role of the media as that of guiding public opinion.[13] In contrast to his predecessor, who has referred to the media in more general terms, Xi has specifically pointed to official, commercial and new media as all being unified by the objective of 'correct guidance' of public opinion.[14] Some analysts and observers, thereby, note the 'all-dimensional nature' of Xi's control over the media, encompassing all layers of the media ecosystem, from the flagship party media, to competitive commercial outlets to the vibrant social media sphere.[15] The apparent effectiveness of this three-dimensional approach is manifested in the recent success of official media in capturing social media audiences, with top official outlets now out-pacing commercialised press in their popularity online.[16]

In addition to the fusion of repression-propaganda strategies, Xi's deliberate and top-down mode of enforcing vertical accountability is distinctive from the previous leadership. While the Chinese party-state has consistently intended for bottom-up supervision to serve the agenda of top-down oversight, Xi's administration has taken centralised super-vision to a new level. The infamous anti-corruption campaign is the prime manifestation of this trend, as the campaign has been heavily state-managed, with little role assigned to societal forces. Over 100,000 officials have been affected in the course of the largest anti-corruption campaign in Chinese history, including high-level figures such as the former security chief, Zhou Yongkang.[17] The intent appears to be not only to strike at corruption at the highest levels but also to demonstrate the party's ser-iousness in enforcing oversight and thereby threaten officials into com-pliance throughout the party hierarchy. Some facets of this campaign, such as the new disciplinary code (*zhongguo gongchangdang jilu chufen tiaoli*, 中国共产党纪律处分条例), passed on 1 January 2016, resonate with the Mao period. The code, which encompasses a detailed list of offenses and punishments, places any party member under potential

[13] Tom Phillips, 'Love the Party, Protect the Party': How Xi Jinping is Bringing China's Media to Heel', *The Guardian*, 27 February, 2016, available at: www.theguardian.com /world/2016/feb/28/absolute-loyalty-how-xi-jinping-is-bringing-chinas-media-to-heel.

[14] David Bandurski, 'Mirror, Mirror On the Wall', *China Media Project*, 22 February 2016, available at: http://cmp.hku.hk/2016/02/22/39646/.

[15] Ibid.

[16] Maria Repnikova and Fang Kecheng, 'Persuasion 2.0 under Xi: State-Sanctioned Civility Goes Digital', Paper presented at the China Internet Research Conference, Edmonton, 8 May, 2015.

[17] 'China's Anti-Corruption Campaign Ensnares Tens of Thousands More', *Foreign Policy*, 9 January 2015, available at: http://foreignpolicy.com/2015/01/09/chinas-anti-corruption-campaign-ensnares-tens-of-thousands-more/.

scrutiny.[18] This state-led offensive, however, has ironically paralleled its silencing and jailing of anti-corruption activists,[19] who had demanded that high-level officials declare their assets to the public. Central officials, therefore, are driven to manage the campaign from the top, granting little space for bottom-up activists to partake in facilitating oversight.

These shifts in Xi's strategies for upholding political stability, with intensified repression, propaganda and top-down oversight working together to contain societal activism, have undoubtedly affected the scope for critical journalism in recent years. Some journalists interviewed for this book have moved into less politically sensitive endeavours. A senior editor at *Caijing* interviewed back in 2012, for instance, has quit the magazine after facing pressures following a publication of an anti-corruption report, and is now working in a private enterprise, while some investigative journalists at *Caixin* and *Nanfang Dushi*bao have switched to Western media outlets, such as the BBC, or Hong Kong news outlets that still enjoy more independence than their mainland counterparts.[20] Others, especially some journalists at *Nanfang Zhoumo*, which has recently experienced a significant decline in commercial and political freedom, have opted for social entrepreneurship or academic careers abroad.[21]

All this having been said, much of the dynamic interaction between journalists and the state has continued, even as it is being eclipsed by the more 'newsworthy' reports of the party's crackdowns and ideological recalibration. Now, as before, journalists creatively walk the thinning political line and investigate and discuss governance. In the past two years, *Caixin* magazine in particular, has published a number of breakthrough reports on corruption, as well as on other thorny governance issues, such as environmental degradation.[22] These revelatory reports drew criticism and warnings from propaganda authorities, but no other, graver repercussions, such as firing of journalists or detentions, have ensued thus far.[23] Whereas with some exceptions, publications in the

---

[18] Leo Lin, 'To Purge or Not to Purge: China's Anti-Corruption Campaign: A New Code Marks a Return to Maoist Practices', *The Diplomat*, 15 February 2016.

[19] 'China Jails Corruption Activists', *BBC News*, 11 March 2015, available at: www.bbc.com/news/world-asia-china-27917234.

[20] The author has followed up on career shifts of many of the interviewees via communication online, as well as in person during a visit to Beijing in June–July 2016.

[21] Maria Repnikova and Kecheng Fang, 'Behind the Fall of China's Greatest Newspaper', *Foreign Policy*, 30 January 2015, available at: http://foreignpolicy.com/2015/01/29/south ern-weekly-china-media-censorship/.

[22] The most famous investigative coverage by *Caixin* concerns corruption of China's fallen security chief, Zhou Yongkang. A forty-five-page compilation of reports is still available on the magazine's website: http://china.caixin.com/2014-10-22/100741777.html.

[23] The author has followed up on *Caixin* developments through several Skype conversations with their reporters.

Nanfang Media Group have pursued less critical coverage under Xi,[24] China's largest internet portals, Tencent and Sohu, have emerged as new platforms for in-depth reporting.[25] Even though in July 2016 the party-state has cracked down on independent news reporting by social media platforms,[26] informal follow-ups with journalists working for these news platforms in July 2016 and February 2017 reveal that they resumed reporting, again pointing at the improvised engagement between journalists and officials.[27] In the past two years, we are also seeing a development of state-sanctioned digital-only news outlets, such as *Pengpai* and *Jiemian*, that have carried more professional political and economic reporting, including investigative journalism. Moreover, some journalists continue to publish as freelancers through online channels, according to the latest follow-up interviews, while others embrace new creative platforms for sending a powerful political message. A documentary criticising China's environmental policy by Chai Jing, a former investigative journalist at CCTV, for instance, has attracted millions of views, including from

[24] The issues for the decline of the group are more complex than Xi's media crackdown and involve local-level and commercial pressures. For a detailed examination of *Nanfang Zhoumo*, see Maria Repnikova and Kecheng Fang, 'Behind the Fall of China's Greatest Newspaper', *Foreign Policy*, 30 January 2015, available at: www.tealeafnation.com/2015/01/behind-the-fall-of-chinas-greatest-newspaper/.

[25] In the past several years, Tencent has intensified its journalism platform, including a separate unit involved in in-depth reporting. The most striking investigative report recently published by Tencent concerns corruption within China's Red Cross. The report has since been censored, but last time checked it could still be found here: www.weibo.com/p/1001603745261217292574?from=page_100505_profile&wvr=6&mod=wenzhangmod. In July 2016, the party-state has cracked down on news reporting by social media platforms by resurrecting old legislation that outlaws them to pursue independent reporting. Informal follow-ups with journalists working for these news platforms in July 2016 and February 2017 reveal that after waiting out the ban, they continued to report, again pointing at the improvised engagement between journalists and officials.

[26] The party resurrected old legislation that outlaws social media platforms from pursuing independent reporting. For more details, see: Edward Wong and Vanessa Piao, 'China Cracks Down on News Reports Spread via Social Media', *The New York Times*, 5 July 2016, available at: www.nytimes.com/2016/07/06/world/asia/china-internet-social-media.html.

[27] Contacts at Sohu revealed that they took a 'break' after the ban and then changed their platform's name to *Jujiao Renwu* (聚焦人物). For examples of investigative reports post-ban, see Sohu's report on corruption in the medicine testee business: Yao Shun, 'Shi yao liantiao zhong de yaotou: dadian yisheng la danzi yue zhuan 3 wan' (Yaotou role in the chain of medicine testing: the examining doctor gets a profit of 30,000 yuan per month), *Jujiao Renwu*, 31 December, 2016, available at: http://mt.sohu.com/20161231/n47747 2896.shtml. Tencent Lengjing, a financial investigative news site on Tencent platform, for instance, published an investigation into the development of China's P2P lending industry. See: Zhou Chun, 'Wang dai zhoubian chanye diaocha: juejinzhe xiaotui du shuizhe anzai?' (Investigation into P2P Lending Industry: As Opportunitists Fade Away, Where are the Service Providers?), *Lengjing Tengxun*, 14 November 2016, available at: http://finance.qq.com/original/lenjing/wangdai.html.

central officials, stretching the limits of permissible public discourse on a topic of high public concern.[28] Other journalists are deploying social media platforms to start media enterprises that would present news features online. In June 2016, for instance, a team of journalists at *Pengpai* left to start their own media company, Pear Video, that does digital video reporting and in-depth features.[29] In addition to mainland-based outlets, new creative initiatives are springing up in Hong Kong. The Initium, a new media start-up in Hong Kong, that projects itself as the 'quality digital media for the global Chinese community', has captured four million monthly views as of March 2016, with much of the readership originating from mainland China (accessed via VPN).[30] Other than more news-oriented platforms and outlets, new genres, such as creative non-fiction and satirical talk shows online are exploding in China to the point that they are becoming lucrative businesses.[31] While politics may be getting harder to talk about, savvy writers, journalists and producers are turning to novel literary expressions to engage with complex societal issues that are implicitly linked to politics. These developments point to the importance of stretching the notion of the 'political' in the Chinese context and thinking of cultural and literary expressions as having a political resonance in a society with tightening government controls. In short, pockets of critical journalism have shrunk, but have managed to survive and redefine themselves in the Xi era.

These examples, and many more point to the fact that although the socio-political context in the past four years has undergone some changes, the rules of the game for journalist-state interactions have remained largely the same. The fluid collaboration framework, introduced in this book, continues to underpin the persisting coexistence between critical

[28] Mark Tran, 'Phenomenal Success for New Film That Criticises China's Environmental Policy', *The Guardian*, 11 March 2015, available at: www.theguardian.com/world/2015/mar/02/chinaenvironmental-policy-documentary-under-the-dome-chai-jing-video.

[29] For more on Pear Video, see: Manya Koetse, 'The Rise of Pear Video (梨视频): Making Short News Videos Trending on Chinese Social Media', *What's On Weibo*, 13 January 2017, available at: www.whatsonweibo.com/rise-pear-video-梨视频-making-short-news-videos-trending-chinese-social-media/.

[30] 'New Hong Kong Media Startup Attempts to Capture Chinese Global Market', *World Association of Newspapers and News Publishers*, 2 March 2016, available at: http://bit.ly/1WWngKX. The capture of mainland Chinese market was revealed in recent interviews with one of the leading editors at The Initium.

[31] On the boom in creative non-fiction, see: Tabitha Speelman, 'Telling True Stories is a Booming Business in China', *Supchina*, 17 January 2017, available at: http://supchina.com/2017/01/18/telling-true-stories-is-a-booming-business-in-china/. On talk shows and general digital creativity under Xi, see: Maria Repnikova and Kecheng Fang, 'China's New Media: Pushing the Boundaries Without Being Political', *Foreign Affairs*, 12 October 2016, available at: www.foreignaffairs.com/articles/china/2016-10-12/chinas-new-media.

journalists and the party-state under Xi's leadership. As for shared objectives, the regime continues to engage media oversight in selective policy agenda, and journalists, in their professional writings, still conform to the political status quo.

The official disregard for public opinion feedback loops is not anywhere near absolute. While consultative channels have been less explicitly invoked under Xi's leadership, media supervision still remains in the shadows of the party's media policy, and authorities have indirectly engaged the media in some governance campaigns. As with the official discourse in the Hu-Wen period, the media supervision role has been invoked by central leadership in conjuncture with propaganda policy. A summary of Xi's media policy, published in *Renmin Ribao*, stated that 'supervision by public opinion and positive propaganda are unified',[32] implying that the former is only welcomed in so far as it helps the latter – the logic prevalent in the past decade, as explained in Chapter 3. As for initiatives to collaborate with the media, some media and individual journalists appear to have been allowed to facilitate the party's oversight agenda by being granted unprecedented space for critically examining individuals, groups and issues already under official scrutiny. In the case of corruption, for instance, *Caixin* has published a number of hard-hitting reports about officials investigated by the party, including several on Zhou Yongkang, and the magazine has even opened a special unit for anti-corruption investigations. Follow-up conversations with *Caixin* journalists suggest that the magazine was unofficially granted this collaborator role, as evident by its surprising ability to get away with high-level investigations.[33] In the case of the environmental campaign, the state-driven cooperation is less explicit, but yet still present. The Environmental Minister, for instance, has complimented Chai Jing's documentary, 'Under the Dome', for facilitating public discussion on pollution.[34] And while the film has by now been shuffled into the red zone, the authorities are prioritising the issue at high-level meetings, including at the Eleventh and Twelfth National People's Congresses.[35]

---

[32] Bandurski, 'Mirror, Mirror on the Wall'.

[33] The exact phrasing used by a journalist from Caixin magazine was 'invited to investigate' – suggesting that there were signals received by top editors to report on specific individuals.

[34] Anthony Kuhn, 'The Anti-Pollution Documentary That's Taken China By Storm', *NPR.org*, 14 May 2015, available at: www.npr.org/blogs/parallels/2015/03/04/3906890 33/the-anti-pollution-documentary-thats-taken-china-by-storm.

[35] 'Environmental Issues Top Major Legislative Meeting in China – US News', *US News & World Report*, 12 March 2015, available at: www.usnews.com/news/world/articles/2015/03/ 07/environmental-issues-top-major-legislative-meeting-in-china; 'China to Complete Environmental Supervision Reform in Two Years', *Xinhua News*, 11 March 2016, available at: http://news.xinhuanet.com/english/2016–03/11/c_135179328.htm.

There has also been notable tolerance and responsiveness to investigative coverage of some national crises. The aftermath of the deadly chemical explosion in Tianjin, for instance, one of the worst man-made disasters in China's recent history, saw a number of in-depth media investigations, including those conducted by *Caijing* and *Caixin*, but also by more mainstream outlets, like *Xinjing Bao*, and new media platforms like Tencent and Netease.[36] The topics investigated include the offending company's access to registration permits for storing the toxic materials, the ownership structure of the company and the deadly fate of the innocent fire fighters. As in the Hu-Wen period, the state's limited tolerance for these reports was combined with a demonstrative policy response in the form of investigations and public punishment, with 123 people punished for the Tianjin explosion.[37]

As for critical journalists' continuing implicit support for the status quo, the major investigations and critical reports introduced above have either directly corresponded to the party-state's agenda, as was the case with corruption stories; or looked at specific failures associated with disasters, targeting primarily local officials and company managers, as was the case with investigations of Tianjin, and has been the pattern over the past decade; or they looked at the mainly human interest side of the stories (via literary non-fiction genre) as has been the focus of *Nanfang Zhoumo*.

In maintaining their fluid collaboration, guarded improvisation has remained at the heart of the official-journalists' interactions. A substantial ambiguity is notable in the official mode of facilitating, guarding and responding to media supervision. The endorsement of media oversight is even more muted and indirect than it was under Hu-Wen's leadership, with supervision only mentioned in passing and in unison with the media propaganda role. As for guarding the spaces for investigative journalism, despite the heightened emphasis on what appears as strategic pre-emptive control of dissent via repression and deliberative coercive measures, the number of journalists jailed represents a small minority of the total, and the official management of the media still primarily relies on ad hoc restrictions, some being applied prior to publication, others in its aftermath. The official reaction to Chai Jing's environmental documentary is a vivid manifestation of these dynamics. The authorities allowed the controversial film to run on social media for days before issuing a censorship ban.[38] It appears that as with other critical reporting discussed in this book, the officials were waiting to get a sense of public reactions online before obliterating the sensitive content and crafting a high-level policy response. Tianjin investigations were also mildly pre-censored, and further restricted post-factum, but journalists were still implicitly granted a short window to carry out their reporting.[39] Paralleling the dynamics that emerged in the last years of the Hu-Wen administration, breaking stories on the disaster first appeared on social media, making full concealment an impossible strategy, and forcing authorities to adapt on the spot.[40] In responding to media investigations of major crises, the official reaction continued to feature a degree of improvisation, with immediate responsiveness being fused with more ambivalent policies on systemic reform, as similar man-made disasters have kept reoccurring over time. The Tianjin explosion, for instance, was followed by the collapse of an illegal waste dump in Shenzhen, killing eighty-five people.[41] The incident, again, was marred by corruption and ineffective local-level oversight – the same systemic ills that have underpinned the school scandal and the mining disasters in the Hu-Wen era.

As for journalists, they have continued to creatively improvise with restrictions by deploying the toolkits of the Hu-Wen era, including by spreading news via social media and outrunning the censors. In the aftermath of a censorship ban, journalists have at times succeeded in sharing their reports with the public online. In the case of a recently banned Tencent report on Red Cross corruption, for instance, a version of the article was made available on Weibo.[42] As demonstrated throughout this book, moreover, critical journalists also continue to be the provocateurs of interactive improvisation by outrunning censorship and delving into topics deemed as potentially sensitive by the regime. 'The restrictions will come sooner or later, so we have to get a move on! Let the bans race against truth!' shared a journalist investigating Tianjin, cited in the analytical report on the crisis.[43] In the process of conducting investigations, journalists have also continued to actively navigate the official pressures

---

[38] Editorial Board, 'A Documentary on Air Pollution Sparks a Code Red in China', *The Washington Post*, 9 March 2015, available at: www.washingtonpost.com/opinions/a-documentary-on-air-pollution-sparks-a-code-red-in-china/2015/03/09/c0fd352a-c5e5-11e4-a199-6cb5e63819d2_story.html.

[39] Xiao, 'Chinese Media and the Tianjin Disaster'.   [40] Ibid.

[41] Shannon Tiezzi, ' Construction Waste Landslide Buries 85 in Shenzhen', *The Diplomat*, 22 December 2015, available at: http://thediplomat.com/2015/12/construction-waste-landslide-buries-85-in-shenzhen/.

[42] www.weibo.com/p/1001603745261217292574?from=page_100505_profile&wvr=6&mod=wenzhangmod.

[43] Xiao, 'Chinese Media and the Tianjin Disaster'.

by collaborating online. When Weibo became too restricted, journalists switched to Weixin – a more segmented platform, as it requires permission to enter a specific chat circle – but also a more private channel, allowing journalists to communicate in smaller, closed groups. Surveillance over Weixin has recently intensified, but thus far it still constitutes a widely used mechanism for collaborating and bypassing censorship for Chinese journalists. The creativity underpinning the back-and-forth engagements between journalists and authorities, therefore, has not dissipated, but on the contrary, has appeared to amplify in the context of a more sensitive political climate.

The fluid collaborative ties between critical journalists and party officials, however, are also beginning to feature new tensions and expressions that may shift into more radical engagements between the two parties in the future. Namely, as the party-state, and especially President Xi, has become more vocal about enforcing, expanding and refining the media propaganda role, and as widespread crackdowns on social media continue, some journalists and public intellectuals have begun to openly question censorship and debate official media policy. This is something that we haven't seen much of in the Hu-Wen era, with the exception of the *Nanfang Zhoumo* incident in 2013, as discussed earlier in this book. Ren Zhiqiang, a social media celebrity and a high-profile real estate tycoon, quoted Leo Tolstoy on his social media post as a rebuke to the party's intensifying censorship: 'Ignorance in itself is neither shameful nor harmful. Nobody can know everything. But pretending that you know what you actually do not know is both shameful and harmful'.[44] This post attracted thirty-seven million views before Ren's account was deleted by authorities. Weeks after President Xi made his paramount media address, *Caixin* magazine published an interview about the importance of free speech with a prominent Shanghai academic and political adviser, Jiang Hong. The article was quickly censored, but *Caixin* struck against censorship by posting an article on its English-language website, titled as 'Story about Adviser's Free Speech Comments Removed from Caixin Website'.[45] Directly publicising and exposing the state censorship apparatus is unprecedented for this magazine. Even some members of official media channels, typically reticent in their online expression of political critique, have recently voiced their disappointment with the narrowing

[44] Josh Chin, 'China's Censorship Clampdown Stirs a Pushback', *The Wall Street Journal*, 29 February 2016, available at: www.wsj.com/articles/chinas-social-media-muzzling-of-ren-zhiqiang-highlights-clampdown-1456765492.
[45] Tom Phillips, 'Chinese Magazine Challenges Government Over Censorship', *The Guardian*, 8 March 2016, available at: www.theguardian.com/world/2016/mar/08/chinese-magazine-challenges-government-censorship-organ.

space for public discussion. 'China should open up more channels for criticism and suggestions and encourage constructive criticism', read a 14 February 2016 Weibo post by Hu Xijin, the editor of *Global Times*.[46] In March 2016, an open letter signed as 'loyal party members', and calling for President Xi's resignation, was posted on a new state-run website, *Wujie*.[47] The letter attributed recent political, economic, ideological and cultural tensions to Xi's centralisation of power. Informal follow-up interviews with critical journalists over the past year suggest that practising journalists are increasingly wary of the challenging political climate and disappointed by the intensity of restrictions on their work, which leaves less space for meaningful journalism that would benefit as much the party's governance as the society at large. With the exception of the open letter, which has attracted much speculation, individual expressions of critique have thus far still called for constructive solutions and openings that are aligned with the party's governance agenda – the same rhetoric expressed by journalists interviewed in this book. As in the past, these individual expressions and incidents have not translated into an organised societal or media stance against censorship. The sparks of debate about media policy, however, signal the new fractures that arise between journalists and officials when the party-state narrows collaboration and escalates repression and ideology in its engagement with the media and the broader public.

The evolving relationship between China's critical journalists and the party-state underscores that the tensions between the pay-offs and the costs embedded in maintaining limited media supervision, bottom-up activism and fluid consultative governance are increasingly coming onto the surface. As already evident from the analysis of the Hu-Wen era, flexible consultations, including those via the media channels, appear to facilitate political resilience in the short term, while carrying significant political vulnerabilities in the long term. The conflicting agenda of local officials vis-à-vis the media, the centre's weak response to systemic issues and the rising public expectations of official responsiveness – are all by-products of fluid consultations that are ever more apparent in the Xi era. Unlike Putin's more disconnected and state-dominated model for governing society, the Chinese dynamic consultative model is proving more challenging to sustain. President Xi appears to be acutely aware of these challenges, and has opted for downplaying consultations in favour of

---

[46] Chin, 'China's Censorship Clampdown Stirs a Pushback'.
[47] 'Loyal Party Members Urge Xi's Resignation', *China Digital Times*, 16 March 2016, available at: http://chinadigitaltimes.net/2016/03/open-letter-devoted-party-members-urge-xis-resignation/. Conversations with former Wujie journalists in the summer of 2016 suggest that the publication was due to a technical error rather than political intent, but it nonetheless remains puzzling as to who were the originators of this letter. Wujie was shut down quickly after this controversy.

recentralising his political base and silencing opposing voices, while still tolerating some narrow, tightly managed interactions with society. In some ways, Xi's approach resembles more the Putin-style personalistic governance than that of the Leninist one-party system. At the same time, critical actors, including journalists, are not entirely silenced, and they persist in navigating the often-conflicting signals coming from the state. As we continue to observe the evolution of these dynamics, the framework of a fluid collaboration will remain an important instrument not only for gauging a more comprehensive picture of these changes but also for grasping when the shifts may signal larger political transformations. If the fractures between journalists and officials intensify and evolve into a disconnected relationship, akin to that of the Russian case, it may signal a potential radicalisation of critical voices and a rising insecurity of the party apparatus about bottom-up threats to its survival, which would in turn lead us to question its adaptive capacity in the long term. As some China watchers are once again starting to predict the doom of China's one-party system, the engagement between critical journalists and party authorities is an ever-important lens that illuminates the driving tensions in China's evolving polity.

Turning back to the field of comparative authoritarianism, the contested collaboration between China's critical journalists and the party-state points to the importance of a broader treatment of participatory channels in non-democracies, and a stronger emphasis on examining the process whereby they are negotiated between the state and society and the opportunities they present for constructive input of public preferences into the policy arena. The analysis and reflections on journalist-state relations in the Xi period further highlight the significance of ambiguity as a feature that can simultaneously sustain and erode bottom-up participation in authoritarian contexts. Xi's escalation of the climate of uncertainty has at once inhibited constructive media criticism, and provoked more creative negotiation of censorship, including the very questioning of roles that the media should play by some Chinese media professionals and intellectuals. While this book has demonstrated that bounded political openings under authoritarianism may serve alternative governance purposes beyond cosmetic image construction or democratisation, the reflection on the Xi period further underscores not only the ambiguity and vulnerability of these feedback channels but also their importance in informing us of the evolution of a given authoritarian system. The shifts in media supervision under Xi, for instance, may signify China's drift away from the model of consultative and responsive authoritarianism explained in Chapter 2, which in turn may invite new comparative research into bases for legitimacy and public support under authoritarianism.

Beyond China and authoritarian politics, the conclusions in this book transcend contextual boundaries and have interesting implications in a broader comparative perspective. Specifically, there are important points of convergence in media practices between democratic and non-democratic contexts, often overlooked in the existing scholarship that tends to emphasise distinctions. The common association of investigative journalism and the media watchdog role with democracies is outdated, as a limited media oversight role can be sustainable even in repressive media environments, like China. Moreover, critical journalists appear to share some common challenges across political contexts. Recent studies on journalism in the West, namely in the United States, for instance, find the media oversight role increasingly under threat, as journalists struggle to manage political pressures of having to maintain relationships with power holders[48] and deal with intensifying government surveillance.[49] Under the Obama administration, journalists have not only faced the threat of spying accusations but also the challenge of securing access to insider sources as self-censorship has veiled over the government apparatus. Most recently, President Trump has declared professional news media 'the enemy of the American people' and repeatedly dismissed reports critical of his policies as 'fake news',[50] further rupturing the relations between the media and the state, and suggesting more barriers are to come on media's attempts to hold power accountable. Though undoubtedly more pervasive and more institutionalised, political pressures, including surveillance, persecution, limits on official information access, as well as official hostility towards explicit criticism, are all common in China, as shown throughout this book, and as evident in the analysis of the Xi period. Self-censorship is also a powerful force across political contexts, as journalists' voluntary collusion with high-level political interests complicates their potential for exercising full-scale oversight over political decision-making. As demonstrated by the inability of the elite US media to provide a counter-frame to the official discourse on the war in Iraq,[51] journalists can be co-opted in the government apparatus

---

[48] Bartholomew H. Sparrow, *Uncertain Guardians: The News Media as a Political Institution* (Baltimore, London: Johns Hopkins University Press, 1999).

[49] An extensive report released in 2014 by the American Civil Liberties Union and Human Rights Watch, drawing on interviews with many journalists from top US media outlets, shows that government surveillance has complicated journalists' work. See www.aclu.org/human-rights-national-security/report-finds-nsa-surveillance-harming-journalism-and-law.

[50] 'Trump Declares Media "The Enemy of the American People"', *AlJazeera*, 18 February 2017, available at: www.aljazeera.com/news/2017/02/trump-declares-media-enemy-american-people-170218044918267.html.

[51] W. Lance Bennett, Regina G. Lawrence, and Steven Livingston, *When the Press Fails: Political Power and the News Media from Iraq to Katrina*, Reprint edition (Chicago, IL; Bristol: University Of Chicago Press, 2007).

regardless of the political system. The specific reasoning guiding their decisions to self-censor may differ, but the outcome in the form of collaboration with authorities is the same across contexts. It is timely, therefore, to view distinctions in media control and media oversight as different shades of grey, as opposed to opposing absolutes engrained in authoritarian or democratic systems. New comparative research is needed into how media oversight is being exercised amidst political restrictions, including investigation into divergent resistance practices, as well as into potential trans-border collaborative efforts led by journalists in their attempts to navigate sophisticated political efforts to minimise transparency.

Appendix A   List of Interviews

	China	
	Journalists	
CJ01	Anchor at CCTV's *Mian dui Mian* programme	August 2009
CJ02	Former editor at *Bingdian*	September 2009
CJ03	Legal correspondent at *Caijing*	September 2009
CJ04	Investigative journalist at *Caijing*	October 2009
CJ05	Investigative journalist at *Caijing*	October 2009
CJ06	Editor at *Bolian* blog, former Xinhua journalist and editor	October 2009
CJ07	Reporter at *Renmin Ribao*	October 2009
CJ08	Editor-in-chief at *Daxuesheng* magazine	October 2009
CJ09	Online editor at *Jingji Guanchabao*	October 2009
CJ10	Investigative journalist at *Nanfang Renwu Zhoukan*	October 2009
CJ11	Investigative journalist at *Nanfang Dushibao*	October 2009
CJ12	Editor at *Sohu* blog	October 2009
CJ13	Former managing editor at *Caijing*, now managing editor at *Caixin*	November 2009
CJ14	Op-ed editor at *Xinjing Bao*	November 2009
CJ15	Editor-in-chief of international news at Xinhua News Agency	November 2009
CJ16	Investigative journalist at *Caijing* (now at Caixin)	November 2009
CJ17	Investigative journalist at *China Economic Times*	November 2009
CJ18	Investigative journalist at *Nanfang Dushibao*	November 2009
CJ19	Online editor at *Caijing*	November 2009
CJ20	Investigative journalist at *Zhongguo Qingnian Bao*	November 2009
CJ21	Producer at *Mian dui Mian*	November 2009
CJ22	Editor at *Bingdian*	November 2009
CJ23	Features and investigative journalist at Xinhua News Agency	December 2009
CJ24	Senior investigative journalist at *Zhongguo Qingnian Bao*	June 2012
CJ25	Editor-in-chief at *Caijing*	June 2012
CJ26	Former editor at *Nanfang Zhoumo*, now a legal correspondent in Beijing	July 2012
CJ27	Op-ed editor at *Xinjing Bao*	July 2012
CJ28	Editor-in-chief of the investigative unit at *Zhongguo Jingji Guanchabao*	July 2012

(*cont.*)

	China	
	Journalists	
CJ29	Investigative journalist at *Caijing*	July 2012
CJ30	Editor at *Nanfang Dushibao*	July 2012
CJ31	Former editor at *Bingdian*, now an independent journalist	July 2012
CJ32	Former editor at *Nanfang Zhoumo*, now editor at *Tencent*	July 2012
CJ33	Producer at *Xinwen Diaocha*, CCTV	July 2012
CJ34	Reporter at *Caixin*	July 2012
CJ35	Reporter at *Caixin*	July 2012
CJ36	Editor at *Caixin (formerly at Caijing)*	July 2012
CJ37	Investigative journalist at *Caijing*	July 2012
CJ38	Features correspondent at *Caijing*	August 2012
CJ39	Investigative journalist at *Caixin*, former *Nanfang Dushibao* journalist	August 2012
CJ40	Former editor at *Nanfang Zhoumo*, now editor at *Yidu*	August 2012
CJ41	Former journalist at *Nanfang Zhoumo*, now journalist at *Yidu*	August 2012
CJ42	Editor at *Huanqiu Shibao*	August 2012
CJ43	Journalist at *Nanfang Dushibao*	August 2012
CJ44	Editor at *Caixin*	August 2012
CJ45	Journalist at *Nanfang Dushibao*	August 2012
CJ46	Journalist at *Nanfang Zhoumo*	August 2012
CJ47	Former investigative journalist at *Caijing*	August 2012
CJ48	Investigative journalist at *Nanfang Zhoumo*	August 2012
CJ49	Journalist at *Nanfang Dushibao*	August 2012
CJ50	Investigative journalist at *Nandu Zhoukan*	August 2012
CJ51	Investigative journalist at *Jingji Guanchabao*	August 2012
CJ52	Senior journalist at *Caijing*	August 2012
CJ53	Journalist at *Nanfang Renwu Zhoukan*	August 2012
CJ54	Journalist at *Caixin*	August 2012
CJ55	Journalist at *Nanfang Zhoumo*	August 2012
CJ56	Investigative journalist at *Nanfang Dushibao*	August 2012
CJ57	Investigative journalist at *Nanfang Nongcun*	August 2012
CJ58	Editor at *Global Times* (English version)	August 2012
CJ59	Former investigative journalist at *Nanfang Renwu Zhoukan*	August 2012
CJ60	Journalist at *Bingdian*	August 2012
CJ61	Freelancer and commentator for online platforms	August 2012
CJ62	Retired former investigative reporter for Nanfang Media Group	August 2012
**	Ten additional follow-up interviews with *Caixin* and *Nanfang Zhoumo* journalists were conducted over Skype and WeChat	November 2015– September 2016
***	Ten follow-up interviews were conducted with former editors of *Caijing, Caixin, Nanfang Zhoumo* (all interviewed previously).	June–July 2016

	Scholars and experts	
CSE01	Professor of Journalism and Communication at Tsinghua University	November 2009
CSE02	Professor of Journalism at China's Foreign Studies University	November 2009
CSE03	Professor of Journalism at Beijing University	November 2009
CSE04	Professor of Journalism and Publishing at Beijing University	July 2012
CSE05	Dean of the School of Journalism at Beijing University	July 2012
CSE06	Professor of Media and Law at China's Communication University	July 2012
CSE07	Director at the Anti-Corruption Centre, Beijing University	July 2012
CSE08	Researcher at the Anti-Corruption Centre, Beijing University	July 2012
CSE09	Researcher at the Anti-Corruption Centre, Beijing University	July 2012
CSE10	Dean of the School of Government at Nankai University	July 2012
CSE11	Crisis management scholar, Nankai University	July 2012
CSE12	Professor of Government, Nankai University	July 2012
CSE13	Professor of Government, Nankai University	July 2012
CSE14	Professor of Communications, expert on crisis communications, Renmin University	July 2012
CSE15	Director of the Crisis Management Centre, Tsinghua University	July 2012
CSE16	Director of the Centre for Crisis Management at Renmin University	August 2012
CSE17	Editor of China's Blue Book on Crisis Management and scholar at China's Academy of Social Science (CASS)	August 2012
CSE18	Senior vice president at Hill & Knowlton China	August 2012
CSE19	Media scholar at China's Academy of Social Sciences	August 2012
CSE20	Professor and expert in mining safety, China's Geological University	August 2012
CSE21	Professor of Journalism at China's Foreign Studies University	August 2012
CSE22	Researcher into coal-mining safety, State Council	August 2012
CSE23	Professor and media crisis communication expert at China's Youth University of Political Studies	August 2012
CSE24	Professor of Media and Communications at China's Youth University of Political Studies	August 2012
Media non-governmental organisations		
MNG01	Internews China director	November 2009
MNG02	Internews China vice director	August 2012
MNG03	Internews China director	August 2012
Officials		
COF01	Official at Central Propaganda Department (CPD)	December 2009
COF02	Official at the General Administration of Publication and Press (GAPP)	December 2009

(cont.)

Scholars and experts		
COF03	Official at the GAPP	December 2009
COF04	Former high-ranking official at the State Council, now consultant on food safety/crisis management	July 2012
COF05	Official of the Central Propaganda Department	July 2012
COF06	Former official at the CPD	July 2012
COF07	Former official at the CPD	July 2012
COF08	Vice director of the GAPP	August 2012
COF09	Official in charge of mining safety at the State Council	August 2012

Russia		
Journalists		
RJ01	Editor at *Kommersant Daily*	April 2010
RJ02	Editor at *Novaya Gazeta*	April 2010
RJ03	Editor at *New Times Magazine*	April 2010
RJ04	Political correspondent at *Kommersant Daily*	April 2010
RJ05	Investigative journalist at *Novaya Gazeta*	April 2010
RJ06	Op-ed editor at *Vedomosti*	April 2010
RJ07	Investigative journalist at *Agentura.ru*	April 2010
RJ08	Senior investigative journalist at *Novaya Gazeta*	April 2010
RJ09	Former editor-in-chief of *Itogi* journal	April 2010
RJ10	Former op-ed page editor at *Kommersant Daily*, now independent political commentator (published in most critical outlets)	April 2010
RJ11	Former investigative journalist at *Novaya Gazeta*, correspondent at *Russian Newsweek*	April 2010
RJ12	Editor-in-chief at *Russian Newsweek*	April 2010
RJ13	Editor-in-chief at *Vlast'* magazine	April 2010
RJ14	Former editor-in-chief of US operations of Ria Novosti, Russian official news network	April 2010
RJ15	Journalist at *Moscovskie Novosti*	April 2010
RJ16	Journalist and producer at *Russia Today*	April 2010
Experts and practitioners		
RSE01	Head of the Department of Sociological Research at Levada Centre, Russia's main independent public opinion polling centre	April 2010
RSE02	Head of socio-cultural research at Levada Centre	April 2010
RSE03	Director of the Glasnost Foundation	April 2010
RSE04	Chair of the Carnegie Moscow Centre's Society and Regions Programme and expert on Russian media	April 2010
RSE05	Director of the Carnegie Moscow Centre	April 2010

(cont.)

	Russia	
	Journalists	
RSE06	Vice director of Carnegie Moscow Centre, and expert on Russian civil society	April 2010
RSE07	Deputy director at the Centre for New Media and Society and an expert on Russian television and internet	April 2010
RSE08	Russian media law expert and professor at the Moscow State University	April 2010
RSE09	Dean of the Journalism Department at Moscow State University	May 2010

Appendix B   Interview Guide

The interviews were semi-structured, allowing for the inclusion of additional questions during the interviews. The following table provides the readers with the overarching questions used to guide the interviews. Many other more specific questions were added during the interviews. Not all the topics were covered during a single interview; some were discussed during several interviews, and some follow-up questions were also asked in e-mail correspondence.

Questions for Chinese journalists (including editors)
On political aspirations and yulun jiandu
How do you perceive the political and societal role of the media's oversight role in China? How do you think it has evolved in the past decade?
What are the main features of *yulun jiandu*?
What has motivated you to work for this type of media outlet, to engage in in-depth and investigative reporting?
Do you care about public opinion reactions on your work, how about official reactions?

On political restrictions
What restrictions and challenges do you encounter when routinely reporting on sensitive issues?
Which issues/topics do you find completely inaccessible, which fall into the grey zone?
How have political directives evolved in the past decade?
Which political (censorship) directives and pressures are the most pervasive? Which are the most inhibiting on your work?
What tactics have you used to evade different restrictions? Which restrictions are more possible to evade and how?

On professionalism and corruption
Are there ethical norms and regulations enforced at your media outlet to prevent journalists from engaging in corrupt activities?
How would you assess the overall state of professionalism in Chinese media?
What do you understand by professional and ethical norms guiding investigative and sensitive reporting?
What countries/cases do you aspire to in your work?

(cont.)

On crisis events

Have you received any special directives from authorities about coverage of crisis events?
How do those differ from restrictions placed on investigations of incidents or other sensitive matters?

What kind of directives did you encounter when reporting on the Wenchuan earthquake and coal-mining accidents? Which coal-mining accidents were more challenging to investigate and why?

How do you think the party-state's management of the media following crises changed in the past decade?

What other challenges did you encounter in investigating post-crisis governance failures?

How did you manage the restrictions and pressures in investigating crisis events, especially the Wenchuan earthquake and coal-mining accidents? Which tactics proved most effective and why?

How do you perceive the influence of your investigative and in-depth reports on the official policy response? How about in the cases of the Wenchuan earthquake and coal-mining accidents?

Do you think the authorities have incorporated any of the suggestions you included in your reports? If not, then why not?

Questions for Chinese media scholars
On yulun jiandu *and media oversight*

How do you perceive the developments of the official *yulun jiandu* policy in the past decade?

How do you present *yulun jiandu* to your students?

How would you say the space for critical reporting has evolved in the Hu-Wen era? What shifts and similarities have you observed in comparison to the previous decades?

What are the key features in the official management of the media in the past decade? Did the development of new media alter the state's approach? If so, in what ways?

On media-state relations during crisis events

How do you teach crisis communication to your students? What key roles should Chinese journalists undertake following crisis events?

How do you think the Chinese officials' attitudes change towards *yulun jiandu* reporting following crisis events?

How would you assess the space for media's reporting following major crises in the past decade?

How did *yulun jiandu* reporting play out following the Wenchuan earthquake and coal-mining accidents?

Questions for Chinese crisis management scholars and experts

How has official crisis communication, and crisis management more broadly, changed in the past decade? Which countries did China learn the most from in that respect? What are the most pressing challenges China is facing in crisis management?

What role do you think media plays in crisis management?

In training officials about crisis communication, what are the most frequent questions and concerns that you hear from officials?

How significant is the media supervision role for developing effective crisis management strategies?

(cont.)

To what extent do the relevant authorities respond to media investigations and criticisms following crisis events?

Some media outlets published extensive investigations of the school scandal following the Sichuan earthquake. Have there been reactions from authorities to these investigations? If so, has the system of managing the school safety been transformed, and how?

Several outlets have investigated coal-mining accidents in the past decade, uncovering the corrupt ties between local officials and mine managers behind the frequent accidents. Has there been a policy response to media coverage? If so, what kind?

Questions for governance scholars

How would you evaluate the effectiveness of China's top-down accountability or oversight mechanisms? How would you evaluate the effectiveness of China's bottom-up accountability mechanisms? Has there been a change in the party-state's supervision system in the past decade?

How do you think *yulun jiandu* compares to other supervision mechanisms in terms of its effectiveness, importance to the state, etc.?

How has the attitude of Chinese authorities towards *yulun jiandu* changed in the past decade?

How would you evaluate media-state relations in China in the past decade?

How would you evaluate progress the Chinese government has made in addressing the high coal-mining fatalities in the past decade?

Have there been any policy responses to the investigations into the school scandal following the Wenchuan earthquake?

Questions for Chinese officials

On media policy and yulun jiandu

How would you describe the main changes in China's media policy in the past decade? When it comes to *yulun jiandu*, how has the official perception and encouragement of this media's role changed or evolved?

How has the system of media regulation changed in the past decade? What role, if any, has new media played in these developments?

What are the common misunderstandings, in your view, about China's media landscape?

What are the key challenges you encountered in managing the media?

On media in crisis events

What role do you think media should play during crisis events?

How has media coverage of crises changed in the past decade?

What are the key challenges in managing the media following crisis events? How have you addressed these challenges?

How would you evaluate media reporting of the Wenchuan earthquake? How would you evaluate media reporting of the coal-mining accidents? What improvements do you think are still needed in media coverage of natural and man-made disasters?

* The officials at the State Council were also asked about the specific policies with regard to management of coal-mining accidents, and the role of the media supervision in shifting official policy direction.

(cont.)

Questions for media non-governmental organization practitioners

How has investigative and critical reporting on contentious societal issues evolved in the past decade?

What tactics do journalists use in negotiating the boundaries?

What assistance do you provide to journalists?

What are the key challenges for expanding professional media reporting in China?

Have you worked with Chinese officials and if so, what concerns did they express in their dealings with the media?

Questions for Russian journalists (including editors)

What motivated you to pursue a career in investigative journalism or to work for a critical media outlet?

Which issues would you say are inaccessible to write about in Russia? Which are accessible, but most challenging?

What are the key restrictions you face in reporting, publishing on sensitive issues?

What are the most pressing challenges on conducting investigative, in-depth reporting in Russia beyond political limitations?

How do you deal with these restrictions and challenges?

How would you explain journalistic professionalism in the Russian context?

How would you evaluate the influence of your reporting on society? How would you evaluate the influence of your reporting on the political system?

What do you think is your key political, societal responsibility as a critical journalist?

★ Questions were adjusted for media professionals at official and mainstream outlets.

Questions for Russian media and society experts

How would you say the relationship between the media and the state evolved under Putin? How does it compare to the Gorbachev and the Yeltsin periods?

What role does critical media play in the current political system?

How much do you think the state has used critical media as a feedback mechanism under Putin?

How have media regulations evolved under Putin? What other tactics does the state use to manage critical journalists?

How would you evaluate the community of Russia's critical journalists and its engagement with the state?

Bibliography

Androunas, Elena. *Soviet Media in Transition: Structural and Economic Alternatives*. Westport, CT: Praeger Publishers, 1993.

'Anzhao kexue fazhan guan de yaoqiu qieshi zhuanbian zuofeng: xuexi hu jintao tongzhi zai zhongyang ji-wei di-qi ci quanti huiyi shang de zhongyao jianghua' (Study Comrade Hu Jintao's Speech at the Seventh Plenary Conference of the Central Commission for Inspecting Discipline) (按照科学发展观的要求切实转变作风: 学习胡锦涛同志在中央纪委第七次全体会议上的重要讲话). *Qiushi (Seek Truth)* (求是) no. 5 (2007): 16–19.

Areddy, James T. 'China's Coal Sector has Safety Setback'. *The Wall Street Journal*, 3 September 2012. http://online.wsj.com/article/SB10000872396390443847404577628722372680112.html.

Arksey, Hilary. *Interviewing for Social Scientists: An Introductory Resource with Examples*. London: Sage, 1999.

Bagdikian, Ben H. *The New Media Monopoly*. Boston, MA: Beacon Press, 2004.

Bâli, Asli. 'From Subjects to Citizens? The Shifting Paradigm of Electoral Authoritarianism in Egypt'. *Middle East Law and Governance* 1, no. 1 (2009): 38–89.

Balkin, J.M. 'How Mass Media Stimulate Political Transparency'. *Cultural Values* 3, no. 4 (1999): 393–413.

Balzer, Harley. 'Managed Pluralism: Vladimir Putin's Emerging Regime'. *Post-Soviet Affairs* 19, no. 3 (1 January 2003): 189–227.

Bandurski, David. 'A News Story on School Collapses Tantalizes, Then Disappears'. *China Media Project*, 22 May 2009. http://cmp.hku.hk/2009/05/26/1641/.

Bandurski, David. 'China's Boldest Media: Losing the Battle?' *China Media Project*. 14 August, 2012. 30 July 2013. http://cmp.hku.hk/2012/08/14/25926/.

Bandurski, David and Martin Hala. *Investigative Journalism in China: Eight Cases in Chinese Watchdog Journalism*. Hong Kong; London: Hong Kong University Press, 2010.

Barabantseva, Elena. 'In Pursuit of an Alternative Model? The Modernisation Trap in China's Official Development Discourse'. *East Asia* 29, no. 1 (2011): 63–79.

Barry, Ellen. 'Trial of Russian Activist Aleksei Navalny to Begin'. *The New York Times*, 16 April 2013. www.nytimes.com/2013/04/17/world/europe/trial-of-russian-activist-aleksei-navalny-to-begin.html.

Bauer, Martin W. and George D. Gaskell (eds.). *Qualitative Researching with Text, Image and Sound: A Practical Handbook for Social Research*. London: Sage, 2000.

Baum, Richard. *Burying Mao: Chinese Politics in the Age of Deng Xiaoping*. Princeton: Princeton University Press, 1996.

'Political Implications of China's Information Revolution: The Media, the Minders, and Their Message'. In *China's Changing Political Landscape: Prospects for Democracy*, edited by Cheng Li, 161–185. Washington, DC: Brookings Institution Press, 2008.

'BBC News – Sichuan 2008: A Disaster on an Immense Scale'. www.bbc.co.uk/news/science-environment-22398684.

Becker, Jonathan. 'Lessons from Russia: A Neo-Authoritarian Media System'. *European Journal of Communication* 19, no. 2 (2004): 139–163.

'Beijing Flood Stories Cut from Southern Weekend'. *China Digital Times*. http://chinadigitaltimes.net/2012/07/beijing-flood-stories-cut-southern-weekend/.

Belin, Laura. 'Politics and Mass Media under Putin'. In *Russian Politics under Putin*, edited by Ross Cameron, 133–155. Manchester; New York: Manchester University Press, 2004.

Bellin, Eva. 'Reconsidering the Robustness of Authoritarianism in the Middle East: Lessons from the Arab Spring'. *Comparative Politics* 44, no. 2 (2012): 127–149.

Bennett, Lance W. 'The Media and Democratic Development: The Social Basis for Political Communication'. In *Communicating Democracy: The Media and Political Transitions*, edited by Patrick H. O'Neil, 195–207. Boulder, CO: Lynne Rienner Publishers, 1998.

Bennett, Lance W., Regina G. Lawrence, and Steven Livingston. *When the Press Fails: Political Power and the News Media from Iraq to Katrina*. Chicago, IL; Bristol: University of Chicago Press, 2007.

Berg, S. 'Snowball Sampling'. In *Encyclopaedia of Statistical Sciences*, edited by Samuel Kotz and Norman L. Johnson, 528–532. New York: John Wiley and Sons, 1988.

Bermeo, Nancy. *Liberalization and Democratization: Change in the Soviet Union and Eastern Europe*. Baltimore: Johns Hopkins University Press, 1992.

Bialer, Seweryn (ed.). *Politics, Society, and Nationality Inside Gorbachev's Russia*. Boulder, CO: Westview, 1988.

Bijian, Zheng. 'China's "Peaceful Rise" to Great-Power Status'. *Foreign Affairs* 84 (5)(2005): 18–24.

Binyan, Liu. 'After Tiananmen Square, a "Dark Age" for Press Freedom in China'. *Nieman Reports*, 28 August 2014.

Birch, Sarah. *Elections and Democratization in Ukraine*. Basingstoke: Macmillan, 2000.

Boin, Arjen. *The Politics of Crisis Management: Public Leadership under Pressure*. Cambridge: Cambridge University Press, 2005.

Boswell, T. *Revolution in the World-System*. New York; London: Greenwood Publishing Group, 1989.

Bovt, Georgy. 'The Russian Press and Civil Society: Freedom of Speech vs. Freedom of Market'. In *Civil Society and the Search for Justice in Russia*, edited by Christopher Marsh and Nikolas K. Gvosdev. Lanham, MD; Oxford: Lexington Books, 2002: 91–104.

Boyatzis, Richard E. *Transforming Qualitative Information: Thematic Analysis and Code Development*. Thousand Oaks, CA; London: Sage Publications, 1998.

Brady, Anne-Marie. *China's Thought Management*. Abingdon, OX; New York: Routledge, 2012.

Marketing Dictatorship: Propaganda and Thought Work in Contemporary China. Lanham, MD; Plymouth: Rowman & Littlefield, 2008.

'We Are All Part of the Same Family': China's Ethnic Propaganda'. *Journal of Current Chinese Affairs* 41, no. 4 (2013): 159–181.

Brandt, Loren and Thomas Rawski. *China's Great Economic Transformation*. Cambridge: Cambridge University Press, 2008.

Branigan, Tania. 'Anti-Pollution Protesters Halt Construction of Copper Plant in China', The Guardian. 3 July 2012. www.theguardian.com/world/2012/jul/03/china-anti-pollution-protest-copper.

'Snowstorms Cause Havoc in China'. *The Guardian*, 28 January 2008.

'Wang Keqin and China's Revolution in Investigative Journalism'. *The Guardian*, 23 May 2010.

Brenderbach, Martin. 'Public Opinion – A New Factor Influencing the PRC Press'. *Asien* 96 (July 2005): 29–45.

Brown, Archie. *The Gorbachev Factor*. Oxford: Oxford University Press, 1996.

The Rise and Fall of Communism. London: Bodley Head, 2009.

Brynen, Rex, Bahgat Korany, and Paul Noble. *Political Liberalization and Democratization in the Arab World*. Boulder, CO: Lynne Rienner, 1995.

Bunce, Valerie J. and Sharon L. Wolchik. *Defeating Authoritarian Leaders in Postcommunist Countries*. Cambridge: Cambridge University Press, 2011.

Büsgen, M. 'NGOs and the Search for Chinese Civil Society Environmental Non-Governmental Organisations in the Nujiang Campaign'. *ISS Working Paper* 422 (February 2006): 1–61. http://repub.eur.nl/res/pub/19180/wp422.pdf.

Cabestan, Jean-Pierre. 'Is China Moving Towards "Enlightened" But Plutocratic Authoritarianism?' *China Perspectives* no. 55 (2004). http://chinaperspectives.revues.org/412.

Cairns, Christopher. 'Prerequisites for Selective Censorship: Leaders' Evolving Beliefs and Bureaucratic Re-Centralization'. PhD Dissertation, Chapter 3. Cornell University, 2016.

Cao Haili, Chang Hongxiao, Wu Yan, and Li Jing (曹海丽, 常红晓, 吴燕, 林靖). 'Zhenhan zhongguo: jiuyuan pian: juguo jiuzai' (China Shocked: The Rescue Edition: The Whole Nation Provides Disaster Relief) (震撼中国·救援篇：举国救灾). *Caijing*, 26 May 2008.

Carlson, Allen, Mary Gallagher, Kenneth Lieberthal, and Melanie Manion. *Contemporary Chinese Politics: New Sources, Methods, and Strategies*. New York: Cambridge University Press, 2010.

Carothers, Thomas. 'The End of the Transition Paradigm'. *Journal of Democracy* 13, no. 1 (2002): 5–21.

'Censorship, Prosecution Drive Exodus of Opinion Leaders from China's Sina Weibo'. *Global Voices Advocacy*, 6 January 2015. http://advocacy.globalvoice sonline.org/2014/01/06/censorship-prosecution-drive-exodus-of-opinion-le aders-from-chinas-sina-weibo/.

Cerf, Christopher, Marina Albee, Lev Gushchin, and Vitalii Korotych *Voices of Glasnost: Letters from the Soviet People to Ogonyok Magazine*. London: Kyle Cathie, 1990.

Chaisty, Paul and Stephen Whitefield. 'Forward to Democracy or Back to Authoritarianism? The Attitudinal Bases of Mass Support for the Russian Election Protests of 2011–2012'. *Post-Soviet Affairs* (June 2013): 1–17.

'Charter 08'. *Foreign Policy*, 8 October 2010. www.foreignpolicy.com/articles/20 10/10/08/charter_08.

Chang, Jack. 'Environmental Issues Top Major Legislative Meeting in China-US News'. *US News & World Report*. 7 March 2015. 12 March 2015. www.usn ews.com/news/world/articles/ 192015/03/07/environmental-issues-top-majo r-legislative-meeting-in-china.

Cheek, Timothy. *The Intellectual in Modern Chinese History*. Cambridge, United Kingdom: Cambridge University Press, 2015.

Cheek, Timothy and Tony Saich (eds.). *New Perspectives on State Socialism in China*. Armonk, NY: M.E. Sharpe, 1997.

Chen Baocheng (陈宝成). 'Guangdong sheng-wei xuanchuanbu fubuzhang zhuanren nanfang baoye dangwei shuji' (Vice-Minister of the Guangdong Department of Propaganda was Transferred to the Position of the Party Secretary of the Nanfang Press Group) (广东省委宣传部副部长转任南方报业党委书记). *Caixin* (财新网). 3 May 2012. http://news.sohu.com/2012050 3/n342262531.shtml.

Chen, Cheng. 'Institutional Legitimacy of an Authoritarian State: China in the Mirror of Eastern Europe'. *Problems of Post-Communism* 52, no. 4 (2005): 3–13.

Chen, Hong, Hui Qi, Ruyin Long, and Maolong Zhang,. 'Research on 10-year Tendency of China Coal Mining Accidents and the Characteristics of Human Factors'. *Safety Science* 50, no. 4 (2012): 745–770.

Chen Huiying (陈慧颖). 'Zhenhan zhongguo, jinjibian: baoxian: buneng cheng-shou zhi qing' (China Shocked, Economics Edition: Insurance: Cannot Bear It) (震撼中国·经济篇：保险：不能承受之轻). *Caijing*, 26 May 2012.

Chen Jiang (陈江). 'Zhiming 43 fenzhong' (Fatal 43 Minutes) (致命43分钟). *Nanfang Zhoumo*. 26 November 2009.

Chen Lidan. 'Wo guo yulun jiandu de lilun yu jiangou' (*Yulun Jiandu*'s Theoretical Construction in China) (我国舆论监督的理论与建构). *Xinwen Jie* (*Press Circles*) (新闻界). April 2004: 24.

Chen, Ni. 'Institutionalizing Public Relations: A Case Study of Chinese Government Crisis Communication on the 2008 Sichuan Earthquake'. *Public Relations Review* 35, no. 3 (2009). www.deepdyve.com/lp/elsevier/ institutionalizing-public-relations-a-case-study-of-chinese-government-T8rsWktINa.

Chen, Ni. 'Beijing's Political Crisis Communication: An Analysis of Chinese Government Communication in the 2009 Xinjiang Riot'. *Journal of Contemporary China* 21, no. 75 (2012): 461–479.

Chen Yiming (陈一鸣). 'Beichuan zhongxue: xiaoxin liaoshang' (Beichuan Middle School: Careful Healing) (北川中学：小心疗伤). *Nanfang Zhoumo*, 29 May 2008.

Chengju, Huang. 'The Development of a Semi-Independent Press in Post-Mao China: An Overview and a Case Study of Chengdu Business News'. *Journalism Studies* 1, no. 4 (2000): 649–664.

Chengpeng, Li. 'Patriotism With Chinese Characteristics'. *The New York Times*, 25 May 2012. www.nytimes.com/2012/05/26/opinion/patriotism-with-chinese-characteristics.html.

Cheung, Anne S.Y. 'Public Opinion Supervision – A Case Study of Media Freedom in China'. *Columbia Journal of Asian Law* 20, no. 2 (2007): 357–384.

'China Jails "New Citizens' Movement"'. *BBC News*. 19 June 2014. 11 March 2015. www.bbc.com/news/world-asia-china-27917234.

'China: International Energy Data and Analysis'. *U.S. Energy Information Administration* www.eia.gov/beta/international/analysis.cfm?iso=CHN.

'China Media Bulletin: Issue No. 88'. 14 June 2013. www.freedomhouse.org/c mb/88_061313.

Cho, Li-Fung. 'The Emergence, Influence, and Limitations of Watchdog Journalism in Post-1992 China: A Case Study of Southern Weekend'. Unpublished PhD Dissertation. University of Hong Kong: Journalism and Media Studies Centre, 2007.

Chŏng, Chae-ho and Jae Ho Chung. *China's Crisis Management*. London: Routledge, 2012.

Chongjian wenchuan – renlei kangzheng, jiuzai shi de qiji (Rebuilding Wenchuan – A Miracle in Quake Proof Provision of Disaster Relief in Human History) (重建汶川－人类抗争救灾是的奇迹). Beijing: Dizhen chubanshe (Earthquake Publishing House), 2012.

Clarke, Gerard. *The Politics of NGOs in South-East Asia: Participation and Protest in the Philippines*. London: Routledge, 1998.

Cody, Edward. 'In China, Flooding Traps 172 Miners Underground'. *The Washington Post*, 18 August 2007. www.washingtonpost.com/wp-dyn/con tent/article/2007/08/17/AR2007081702315.html.

Cohen, Stephen F. *The Voices of Glasnost: Interviews with Gorbachev's Reformers*. New York; London: Norton, 1990.

Collier, David and James Mahoney. 'Insights and Pitfalls: Selection Bias in Qualitative Research'. *World Politics* 49, no. 1 (1996): 56–91.

Collier, David and Steven Levitsky. 'Democracy with Adjectives: Conceptual Innovation in Comparative Research'. *World Politics* 49, no. 3 (1997): 430–451.

Colton, Timothy J. and Jerry F. Hough. *Growing Pains: Russian Democracy and the Election of 1993*. Washington, DC: Brookings Institution Press, 1998.

Colton, Timothy J. and Michael McFaul. *Popular Choice and Managed Democracy the Russian Elections of 1999 and 2000*. Washington, DC: Brookings Institution Press, 2003.

'Concern for Women's Rights Activists Detained in China'. *BBC News*, 9 March 2015. www.bbc.com/news/world-asia-china-31792608.

Coronel, Sheila S. and Howie G. Severino. *Investigative Reporting for Television in Southeast Asia*. Quezon City, Philippines: Philippine Center for Investigative Journalism, 2006.

Cui Baoguo (催保国). *2010 nian: zhongguo chuanmei chanye fazhan baogao (2010: Report on Development of China's Media Industry)* (2010年: 中国传媒产业发展报告).Beijing: Social Sciences Academic Press, 2010.

Curran, James and Jean Seaton. *Power Without Responsibility: The Press, Broadcasting and the Internet in Britain*. London; New York: Routledge, 2009.

Curran, James and Myung-Jin Park. *De-Westernizing Media Studies*. London: Routledge, 2000.

Curry, Jane L. and Joan Dassin. *Press Control Around the World*. New York: Praeger, 1982.

Dalpino, Catharin E. *Deferring Democracy: Promoting Openness in Authoritarian Regimes*. Washington, DC: Brookings Institution Press, 2000.

Davies, Gloria. *Worrying about China: The Language of Chinese Critical Inquiry*. Cambridge, MA; London: Harvard University Press, 2007.

De Burgh, Hugo. *The Chinese Journalist: Mediating Information in the World's Most Populous Country*. London: RoutledgeCurzon, 2003.

Investigative Journalism: Context and Practice. London: Routledge, 2004.

'Kings Without Crowns? The Re-Emergence of Investigative Journalism in China'. *Media, Culture & Society* 25, no. 6 (2003): 801–820.

De Certeau, Michel. *The Practice of Everyday Life*. Berkeley: University of California Press, 1984.

DeLong-Bas, Natana J. 'The New Social Media and the Arab Spring'. *Oxford Islamic Studies Online*. www.oxfordislamicstudies.com/Public/focus/essay0611_social_media.html.

Dombernowsky, Laura. 'Chinese Journalism Students: Balancing Competing Values'. In *Chinese Investigative Journalists' Dreams*, edited by Marina Svensson, Elin Saether, and Zhi'an Zhang, 53–75. Plymouth, UK: Lexington Books, 2014.

Denyer, Simon. 'Arrest of Inspirational Editor Shen Hao Marks End of an Era for Chinese Journalism'. *The Washington Post*, 9 January 2015. www.washingtonpost.com/world/asia_pacific/arrest-of-inspirational-editor-shen-hao-marks-end-of-an-era-for-chinese-journalism/2015/01/09/4e7e9ece-8924-11e4-ace9-47de1af4c3eb_story.html.

'Detentions of Chinese Activists Tripled Last Year: Report'. *Radio Free Europe*, 3 March 2014. www.rfa.org/english/news/china/detentions-03032014182151.html.

Dewhirst, Martin. 'Censorship in Russia: 1991 and 2001'. In *Russia after Communism*, edited by Rick Fawn and Stephen White, 21–34. London: Frank Cass Publishers, 2002.

Diamant, Neil J., Stanley B. Lubman, and Kevin J. O'Brien. *Engaging the Law in China: State, Society, and Possibilities for Justice*. Stanford, CA: Stanford University Press, 2005.

Diamond, Larry J. *Developing Democracy: Toward Consolidation*. Baltimore; London: Johns Hopkins University Press, 1999.

Diamond, Larry J. and Juan J. Linz. 'Introduction: Politics, Society, and Democracy in Latin America'. In *Democracy in Developing Countries: Latin America*, edited by Larry J. Diamond, Juan J. Linz, and Seymour M. Lipset. Boulder, CO: Lynne Rienner Publishers, 1999.

Diamond, Larry J., Juan J. Linz, and Seymour M. Lipset. 'Introduction: What Makes for Democracy?' In *Politics in Developing Countries: Comparing Experiences with Democracy*, edited by Larry Diamond, Juan J. Linz, and Seymour M. Lipset, 1–66. London: Lynne Rienner Publishers, 1995.

Diamond, Larry J. and Leonardo Morlino. *Assessing the Quality of Democracy*. Baltimore: Johns Hopkins University Press, 2005.

Diamond, Larry J., Marc F. Plattner, and Philip J. Costopoulos. *Debates on Democratization*. Baltimore: Johns Hopkins University Press, 2010.

Dickson, Bruce J. *Red Capitalists in China: The Party, Private Entrepreneurs, and Prospects for Political Change*. New York, NY: Cambridge University Press, 2003.

Dijk, Van and Teun A. 'Principles of Critical Discourse Analysis'. *Discourse & Society* 4, no. 2 (1993): 249–283.

Dillon, Nara. 'Governing Civil Society: Adapting Revolutionary Methods to Serve Post-Communist Goals'. In *Mao's Invisible Hand: The Political Foundations of Adaptive Governance*, edited by Sebastian Heilmann and Elizabeth J. Perry, 138–165. Cambridge, MA; London: Harvard University Asia Center, 2011.

Dimitrov, Martin K. 'Popular Autocrats'. *Journal of Democracy* 20, no. 1 (2008): 78–81.

Ding Buzhi and Zhu Hongjun (丁补之，朱红军). 'Mianzhu fuxin er xiao: daota jiaoshe shi zenmeyang jiancheng de?' (Mianzhu Fuxin Number 2 School: How was the Collapsed School Building Constructed?) (绵竹富新二小：垮塌校舍是怎样建成的). *Nanfang Zhoumo*, 29 May 2008.

Dittmer, Lowell. 'The Structural Evolution of "Criticism and Self-Criticism" '. *The China Quarterly* 56 (1973): 708–729.

Donohue, George A., Phillip J. Tichenor, and Clarice N. Olien, 'A Guard Dog Perspective on the Role of Media'. *Journal of Communication* 45, no. 2 (1995): 115–132.

'Dozens Die in China Train Crash'. *BBC*, 24 July 2011. www.bbc.co.uk/news/world-asia-pacific-14262276.

Duchâtel, Mathieu and François Godement, 'China's Politics under Hu Jintao'. *Journal of Current Chinese Affairs* 38, no. 3 (2009): 3–11.

Duncan, Maxim. 'China Families Protest Mine Disaster; Toll Hits 104'. *Reuters*, 23 November 2009. www.reuters.com/article/2009/11/23/us-china-mine-explosion-idUSTRE5AK08Y20091123.

'Duonan heyi xingbang' (How to Rejuvenate a Country from Many Disasters) (多难何以兴邦). *Nanfang Zhoumo*, 5 June 2008.

Du Junfei. 'The Road to Openness: The Communication Legacy of the Wenchuan Earthquake'. In *Convulsion: Media Reflections*, edited by Liang,

116–125. Beijing: China Democracy and Legal System Publishing House, 2008.

Editorial Board. 'A Documentary on Air Pollution Sparks a Code Red in China'. *The Washington Post*, 9 March 2015. www.washingtonpost.com/opinions/a-documentary-on-air-pollution-sparks-a-code-red-in-china/2015/03/09/c0f d352a-c5e5-11e4-a199-6cb5e63819d2_story.html.

Eickelman, Dale F. and Jon W. Anderson. *New Media in the Muslim World: The Emerging Public Sphere*. Bloomington, IN: Indiana University Press, 2003.

Esarey, Ashley. 'Cornering the Market: State Strategies for Controlling China's Commercial Media'. *Asian Perspectives* 29, no. 4 (2005): 37–83.

Esarey, Ashley and Xiao Qiang. 'Political Expression in the Chinese Blogosphere: Below the Radar'. *Asian Survey* 48, no. 5 (2008): 752–777.

Esherick W. Joseph and Jeffrey W. Wasserstrom. 'Acting Out Democracy: Political Theater in Modern China'. *The Journal of Asian Studies* 49(4) (1990): 835–865.

Fairclough, Gordon. 'Eleven Schools Collapsed in Quake'. *Wall Street Journal*, 15 April 2010. http://online.wsj.com/article/SB10001424052702304628 704575185431052701868.html.

Fairclough, Norman. *Language and Power*. Harlow: Longman, 2001.

Farid, May. 'China's Grassroots NGOs and the Local State: Mechanisms of Influence and the Expansion of Rights'. *SSRN eLibrary* (2011). http://pape rs.ssrn.com/abstract=1899937.

Federman, Adam. 'Moscow's New Rules'. *Columbia Journalism Review* (January/ February 2010). www.cjr.org/feature/moscows_new_rules.php.

Feldbrugge, Ferdinand J.M. *Samizdat and Political Dissent in the Soviet Union*. Leiden: A.W. Sijthoff, 1975.

Ferdinand, Peter. *The Internet, Democracy and Democratization*. London: Cass, 2000.

Fewsmith, Joseph. 'Review of China's Democratic Future: How It Will Happen and Where It Will Lead'. *Taiwan Journal of Democracy* 1, no. 2 (2005): 151–154.

Finkelstein, David M. and Maryanne Kivlehan. *China's Leadership in the 21st Century: The Rise of the Fourth Generation*. London: M.E. Sharpe, 2003.

Fisher, Julie. *Nongovernments: NGOs and the Political Development of the Third World*. Hartford, CT: Kumarian Press, 1997.

Fossato, Floriana. 'The Russian Media: From Popularity to Distrust'. *Current History* 100, no. 648 (2001): 343–347.

Fossato, Floriana and John Lloyd. *The Web That Failed: How Opposition Politics and Independent Initiatives are Failing on the Internet in Russia*. Oxford: Reuters Institute for the Study of Journalism, 2008.

Foster, Kenneth W. 'Associations in the Embrace of an Authoritarian State: State Domination of Society?' *Studies in Comparative International Development* 35, no. 4 (1 December 2001): 84–109.

'Four Years on: What China Got Right When Rebuilding after the Sichuan Earthquake'. 11 May 2012. http://blogs.worldbank.org/eastasiapacific/fo ur-years-on-what-china-got-right-when-rebuilding-after-the-sichuan-earthquake.

Fu Jianfeng and Yao Yijiang (傅剑锋, 姚忆江). 'Jianshe bu zhuanjia rending ju yuan zhongxue shi wenti jianzhu – ju yuan zhongxue daota beiju diaocha' (The Experts from the Construction Department Firmly Believe That the Construction of the Ju Yuan Middle School has a Problem – The Investigation into the Yu Juan Middle School's Tragic Collapse) (建设部专家认定聚源中学是问题建筑 –聚源中学倒塌悲剧调查). *Nanfang Zhoumo*, 29 May 2008.

Fukuyama, Francis. 'The Patterns of History'. *Journal of Democracy* 23, no. 1 (2012).

Gandhi, Jennifer. '*Coordination among Opposition Parties in Authoritarian Regimes*'. Princeton: Princeton University, 2008.

Gandhi, Jennifer and Ellen Lust-Okar. 'Elections under Authoritarianism'. *Annual Review of Political Science* 12, no. 1 (2009): 403–422.

Gang, Qian. 'Why Southern Weekly?' *China Media Project*, 18 February 2013. http://cmp.hku.hk/2013/02/18/31257/.

Gang, Qian and David Bandurski. 'China's Emerging Public Sphere: The Impact of Media Commercialization, Professionalism, and the Internet in an Era of Transition'. In *Changing Media, Changing China*, edited by Susan L. Shirk, 38–77. Oxford; New York: Oxford University Press, 2011.

Ganguly, Sumit. 'Bangladesh and India'. In *Assessing the Quality of Democracy*, edited by Larry J. Diamond and Leonardo Morlino. Baltimore: Johns Hopkins University Press, 2005.

Gao, Li and James Stanyer, 'Hunting Corrupt Officials Online: The Human Flesh Search Engine and the Search for Justice in China'. *Information, Communication and Society* 17 (2014): 814–829.

Gao Mingyong (高明勇). *Weibo wen zheng de 30 tang ke (30 Lessons from Interviews with Officials about Weibo) (*微博问政的30堂课*)*. Hangzhou, China: Zhejiang renmin chubanshe (Zhejiang People's Publishing House) (浙江人民出版社), 2012.

Gardels, Nathan. 'The Price China has Paid: An Interview with Liu Binyan'. *The New York Review of Books*, 19 January 1989. www.nybooks.com/articles/arc hives/1989/jan/19/the-price-china-has-paid-an-interview-with-liu-bin/.

Gehlbach, Scott. 'Reflections on Putin and the Media'. *Post-Soviet Affairs* 26, no. 1 (2010): 77–87.

Gerring, John. *Case Study Research: Principles and Practices*. Cambridge: Cambridge University Press, 2007.

Gibbs, Joseph. *Gorbachev's Glasnost: The Soviet Media in the First Phase of Perestroika*. College Station, TX: Texas A&M University Press, 1999.

Gilley, Bruce. *China's Democratic Future: How It Will Happen and Where It Will Lead*. New York: Columbia University Press, 2004.

'Democratic Enclaves in Authoritarian Regimes'. *Democratization* 17, no. 3 (2010): 389–415.

Gilley, Bruce and Larry Diamond. *Political Change in China: Comparisons with Taiwan*. Boulder, CO: Lynne Rienner Publishers, 2008.

Ginsburg, Tom. 'Administrative Law and the Judicial Control of Agents in Authoritarian Regimes'. In *Rule by Law: The Politics of Courts in Authoritarian Regimes*, edited by Tom Ginsburg and Tamir Moustafa, 58–73. New York, NY: Cambridge University Press, 2008.

Givens, John Wagner and Maria Repnikova. 'Advocates of Change in Authoritarian Regimes: How Chinese Lawyers and Chinese and Russian Journalists Stay Out of Trouble'. *SSRN eLibrary* (2011). http://papers.ssrn .com/abstract=1911590.

Gong, Ting. 'Dangerous Collusion: Corruption as a Collective Venture in Contemporary China'. *Communist and Post-Communist Studies* 35, no. 1 (2002): 85–103.

Gorbachev, Mikhail S. *Memoirs*. London: Bantam, 1997.

Perestroika. London: Collins, 1987.

Gorbachev, Mikhail and Zdeněk Mlynář. *Conversations with Gorbachev: On Perestroika, the Prague Spring, and the Crossroads of Socialism*. New York; Chichester: Columbia University Press, 2013.

Gordon, Kim. 'China Speaks Out'. *Prospect*, 20 March 1999. www.prospectma gazine.co.uk/1999/03/chinaspeaksout/.

Graber, Doris A. *Mass Media and American Politics*. Washington, DC: CQ Press, 2005.

Greenslade, Roy. 'China Launches Attack on Tibet Coverage'. *The Guardian*, 25 March 2008. www.theguardian.com/media/greenslade/2008/mar/25/ chinalaunchesattackontibet.

Griffiths, P., M. Gossop, B. Powis, and J. Strang. 'Reaching Hidden Populations of Drug Users by Privileged Access Interviewers: Methodological and Practical Issues'. *Addiction* 88, no. 12 (1 December 1993): 1617–1626.

Gross, Natalie. 'Glasnost: Roots and Practice'. *Problems of Communism* (November 1987): 69–80.

Guan Jun (关军). 'Daping haishi zouchu yangxing' (Daping is Beginning to Come Out of the Shadow) (大平开始走出阴影). *Nanfang Zhoumo*, 27 October 2005.

'Guanyu chengli jiaoyubu wenchuan dizhen zaihou xuexiao huifu chongjian gongzuo lingdao xiaozu de tongzhi' (The Ministry of Education Notice about the Establishment of the Ministry of Education's Leadership Group Concerning the Work on the Recovery and Reconstruction of Schools Following the Wenchuan Earthquake) (教育部关于成立教育部汶川地震灾后学校恢复重建工作领导小组的通知). Zhonghua renmin gonghe guo jiaoyubu (Ministry of Education of the People's Republic of China) (中华人民共和教育部), 11 June 2008. www.moe.gov.cn/publicfiles/business/htm lfiles/moe/moe_2083/200806/xxgk_62880.html.

'"Guanmei Goujie" Zheng Jie' (Correctly Separating the Collision between Officials and Mining Managers) (官煤勾结征解) *Caijing*, 22 October 2005.

Guoguang, Wu. 'One Head, Many Mouths: Diversifying Press Structures in Reform China'. In *Power, Money, and Media: Communication Patterns and Bureaucratic Control in Cultural China*, edited by Chin-Chuan Lee, 45–68. Evanston: Northwestern University Press, 2000.

Hackett, Robert. 'Media Reform: Democratizing the Media, Democratizing the State'. *Canadian Journal of Communication* 28, no. 3 (2003).

Hallin, Daniel C. *Comparing Media Systems: Three Models of Media and Politics*. Cambridge: Cambridge University Press, 2004.

Halper, Stefan. *The Beijing Consensus: Legitimizing Authoritarianism in Our Time.* New York, NY: Basic Books, 2012.

Han, Rongbin. 'Manufacturing Consent in Censored Cyberspace: China's "Fifty-Cent Army"'. *Journal of Current Chinese Affairs* 44, no. 2 (2015).

'Defending Authoritarian Regime On-line: China's "Voluntary Fifty-cent Army"'. *The China Quarterly* 224 (2015): 1006–1025.

Haraszti, Miklos. *The Velvet Prison: Artists under State Socialism.* New York, NY: Basic Books: 1987.

Hassid, Jonathan. 'China's Contentious Journalists: Reconceptualizing the Media'. *Problems of Post-Communism* 55, no. 4 (2008): 52–61.

China's Unruly Journalists: How Committed Professionals are Changing the People's Republic. London and New York: Routledge, 2015.

'Controlling the Chinese Media: An Uncertain Business'. *Asian Survey* 48, no. 3 (1 June 2008): 414–430.

'Four Models of the Fourth Estate: A Typology of Contemporary Chinese Journalists'. *The China Quarterly* 208 (2011): 813–832.

'Safety Valve or Pressure Cooker? Blogs in Chinese Political Life'. *Journal of Communication* 62, no. 2 (2012): 212–230.

Hassid, Jonathan and Maria Repnikova. 'Why Chinese Print Journalists Embrace the Internet'. *Journalism* 17, no. 7 (2016): 882–898.

He, Alex Jingwei, Genghua Huang. 'Fighting for Migrant Labor Rights in the World's Factory: Legitimacy, Resource Constraints and Strategies of Grassroots Migrant Labor NGOs in South China'. *Journal of Contemporary China* 24 (2015): 471–492.

He, Baogang and Mark E. Warren. 'Authoritarian Deliberation: The Deliberative Turn in Chinese Political Development'. *Perspectives on Politics* 9, no. 02 (2011): 269–289.

He, Baogang and Stig Thøgersen, 'Giving the People a Voice? Experiments with Consultative Authoritarian Institutions in China'. *Journal of Contemporary China* 19, no. 66 (2010): 675–692

Heilmann, Sebastian. 'Policy Experimentation in China's Economic Rise'. *Studies in Comparative International Development (SCID)* 43, no. 1 (2008): 1–26.

'Policy-Making through Experimentation: The Formation of a Distinctive Policy Process'. In *Mao's Invisible Hand: The Political Foundations of Adaptive Governance,* edited by Sebastian Heilmann and Elizabeth J. Perry, 62–102. Cambridge, MA; London: Harvard University Asia Center, 2011.

Hem, Mikal. 'Evading the Censors: Critical Journalism in Authoritarian States'. Reuters Institute Fellowship Paper, University of Oxford, Trinity Term, 2014.

Herman, Edward S. and Noam Chomsky. *Manufacturing Consent: The Political Economy of Mass Media.* New York: Pantheon Books, 1988.

Heydemann, Steven. 'Upgrading Authoritarianism in the Arab World'. Saban Center Analysis Paper Series no. 13 (October 2007). www.brookings.edu/papers/2007/10arabworld.aspx.

Hildebrandt, Timothy. *Social Organizations and the Authoritarian State in China.* Cambridge; New York: Cambridge University Press, 2013.

Hille, Kathrin. 'China: Citizens United'. *Financial Times*, 29 July 2013. www.ft
.com/intl/cms/s/0/39cf53e8-f829-11e2-b4c4-00144feabdc0.html#axz
z2aw4gfb52.
'Real Name Rule to Add to Sina Weibo's Woes'. *Financial Times*, 28 February
2012. www.ft.com/intl/cms/s/0/e995b7aa-6201-11e1-807 f-00144feabdc0
.html#axzz2cRu2f1qm.
Ho, Peter and Richard L. Edmonds (eds.). *China's Embedded Activism:
Opportunities and Constraints of a Social Movement*. Abingdon; New York:
Routledge, 2008.
Holmes, Stephen. 'Conclusion: The State of the State in Putin's Russia'. In *The
State after Communism*, edited by Timothy J. Colton and Stephen Holmes,
299–311. Lanham, MD; Oxford: Rowman & Littlefield, 2006.
Hopkins, Mark W. *Mass Media in the Soviet Union*. New York: Pegasus, 1970.
Horsley, Jamie P. 'China Adopts First Nationwide Open Government
Information Regulations'. 24 April 2007. www.law.yale.edu/documents/pd
f/Intellectual_Life/Ch_China_Adopts_1st_OGI_Regulations.pdf.
Hou Fangyu (侯方域). 'Nanfang Shibian' (Southern Incident) (南方事變).
Yangguang Shiwu Zhoukan (阳光时务周刊), 9 August 2012. www.isunaf
fairs.com/?p=10133.
'How Officials can Spin the Media'. *China Media Project*. 21 April 2012. http://
cmp.hku.hk/2010/06/19/6238/.
Howard, Marc M. *The Weakness of Civil Society in Post-Communist Europe*.
Cambridge: Cambridge University Press, 2003.
Hsing, You-tien and Ching Kwan, Lee. *Reclaiming Chinese Society: The New Social
Activism*. London: Routledge, 2009.
Hu Baijing (胡百精, ed.). 'Ziran zainan zhong de weiji guanli zhenglu yu shehui
dongyuan moshi – yi '5.12' dizhen we ge an' (The Crisis Management
Strategy and Societal Mobilisation Model during Natural Disasters – The
Case Study of the '5.12' earthquake) (自然灾难中的微机管理策略与社会动
员模式 – 以'5.12地震为个案). In *Zhongguo weiji guanli baogao 2008–2009
(The Report of China's Crisis Management in 2008–2009)* (中国危机管理报告
2008–2009), 148–176. Beijing, China: Zhongguo Renmin daxue chubanshe
(Renmin University Press), 2009.
Hu Dejia. *Dui hu jintao 'tidao yulun jiandu' de lijie (The Understanding of Hu Jintao's
Mention of Strengthening Yulun Jiandu)* (对胡锦涛提到舆论监督的理解).
Beijing: China Youth University for Political Sciences, 2008.
'Hu jintao zai renmin ribao kaocha gongzuo de jianghua' (Hu Jintao's Speech
While Investigating the Work of *People's Daily*) (胡锦涛在人民日报考察工作
的讲话). *Xinhua News*, 26 June 2008. http://news.xinhuanet.com/politics/2
008-06/26/content_8442547.htm.
Hu Shuli. 'The Rise of the Business Media in China'. In *Changing Media,
Changing China*, edited by Susan Shirk, 77–91. Oxford; New York: Oxford
University Press, 2011.
Hu Shuli (胡舒立). 'Fuxin kuangnan zai bi meikuang gaige' (Fuxin Mining
Disaster is Again Forcing the Reform of the Mining Industry) (阜新矿难再
逼煤矿改革). *Caijing*, 21 February 2005. http://magazine.caijing.com.cn/20
05-05-08/110061290.html.

'Hu Shuli Leaves Caijing, China's Boldest News Magazine'. *Huffington Post*, 9 November 2009. www.huffingtonpost.com/2009/11/09/hu-shuli-leaves-caij ing-c_n_350703.html.

Huang, Ronggui and Xiaoyi Sun. 'Weibo Network, Information Diffusion and Implications for Collective Action in China'. *Information, Communication & Society*, 17 no. 1 (2013): 86–104.

Huang Xiuli (黄秀丽). 'Zhongzui zhikong yizai zuji kuangnan?' (The Meaning of Felony Accusation Lies in Blocking Mining Accidents?) (重罪指控意在阻击矿难?). *Nanfang Zhoumo*, 17 September 2010. www.infzm.com/content/50126.

Huckin, Thomas N. 'Critical Discourse Analysis'. In *Functional Approaches to Written Text: Classroom Applications*, edited by Tom Miller, 1997. http://eca .state.gov/education/engteaching/pubs/BR/functionalsec3_6.htm.

Hui, Dennis and Lai Hang. 'Politics of Sichuan Earthquake, 2008'. *Journal of Contingencies and Crisis Management* 17, no. 2 (2009): 137–140.

Hung, Chin-Fun. 'China's Changing State-Society Relations in the Internet Age: Case Study of Zhao Zuohai'. *International Journal of China Studies* 3, no. 3 (2012): 363–381.

Huntington, Samuel P. *The Third Wave: Democratization in the Late Twentieth Century*. Norman; London: University of Oklahoma Press, 1991.

Illarionov, Andrei. 'The Siloviki in Charge'. *Journal of Democracy* 20, no. 2 (2009): 69–72.

Inwood, Heather. 'Multimedia Quake Poetry: Convergence Culture after the Sichuan Earthquake'. *The China Quarterly* 208 (2011): 932–950.

Jacobs, Andrew and Edward Wong. 'China Reports Student Toll for Quake'. *The New York Times*, 8 May 2009. www.nytimes.com/2009/05/08/world/asia/08 china.html.

Jankowski, Nick and Klaus Bruhn Jensen. *A Handbook of Qualitative Methodologies for Mass Communication Research*. London: Routledge, 1991.

Jenkins, Henry, David Thorburn, and Brad Seawell. *Democracy and New Media*. Cambridge, MA: London, 2003.

Jensen, Klaus and Nick Jankowski. *A Handbook of Qualitative Methodologies for Mass Communication Research*. London: Routledge, 1991.

Jiang, Jessie. 'China's Rage over Toxic Baby Milk'. *Time*. 16 April 2012. www .time.com/time/world/article/0,8599,1842727,00.html.

Jiang, Min. 'Authoritarian Deliberation on Chinese Internet'. *Electronic Journal of Communication* 20, no. 3&4 (2010).

Jianzhu gongcheng kangzhen shefang fenlei biaozhun (*Standard for Classification of Seismic Protection of Buildings' Construction*) (建筑工程抗震设防分类标准). Zhonghua renmin gonghe he guo zhufang he chengxiang jianzhu bu; guojia zhiliang jiandu jianyan jianyi zongju (People's Republic Housing and Town and County Construction Bureau; the State's Quality Supervision and Quarantine Inspection Central Headquarters) (中华人民共和国住房和城乡建设部; 国家质量监督检验检疫总局), 30 May 2008. http://wenku.baidu.co m/view/8f818f2e3169a4517723a3e1.html.

'Jiaoyubu jianshebu xiuding nongcun xuexiao jianshe biaozhun 12 yue qi shishi' (Department of Education and Construction Revise the Standards for Construction of Schools in Rural Areas to Take Effect at the Beginning of December) (教育部建设部修订农村学校建设标准12月起实), *Zhongguo Wang* (中国网), 24 November 2008. www.china.com.cn/news/2008-11/24/content_16817976.htm.

Johnson, Chalmers. *Peasant Nationalism and Communist Power: The Emergence of Revolutionary China, 1937–1945*. Stanford, Stanford University Press, 1962.

Johnson, Ian. 'Is Democracy Chinese? An Interview with Journalist Chang Ping'. *NYRblog*, 27 January 2012. www.nybooks.com/blogs/nyrblog/2012/jan/27/is-democracy-chinese-chang-ping-interview/.

Joseph, Richard A. *State, Conflict, and Democracy in Africa*. Boulder, CO: Lynne Rienner Publishers, 1999.

Ju Jing (鞠靖). 'Shendu baodao shengchan fangshi de xin bianhua: shendu baodao jizhe QQ qun chutan' (A New Change in the Mode of Production of In-Depth Reporting: A First Exploration of QQ Groups among In-Depth Journalists) (深度报道生产方式的新变化: 深度报道记者QQ群初探). *Xinwen Jizhe (Journalist)* (新闻记者) no. 1 (2012).

Jun, Jing. 'Environmental Protests in Rural China'. In *Chinese Society: Change, Conflict and Resistance*, edited by Elizabeth J. Perry and Mark Selden, 143–160. London: Routledge, 2000.

Kaiman, Jonathan. 'China Cracks down on Social Media with Threat of Jail for "Online Rumors"'. *The Guardian*, 10 September 2013. www.theguardian.com/world/2013/sep/10/china-social-media-jail-rumours.

Kamrava, Mehran and Frank O. Mora. 'Civil Society and Democratisation in Comparative Perspective: Latin America and the Middle East'. *Third World Quarterly* 19, no. 5 (15 December 1998): 893–915.

Katzenstein, Peter J. *A World of Regions: Asia and Europe in the American Imperium*. Ithaca, NY: Cornell University Press, 2005.

Keane, John. *The Media and Democracy*. Cambridge: Polity Press, 1991.

Khamis, Sahar and Katherine Vaughn. 'Cyberactivism in the Egyptian Revolution: How Civic Engagement and Citizen Journalism Tilted the Balance'. *Arab Media & Society* no. 14 (Summer 2011).

Kim, Lucian and Maria Levitov. 'Russia Heat Wave May Kill 15,000, Shave $15 Billion of GDP'. *Bloomberg*, 10 August 2010. www.bloomberg.com/news/2010-08-10/russia-may-lose-15-000-lives-15-billion-of-economic-output-in-heat-wave.html.

King, Gary, Jennifer Pan, and Margaret Roberts. 'How Censorship in China Allows Government Criticism but Silences Collective Expression'. *American Political Science Review* 107, no. 2 (May 2013): 1–18.

Koltsova, Olessia. *News Media and Power in Russia*. London: Routledge, 2006.

Korotych, Vitaliĭ O. and Cathy Porter. *The Best of Ogonyok: The New Journalism of Glasnost*. London: Heinemann, 1990.

Kraus, Richard Curt. *The Party and the Arty in China: The New Politics of Culture*. Lanham, MD: Rowman & Littlefield Publishers, 2004.

'Kuangnan tanyuan' (Extensive Investigation into the Roots of Coal-Mmining Accidents) (矿难探源). *Caijing*, 29 December 2005.

Kuhn, Anthony. 'The Anti-Pollution Documentary That's Taken China by Storm'. *NPR News*. 4 March, 2015. 14 March 2015. www.npr.org/blogs/pa

rallels/2015/03/04/390689033/the-anti-pollution-documentary-thats-taken-china-by-storm.

Lachapelle, Jean, Lucan A. Way, and Steven Levitsky. 'Crisis, Coercion, and Authoritarian Durability: Explaining Diverging Responses to Anti-Regime Protest in Egypt and Iran.' *SSRN eLibrary* (2012). http://papers.ssrn.com/abstract=2142721.

LaFraniere, Sharon. 'School Construction Critic Gets Prison Term in China'. *The New York Times*, 23 November 2009. www.nytimes.com/2009/11/24/world/asia/24quake.html?_r=0.

LaFraniere, Sharon and Jonathan Ansfield. 'Editor Gets Fired after Criticizing Chinese Registration System'. *The New York Times*, 9 May 2010.

Lagerkvist, Johan. 'New Media Entrepreneurs in China: Allies of the Party-State or Civil Society?' *Journal of International Affairs* 65, no. 1 (2011): 169–182
'The Legacy of the 1989 Beijing Massacre: Establishing Neo-Authoritarian Rule, Silencing Civil Society'. *International Journal of China Studies* 5 no. 2 (2014): 349–369.

Lai, Dennis and Hang Hui. 'Research Note: Politics of Sichuan Earthquake'. *Journal of Contingencies and Crisis Management* 17 no. 2 (2009): 138.

Lai, Karyn. *An Introduction to Chinese Philosophy*. Cambridge; New York: Cambridge University Press, 2008.

Lakoff, George. *Don't Think of an Elephant: Know Your Values and Frame the Debate*. White River Junction, VT: Chelsea Green Publishing Co, 1990.

Lan, Yuxin. 'Coverage of the Wenchuan Earthquake: An Overview'. *The China Nonprofit Review* 1, no. 2 (2009): 221–245.

Landry, Pierre F. *Decentralized Authoritarianism in China: The Communist Party's Control of Local Elites in the Post-Mao Era*. Cambridge: Cambridge University Press, 2008.

Landry, Pierre F. and Daniela Stockmann. 'Crisis Management in an Authoritarian Regime: Media Effects during the Sichuan Earthquake by Pierre F. Landry, Daniela Stockmann'. *SSRN eLibrary* (2009). http://papers.ssrn.com/sol3/papers.cfm?abstract_id=1463796.

Landry, Pierre F., Deborah Davis, and Shiru Wang. 'Elections in Rural China: Competition Without Parties'. *Comparative Political Studies* 43, no. 6 (1 June 2010): 763–790.

Larson, Christina. 'In China, Politically Connected Firms have Higher Worker Death Rates'. *BusinessWeek*, 28 January 2013. www.businessweek.com/articles/2013-01-28/in-china-corrupt-officials-and-worker-deaths#p1.

Lee, Ching Kwan. *Against the Law: Labor Protests in China's Rustbelt and Sunbelt*. Berkeley: University of California Press, 2007.

Lei, Ya-Wen. 'The Political Consequences of the Rise of the Internet: Political Beliefs and Practices of Chinese Netizens'. *Political Communication* 28 (2011): 291–322.

Lemos, Gerard. *The End of the Chinese Dream: Why Chinese People Fear the Future*. New Haven, CT: Yale University Press, 2012.

Leng, Shujie and David Wertime. 'China's Anti-Corruption Campaign Ensnares Tens of Thousands More'. *Foreign Policy*. 9 January, 2015. 11 March 2015.

http://foreignpolicy.com/2015/01/09/chinas-anti-corruption-campaign-ensn ares-tens-of-thousands-more/.

Levitsky, Steven and Lucan A. Way. 'The Rise of Competitive Authoritarianism'. *Journal of Democracy* 13, no. 2 (2002): 51–65.

Competitive Authoritarianism: Hybrid Regimes After the Cold War. 1st ed. New York, NY: Cambridge University Press, 2010.

Levy, Richard. 'Village Elections, Transparency, and Anticorruption: Henan and Guangdong Provinces'. In *Grassroots Political Reform in Contemporary China*, edited by Elizabeth J. Perry and Merle Goldman, 20–47. Cambridge; London: Harvard University Press, 2007.

Li, Jinquan. *Voices of China: The Interplay of Politics and Journalism*. New York; London: Guilford Press, 1990.

Li Wei'ao (李微敖). 'Hegang "Renwei" Kuangnan' (Hegang 'Man-Made' Mining Accident) (鹤岗'人为'矿难). *Caijing*, 6 December 2009.

Li Wei'ao, Gao Shengke, and Dong Yuxiao (李微敖, 高耘科, 董欲晓). 'Chuan zhen chongjian de zhangdan' (Sichuan Earthquake Reconstruction Bill) (川 震重建的帐单). *Caijing*, 7 May 2012.

Li Zixin (李梓新). *Zainan ruhe baodao (How Disasters Are Reported)* (灾难如何报 道). Nanfang Ribao Chubanshe (Southern Newspaper Press) (南方日报出版 社), 2009.

Lieberthal, Kenneth. *Governing China: From Revolution through Reform*. New York; London: W.W. Norton, 2004.

Lieberthal, Kenneth and Michel Oksenberg. *Policy Making in China*. Princeton: Princeton University Press, 1988.

Liebman, Benjamin L. 'The Media and the Courts: Towards Competitive Supervision?' *The China Quarterly* 208 (2011): 833–850.

'Watchdog or Demagogue? The Media in the Chinese Legal System'. *Columbia Law Review* 105, no. 1 (1 January 2005): 1–157.

Ligachev, E.K. *Inside Gorbachev's Kremlin: The Memoirs of Yegor Ligachev*. Boulder, CO; Oxford: Westview Press, 1996.

Lim, Louisa. *The People's Republic of Amnesia*. New York, NY: Oxford University Press: 2015.

Lin, Yutang. *A History of the Press and Public Opinion in China*. Chicago: The University of Chicago Press, 1936.

Link, Perry. 'China: The Anaconda in the Chandelier'. *The New York Review of Books*, 11 April 2002. www.nybooks.com/articles/archives/2002/apr/11/chin a-the-anaconda-in-the-chandelier/.

The Uses of Literature: Life in the Socialist Chinese Literary System. Princeton: Princeton University Press, 2000.

Evening Chats in Beijing. New York: Norton, 1992.

Linz, Juan J. *Totalitarian and Authoritarian Regimes*. Boulder, CO; London: Lynne Rienner Publishers, 2000.

Lipman, Maria. 'Rethinking Russia: Freedom of Expression Without Freedom of Press'. *SIPA Journal of International Affairs* 63 (2010): 153–169.

'Russia's No-Participation Pact'. *Carnegie Endowment for International Peace*, 30 March 2011. http://carnegieendowment.org/2011/03/30/russia-s-no-partici pation-pact/bmkg.

Littlefield, Robert and Andrea Quenette. 'Crisis Leadership and Hurricane Katrina: The Portrayal of Authority by the Media in Natural Disasters'. *Journal of Applied Communication Research* 35, no. 1 (2007): 26–47.

Liu, Xiabo. 'Corruption Lingers in the Shadows of the Chinese Media'. *China Perspectives* 54 (2004): 45–48.

'Looking Back on Chinese Media Reporting of School Collapses'. *China Media Project*, 7 May 2009. http://cmp.hku.hk/2009/05/07/1599/.

Lopez-Pintor, Rafael and Leonardo Morlino. 'Italy and Spain'. In *Assessing the Quality of Democracy*, edited by Larry J. Diamond and Leonardo Morlino, 85–123. Baltimore: Johns Hopkins University Press, 2005.

Lorentzen, Peter L. 'China's Strategic Censorship'. *American Journal of Political Science* 58, no. 2 (2014): 402–414.

Lorentzen, Peter L., Pierre F. Landry, and John K. Yasuda. 'Undermining Authoritarian Innovation: The Power of China's Industrial Giants', *The Journal of Politics* 76, no. 1 (2014): 182–194.

Louw, Eric. *The Media and Political Process*. London: Sage, 2010.

Lubman, Stanley B. *Bird in a Cage: Legal Reform in China after Mao*. Stanford: Stanford University Press, 1999.

Lux, Steven J. and Jeffrey D. Straussman. 'Searching for Balance: Vietnamese NGOs Operating in a State-Led Civil Society'. *Public Administration and Development* 24, no. 2 (May 2004): 173–181.

Lynch, Daniel C. *After the Propaganda State: Media, Politics, and 'Thought Work' in Reformed China*. Stanford, CA: Stanford University Press, 1999.

Lynch, Marc. 'Tunisia and the New Arab Media Space'. *Foreign Policy Blogs*, 15 January 2011. http://lynch.foreignpolicy.com/posts/2011/01/15/tunisia_and_the_new_arab_media_space.

Ma Changbo (马昌博). 'Tunlan kuangnan: an jian shengzhang de lei yu tong' (Tunlan Mining Accident: The Tiredness and Pain of the Provincial Governor) (屯兰矿难：'安监省长'的累与痛). *Nanfang Zhoumo*, 26 February 2009.

'Weixian "feng kou fei" an: jiu jizhe quan bei panxing' (Weixian's Case of 'shut Up fees': Nine Journalists have been Completely Sentenced) (蔚县'封口费'案：九记者全被判刑). *Nanfang Zhoumo*, 1 April 2010.

MacDonald, Adam P. 'From Military Rule to Electoral Authoritarianism: The Reconfiguration of Power in Myanmar and Its Future'. *Asian Affairs: An American Review* 40, no. 1 (2013): 20–36.

MacIntyre, Donald. 'Rumours of the Death of Investigative Journalism Are Greatly Exaggerated'. In *Investigative Journalism: Dead or Alive*, edited by John Mair and Richard Lance Keeble. Suffolk: Abramis Academic Publishing, 2011.

MacKinnon, Rebecca. 'China's "Networked Authoritarianism"'. *Journal of Democracy* 22, no. 2 (2011): 32–46.

'Flatter World and Thicker Walls? Blogs, Censorship and Civic Discourse in China'. *Public Choice* 134, no. 1–2 (1 January 2008): 31–46.

'China's Censorship 2.0: How Companies Censor Bloggers'. *First Monday* 14 (2) (2009).

Magnier, Mark. 'China Tightens Media Limits Loosened in Quake'. *Los Angeles Times*, 5 June, 2008; http://articles.latimes.com/2008/jun/05/world/fg-rollback5.

Makley, Charlene. 'Spectacular Compassion'. *Critical Asian Studies* 46 no. 3 (2014): 371–404.

Manion, Melanie. *Corruption by Design: Building Clean Government in Mainland China and Hong Kong*. Cambridge, MA: Harvard University Press, 2004.

Martin, Nicholas. 'Safety, Media Coverage and Provincial SOEs: Explaining Ownership Variation in Chinese Coal-Industry Restructuring', Working Paper 2013-39 (2013); available at: https://papers.ssrn.com/sol3/papers.cfm?abstract_id=2351473.

Mauldin, William and Alexander Kolyandr. 'Moscow Editor Fired Over Coverage of Putin'. *Wall Street Journal*, 14 December 2011. http://online.wsj.com/article/SB10001424052970203518404577096083626131686.html.

McFaul, Michael. *Between Dictatorship and Democracy: Russian Post-Communist Political Reform*. Washington, DC: Carnegie Endowment for International Peace, 2004.

'Lessons from Russia's Protracted Transition from Communist Rule'. *Political Science Quarterly* 114, no. 1 (1 April 1999): 103–130.

'Transitions from Postcommunism'. *Journal of Democracy* 16, no. 3 (2005): 5–19.

McFaul, Michael and Maria Lipman. '"Managed Democracy" in Russia: Putin and the Press'. *The Harvard International Journal of Press/Politics* 6, no. 3 (2001): 116–127.

'Putin and the Media'. In *The Putin Russia: Past Imperfect, Future Uncertain*, edited by Dale Herspring, 63–84. New York, NY: M.E. Sharpe, 2003.

McManus, John H. *Market-Driven Journalism: Let the Citizen Beware?* Thousand Oaks: Sage, 1994.

McNabb, David E. *Research Methods for Political Science: Quantitative and Qualitative Methods*. Armonk, NY; London: M.E. Sharpe, 2004.

McNair, Brian. *Glasnost, Perestroika and the Soviet Media*. London: Routledge, 1991.

McQuail, Denis. 'Accountability of Media to Society Principles and Means'. *European Journal of Communication* 12, no. 4 (1 December 1997): 511–529.

McReynolds, Louise. *The News under Russia's Old Regime: The Development of a Mass-Circulation Press*. Princeton: Princeton University Press, 1991.

'Media Watchdog Ranks Russia 9th in Unsolved Journalist Killings'. *The Moscow Times*, 3 May 2013. www.themoscowtimes.com/news/article/media-watchdog-ranks-russia-9th-in-unsolved-journalist-killings/479543.html.

Medvedev, Grigori. *No Breathing Room: The Aftermath of Chernobyl*. New York: Basic Books, 1994.

Mercer, Claire. 'NGOs, Civil Society, and Democratization: A Critical View of the Literature'. *Progress in Development Studies* 2, no. 1 (2002): 5–22.

Mertha, Andrew. Review of 'China's Democratic Future: How It Will Happen and Where It Will Lead'. *Perspectives on Politics* 4, no. 03 (2006): 613–614.

'"Fragmented Authoritarianism" 2.0: Political Pluralization in the Chinese Policy Process'. *The China Quarterly* 200 (2009): 995–1012.

'Society in the State: China's Nondemocratic Political Pluralization'. In *Chinese Politics: State, Society, and the Market,* edited by Peter Hays and Stanley Rosen, 69–84. Abingdon, Oxon; New York, NY: Routledge.

The Politics of Piracy: Intellectual Property in Contemporary China. Ithaca, NY: Cornell University Press, 2005.

Michelson, Ethan. 'Lawyers, Political Embeddedness, and Institutional Continuity in China's Transition from Socialism'. *American Journal of Sociology* 113, no. 2 (2007): 352–414.

Mickiewicz, Ellen. *Television, Power, and the Public in Russia.* Cambridge, UK; New York: Cambridge University Press, 2008.

Migdal, Joel S. *State in Society; Studying How States and Societies Transform and Constitute One Another.* Cambridge: Cambridge University Press, 2001.

Mill, John Stuart. *On Liberty.* Boston, MA: Ticknor and Fields, 1863.

Ming Shuliang (明叔亮). 'Dianxin: cuiruo de yinji tongxin' (Telecommunications: Weak Disaster Response) (震撼中国·经济篇：电信：脆弱的应急通信). *Caijing,* 26 May 2008.

Moeller, Susan D. *Compassion Fatigue: How the Media Sell Disease, Famine, War and Death.* London: Routledge, 1999.

Moore, Malcolm. 'Barack Obama's Exclusive Interview with the Chinese Media'. *Telegraph Blogs,* 19 November 2009. http://blogs.telegraph.co.uk/news/malcolmmoore/100017310/barack-obamase-exclusive-interview-with-the-chinese-media/.

Morozov, Evgeny. 'Moldova's Twitter Revolution'. *Foreign Policy Blogs,* 7 April 2009. http://neteffect.foreignpolicy.com/posts/2009/04/07/moldovas_twitter_revolution.

Morse, Yonatan L. 'The Era of Electoral Authoritarianism'. *World Politics* 64, no. 01 (2012): 161–198.

Mughan, Anthony and Richard Gunther. 'The Political Impact of the Media: A Reassessment'. In *Democracy and the Media: A Comparative Perspective,* edited by Anthony Mughan and Richard Gunther, 402–449. New York: Cambridge University Press, 2000.

Mulvenon, James C. 'China: Conditional Compliance'. In *Coercion and Governance in Asia: The Declining Political Role of the Military,* edited by Muthiah Alagappa, 317–321. Stanford, CA: Stanford University Press, 2001.

Nan Xianghong (南香红). *Juzai shidai de meiti caozuo (Media Operations in the Disaster Era)* (巨灾时代的美体操作). Guangzhou: Nanfang Daily Press, 2009.

Nan Zhenzhong (南振中). 'Yulun jiandu shi weihu renmin qunzhong genben liyi de zhongyao tujin' (*Yulun Jiandu* is an Important Channel for Protecting the Basic Interests of the Masses) (舆论监督是维护人民群众根本利益的重要途径). *Qiushi (Seek Truth)* (求是) no. 12 (2005): 26–29.

Nathan, Andrew J. 'Authoritarian Resilience'. *Journal of Democracy* 14, no. 1 (2003): 6–17.

Naughton, Barry J. 'China's Distinctive System: Can It Be a Model for Others?' *Journal of Contemporary China* 19, no. 65 (2010): 437–460.

The Chinese Economy: Transitions and Growth. Cambridge, MA: MIT Press, 2007.

Naughton, Barry J. and Dali L. Yang (eds.). *Holding China Together: Diversity and National Integration in the Post-Deng Era*. New York: Cambridge University Press, 2004.

Neuman, Scott. 'Chinese Activist Tells of "Crazy Retaliation" Against His Family'. *NPR.org*. 10 May 2012. www.npr.org/blogs/thetwo-way/2012/05/10/152412388/chinese-activist-tells-of-crazy-retailation-against-his-family.

'Niandu huati zhuizong 2005 nian de kuangnan' (End-of-the-Year Topic Focuses on 2005 Coal-Mining Accidents) (年度话题追踪 2005年的矿难). *Caijing*, 26 December 2005.

Nie, Xiaofeng. 'China Should Pay Greater Attention to Supervision by Public Opinion'. *Xinhua Hong Kong Services*, 17 April 1998.

'No More Survivors in China Blast'. *BBC*, 1 December 2004, http://news.bbc.co.uk/1/hi/world/asia-pacific/4053795.stm.

Norris, Pippa, Montague Kern, and Marion Just (eds.). *Framing Terrorism: The News Media, the Government and the Public*. New York; London: Routledge, 2003.

Nove, Alec. *Glasnost in Action: Cultural Renaissance in Russia*. Boston; London: Unwin Hyman, 1989.

Oates, Sarah. *Revolution Stalled: The Political Limits of the Internet in the Post-Soviet Sphere*. New York: Oxford University Press, 2013.

O'Brien, Kevin J. *Rightful Resistance in Rural China*. New York: Cambridge University Press, 2006.

'Chinese People's Congresses and Legislative Embeddedness: Understanding Early Organizational Development'. *Comparative Political Studies* 27, no. 1 (1994).

(ed.). *Popular Protest in China*. Cambridge, MA: Harvard University Press, 2009.

'Villagers, Elections, and Citizenship in Contemporary China'. *Modern China* 27, no. 4 (2001): 407–435.

O'Donnell, Guillermo. 'Horizontal Accountability in New Democracies'. In *The Self-Restraining State: Power and Accountability in New Democracies*, edited by Andreas Schedler, Larry J. Diamond, and Marc F. Plattner, 59–63. Boulder, CO: Lynne Rienner Publishers, 1999.

O'Sullivan, John and Ari Heinonen. 'Old Values, New Media'. *Journalism Practice* 2, no. 3 (2008): 357–371.

Ogden, S. *Inklings of Democracy in China*. Cambridge, MA: Harvard University Press, 2002.

Olcott, Marina B. and Marina Ottaway. 'Challenge of Semi-Authoritarianism'. Carnegie Endowment for International Peace Paper, 1 October 1999. http://carnegieendowment.org/1999/10/01/challenge-of-semi-authoritarianism/cm8.

Olson, Richard S. and A. Cooper Drury. 'Un-Therapeutic Communities: A Cross-National Analysis of Post-Disaster Political Unrest'. *International Journal of Mass Emergencies and Disasters* 15, no. 2 (1997): 221–238.

Osnos, Evan. 'Boss Rail'. *The New Yorker*, 22 October 2012. www.newyorker.com/reporting/2012/10/22/121022fa_fact_osnos?currentPage=all.

'Qinghai Earthquake'. *The New Yorker Blogs*, 14 April 2010. www.newyorker.com/online/blogs/evanosnos/2010/04/qinghai-earthquake.html.

'How a High-Speed Rail Disaster Exposed China's Corruption: The New Yorker'. *The New Yorker*, 22 October 2012. www.newyorker.com/report ing/2012/10/22/121022fa_fact_osnos.

Ottaway, Marina. *Democracy Challenged: The Rise of Semi-Authoritarianism*. Washington, DC: Carnegie Endowment for International Peace, 2003.

Paige, Jeffery M. (Revolution and the Agrarian Bourgeoisie in Nicaragua). CRSO Working Paper. Center for Research on Social Organization. Ann Harbor: The University of Michigan, 1988.

Park, Myung-Jin and James Curran. *De-Westernising Media Studies*. London: Routledge, 2000.

Patterson, Thomas E. 'Bad News, Bad Governance'. *The Annals of the American Academy of Political and Social Science* 546, no. 1 (1 July 1996): 97–108.

Pavlik, John V. *Journalism and New Media*. New York, NY: Columbia University Press, 2001.

Peerenboom, Randall. *China's Long March Toward Rule of Law*. Cambridge, UK: Cambridge University Press, 2002.

Pei, Minxin. *From Reform to Revolution: The Demise of Communism in China and the Soviet Union*. Cambridge, MA; London: Harvard University Press, 1994.

China's Trapped Transition: The Limits of Developmental Autocracy. Cambridge, MA: Harvard University Press, 2009.

Pelling, Mark and Kathleen Dill. 'Disaster Politics: Tipping Points for Change in the Adaptation of Sociopolitical Regimes'. *Progress in Human Geography* 34, no. 1 (1 February 2010): 21–37.

Perry, Elizabeth J. *Anyuan: Mining China's Revolutionary Tradition*. Berkeley, CA: University of California Press, 2012.

'Studying Chinese Politics: Farewell to Revolution?' *The China Journal* no. 57 (2007).

Perry, Elizabeth J. and Mark Selden. *Chinese Society: Change, Conflict and Resistance*. London; New York: Routledge, 2010.

Perry, Elizabeth J. and Merle Goldman. *Grassroots Political Reform in Contemporary China*. Cambridge, MA: Harvard University Press, 2009.

Perry, Elizabeth J. and Sebastian Heilmann. 'Embracing Uncertainty: Guerrilla Policy Style and Adaptive Governance in China'. In *Mao's Invisible Hand: The Political Foundations of Adaptive Governance*, edited by Sebastian Heilmann and Elizabeth J. Perry, 1–30. Cambridge, MA; London: Harvard University Asia Center, 2011.

Peruzzotti, Enrique and Catalina Smulovitz. 'Societal Accountability in Latin America'. *Journal of Democracy* 11, no. 4 (2000): 147–158.

Phillips, Tom. 'China Underreporting Coal Consumption by up to 17%, Data Suggests'. *The Guardian*. 4 November 2015. www.theguardian.com/world/2015/nov/04/china-underreporting-coal-consumption-by-up-to-17-data-suggests.

Pi Chuanrong (皮传荣). 'Wenchuan dizhen meiti baodao zhi fansi' (Reflections on the Media Reporting of the Wenchuan Earthquake) (汶川地震媒体报道之反思). *Xinan Mingzu Daxue Xuebao* (西南民族大学学报) no. 8 (2008): 149–204.

Pilger, John (ed.). *Tell Me No Lies: Investigative Journalism and Its Triumphs.* London: Cape, 2004.

Ping Xiang (冯翔). 'Shisi Feng Hexin Yu Yi Ci Kuangnan' (Fourteen Congratulatory Letters and One Mining Disaster) (十四封贺信与一次矿难). *Nanfang Zhoumo*, 1 April 2010.

Plattner, Marc F. and Larry J. Diamond. 'Rethinking Civil Society'. *Journal of Democracy* 5, no. 3 (1994): 4–18.

Politkovskaya, Anna. *A Small Corner of Hell: Dispatches from Chechnya.* Translated by Alexander Burry and Tatiana Tulchinsky. University Of Chicago Press, 2003.

'President Vladimir Putin Took Part in the 59th World Newspaper Congress'. *The Ministry of Foreign Affairs of the Russian Federation*, 5 June 2006. www .mid.ru/bdomp/brp_4.nsf/e78a48070f128a7b43256999005bcbb3/715106c a4d6f2911c32571850043f9af!OpenDocument.

'Profile: Mikhail Khodorkovsky'. *BBC*, 30 December 2010, sec. Europe. www .bbc.co.uk/news/world-europe-12082222.

Protess, David L. and Fay Lomax Cook. *The Journalism of Outrage: Investigative Reporting and Agenda Building in America.* New York, NY: Guilford Press, 1992.

Przeworski, Adam and Fernando Limongi. 'Modernization: Theories and Facts'. *World Politics* 49, no. 02 (1997): 155–183.

Przeworski, Adam, Susan Carol Stokes, and Bernard Manin. *Democracy, Accountability, and Representation.* Cambridge, UK; New York: Cambridge University Press, 1999.

'Putin's Comments on Politkovskaya Anger Activists'. *RadioFreeEurope/ RadioLiberty*, 11 October 2006. www.rferl.org/content/article/1071942 .html.

Qian Pinfang (钱平凡) and Zhou Jianyi (周健奇). *Wo guo tigao meikuang anquan shengchan shuiping de cuoshi yu Jingyan* (My Country's Policies and Experiences in Improving Mining Safety Level) (我国提高煤矿安全生产水平的措施与经验). Guowuyuan fazhan yanjiu zhongxin diaocha yanjiu bao-gao (The Development Research Centre of the State Council Research Report) (国务院发展研究中心调查研究报告). Guowuyuan fazhan zhongxin (Development Research Centre of the State Council) (国务院发展研究中心), 2011.

Qiang, Xiao. 'The Rise of Online Public Opinion and Its Political Impact'. In *Changing Media, Changing China*, edited by Susan Shirk, 202–225. Oxford, UK; New York: Oxford University Press, 2011.

Qiu, Jack Lingchuan. 'Virtual Censorship in China: Keeping the Gate between Cyberspaces'. *International Journal of Communication Law and Policy*, 4 (1999/2000):1–25.

Qu, Yan., Philip Fei Wu, and Xiaoqing Wang. 'Online Community Response to Major Disaster: A Study of Tianya Forum in the 2008 Sichuan Earthquake'. Proceedings of the 42nd Hawaii International Conference on *System Sciences* (2009).

'Quake Parents Protest in Sichuan'. *Radio Free Asia*, 11 January 2012. www.rfa .org/english/news/china/parents-01112012151815.html.

2009 quanguo xinwen chubanye jiben qingkuang (*Overview of All News Publications in 2009*) (*2009 全国新闻出版业基本情况*) General Administration of the Press and Publication of the People's Republic of China (GAPP), 7 September 2009. www.gapp.gov.cn/cms/html/21/493/201009/702538.html.

Raymond, Fishman and Yongxiang, Wang. 'The Unsafe Side of Chinese Crony Capitalism'. *Harvard Business Review* (February 2013).

Reilly, James. *Strong Society, Smart State: The Rise of Public Opinion in China's Japan Policy*. New York: Columbia University Press, 2012.

Remington, Thomas F. *Politics in Russia*. Boston; London: Longman, 2009.

Repnikova, Maria. 'China's Journalists are No Revolutionaries'. *Wall Street Journal*, 15 January 2013. http://online.wsj.com/article/SB1000142412788 732423510457824420354612291 8.html.

'Partial Political Liberalisation in an Authoritarian Regime: A Case Study of China's Media Politics'. MPhil Dissertation, University of Oxford, 2009.

'Information Management During Crisis Events: A Case Study of Beijing Floods of 2012'. *Journal of Contemporary China* 26, no. 105 (2017): 1–15.

'Thought Work Contested: Ideology and Journalism Education in China'. *The China Quarterly* 230 (2017).

Repnikova, Maria and Kecheng Fang. 'Behind the Fall of China's Greatest Newspaper'. *Foreign Policy*. 30 January 2015. www.tealeafnation.com/2015 /01/behind-the-fall-of-chinas-greatest-newspaper/.

'Reporter Who Wrote about Kremlin Slush Fund Banned from Reentering Russia'. *Reporters without Borders*, 18 December 2007. http://archives.rsf.or g/article.php3?id_article=24793.

Richardson, John E. *Analysing Newspapers: An Approach from Critical Discourse Analysis*. Basingstoke; New York: Palgrave Macmillan, 2007.

Richter, Andrei. *Post-Soviet Perspective on Censorship and Freedom of the Media*. *International Communication Gazette* 70, no. 5 (2008).

'Rising Protests in China'. *The Atlantic*, 17 February 2012. www.theatlantic.com/ infocus/2012/02/rising-protests-in-china/100247.

Rodriguez-Llanes, Jose M., Femke Vos, Regina Below, and Debarati Guha Sapir (Eds.) *Annual Disaster Statistical Review 2008: The Numbers and Trends*. Belgium Centre for Research on the Epidemiology of Disasters, 2009.

Roeder, Philip G. *Red Sunset: The Failure of Soviet Politics*. Princeton: Princeton University Press, 1993.

Rohde, David. 'China's Newest Export: Internet Censorship'. *Reuters*, 17 November 2011. http://blogs.reuters.com/david-rohde/2011/11/17/chinas- newest-export-internet-censorship/.

Rose, Richard, William Mishler, and Christian Haerpfer. *Democracy and its Alternatives: Understanding Post-Communist Societies*. Baltimore: John Hopkins University Press, 1998.

Rose, Richard, William Mishler, and Neil Munro. *Popular Support for an Undemocratic Regime: The Changing Views of Russians*. Cambridge; New York: Cambridge University Press, 2011.

Rosen, Stanley. 'Retrofitting the Steel Frame: From Mobilizing the Masses to Surveying the Public'. In *Mao's Invisible Hand: The Political Foundations of Adaptive Governance in China*, edited by Sebastian Heilmann and Elizabeth J. Perry, 237–269. Cambridge, MA; London: Harvard University Press Asia Center, 2011.

Ross, Cameron. 'Regional Elections and Electoral Authoritarianism in Russia'. *Europe-Asia Studies* 63, no. 4 (2011): 641–661.

Rowen, Henry S. 'When Will the Chinese People Be Free?' *Journal of Democracy* 18, no. 3 (2007): 38–52.

'Russian Journalist Wins Peter Mackler Award'. *RIA Novosti*. 17 April 2012. http://en.rian.ru/russia/20100823/160300552.html.

Saich, Tony. 'Negotiating the State: The Development of Social Organizations in China'. *The China Quarterly* 161 (1 March 2000): 124–141.

Sakwa, Richard. *Gorbachev and His Reforms, 1985–1990*. Upper Saddle River, NJ: Prentice Hall College Div, 1991.

'Regime Change from Yeltsin to Putin: Normality, Normalcy or Normalisation?' In *Russian Politics under Putin*, edited by Ross Cameron, 17–39. Manchester; New York: Manchester University Press, 2004.

Salame, Ghassan. *Democracy without Democrats?: The Renewal of Politics in the Muslim World*. London: I.B. Tauris, 1994.

Saleh, Yasmine and Tom Finn. 'Egypt Forces Assault Protest Camp, Many Scores Shot Dead'. *Reuters*, 14 August 2013. www.reuters.com/article/201 3/08/14/us-egypt-protests-idusbre97c09a20130814.

Schedler, Andreas. 'Conceptualizing Accountability'. In *The Self-Restraining State: Power and Accountability in New Democracies*, edited by Andreas Schedler, Larry Diamond, and Marc F. Plattner, 13–28. Boulder, CO; London: Lynne Rienner Publishers, 1993.

'The Menu of Manipulation'. *Journal of Democracy* 13, no. 2 (2002): 36–50.

'The New Institutionalism in the Study of Authoritarian Regimes'. *SSRN eLibrary* (2009). http://papers.ssrn.com/sol3/papers.cfm?abstract_id=1451602.

Electoral Authoritarianism. L. Rienner, 2006.

Schmitter, Philippe C. 'The Limits of Horizontal Accountability'. In *The Self-Restraining State: Power and Accountability in New Democracies*, edited by Andreas Schedler, Larry J. Diamond, and Marc F. Plattner, 59–63. Boulder, CO: Lynne Rienner Publishers, 1999.

Schneider, Florian and Yin-Jye Hwang. 'The Sichuan Earthquake and the Heavenly Mandate: Legitimizing Chinese Rule through Disaster Discourse'. *Journal of Contemporary China* 23, no. 88 (2014): 636–656.

Schulz, Sandra. 'The Courage of the Few: Dozens Targeted in Chinese Crackdown on Critical Voices'. *Spiegel Online*, 20 April 2011. www.spiegel .de/international/world/the-courage-of-the-few-dozens-targeted-in-chinese-crackdown-on-critical-voices-a-758152.html.

Schumpeter, Joseph A. *Capitalism, Socialism, and Democracy*. Mansfield Centre, CT: Martino, 2011.

Shieh, Shawn and Guosheng Deng. 'An Emerging Civil Society: The Impact of the 2008 Sichuan Earthuake on Grass-Roots Associations in China'. *The China Journal* 65 (2011): 181–194.

Scotton, James F. *New Media for a New China*. Oxford: Wiley-Blackwell, 2010.

Sequeira, Consuelo Cruz. 'Mistrust and Violence in Nicaragua: Ideology and Politics'. *Latin American Research Review* 30, no. 1 (January 1995): 212.

Shambaugh, David. *China's Communist Party: Atrophy and Adaptation*. Berkeley, CA; London: University of California Press, 2008.

China Goes Global: The Partial Power. New York; Oxford: Oxford University Press, 2013.

'China's Propaganda System: Institutions, Processes and Efficacy'. *The China Journal* 57 (1 January 2007): 25–58.

Modernizing China's Military: Progress, Problems, and Prospects. Berkeley; London: University of California Press, 2002.

'The Coming Chinese Crackup'. *Wall Street Journal*, 6 March 2015. www.wsj .com/articles/the-coming-chinese-crack-up-1425659198.

Shen Liang (沈亮). '"Qing ji hui" 169 suo xiwang xiaoxue jiben wanhao – zhuanfang nan dou gongyi jijinhui fu lishizhang jian mishuzhang, zhongguo qing-shaonian fazhan jijin qian chuangbanren xu yong guang' (Qing Ji Hui 169 Primary Schools Are Basically Intact – Report Based on Interviews with the Vice-Chair of the Nan Dou Public Goods/Welfare Foundation, Secretary Jian, and the Founder of China's Young People Development Fund, Xu Yong Guang) ("青基会"169所希望小学基本完好—专访南都公益基金会副理事长兼秘书长、中国青少年发展基金会前创办人徐永光). *Nanfang Zhoumo*, 29 May 2008.

Shen Liang and Yang Ruichun (沈亮, 杨瑞春). 'Zhongguo hongshizihui zhimian xinren fengbo' (China's Red Cross Faces Crisis of Public Confidence) (中国红十字会直面信任风波). *Nanfang Zhoumo*, 5 June 2012.

Shevtsova, Lilia. 'The Return of Personalized Power'. *Journal of Democracy* 20, no. 2 (2009): 61–65.

'The Limits of Bureaucratic Authoritarianism'. *Journal of Democracy* 15, no. 3 (2004): 67–77.

'Russia's Hybrid Regime'. *Journal of Democracy* 12, no. 4 (2001): 65–70.

Shi Ping (石平). 'Lingdao ganbu xuexi guanyu zai yulun jiandu xia gongzuo' (Leading Cadres Learning to Work Under Public Opinion Supervision) (领导干部应习惯于在舆论监督下工作). *Qiushi (Seek Truth)* (求是) no. 14 (2009): 53–54.

Shi, Tianjian. *Political Participation in Beijing.* Cambridge; London: Harvard University Press, 1997.

Shirk, Susan L. (ed.). *Changing Media, Changing China.* New York; Oxford: Oxford University Press, 2010.

China: Fragile Superpower: How China's Internal Politics Could Derail Its Peaceful Rise. New York; Oxford: Oxford University Press, 2007.

Shlapentokh, Vladimir. *Soviet Intellectuals and Political Power: The Post-Stalin Era.* London; New York: I.B. Tauris, 1990.

'Should Journalists Participate in the Protests?' *Russia Beyond The Headlines*, 12 April 2012. http://rbth.ru/articles/2012/04/12/should_journalists_participa te_in_the_protests_15304.html.

'Sichuan sheng nei gongji 5335 ming xuesheng zai wenchuan dizhen zhong yunan huo shizong' (5,335 Students were Killed or Went Missing in Sichuan Province during the Wenchuan Earthquake) (四川省内共计5335名学生在汶川地震中遇难或失踪). *Xinhuanews* (新华社), 7 May 2009. http://news.xi nhuanet.com/newscenter/2009–05/07/content_11328503.htm.

Shu Mei (舒眉). 'Zaihou jinrong: xuqiu bi congqian geng poqie' (Post-Disaster Finance: The Demand is More Pressing Than Before) (灾后金融：需求比从前更迫切). *Nanfang Zhoumo*, 5 June 2008.

Shue, Vivienne. 'Legitimacy Crisis in China?' In *State and Society in 21st Century China: Crisis, Contention, and Legitimation*, edited by Peter H. Gries and Stanley Rosen. New York: Routledge, 2004.

The Reach of the State: Sketches of the Chinese Body Politic. Stanford: Stanford University, 1988.

Simon, Roger. *Gramsci's Political Thought: An Introduction.* London: Lawrence & Wishart, 2002.

Singerman, Diane. *Avenues of Participation: Family, Politics, and Networks in Urban Quarters of Cairo.* Princeton, NJ: Princeton University Press, 1996.

Sklar, Richard L. 'Developmental Democracy'. *Comparative Studies in Society and History* 29, no. 04 (1987): 686–714.

Slater, Dan and Joseph Wong,. 'The Strength to Concede: Ruling Parties and Democratization in Developmental Asia'. *Perspectives on Politics* 11, no. 3 (2013): 717–733.

Slater, Dan and Sofia Fenner. 'State Power and Staying Power: Infrastructural Mechanisms and Authoritarian Durability'. *Journal of International Affairs* 65, no. 1 (2011): 15–29.

Smith, Roberta. 'Ai Weiwei Survey in Washington'. *The New York Times*, 11 October 2012. www.nytimes.com/2012/10/12/arts/design/ai-weiwei-survey-in-washington.html.

Song, Yingyi. 'A Glance at the Underground Reading Movement during the Cultural Revolution'. *Journal of Contemporary China* 16, no. 1 (2007): 325–333.

Sorace, Christian. 'China's Vision for Developing Sichuan's Post-Earthquake Countryside: Turning Unruly Peasants into Grateful Urban Citizens'. *The China Quarterly* 218 (2014): 404–424.

'The Communist Party Miracle? The Alchemy of Turning Post-Disaster Reconstruction into Great Leap Development'. *Comparative Politics* 208 (2014): 404–427.

Sparks, Colin and Anna Reading. *Communism, Capitalism and the Mass Media.* London: Thousand Oaks, 1998.

'Understanding Media Change in East-Central-Europe'. *Media Culture & Society* 16, no. 2 (1994): 243–270.

Sparrow, Bartholomew H. *Uncertain Guardians: The News Media As a Political Institution.* Baltimore; London: Johns Hopkins University Press, 1999.

Spires, Anthony J. 'Contingent Symbiosis and Civil Society in an Authoritarian State: Understanding the Survival of China's Grassroots NGOs'. *American Journal of Sociology* 117, no. 1 (July 2011): 1–45.

Stark, David and László Bruszt. *Postsocialist Pathways: Transforming Politics and Property in East Central Europe.* Cambridge: Cambridge University Press, 1998.

'State Team to Probe Coal Mine Disaster'. *China Daily*, 12 December 2007. www.chinadaily.com.cn/china/2007-12/10/content_6308335.htm.

Statistical Reports on the Internet Development in China. China Internet Network Information Center (CNNIC), January 2012.

Steinhardt, Christoph H. 'From Blind Spot to Media Spotlight: Propaganda Policy, Media Activism and the Emergence of Protest Events in the Chinese Public Sphere'. *Asian Studies Review* 39, no. 1 (2015): 119–137.

Stern, Rachel E. *Environmental Litigation in China: A Study in Political Ambivalence*. Cambridge, New York: Cambridge University Press, 2013.

Stern, Rachel E. and Jonathan Hassid. 'Amplifying Silence Uncertainty and Control Parables in Contemporary China'. *Comparative Political Studies* 45, no. 10 (1 October 2012): 1230–1254.

Stern, Rachel E. and Kevin J. O'Brien. 'Politics at the Boundary Mixed Signals and the Chinese State'. *Modern China* 38, no. 2 (1 March 2012): 174–198.

Stockmann, Daniela. *Media Commercialization and Authoritarian Rule in China*. New York: Cambridge University Press, 2012.

'Who Believes Propaganda? Media Effects during the Anti-Japanese Protests in Beijing'. *The China Quarterly* 202 (2010): 269–289.

Stockmann, Daniela and Mary E. Gallagher. 'Remote Control: How the Media Sustain Authoritarian Rule in China'. *Comparative Political Studies* 44, no. 4 (1 April 2011): 436–467.

Stoner-Weiss, Kathryn. 'Russia: Authoritarianism Without Authority'. *Journal of Democracy* 17, no. 1 (2006): 104–118.

(Successor of Internews Suspends Activity after Police Search). Committee to Protect Journalists, 23 April 2007. http://cpj.org/2007/04/successor-of-inter news-russia-suspends-activity-af.php.

Sullivan, Jonathan. 'China's Weibo: Is Faster Different?' *New Media & Society* (7 February 2013).

Sun, Wanning and Jenny Chio (eds.). *Mapping Media in China: Region, Province, Locality*. New York, NY: Routledge, 2012.

Sun, Xupei. *An Orchestra of Voices: Making the Argument for Greater Speech and Press Freedom in the People's Republic of China*. Westport, CT: Greenwood Publishing Group, 2001.

'Press Laws Save Media from Political Tangles'. *Global Times*, 13 May 2010.

Svensson, Marina. 'Media and Civil Society in China: Community Building and Networking among Investigative Journalists and Beyond'. *China Perspectives* 3 (2012): 19–28.

Swanson, David L. 'Transnational Trends in Political Communication: Conventional Views and New Realities'. In *Comparing Political Communication: Theories, Cases, and New Challenges*, edited by Frank Esser and Barbara Pfetsch, 45–63. New York: Cambridge University Press, 2004.

Tai, Zixue and Tao Sun. 'Media Dependencies in a Changing Media Environment: The Case of the 2003 SARS Epidemic in China'. *New Media & Society* 9(6) (2007): 987–1009.

Tang, Beibei. 'The Discursive Turn: Deliberative Governance in China's Urbanized Villages'. *Journal of Contemporary China* 24 (2015): 137–157.

Tang Guozhong (唐国忠). 'Shanjie shandai shanyong shanguan xinwen meiti' (Skilfully Understand, Treat, Use, and Manage News Media) (善解善待善用善管新闻媒体). *Qiushi (Seek Truth)* (求是) no. 3 (2008).

Taylor, Alan. 'Rising Protests in China'. *The Atlantic*, 12 February 2012. www .theatlantic.com/infocus/2012/02/rising-protests-in-china/100247.

Taylor, Matthew. 'Media Relations in Bosnia: A Role for Public Relations in Building Civil Society'. *Public Relations Review* 26 (2000): 1–14.

Teets, Jessica C. 'Let Many Civil Societies Bloom: The Rise of Consultative Authoritarianism in China'. *The China Quarterly* 213 (2013): 19–38.

Tettey, Wisdom J. *Media Pluralism, Democratic Discourses and Political Accountability in Africa.* Harvard-World Bank Workshop: Harvard University, 29 May 2008. www.hks.harvard.edu/fs/pnorris/Conference/Co nference%20papers/Tettey%20Africa.pdf.

'The Battle for Moscow: Russian Opposition at Odds over Path for Future— Spiegel Online'. *Spiegel*, 14 March 2012. www.spiegel.de/international/eur ope/anti-putin-protests-continue-in-moscow-a-820900.html.

'The Dangers of Mining Around the World'. *BBC*, 14 October 2010. www.bbc .co.uk/news/world-latin-america-11533349.

Thornton, Patricia M. 'Censorship and Surveillance in Chinese Cyberspace: Beyond the Great Firewall'. In *Chinese Politics: State, Society and the Market*, edited by Peter Hays Gries and Patterson, 262–284. London and New York: Routledge, 2009.

'China's Democratic Future: How It Will Happen and Where It Will Lead by Bruce Gilley'. *Political Science Quarterly* 120, no. 2 (2005): 338–339.

Tilly, Charles. *From Mobilization to Revolution.* New York: McGraw-Hill, 1978.

Tong, Jingrong. *Investigative Journalism in China: Journalism, Power, and Society.* London: Continuum, 2011.

'Press Self-Censorship in China: A Case Study in the Transformation of Discourse'. *Discourse & Society* 20, no. 5 (1 September 2009): 593–612.

'The Crisis of the Centralized Media Control Theory: How Local Power Controls Media in China'. *Media, Culture & Society* 32, no. 6 (1 November 2010): 925–942.

Tong, Jingrong and Colin Sparks. 'Investigative Journalism in China Today'. *Journalism Studies* 10, no. 3 (2009): 337–352.

Tran, Mark. 'Phenomenal Success for New Film That Criticises China's Environmental Policy'. *The Guardian*, 11 March 2015.www.theguardian.co m/world/ 192015/mar/02/china- environmental-policy-documentary-under-the-dome-chai-jing-video.

Truex, Rory. 'Consultative Authoritarianism and Its Limits'. *Comparative Political Studies* 50, no. 3 (2014): 329–361.

'Who Believes in *People's Daily*? Bias and Trust in Authoritarian Media'. Paper Presented at the Comparative Politics Seminar, University of Pennsylvania, 10 April 2015.

Tsai, Lily L. *Accountability Without Democracy: Solidary Groups and Public Goods Provision in Rural China.* New York; Cambridge: Cambridge University Press, 2007.

Tsang, Steve. 'Consultative Leninism: China's New Political Framework'. *Journal of Contemporary China* 18, no. 62 (2009): 865–880.

Tu, Jianjun. 'Coal Mining Safety: China's Achilles' Heel'. *China Security* 3 (2007): 36–53.

'Safety Challenges in China's Coal Mining Industry'. *The Jamestown Foundation, China Brief,* 15 March 2006. www.asianresearch.org/articles/29 97.html.

Voltmer, Katrin. 'The Media, Government Accountability, and Citizen Engagement'. In *Public Sentinel: News Media & Governance Reform*, edited by Pippa Norris, 137–163. Washington, DC: The World Bank, 2010.

Waisbord, Silvio Ricardo. *Watchdog Journalism in South America: News, Accountability, and Democracy*. New York: Columbia University Press, 2000.

Walker, Christopher and Sarah Cook. 'China's Export of Censorship'. *Far Eastern Economic Review*. 12 October 2009. www.freedomhouse.org/article/chinas-export-censorship.

Wang Fengxiang (王风翔). 'Dizhen zaihai de weiji baodao – yi 2008 nian sichuan wenchuan dizhen, 2010 nian qinghai baoshu dizhen de weiji baodao weilie' (Reporting of Earthquake Disasters – Case Studies of 2008 Sichuan Wenchuan Earthquake and the 2010 Qinghai Baoshu Earthquake) (地震灾害的危机报告－以2008年四川汶川地震，2010年青海宝树地震的危机报告为例). In *Zhongguo weiji guanli baogao* (*Blue Book on Crisis Management*) (中国危机管理报告), 130–149. Beijing: Social Sciences Academic Press, 2011.

Wang, Haiyan. 'How Big Is the Cage? An Examination of Local Press Autonomy in China'. *Westminster Papers in Communication and Culture* 7, no. 1 (2010): 56–72.

The Transformation of Investigative Journalism in China: From Journalists to Activists. London: Lexington Books, 2016.

Wang Heyan (王和岩). 'Weixian kuangnan "miehuo zhan"' (The Struggle to "Put Out a Fire" after Weixian Coal-Mining Accident) (蔚县矿难'灭火战'). *Caijing*, 22 February 2009.

Wang, Qinghua and Gang Guo,. 'Yu Keping and Chinese Intellectual Discourse on Good Governance'. *The China Quarterly* 224 (2015): 985–1005.

Wang, Shaoguang. 'Changing Models of China's Policy Agenda Setting'. *Modern China* 34, no. 1 (1 January 2008): 56–87.

'Regulating Death at Coalmines: Changing Mode of Governance in China'. *Journal of Contemporary China* 15, no. 46 (2006): 1–30.

Wang Yichao, Wang Heyan, and Li Hujun (王以超, 王和岩, 李虎军). 'Zhenhan zhongguo: keji pian: kan bu jian de zhan xian' (China Shocked: The Science Section: The Invisible Battle Front) (震撼中国·科技篇：看不见的战线). *Caijing*, 26 May 2008.

Wasserstrom, Jeffrey. 'Illuminating the Misleading Takes on China 20 Years Since Tiananmen'. *The Huffington Post*. 5 July 2009. www.huffingtonpost.com/jeffrey-wasserstrom/illuminating-and-misleadi_b_211610.html.

Wedeen, Lisa. *Ambiguities of Domination: Politics, Rhetoric, and Symbols in Contemporary Syria*. Chicago, IL: University of Chicago Press, 1999.

Weerakkody, Niranjala. *Research Methods for Media and Communication*. South Melbourne, VIC; Oxford: Oxford University Press, 2009.

Weller, Robert P. 'Responsive Authoritarianism'. In *Political Change in China: Comparisons with Taiwan*, edited by Bruce Gilley and Larry Diamond, 117–183. Boulder, CO; London: Lynne Rienner Publishers, 2008.

Wen-Hsuan. 'A Unique Pattern of Policymaking in China's Authoritarian Regime: The CCP's Neican/Pishi Model'. *Asian Survey* 55, no. 6 (2015): 1093–1115.

Wen Xiu, Zhang Yuzhe, and Li Zhigang (温秀, 张宇哲, 历志钢). 'Zhenhan Zhongguo, Jingji Bian: Yinhang: Duochong Fengxian' (Banks: Multiple Risks) (震撼中国·经济篇: 银行: 多重风险). *Caijing*, 26 May 2012.

Wen Xueguo (文学国) and Fan Zhengqing (范正青) (eds.) 'Sichuan zaihou chongjian moshi: fazhanxing chongjian' (The Model of Sichuan's Post-disaster Reconstruction: The Development Type of Reconstruction) (四川灾后重建模式: 发展型模式). In *Zhongguo weiji guanli baogao* (*Blue Book on China's Crisis Management*) (中国危机管理报告), 103–130. Beijing: Social Sciences Academic Press, 2011.

'Wenchuan dizhen 5335 xuesheng yunan shizong' (5,335 Students Were Killed and Missing in the Wenchuan Earthquake) (汶川地震5335学生遇难失踪). *Nanfang Dushibao*, 8 May 2009.

White, Stephen. *After Gorbachev*. Cambridge: Cambridge University Press, 1993.

Media, Culture, and Society in Putin's Russia. Basingstoke: Palgrave MacMillan, 2008.

Understanding Russian Politics. Cambridge: Cambridge University Press, 2011.

Whitehead, Laurence. *Democratization: Theory and Experience*. Oxford: Oxford University Press, 2002.

Winston, David. 'From Yeltsin to Putin'. *Hoover Policy Review* 100 (2000). www.hoover.org/publications/policy-review/article/7127.

Wodak, Ruth. *Qualitative Discourse Analysis in the Social Sciences*. Basingstoke, UK: Palgrave Macmillan, 2008.

Wodak, Ruth and B. Busch. 'Approaches to Media Texts'. In *The Sage Handbook of Media Studies*, edited by John H. Downing, 105–123. Thousand Oaks, CA; London: Sage, 2004.

Wodak, Ruth and Michał Krzyżanowski. *Qualitative Discourse Analysis in the Social Sciences*. Basingstoke: Palgrave Macmillan, 2008.

Wong, Edward. 'Editor Reviewing China Quake Deaths Is Sentenced'. *The New York Times*. 9 February 2010. www.nytimes.com/2010/02/10/world/asia/10 quake.html.

Wong, Edward and Vanessa Piao. 'China Cracks Down on News Reports Spread via Social Media'. *The New York Times*. 5 July 2016. www.nytimes.com/20 16/07/06/world/asia/china-internet-social-media.html.

Wright, Mary C. 'A Review Article: The Pre-Revolutionary Intellectuals of China and Russia'. *The China Quarterly* 6 (1961): 175–179.

Wright, Tim. *The Political Economy of the Chinese Coal Industry: Black Gold and Blood-Stained Coal*. London: Routledge, 2012.

Wu Bingqing (吴冰清). '"Miaopu xingdong" de xuexiao weihe yili bu dao – miaopu xingdong yiwu zongganshi liang jianha zhuanfang' (Why the Miaopo Xingdong Schools Didn't Collapse – An Interview with the Secretary-General of the Miapu Xingdong Philanthropic Organisation) (苗圃行动'的学校为何屹立不倒? —'苗圃行动'义务总干事梁建华专访). *Nanfang Zhoumo*, 29 May 2008.

Wu, Guoguang. 'One Head, Many Mouths: Diversifying Press Structures in Reform China'. In *Power, Money, and Media: Communication Patterns and Bureaucratic Control in Cultural China*, edited by Chin-Chuan Lee, 45–68. Evanston: Northwestern University Press, 2000.

Wu, Shiwen. 'Contentious Discourse and Dynamic Frames: Interplay among Online Public Opinion, Media Reporting, and Government Discourse with Respect to Social Events'. Working Paper Presented at the Media Activism Research Collective, Annenberg School for Communication, University of Pennsylvania. 4 December 2015.

Xia Yu (夏榆). 'Jiuyuan de liliang bu zai renshu, zai zhuanye nengli' (The Strength or Rescue Operations is Not in Numbers, but in Professionalism) (救援的力量不在人数,在专业能力). *Nanfang Zhoumo*, 29 May 2008.

Xiabo, Liu. 'Listen Carefully to the Voices of the Tiananmen Mothers'. *No Enemies, No Hatred*. Cambridge, MA: Harvard University Press: 2013.

Xie Miaofang and Hu Yazhu (谢苗枫,胡亚柱). 'Sichuan sheng jiaoyuting guina xiaoshe daota wu dian yuanyin' (Sichuan Province Department of Education Gives Five Reasons Why the Schools Collapsed) (四川省教育厅归纳校舍倒塌五点原因). *Nanfang Ribao*, 28 May 2008. http://news.qq.com/a/2008052 8/000849.htm.

Xie Yungeng (谢耘耕). *Zhongguo shehui yuqing yu weiji guanli lanpishu (The Report on Chinese Social Opinion and Crisis Management)* (中国社会与微机管理报告). Beijing: Social Sciences Academic Press, 2012.

Xin, Xin. 'The Impact of "Citizen Journalism" on Chinese Media and Society'. *Journalism Practice* 4, no. 3 (2010): 333–344.

Xu, Bin. 'Durkheim in Sichuan: The Earthquake, National Solidarity, and the Politics of Small Things'. *Social Psychology Quarterly* 72, no. 1 (2009): 5–8.

'For Whom the Bell Tolls: State-Society Relations and the Sichuan Earthquake Mourning in China'. *Theory Soc* 42 (2013): 509–542.

'Consensus Crisis and Civil Society: The Sichuan Earthquake Response and State-Society Relations'. *The China Journal* 17 (2014): 91–108.

Xu, Jian. *Media Events in Web 2.0 China: Interventions of Online Activism.* Eastbourne: Sussex Academic Press, 2016.

'Xuese xiao meiyao' (Blood Stained Small-Scale Mining Operations) (血色小煤窑). *Caijing*, 5 April 2003.

Yang Anjiang (阳安江). 'Qianghua jiandu, tuijin chengfan tixi jianshi' (Strengthen Supervision, Move Forward the Implementation of the Self-Restraint System) (强化监督,推进惩防体系建设). *Qiushi (Seek Truth) (*求是*)* no. 5 (2005): 36–37.

Yang Binbin, Zhao Hejuan, Li Zhigang, Chang Hongxiao, Zhang Yingguang, and Chenzhong Xiaolu (杨彬彬, 赵何娟, 历志钢, 常红晓, 张映光, 陈中小路). 'Xiaoshe yousi lu' (The Worrisome Record of the School Buildings) (校舍忧思录). *Caijing*, 9 June 2008.

Yang, Dali. *Remaking the Chinese Leviathan: Market Transition and the Politics of Governance in China.* Stanford: Stanford University Press, 2005.

Yang, Guobin. *The Power of the Internet in China: Citizen Activism Online.* New York; Chichester: Columbia University Press, 2009.

Yang, Guobin and Min Jiang. 'The Networked Practice of Online Political Satire in China: Between Ritual and Resistance'. *International Communication Gazette*. February 2015.

Yang Shaohua (杨绍华). 'Anzhao kexue fazhan guan de yaoqiu qieshi zhuanbian zuofeng: xuexi hu jintao tongzhi zai zhongyang ji-wei di-qi ci quanti huiyi shang de zhongyao jianhua' (Study Comrade Hu Jintao's Speech at the Seventh Plenary Conference of the Central Commission for Inspecting Discipline) (按照科学发展观的要求切实转变作风—学习胡锦涛同志在中央纪委第七次全体会议上的重要讲话). *Qiushi*, July 2007.

Yang, Stevenson. 'The Absent-Minded Reform of China's Media'. In *China's Leadership in the 21st Century: The Rise of the Fourth Generation*, edited by David M. Finkelstein and Maryanne Kivlehan, 223–249. Armonk, NY: M. E. Sharpe, 2002.

Yao Shun (姚舜). Shi yao liantiao zhong de yaotou: dadian yisheng la danzi yue zhuan 3 wan (Yaotou role in the chain of medicine testing: the examining doctor gets a profit of 30,000 yuan per month) (试药链条中的药头：打点医生拉单子月赚**3**万). *Jujiao Renwu*. 31 December 2016; http://mt.sohu.com/20161231/n477472896.shtml.

Yardley, Jim. 'Violence in Tibet as Monks Clash with the Police'. *The New York Times*, 15 March 2008.

'Yi ge kuangzhu de facai shi' (A Story of How One Mining Manager Became Wealthy) (一个矿主的发家史). *Nanfang Zhoumo*, 18 August 2005.

Yin, Liangen and Haiyan Wang. 'People-Centred Myth: Representation of the Wenchuan Earthquake in China Daily'. *Discourse & Communication* 4, no. 4 (2010): 383–398.

Yu, Sun. *Lessons from SARS Coverage*. Nieman Reports, Winter 2003. www.nieman.harvard.edu/reportsitem.aspx?id=100974.

Yuan Wan (袁玥). 'Duo ming de shi jianzhuwu er bu shi dizhen – bei hushi de kanzheng shifang wenti' (The Loss of Life Is from the Constructions Not from the Earthquake – the Ignored Question of Quake-proof Fortifications) (夺命的是建筑物而不是地震—被忽视的抗震设防问题). *Nanfang Zhoumo*, 29 May 2008.

Yurchak, Alexei. *Everything Was Forever, Until It Was No More: The Last Soviet Generation*. Princeton; Oxford: Princeton University Press, 2006.

Zakaria, Fareed. 'The Rise of Illiberal Democracy'. *Foreign Affairs* 76, no. 6 (1997): 22.

Zassoursky, Ivan I. *Mass Media Vtoroi Respubliki* (*Mass Media of the Second Republic*). Moscow: Moscow State University, 1999.

Zelizer, Barbie. 'How Communication, Culture, and Critique Intersect in the Study of Journalism'. *Communication, Culture & Critique* 1, no. 1: 86–91.

Zhang Huixin (张惠新). 'Jinyibu tigao fanfuchanglian jianshe kexuehua shuiping' (Go a Step Further in Improving the Scientific Standards of Opposing Corruption and Advocating Honesty) (进一步提高反腐倡廉建设科学化水平). *Qiushi (Seek Truth)* (求是) no. 23 (2010): 15–17.

Zhang, Xiantao. *The Origins of the Modern Chinese Press*. Milton Park: Routledge, 2007.

Zhang, Xiaoling. 'From Totalitarianism to Hegemony: The Reconfiguration of the Party-State and the Transformation of Chinese Communication'. *Journal of Contemporary China* 20, no. 68 (2011): 103–115.

'From Totalitarianism to Hegemony: The Reconfiguration of the Party-State and the Transformation of Chinese Communication'. *Journal of Contemporary China* 20, no. 68 (2010): 103–115.

Zhang Yingguang, Cheng Zhongxiaolu, and Yang Binbin (张映光, 陈中小路, 杨彬彬). 'Gongjian jianzhu hechu bu lao' (Where to Mend Strong Public Construction) (公共建筑何处补牢). *Caijing*, 9 June 2008.

Zhang Yue and Tan Ailing (张悦, 覃爱玲). 'Jiuzhou tiyuguan: xingcun beichuan de biaoqing' (Jiuzhou Gymnasium: Beichuan Expression Survives) (九洲体育馆：幸存北川的表情). *Nanfang Zhoumo*, 29 May 2008.

Zhang Zhi'an (张志安). *Jizhe ruhe zhuanye: shendu baodao jingyingde zhiye yishi yu baodao celu (Journalists' Professionalism: The Professional Awareness and Reporting Strategies of In-Depth Journalists)* (记者如何专业：深度报道精英的职业意识与报道策落). Guangzhou: Nanfang Ribao Chubanshe （南方日报出版社), 2007.

'Zhao Death Shows Limits of China's Media Freedom'. *The Epoch Times*, 27 January 2005. www.theepochtimes.com/news/5-1-27/26079.html.

Zhao Peixi (赵培玺). 'Xinwen jianduzhe bixu ziwo jiandu' (News Supervisors Must Supervise Themselves). *Qiushi (Seek Truth)* (求是) 14 (2005): 55.

Zhao, Suisheng. 'The China Model: Can It Replace the Western Model of Modernization?' *Journal of Contemporary China* 19, no. 65 (2010): 419–436.

Zhao, Yuezhi. 'From Commercialization to Conglomeration: The Transformation of the Chinese Press Within the Orbit of the Party State'. *Journal of Communication* 50, no. 2 (2000): 3–26.

Communication in China: Political Economy, Power, and Conflict. Lanham, MD; Plymouth: Rowman & Littlefield, 2008.

Media, Market, and Democracy in China: Between the Party Line and the Bottom Line. Urbana, IL: University of Illinois Press, 1998.

'Watchdogs on Party Leashes? Contexts and Implications of Investigative Journalism in Post-Deng China'. *Journalism Studies* 1, no. 4 (2000): 577–597.

Zhao, Yuezhi and Sun Wusan. 'Public Opinion Supervision: Possibilities and Limits of the Media in Constraining Local Officials'. In *Grassroots Political Reform in Contemporary China*, edited by Elizabeth J. Perry and Merry Goldman, 303–324. Cambridge and London: Cambridge University Press, 2007.

Zhou Chun (周纯). 'Wang dai zhoubian chanye diaocha: juejinzhe xiaotui mai shuizhe anzai?' (Investigation into P2P Lending Industry: As Opportunitists Fade Away, Where are the Service Providers?) (网贷周边产业调查：掘金者消退卖水者安在). *Lengjing Tengxun*. 14 Novemer, 2016; http://finance.qq.com/original/lenjing/wangdai.html.

Zhou Fengzhen (周奉真). 'Maikefeng shidai yulun yindao wenti' (The Question of Guidance of Public Opinion in the Microphone Era) (麦克风时代'与舆论引导问题). *Qiushi (Seek Truth)* (求是)4 (2010): 21–22.

Zhou Haibin (周海滨). 'Zhenhai diaocha zu pilu wenchuan dizhen xiaoshe sunhui yanzhong yuanyin' (The Group That Investigated the Earthquake Uncovered the Key Reasons Behind the Schools' Ruins) (震害调查组披露汶川地震校舍损毁严重原因). *Zhongguo Jingji Zhoukan*, 25 May 2009. http://

news.ifeng.com/mainland/special/512dizhenyizhounian/zuixinbaodao/2009
05/0525_6415_1172036.shtml.

Zhou, He. 'Working with a Dying Ideology: Dissonance and its Reduction in
Chinese Journalism'. *Journalism Studies* 1, no. 4 (2000): 599–616.

Zhu Hongjun (朱红军). '*Dongqi zhongxue: canju huoke bimian*' (Dongqi Middle
School: Could Tragedy Have Been Averted?) (东汽中学：惨剧如何避免).
Nanfang Zhoumo., 29 May 2008.

Zhu Liyi and Tan Hao (失立毅，谭浩). 'Wenchuan dizhen yijing zaocheng
69196 ren yunan 18379 ren shizong' (Wenchuan Earthquake Already
Incurred 69196 Deaths and 18379 Missing) (汶川地震已经造成69196人遇
难18379人失踪). *Xinwen Zhongxin*. 6 July 2008. http://news.sina.com.cn/c/
2008-07-06/162615881691.shtml.

Zhu Tao (朱弢) and Wang Heyan (王和岩). 'Tunlan kuangnan nan ciren ze'
(Tunlan Mining Accident: Difficult to Brush Off Responsibility) (屯兰矿难
难辞人责). *Caijing*, 2 March 2009. http://magazine.caijing.com.cn/2009-03-
01/110075360.html.

'Zhuiwen xinning kuangnan' (Examining Xinning Mining Accident) (追问兴
宁矿难). *Caijing*, 22 August 2005.

Zhu, Ying. *Two Billion Eyes – the story of China Central Television*. New York, NY:
The New Press, 2014.

Zong He (综合). 'Jia renshu, Jia shijian, Jia tuzhi: Henan "Luoshengmen" kuangnan pu jianguan loudong' (Fake Number of People, Fake Time, Fake
Drawing: Henan "Luoshengmen" Mine Accident Exposure of
Management Leaks) (假人数，假时间，假图纸河南'罗生门'矿难曝监管漏
洞). *Nanfang Zhoumo*, 5 January 2011. www.infzm.com/content/53499.

'Zuoyun kuangnan zhi sheng yiqi' (Zuoyun Mine Disaster Only Saved by
Miracle) (左云矿难只剩奇迹). *Caijing*, 29 May 2006.

Index

CPSIA information can be obtained
at www.ICGtesting.com
Printed in the USA
LVHW081715080119
603029LV00023BA/338/P